The Pleasure of the Crown

Anthropology, Law and First Nations

THE PLEASURE OF THE CROWN

Anthropology, Law and First Nations

Dara Culhane

Talonbooks
1998

Published with the assistance of the Canada Council

Talon Books Ltd.
#104—3100 Production Way
Burnaby, British Columbia, V5A 4R4, Canada

Typeset in Adobe Caslon and printed and bound in Canada by Hignell Book Printing.

First printing: January 1998.

Talonbooks are distributed in Canada by General Distribution Services, 30 Lesmill Road, Don Mills, Ontario, Canada M3B 2T6; Tel.:(416) 445-3333; Fax:(416) 445-5967.

Talonbooks are distributed in the U. S. A. by General Distribution Services Inc., 85 Rock River Drive, Suite 202, Buffalo, New York, U.S.A. 14207-2170; Tel.:1-800-805-1083; Fax:1-800-481-6207.

Canadian Cataloguing in Publication Data

Culhane, Dara, 1950-

The pleasure of the Crown
Includes bibliographical references.
ISBN 0-88922-315-7

1. Kitksan Indians—Claims. 2. Wet'suwet'en Indians—Claims.
3. Kitksan Indians—Land tenure. 4. Wet'suwet'en Indians—Land tenure.
5. Land tenure—Law and legislation—British Columbia—Cases.
6. Law and anthropology. I. Title.
KEB529.5.L3C84 1997   346.71104'32'089772   C97-911081-5
KF8208.C84 1997

for feral travelers in the vast emptiness

TABLE OF CONTENTS

PART VIII: AD INFINITUM (Going on Forever, into Infinity)

PART IX: IN FUTURO (In the Future)

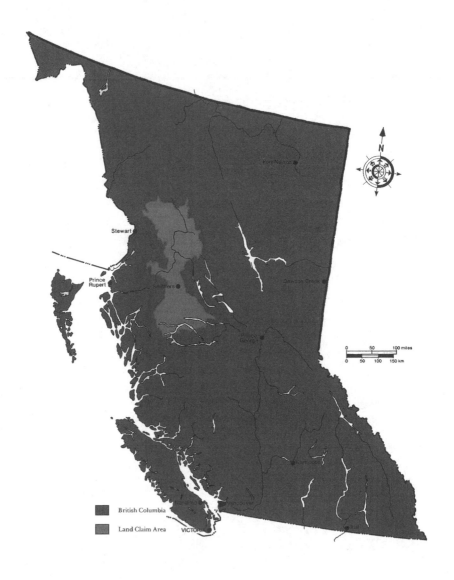

Generalized map of British Columbia showing Territories claimed by Gitksan and Wet'suwet'en Peoples (not to scale).

PART I

JUSTITIA OMNIBUS

(JUSTICE FOR ALL)

Chapter 1: How Did the Crown Acquire Title?

The Indian elders in British Columbia question why they must subject their relationship to the land to a non-Indian court's strict scrutiny: why they must explain their use of the land to obtain 'rights' abstractly defined by others.

They believe that the Indians have rights to their land because their people go back with the land for thousands of years. What they do not understand is how the Crown acquired its 'rights' to their land.
—Lawyer Louise Mandell, 1987, *Native Culture on Trial.*

The Long and the Short of It

Law, we are taught to believe by our educational institutions, embodies justice. Our courts' formal rules of evidence, and their procedures, enable the discovery of truth through the application of reason. "Judicial neutrality"—the absence of bias among judges—guarantees that fair and equitable resolutions to disputes between any and all people(s) will be arrived at. Equality before the law, we are told, is the linchpin of the Canadian judicial system; and justice, we are assured, is the outcome of legal processes. It follows from these official premises, and by this reasoning, that if contemporary Canadian sovereignty and Crown title and rights to land are confirmed by law, they must have been justly acquired.

Of course, in these cynical times, few claim the Canadian legal system is infallible. Charges that interests other than the pursuit of justice may be at play in legal processes do not usually generate widespread alarm. Increasingly, we understand that what we call "facts" are frequently matters of interpretation that reflect particular points of view rather than unequivocal certainty. We have come to appreciate that something called "culture," and more specifically, "cultural differences," come between Aboriginal[1] peoples and Canadian law, disrupting communication and mutual understanding. Suggestions that judges' decisions often reflect prejudices common in contemporary society at large, rather than being strictly determined by exclusively legal concerns, are hardly shocking revelations.

However, periodically a particular judicial decision comes to public attention that shocks even the most complacent or embittered cynic. Allan McEachern, the former Chief Justice of the Supreme Court of British Columbia, created just such a controversy when he handed down his 1991 judgment against the Aboriginal claimants in the high profile Gitksan[2] and Wet'suwet'en[3] land rights case, also known as the case of *Delgamuukw v. The Queen*. Judge McEachern ruled that, before Europeans arrived in the late eighteenth century, the First Nations had been too "primitive" to have had property laws or institutions of governance. Today, he declared, they have no Aboriginal rights whatsoever. Charges of racism were hurled at the judge. He was accused of shamelessly favouring the interests of big forestry companies and non-Aboriginal elites against the rights of First Nations. The Chief Justice defended himself, using the letter of the law as his shield. He protested that he was compelled by historical precedents to repeat the rulings of previous judges that dated back hundreds of years. Chief Justice McEachern admitted that his decision might not be *just*, but he was convinced that it was definitely *legal*.

Indeed, law and justice have not always walked hand in hand through British Columbia's history, and nowhere is the distance between them greater than on the question of Aboriginal title and rights. How *did* the British Crown acquire its rights to the territory we now call British Columbia? Many Canadians would respond, with pride, that unlike Americans, we gained sovereignty over the lands we live on, and established political jurisdiction over its Indigenous inhabitants, through the rule of law, rather than by military force.

In fact, the Crown acquired its title to First Nations' lands and resources by simply asserting sovereignty and ignoring Aboriginal title *in contravention of British colonial law*. British and then Euro-Canadian rule was enacted by sheer force of numbers as settlers overwhelmed fragments of Aboriginal populations who had survived the first waves of epidemic diseases brought by European fur traders during the eighteenth century. Aboriginal peoples were simply deemed, by law, not to exist. The colonists then established their own legal regime that validated their self-proclaimed sovereignty and jurisdiction. For over 100 years, the governments and the courts of the Province of British Columbia have defended their predecessors' initial trespass on Aboriginal lands, and their transgression of British law, by whatever means necessary: coercion, deceit, compromise, seduction, force. Law.

Aboriginal peoples have steadfastly insisted that they surrendered neither ownership of their lands, nor their political autonomy. Nor did they cease to exist. However, it was not until the late 1960s that First Nations—after over a century of petitioning—succeeded in compelling Canadian courts to begin adjudicating their disputes with the governments about who owns the land in British Columbia.

When called upon to justify its actions in law, the Province of British Columbia retreats to a legal fortress, the cornerstone of which is the mystical "original moment" when Britain asserted sovereignty over First Nations in British Columbia, often without their knowledge, and always without their consent. The Crown's defense begins by giving legal sanction to this crude act of aggression, and then proceeds from this starting point to call upon a range of social theories, historical fictions, and popular "common sense" ignorance and prejudice to justify its actions. Crown lawyers present as evidence stereotypical caricatures of Aboriginal peoples as "backward" and "primitive" when Europeans arrived. Grisly tales of "war-like savages" are juxtaposed with an heroic epic of "advanced" and "civilized" white settlers who, it is claimed, brought Christianity, reason, and the rule of law to the untamed wilderness of British Columbia. The stark contrast in "development" between the two "races," the Crown argues, made the superimposition of British sovereignty over Aboriginal sovereignty a "natural" outcome of the "progress" of history, and rendered inevitable the subordination of Aboriginal peoples to non-Aboriginal governance. A short answer to the Aboriginal elders' question is that the Crown acquired its 'rights' to their land by simply seizing it: through the force of law.

How could this have happened in this way? Here, in British Columbia, in Canada? More importantly, how can this violation of values that many Canadians hold dear—like respect for the rule of law, a belief in equality, and a commitment to human rights—continue to be legitimized in the 1990s? These are the questions that shape this book. By looking behind, around, and through the interconnections between law, history, culture, and power, I offer a long answer to the elders' question.

Human Being, Citizen, Anthropologist

The landmark case of *Delgamuukw v. The Queen* heard in British Columbia during 1987-1991 represented a crystallizing moment in the history of Aboriginal peoples and the law in British Columbia. All the variously interested parties to the dispute came together in one forum to present their positions, their arguments, and their supporting evidence. History followed them into the courtroom, and they carried the future out with them when they left.

I wrote this book as a contribution to the ongoing discussions that are taking place in British Columbia and Canada about the possibilities for justice in Aboriginal/non-Aboriginal relations; as a commentary on a particular dispute in one corner of the globe that is linked to more general struggles for social justice around the world; and, as an intervention in debates in the academic fields of anthropology and law. I write as a human being, a citizen, and an anthropologist. I present an explanation of issues and events that is necessarily one interpretation among many possibilities. Like any account, mine arises from and is shaped by some fundamental assumptions, principles, experiences and positions that I will set out as honestly as I can.

My inquiry begins and ends with the basic claim that all human beings are fundamentally equal and worthy of respect, and the simple assertion that Canadian law should reflect these principles, both in theory and in practice. My argument is that, in relation to Aboriginal peoples, this has not historically been, nor is it now, the case. I have come to this conclusion by way of a number of different paths.

Long before I began this study of the *Delgamuukw v. R.* case, (and former Chief Justice Allan McEachern's *Reasons for Judgment*); and long before I had ever heard of the Gitksan or Wet'suwet'en First Nations, I was imbued as a child with certain understandings of both the danger of the law when it is abused as a weapon of terror, and of the promise of the law when it is employed to achieve and protect justice. Members of my Irish father's family were assassinated by English soldiers in the early years of this century: I was raised with few illusions about British justice. My mother's Jewish family fled pogroms in Czarist Russia and witnessed the Holocaust: I was taught to respect law as an alternative to brutality, and to value scholarship in the service of justice. These general understandings represent, to me, who I am and, as such, they shape how I interpret the world I live in.

I began thinking seriously about the particular questions that constitute the subject matter of this book in the early 1970s, when I married a First Nations man, lived in his reserve community on the Central Coast of British Columbia, and became involved in the movement for recognition of Aboriginal title.[4] I cannot remember when I first began to "believe" the simple truth that British Columbia First Nations hold unsurrendered Aboriginal title to their lands. If I ever thought differently, and there indeed was such a "moment of revelation" when I changed my mind, it happened so long ago that I cannot recall it now. For as long as I can remember, this position has appeared to me as simple common sense: Aboriginal peoples were here, Europeans arrived. No wars of conquest were fought, no treaties were entered into. Hence, no Aboriginal title or rights were surrendered. These issues remain unresolved, so mutually-respectful negotiations should begin. These fundamental factual and moral "truths" are, to me, obvious. Nothing I have heard, seen, read, learned or experienced in the last twenty-five years has caused me to think or feel differently.

I have brought up two Aboriginal children in contemporary British Columbia. I know something of the depths of racism in this province and in this country. I recognize, in the erudite language of the law, the same cruelty I have seen and heard directed to Aboriginal people in Canadian schools, hospitals, legislatures and many other "public" spaces. As a human being, I consider racism a violation of human rights. This is the first premise from which I write.

Sometime during the last twenty or so years, I also began to understand how the denial of Aboriginal title and rights in this context was simultaneously a denial of human equality. This understanding emerged first from learning how British and Canadian property law differentiates between categories of citizens according to their relationship to private property: fully "matured" citizens may own land, and others may not. These legal classifications mirror, and are mirrored by, cultural beliefs that accord greater value and worth to persons with property, than to those without. Ownership of private property stands as both criteria for, and evidence of, successful citizenship. Knowing this, when I hear Aboriginal people say that they are deeply hurt when governments and courts repeatedly refuse to recognize Aboriginal title and acknowledge Aboriginal rights, I interpret the injury they express as reflecting their very perceptive understanding of the meaning and value of property in the dominant Canadian culture, and the law's reflection of these meanings. That is to say, regardless of how diverse Aboriginal peoples may feel about property, they know how Canadian law feels about it, and they therefore rightly ascertain that they are being insulted—treated as second class citizens—by the law.

As a citizen, I wish to live in a just and democratic nation, and I object to the fact that Canadian sovereignty relies for its legitimacy on assumptions of human inequality: of European superiority and Aboriginal inferiority. The second premise I write from takes the form of an assertion of the democratic authority of a citizen to critique the law, and to insist that its practices accord with its avowed principles in ways that are comprehensible and transparent to the average person. I am neither a lawyer nor a legal scholar. I am, in this professional way, an "outsider" looking at the law. But as a citizen I am inevitably and irrevocably "inside" the law. The law claims to speak in the name of all people, and therefore the people should be able to discern the law's reasoning and the factual foundation it claims to rest on. All this I learned from my parents and other wise people. I brought these understandings and points of view with me when I began studying anthropology in 1982.

Anthropology, historically, has been about western intellectuals investigating the ways of life—the "cultures"—of those classified as "others" in dominant European social theory: non-western, non-industrial, Indigenous peoples; and, to a lesser extent, marginalized groups within the borders of western nations. One of the central tasks of this traditional anthropology was identified as that of cross-cultural translation. Anthropologists sought to immerse themselves in the lives of the people they studied and, in this way, to achieve an "insider's" point of view. The next step in the anthropological enterprise was then to describe and explain—to translate and represent—these "Native points of view," and their different cultural perspectives on the human condition, to western audiences.

Contemporary anthropology questions many of the foundations of this academic discipline. Most importantly, classical anthropology is undergoing a thorough re-examination by those "subjects" who were constituted as "objects" of study by earlier generations of ethnographers. Formerly colonized peoples, members of minority communities in the west, women, and other "Others" who were historically written about and analyzed by anthropologists, are turning the microscope around and scrutinizing those who originally examined them. They are reading and critiquing traditional ethnographic representations of themselves; conducting their own research into the cultures of both colonizers and colonized, oppressors and oppressed; producing a critical "anthropology of anthropology." More and more, western and non-western anthropologists are studying their own societies: exploring the cultures they are always already immersed in, re-examining the histories that have produced them, and questioning their own taken-for-granted assumptions about the past, the present, and the future. This process is exciting and profoundly challenging. Errors in fact are being corrected. Alternative explanations of world history are being considered. Diverse visions of possible futures are being contemplated. We now struggle to read the "great works" of the European intellectual tradition through the eyes of these "Others." It is now marginalized peoples' analyses of the centres, as well as of the margins, that we must try to grasp.

Traditionally, an anthropologist might be expected to study the cultural beliefs and practices that First Nations draw on to support their appeals for legal recognition of Aboriginal title. I recognize and respect the fact that it is a consequence of persistent Aboriginal resistance that these issues are before the courts at all. Aboriginal litigants perpetually challenge the law, and occasionally jurists acknowledge some legitimacy to their claims. In these ways, First Nations have influenced Canadian law significantly. But I did not undertake this study for the purpose of learning what the evidence and testimony presented in *Delgamuukw v. R.* might tell us about Gitksan and Wet'suwet'en cultures and histories, or to unravel how legal strategies have shaped the representation of such issues in the courtroom. These are interesting questions, of course. But they are not the questions that have guided my inquiry. Rather, I take as given—as "common sense"—that the Gitksan's and Wet'suwet'en's fundamental position is valid. That is, I take for granted that regardless of what forms their social structures and cultural beliefs took at the time, they owned the territory in dispute when the British arrived in the eighteenth century, and they have not ceded, sold, lost or surrendered their title or rights to these lands and their resources under the terms of either Aboriginal, British or Canadian law. The Gitksan and Wet'suwet'en, and other First Nations in British Columbia, have sought recognition by Canadian courts of these facts in order that provincial and federal governments could be compelled to negotiate a mutually respectful relationship with them. First

Nations have sought peaceful co-existence with newcomers who, like my own predecessors, came from many parts of the world—for myriad reasons—to live here, in Canada. I believe this is a just goal, and it is one I share. I take this position to constitute "good sense."[5]

What I consider *not* readily accessible to common sense, and not a reflection of good sense, and therefore in need of explanation and criticism, are the Crown's positions and the evidence and theories relied upon to support them. This book is therefore a project in the anthropology of European colonialism: a study of power and of the powerful. I turn my anthropologist's spyglass on the law, an institution that quintessentially embodies and reproduces Western power. This is the third premise from which I write.

As an anthropologist, I have tried to make sense of the law on Aboriginal title in British Columbia by placing the Gitksan and Wet'suwet'en case within the historical and contemporary political context of British and Canadian relations with First Nations, and considering the ways that law reflects and reinforces Euro-Canadian cultural beliefs, practices and diverse interests. I have explored how law shapes relations between people outside the courtroom as well as inside. Contrary to the image law holds of itself as a world unto itself, I understand law as inextricably enmeshed in society.

The first obligation of any responsible critic is to thoroughly investigate the object of critique, and I have tried to do so. In order to understand the story of *Delgamuukw v. R.*, I read, watched, listened to and discussed commentaries on the case by a wide range of people. I conducted a "close reading" of the various texts of this case: expert witness reports; transcripts of the trial; Reasons for Judgment; academic and popular commentaries on the case itself and the issues it raised. By "close reading," I mean studying the texts not only for their literal or "factual" content, but also to understand the various ways they communicate meanings directly and subtly, by using language in particular ways; by writing and speaking in rhetorical styles; by deploying metaphor and evoking certain images and emotions; by using grammar, and constructing each text as a whole along specific lines. That is to say, I read these documents as cultural texts, using the tools of anthropological and cultural criticism. And, since particular texts do not make sense outside the broader context in which they are written and read, I have also studied related work in the fields of anthropology, history, law, and northwest coast ethnography.

However, Chief Justice Allan McEachern's *Reasons for Judgment* in *Delgamuukw v. R.*, was not written as a work of fiction or ethnography. Judicial rulings carry with them a great deal of power and authority, based largely on assumptions that they represent reasonable and coherent conclusions drawn from a basis in empirical fact. I therefore considered it important to try to understand and critique this text on its own terms first. I began by analyzing the judge's ruling within its own context: the law on Aboriginal title in British Columbia. I considered it as a recent link in a long historical chain of Aboriginal title and rights cases that began when the British Empire began, and gave rise to the legal precedents that continue to shape contemporary judgments. My first task, then, was to trace the history of the law that Chief Justice McEachern claimed forced him to arrive at the ruling that he did.

I conducted my critique from three positions, or points of view. First, I tried to step inside the law to understand it. I asked whether the law has followed its own rules and met its own criteria. As an anthropologist, the question that I sought to answer was whether or not the judge's rulings that relied on history and anthropology reflected reliable findings based on reputable research in these fields. Second, I stepped back outside the law, and read these texts from a position informed by a conventional anthropological critique of ethno-centrism that argues that all of humanity's cultures are worthy of equal respect, and should be understood on their own terms. The rules or values of one culture should not be applied to the evaluation of another. From this perspective, the dominant western culture is but one among many, neither universal nor superior. I asked, "What cultural beliefs and practices did the Crown rely on to make sense of their arguments in *Delgamuukw v. R.*?" Interpreted from this position, the Crown's arguments and the Chief Justice's *Reasons for Judgment* read like archaic, eurocentric, colonial texts, with a uniquely local, British Columbian flavour. Finally, I read and wrote from a third position, that of a critic of the dominant order. From this position, I argue that a critique of ethnocentrism must necessarily be the beginning, but should not be the conclusion, of a project aimed at re-imagining law and justice, and re-thinking how Aboriginal and non-Aboriginal people may live together. From this location on the political margins, I asked questions that address the future, as well as the past: regardless of the *cultural traditions* these texts emerge from, what are the *cultural prescriptions* embedded in the Crown's legal position and Chief Justice McEachern's law. Particularly, what visions of nature and society, what models of human relationships, did the Crown's defense of their position reflect, assert and defend? How are their images represented in the world they would create? What is the way of life they are empowered to command an army to defend? What kind of world/country/ province will we all, Aboriginal and non-Aboriginal, live in if desires like his continue to govern?

My interpretation and analysis therefore emerged from this critical "ethnographic reading" of the texts through which the law, and *Delgamuukw v. R.*, has made itself known to the public. I did not observe the trial, and I have not interviewed or consulted with any of the participants. My writing has been a solitary project, not carried out in collaboration with any representatives of any parties to the dispute. I claim to represent no one but myself. I retell the story of the Gitksan and Wet'suwet'en case, from my point of view, as a detailed account of an important moment in our recent history: a snapshot that artificially freezes time and records the instant so that we may return to it and re-view it, see it from different perspectives, read it in different ways, and learn different lessons from it. Many people have engaged in similar studies and arrived at similar—and different—conclusions, and I have learned a great deal from their work. Believing that what people say is inseparable from how they say—or write—it, I have tried to bring some of these other observers and commentators into conversation with each other on the pages of my text. Of course, it is I who have chosen which of their words to select, and directed at what moments they should speak and to whom. In so doing, I have interrupted, interpreted and appropriated their meanings to my own ends. My sources are not responsible for the uses I have made of their words. Believing too that humour is one of the strongest forms of cultural criticism, when particular moments in this story have struck me as funny or ironic, satirical or sardonic, I have presented them as such. Learning to laugh at ourselves and with others must surely be a worthy goal in the pursuit of justice.

Any account of a process like the trial of *Delgamuukw v. R.* enacted over four years, that involved many people presenting complex evidence, debating obscure points of law, contradicting each other's interpretations of history, disputing understandings of esoteric cross-cultural translations, must necessarily be selective and partial. I have tried to provide enough detail and sufficient references that interested readers may take my account as an entry into, rather than the final word on, or an exit from, the many complex issues this story brings up.

This is not, however, a "dialogue with texts." This is a "dispute with texts," particularly with the texts of the Province of British Columbia's legal arguments in *Delgamuukw v. R.*, and with Chief Justice McEachern's *Reasons for Judgment*. At the same time, this book is not intended to be a polemic expressing an idiosyncratic or unique perspective. I have tried to present a meticulously documented, well-supported, and passionately reasoned, argument. I hope to persuade readers of the soundness of my position, and the weakness of the Crown's; of the injustices of the Crown's actions; and, of the desirability of an alternative vision for the future.

The story of litigation on Aboriginal title and rights in Canada, and particularly in British Columbia, is at one and the same time as remarkably simple as it is extraordinarily complex, as obtuse as it is simple-minded, and as familiar as it is strange. Truth and lies, fact and fiction, noble intentions and shameful motivations crisscross, undercut, and override each other as they dance across the pages of legal texts and treatises, creating a bewildering maze of claims and counter claims, accusations and denials. But when all is said and done, and many possible interpretations have been explored, the important questions remain: Has truth, by anyone's criteria, been told? Has justice, by anyone's measure, been done? Most importantly: how can justice be achieved in the present and protected in the future?

Stories like that of *Delgamuukw v. R.* illustrate how complex, and often contradictory, our feelings about law are. On the one hand, there is widespread cynicism in the public at large about the tenuous relationship between law and justice in Canada, especially in relation to Aboriginal peoples. And, there are hundreds of government reports, and volumes of academic research that support these criticisms. On the other hand, we continue to believe in the *possibility* that the law will be just. Most importantly, we continue to *demand* that the law *should* be just, in both its theories and its practices. We can never cease to insist on this. How could we? Law, after all, is supposed to represent the principles and rules by which we have all agreed to live together in this nation-state, to constitute our particular social and cultural world. To cease trying to hold the law accountable to justice, no less than to condone law answering only to itself, would be to surrender to nihilism, despair and totalitarianism. The consequences of legal rulings are complex and far-reaching. Law's decisions are accompanied by powers of enforcement, including the exclusive right to legitimately use weapons and violence to resolve disputes. None of us can ignore the force of the law: it insists itself upon us in myriad ways every day. When it comes to law, then, critical skepticism, passionate outrage, perpetual hope, sardonic amusement, sheer terror, and utopian dreams of a moral social order are inevitably interwoven in our thinking, feeling, writing and conversation.

My initial goal was to make sense of the law. My next goal was to critique it. My long term goal is to help make the law sensible, and the society it reflects, just. I hope this book will challenge how you think about Aboriginal title and Canadian law, and how you choose to participate in shaping our collective future.

---

1. Language is important. Throughout this text I use a variety of terms to refer to the peoples whose ancestors lived on the North American continent before Europeans. Each term has diverse connotations. "Indigenous" is the most all-encompassing and is the term of global representation chosen by the United Nations. Some people feel it erases the specificity of particular Nations, and suffers from an imprecise time frame, i.e. some people who others consider "settlers" identify themselves as "indigenous" because their families have lived in a region for many generations. "Indian" began with Christopher Columbus' error: landing in the Caribbean, he believed he had reached his destination of India, and so he called the people he encountered "Indians." "Indian" is a term used in many legal documents, and in historical records. Some people find it offensive and feel its continued use reproduces its colonial legacy. "First Nation" is a term of recent emergence that is particularly popular in British Columbia. It is the language used in the *Constitution Act 1982*. Some people, particularly Metis representatives, interpret the "first" in "First Nation" as an implicitly hierarchical term that renders them "Second Nations." "Aboriginal" is also a recent term that encompasses First Nations, Metis, Inuit, and Non-Status people. It is also used in legal documents, including the *Constitution Act 1982*. Some people feel that it is too broad and general and blurs

important differences and erases diversity. I use all these various terms either because they are appropriate to the topic or time frame being discussed, or to the particular context. In unselfconscious contemporary everyday language, I hear all these terms deployed by Aboriginal and non-Aboriginal people and I use all these terms. I have reproduced this normal usage in the text. I regret if any readers are offended by any of these words.

2. In recent years, many Aboriginal nations have adopted spellings of their names that more accurately reflect their own correct pronunciation, replacing those spellings previously developed by Anglophone and Francophone colonial officials to facilitate English or French language and accent versions of Indigenous names. The Gixsan First Nation has adopted a new spelling of their name since this court case. I use the spelling as it appears in documents concerning the case.

3. Similarly, the Witsuwit'en have changed the spelling of their name.

4. The *Indian Act*, as it was when I was married in 1975, conferred "Indian status" on non-Indian women when they married Indian men holding legal status. Conversely, when Indian women married non-Indian men, or Indian men who did not hold legal status, they and their children were dispossessed of their legal status as Indians. According to Canadian law, my marriage transformed me, in the eyes of the law, from a Canadian citizen of Jewish and Irish descent into a "Registered Indian," member of the Nimpkish Band, and ward of the Crown. (The law was changed in 1985 so that today, marriage can neither confer nor take away legal Indian status.)

I understand that, on the basis of my legal classification, some legal analysts would consider me an "interested party" to Aboriginal title and rights litigation. My children would hold entitlements under any treaty or settlement that might result. I do not consider myself an "interested party" in the manner of a potential beneficiary, nor do I think this legalistic aspect of my position significantly influences my analysis of the issues at stake. However, I offer this detailed explanation by way of respecting an obligation to "put all my cards on the table" when engaging in critique and arguments about morality and "interests."

5. The late Antonio Gramsci, an Italian theorist, differentiated between "common sense" and "good sense." "Common sense," he said, consists of widely-held assumptions that are seen as "natural," or in some other sense immutable, and taken for granted. There appears to be no need to question or challenge "common sense" since its "facts" are considered "as obvious as the nose on my face." "Good sense," on the other hand, refers to systematic reflection and conscientious planning based on practical and moral values: the best ideas of an era or populace. I am indebted to Richard Daly for bringing Gramsci's work on this to my attention. See Gramsci 1971.

Chapter 2: In Search of Reason

*It is the law that aboriginal rights exist at the "pleasure of the Crown,"
and they may be extinguished whenever the intention of the Crown to
do so is clear and plain.... The plaintiffs' claims for aboriginal rights are
accordingly dismissed.*
—Chief Justice Allan McEachern, 1991, *Reasons for Judgment, Delgamuukw v. R.*

The Law in its Majesty

Thus spoke Chief Justice Allan McEachern of the British Columbia Supreme
Court as he rendered his long-awaited judgment in the most lengthy and
costly Aboriginal land title litigation in Canadian history. The "Gitksan and
Wet'suwet'en case," also commonly referred to as "the *Delgamuukw case*," or
"*Delgamuukw v. the Queen*," had been four years at trial, beginning in Smithers,
British Columbia, on May 11, 1987, and concluding in Vancouver, B.C., on
March 8, 1991. A total of 318 days of evidence from over 61 witnesses had
been heard, additional evidence had been supplied by affidavit, and legal
argument had taken up an additional 56 days in court. Verbatim transcripts of
testimony now fill 23,503 pages of text, 82 binders of authorities now hold
9,200 pages of exhibits. An estimated 25 million dollars of public funds had
been spent.

The issue before the court can be stated simply: The Gitksan and
Wet'suwet'en had asked for legal recognition of their ownership and jurisdiction over 22,000 square miles of land and resources in the northwest region of
the Province of British Columbia, Canada. They based their claim on the fact
that they are descendants of people who lived there, in the same territory, since
the beginning of time as they conceptualize it. When the Europeans arrived
during what *they* call the eighteenth century, the ancestors of contemporary
Gitksan and Wet'suwet'en peoples were already living there. Neither the
Gitksan nor the Wet'suwet'en ever entered into treaties with Britain or
Canada, the governments representing the interests of the newcomers. Nor
was there a war in which their territory was conquered militarily by the new
colonial forces. Nor were any rights to land or resources ever sold by
Indigenous peoples to any individual settlers, or to the British or Canadian
governments. The Gitksan and Wet'suwet'en, therefore, continue to consider
themselves the rightful owners and governors of the territory in question. They
say they hold "Aboriginal title and rights" to this land.

The Province of British Columbia and the Government of Canada opposed the Gitksan's and the Wet'suwet'en's claims. The Crown asked the court for "a declaration that the Plaintiffs have no right, title or interest in and to the Claim Area, and the resources thereon, thereunder or thereover." Since 1871, when British Columbia joined Canadian Confederation, all successive governments of that province had taken the position that no Aboriginal rights recognizable by "civilized law" existed prior to Britain declaring sovereignty over the territory. And even if those rights had existed, the Province of British Columbia's argument continued, the simple act of assertion of sovereignty by a European power over those lands was sufficient to extinguish any pre-existing Aboriginal title and rights. Legally, the Province of B.C. told First Nations, you do not exist. This position provided the rationale for provincial governments' consistent refusals, until 1990, to participate in any discussions or negotiations with federal government and Aboriginal representatives on Aboriginal title and rights issues.

During the week preceding the release of Chief Justice McEachern's decision in the *Delgamuukw* case, the *Vancouver Sun*, British Columbia's largest circulation daily newspaper, ran a series of articles entitled "Judgment Day" in which spokespeople from government, industry, labour and the general public expressed the view that at least a partial court victory for the Aboriginal plaintiffs was anticipated by all concerned. Gitksan and Wet'suwet'en Tribal Council representative Herb George told the press that he expected to see "the last little trace of honour in the Crown" reflected in the judgment. "We're not naive," George said, "but we can still dream."[1]

There seemed to be good cause for George's cautious optimism. Between 1987, when the *Delgamuukw v. R.* trial began, and 1991, when it concluded, some significant changes had occurred in the legal and political landscape of Aboriginal and non-Aboriginal relations in British Columbia. In 1989, the First Nations Congress, representing most of the 180 First Nations in B.C., had initiated discussions with representatives of the province's leading forestry, fishing and mining companies. The First Nations leaders' goals were to educate the business sector about the historical and legal bases of Aboriginal title, to calm industry fears about potential threats to economic stability in the event of recognition and settlement of Aboriginal claims, and to begin to build a foundation for direct negotiations between industry and First Nations governments on issues of economic development.

Following these conferences, held at the exclusive Whistler Mountain Resort in the traditional territory of the Squamish First Nation, British Columbia Social Credit Premier Bill Vander Zalm appointed a "native affairs advisory council" to serve as a consultative committee. The advisory council held meetings with key players throughout the province during the spring and summer to discuss Aboriginal land claims. *Vancouver Sun* columnist Vaughn

Palmer observed that, "The thinking in government circles is that the court will probably recognize aboriginal title...that it still exists today."[2]

On May 31, 1990, less than a year before Chief Justice McEachern's judgment in the *Delgamuukw* case was delivered, the Supreme Court of Canada had overturned earlier decisions of the British Columbia Supreme Court and the B.C. Court of Appeal in the case of *Regina v. Sparrow*. The Supreme Court concluded that certain Aboriginal rights—in this case the fishing rights of the Musqueam First Nation—had existed in British Columbia prior to the arrival of Europeans; had not been extinguished by the simple assertion of British sovereignty during the colonial era; and were now protected by section 35(1) of the *Constitution Act (1987)*, the supreme law of Canada.

Although the Supreme Court of Canada, in their decision in the *Sparrow* case, upheld the position that, since Britain declared sovereignty, the "underlying title to all land" in Canada is vested in the Crown, they ruled that Aboriginal rights could not be *implicitly* extinguished by the mere declaration that British sovereignty had been asserted. Rather, the Crown would have to *explicitly* express their "clear and plain intention" in order to legally extinguish Aboriginal title to land. The first premise of the Province of British Columbia's position since 1871 had been that no legally-recognizable Aboriginal title existed at the time the British arrived in what is now British Columbia. Therefore, according to the Province of B.C., an *explicit* expression of intent to extinguish title was neither required nor appropriate: what does not exist, could not be recognized. What could not be recognized, need not be extinguished.

The Supreme Court of Canada's rejection of the implicit extinguishment argument in the *Sparrow* case, their reaffirmation of the requirement that the Crown make their intention to extinguish Aboriginal title *explicit*, and their finding that this had not been done, and hence Aboriginal rights still existed in the province, was a significant victory for B.C. First Nations: the provincial government could now be legally required to acknowledge their existence.

The *Sparrow* decision was hailed by many as the judgment that would bring an end to the long—and increasingly contentious—chapter in Canadian legal history in which colonial law, justified by archaic nineteenth-century notions of European superiority and Aboriginal inferiority, had dominated the courts. It was hoped that the *Sparrow* decision would provide the required legal framework within which a new, more equitable relationship between Aboriginal and non-Aboriginal people in Canada could be developed, a relationship that would reflect contemporary commitments to social justice and equality in a multicultural Canada. Lower courts in British Columbia during 1990-1991 had granted several First Nations' applications for injunctions, halting development on their lands until the Aboriginal title question was settled by the courts.

Public opinion polls conducted during 1990 and 1991 had consistently shown that the majority of people in British Columbia thought the provincial government should reconsider its historic refusal to discuss land claims with the First Nations and should proceed, finally, to negotiate an agreement with them. Premier Vander Zalm—heeding the courts, public opinion polls, and increasing pressure from corporate representatives seeking government guarantees that British Columbia could indeed boast a "safe investment climate"—had allowed that the issue of land rights negotiations with First Nations should be revisited. For the first time in the province's 119-year history, a provincial Ministry of Aboriginal Affairs had been inaugurated in the Fall of 1990.

After nearly 100 years of political lobbying for the right to even file such a petition in court, the Nisga'a[3] First Nation—neighbours of the Gitksan and Wet'suwet'en—had been the first to launch a legal claim for recognition of their Aboriginal title in 1969. On March 7th, 1991, the day before Chief Justice McEachern's ruling in the Gitksan and Wet'suwet'en case was handed down, a landmark tripartite agreement between the Nisga'a Tribal Council and the federal and provincial governments was announced.

No one had anticipated what did happen on March 8, 1991.

Chief Justice Allan McEachern had not been swayed by public opinion polls or newspaper editorials, or by the Supreme Court of Canada's *Sparrow* decision, or by the copious evidence in support of the Gitksan and Wet'suwet'en claim that he had listened to for four years. In his 400 page *Reasons for Judgment*, the Chief Justice analyzed the testimony, reviewed the relevant points in law, and then dismissed the Gitksan and Wet'suwet'en claim. No Aboriginal title or rights had pre-existed European settlement, he ruled; and even if they had, they had been extinguished by the simple fact of Britain asserting sovereignty. Treaties had not been made, nor compensation paid, nor Aboriginal consent acquired. Nor were they required, he ruled.

Late One Night at the Legion

Like most everyone else interested in Aboriginal issues, especially in British Columbia, the judgment caught me off guard. The early morning CBC radio news on March 8, 1991, announced that the judgment had been released to the lawyers, who were in a "lock up" with the document until noon.[4] I, too, had assumed that the outcome of this case would be relatively positive for the claimants: an historic turning point in the legal struggle for recognition of Aboriginal title and rights. When I turned on the CBC radio midday news it was not with bated breath or apprehension, but rather with curiosity to know the details of the judgment and what the implications were for all parties to this case. To say I was shocked by what I heard on the radio is an understatement.

During the years 1988 to 1991, I had been a graduate student in Anthropology at the University of British Columbia and at Simon Fraser University. These were also the years that the Gitksan and Wet'suwet'en case was being heard in the British Columbia Supreme Court. While I was not directly involved in the trial in any way, I had followed developments in this case through media, attended public information sessions, special lectures, support demonstrations, benefit dances and fund-raising performances; and bought raffle tickets. Social movements in general, and Aboriginal politics in particular, form both the central focus of my work, and the personal and social milieu in which I live my everyday life. Therefore, the progress of this high-profile court case had been the subject of countless informal discussions among friends and relatives over the course of its four-year duration.

For days following the release of Chief Justice McEachern's ruling, the trial and the judgment were being talked about everywhere I went: at home, at the university, at social gatherings. Everyone I encountered had something to say about the Gitksan and Wet'suwet'en case and the Chief Justice's decision. Most were shocked. Many were outraged. A few were smug. Others were bitter. Some said the Gitksan and Wet'suwet'en should never have gone to court to begin with: what can you expect from the white man's courts? Since when could justice be found in law? Others felt betrayed by a legal system they had previously believed to be fundamentally fair. Some people were critical of the lawyers and the way they had conducted the case—some said they had asked for too much and overwhelmed the judge with mountains of data. Others said they had not asked for enough, and that they should have called even more evidence. Some said the *Delgamuukw* decision was an anomaly and didn't represent the thinking of the judiciary as a whole. Others said the opposite: McEachern had simply used unfashionable words and precedents to express what his colleagues, who had learned to obscure these ideas with more "politically correct" language, really thought.

Anthropologists were insulted by the Chief Justice's wholesale rejection of ethnographic evidence. Many were dismayed that anthropologists like Hugh Brody, Richard Daly and Antonia Mills—who had served as expert witnesses—had been summarily dismissed and reprimanded by the judge for being "advocates" whose participant observation research was not "credible." Others were critical of the anthropology presented, and the anthropologists who had testified on behalf of the Gitksan and Wet'suwet'en: Hugh Brody had been too caustic. Richard Daly had been too obtuse. Antonia Mills had been too ethereal. They had presented too seamless a case. Others said they had indulged themselves in idealism and ideology: empiricism[5] should have ruled the day.

Most Aboriginal people I spoke with were less shocked by the judgment than their non-Aboriginal peers. They were disappointed, and deeply hurt by the Chief Justice's words. More than anything, they were angry at what they saw as the judge having insulted the Chiefs and Elders by his charge that their testimony had been "untrue." Some Aboriginal people muttered resentfully about how much money the lawyers and the expert witnesses had made. Some asked why the anthropologists had ever been involved in the first place. Why hadn't the Gitksan and Wet'suwet'en stood by their own Chiefs and Elders and refused the need for "representation and translation" by white anthropologists?

In an unprecedented gesture, the government of British Columbia bound Chief Justice McEachern's *Reasons for Judgment* in book form and distributed it widely throughout the province. Rumour had it that the Chief Justice hoped his text would form the basis of a public school curriculum. Shock turned to incredulity as the volume circulated among scholars and other people knowledgeable about British Columbia history and Aboriginal cultures. The Canadian Anthropology Society, representing 405 scholars, told the press that the judgment "gratuitously dismisses scientific evidence, is laced with ethnocentric bias and is rooted in the colonial belief that white society is inherently superior."[6] University of British Columbia anthropology Professor Robin Ridington added that "if an Anthropology 100 student wrote anything like that in a paper, not only would you write a lot of red ink over it, you would say 'Look, please come in and talk to me. You have real problems.'"[7]

When I read the *Reasons for Judgment*, I found the text very familiar. I was immersed at university in the study of critiques of colonialism and western culture, written largely by colonized and formerly colonized people. This work focuses on how European social theories classify and represent non-European peoples as inferior "Others," justifying colonial domination and exploitation by western powers. Within the borders of the west, similar processes of "othering" had long legitimated the subordination of women, minorities, gays, lesbians, the poor, the disabled, and political dissidents by dominant classes.[8] Chief Justice McEachern's text read like a caricature of everything I was studying. The rendition the *Reasons for Judgment* offered of British Columbia's history repeats what can be read in the blunt, unselfconscious language of Indian Agents' reports found in archival records, and in the memoirs of pioneers, missionaries and settlers that form the corpus of popular history in B.C.: what political scientist, Paul Tennant, has called "the founding myth of White British Columbians."[9] These local stories of Aboriginal primitivism, European superiority, and the historical inevitability of colonial domination are repeated throughout the colonized world. One can hear very similar stories in Australia, New Zealand, and South Africa. They are self-justifying accounts, told by a colonial people whose ongoing doubts and insecurities about the moral legitimacy of their occupation of Indigenous lands require that these stories be told, and retold. Having lived in a small coastal community in British Columbia for many years, I recognized in the Chief Justice's tome what I had long ago nicknamed the "late one night at the Legion" version of B.C.'s history.

A month or so after the *Delgamuukw* judgment was released, I attended a meeting of anthropologists and historians at the University of British Columbia to discuss how we might responsibly respond. We agreed that we would each write an article on a specific aspect of the anthropological and historical evidence that had been presented during the case. These papers would be compiled in a special edition of the journal, *B.C. Studies*.[10] I chose to write a critique of the opinion report, testimony, and cross-examination of the expert witness who had provided anthropological evidence for the Crown, Dr. Sheila Robinson.

I approached this project expecting to find in Dr. Robinson's evidence an interpretation of facts presented within a coherent, logical argument. I anticipated that I would likely disagree with Robinson's analysis, on a professional basis. Debate, after all, we like to think, is the foundation of scholarly integrity. I was shocked to find that her opinion report did not include an up-to-date review and analysis of relevant theoretical or substantive literature. Instead I found oxymoronic[11] argument, and the substitution of theoretical speculations for empirical facts. I also read the reports and testimony of the anthropologists who testified for the Gitksan and Wet'suwet'en. I found issues to debate with Richard Daly, Antonia Mills and Hugh Brody, but the important difference between their submissions and those made on behalf of the Crown was that the former were meritorious, scholarly documents while the latter were not. The stark contrast between the expert opinion reports in anthropology and history submitted on behalf of the Gitksan and Wet'suwet'en, and those submitted on behalf of the Crown, was alarming in terms of their respective professional credibility. Furthermore, the Gitksan's and Wet'suwet'en's evidence and arguments accorded more obviously with conventional notions of what constitutes facts and logical argument than did the Crown's. Most importantly, the judge's crucial legal findings were based on particular interpretations of history and explanations of cultural differences. Clearly, the Crown's arguments and the testimony of their expert witnesses had appeared the more credible to Chief Justice McEachern. Why? What criteria had the judge used to evaluate the evidence he had heard?

I read more of the transcripts and more of the legal analyses. I found in the texts of the *Delgamuukw v. R.* case an intense debate not only about Aboriginal land rights but also about moral visions, social theories and political strategies. In presenting their cases, the "Plaintiffs" and the "Defendants" disputed how stories would be told about the past, present and future of British Columbia; and about who could tell them. Above all, they competed for the judge's verdict: whose account would the law declare to be "the truth"? Whose story would have an army at its disposal?

I decided to write my doctoral dissertation on the *Delgamuukw* case. I began with law's history.

1. Glavin, Terry 1991: B3.

2. Palmer, Vaughn 1990, quoted in Tennant, P. 1990: 237.

3. Previously, the First Nations of the Nass Valley of British Columbia were called "Nishga." Currently, this First Nation spells its name as "Nisga'a."

4. For a personal account of one lawyer's experience of this event, see Pinder, Leslie Hall 1991.

5. Empiricism is a theory of knowledge usually associated with the natural and physical sciences. Its basic tenets are that all "factual knowledge" originates in observation and experience, and can be falsified by observation and experience. "Empiricism" is usually understood as being opposed to other theories of knowledge that take greater account of the way social-cultural context and the subjectivity of the researcher and the reader can shape the meanings derived from observation and experience.

6. Canadian Press 1991: B3.

7. Ibid.

8. The literature on this subject is huge, multidisciplinary and growing rapidly. Texts that have become classics in the study of European constructions of "others" include: Asad (ed.)1973; Clifford and Marcus (eds.) 1986; Deloria 1969; Fabian 1991; Fanon 1963; McCrane 1989; Trinh T. Minh-ha 1989; Said 1978, 1992; Spivak 1988; Todorov 1982; West 1993; Wolf 1983.

9. Tennant 1991: 76.

10. See Miller (ed.) 1992.

11. An oxymoron is defined as "a combination of contradictory or incongruous words (as *cruel kindness*)," *Webster's New Collegiate Dictionary*, 814.

PART II

TERRA NULLIUS

(UNOCCUPIED, EMPTY LAND)

Chapter 3: Cultures Similar and Different

Law is essentially historical, not just in the sense that the life histories of legal systems can be chronicled, but more importantly in the sense that it is characteristic of law to anchor justification to the past. Time is the soil of the lawyer's thinking.
—Philosopher Gerald Postema, 1991, *On the Moral Presence of Our Past.*

Creating Race in the Interests of Empire

"The point at which a storyteller chooses to begin," Edward Said wrote, "is the first step in the intentional construction of meaning."[1] The Gitksan and Wet'suwet'en begin their story—locate their origins as sovereign peoples with title and rights to specific lands—in "time immemorial," when the Creator placed them on specific territories, and charged them with the responsibility of looking after the sentient beings who lived in and from and with these lands. They adopted the legal term, "time immemorial," as a way of representing and translating—communicating—to English language courts their belief that they have been there since the beginning of time.

Chief Justice McEachern rejected what he considered the "non-specific" nature of Gitksan and Wet'suwet'en history, writing in his *Reasons for Judgment*, "I am not able to conclude on the evidence that the plaintiffs' ancestors used the territory since 'time immemorial' (the time when the memory of man 'runneth not to the contrary'). 'Time immemorial,' as everyone knows, is a legal expression referring to the year 1189 (the beginning of the reign of Richard II), as specified in the Statute of Westminster, 1275."[2]

Another common starting point for legal historians to begin their rendition of the story of European/Aboriginal relations in the Americas is the year Europeans call 1492: when Columbus sailed the ocean blue. The controversies that followed Columbus' arrival in the Caribbean concerning the moral and political legitimacy of conquest and colonialism culminated in the Conference of Valladolid. In 1550, King Charles V of Spain brought together clerics, lawyers and other scholars in the Spanish city of Valladolid and asked them to address the question of whether Indigenous peoples were part of the same human race, or species, as Europeans; and, depending on the answer to this fundamental question, how they should be treated by European colonial powers. The king asked a philosopher, Juan Gines de Sepulveda, and a

Dominican monk, Bartolomeo de Las Casas, to answer the question: "How can conquests, discoveries and settlements in the king's name be made to accord with justice and reason?" Both Sepulveda and Las Casas agreed that all human beings, including Indigenous peoples, were of one species. Both also agreed that it was the duty of Europeans to convert all the world's peoples to Christianity, disagreeing only on method and rationale.

Sepulveda argued, relying on Aristotle, that some races are inferior to others, and that some people are born to slavery. By this reasoning, Europeans, a superior race, were justified in subjugating Indigenous peoples, an inferior race. Sepulveda used stories of cannibalism as evidence of the alleged inherent inferiority of the Indigenous peoples of South America. The technological achievements and complex social organization of the Aztecs and Incas, then as obviously sophisticated by prevailing European standards as they are universally acknowledged to be now, were absent from Sepulveda's analysis. Las Casas argued, on the other hand, that these "Indians" possessed an evolved culture, with social, economic and religious institutions. He claimed that Indigenous peoples were rational beings, fit to be compared to the Greeks and Romans. Las Casas did not argue that Spain should *not* conquer the Indigenous Peoples of the Americas, but rather that its only justification for doing so should be to Christianize them. He was distraught that the cruelty of the conquistadors was inhibiting his mission of conversion.

The choice of the conference at Valladolid as the origin story of European/ Indigenous relations in America, has been popularized in Canada by Judge Thomas Berger, a long time supporter of Aboriginal rights, and well-respected for having headed a public inquiry into the potential impacts of a proposed oil and gas pipeline on the Aboriginal peoples of the Canadian north. In his book, *A Long and Terrible Shadow: White Values, Native Rights in the Americas, 1492- 1992*, Berger writes of the deliberations at Valladolid: "Here was the very debate that I heard centuries later in the Mackenzie Valley Pipeline Inquiry." The "Berger Inquiry" broke with the traditional colonial reliance on non-Aboriginal experts that had historically characterized such processes, and encouraged and respected the participation of Aboriginal communities in its proceedings. The inquiry's findings and recommendations supported the Aboriginal peoples' opposition to the pipeline and their aspirations for local control. Berger proposed a ten-year moratorium on resource development to allow time for environmental and social impact studies to be completed, and for First Nations to consolidate their vision of self determination. (As it turned out, the oil and gas companies eventually abandoned their plans to build the pipeline for "economic reasons": it became an unprofitable proposition.)

The appeal of the Valladolid story, for liberal Canadians like Berger, may in part lie in its archetypal legal story form: a triangle consisting of a good learned person (Las Casas); a bad learned person (Sepulveda); and a benevolent sovereign (Charles), pondering a deeply important and complex issue in a quasi-judicial forum. Berger constructs the law's uninterrupted historical narrative from Columbus' encounters in Central and South America to contemporary Canada. This evokes notions of political conflict rooted in racial or cultural differences, often thought to be universal characteristics of all human societies in all historical periods, and thus to be immutable. The dominant image evoked is easily recognizable in contemporary liberal discourses on multiculturalism and identity-politics: white European colonizers, and brown Indigenous colonized.

While the impact of Spanish colonization on the Americas is important, it is British imperialism and colonial law that is specifically of interest to this story, a story that differs from Spanish colonial history in some important ways. British imperial law traces its origins to the common law tradition that emerged in the fifth century A.D. when the Anglo-Saxons invaded what is now called England and conquered the indigenous Britons. The Anglo-Saxons went on to absorb immigrant Danes and Gauls, others of whom (having become, over the course of the ensuing five centuries, Normans) in turn conquered the Anglo-Saxons in 1066. The Norman conquest of 1066 brought to Great Britain a centralized state and church, and the arbitrary power of the king. Under the Norman-derived legal regime, the king, or sovereign, who mystically embodies the "underlying title to all land" and the implicit consent of all the people to his reign, is said to "hover over the land." The origin of the sovereign's legal title is to be found in this abstract, imaginary vision, made concrete through the exercise of power as the sovereign became the symbolically omnipotent source of law, and his will its practical execution. A feudal regime, sometimes referred to as the "Norman Yoke," was established, against which Anglo-Saxons, Britons, Danes, Gauls and some Normans (now having become English and Scots) waged civil war.[3]

At the same time as Sepulveda and Las Casas were debating in Valladolid, English jurists were confronting similar problems regarding colonization in Ireland. Their dilemma was not precipitated by the sudden "discovery" of seemingly strange and alien peoples. Rather, the problem of justifying expropriations of lands and massacres of native populations that faced British imperial policy-makers was that of *recategorizing* as radically "different" their Irish neighbours who had hitherto been similar and familiar.[4]

That the Irish were Christian was never doubted by the Normans or their successors, but Christianity in Gaelic Ireland did not fully conform to Roman liturgical practice, and many pre-Christian traditions and customs had been only slightly veneered in these territories by Christianity. On this basis, the Irish were classified by British imperial law as atheists or infidels. Although, unlike "certain savage tribes," the Irish were rarely accused of cannibalism, they were described as "little better than Cannibals...."[5] In addition, the English took the Irish practice of transhumance[6] as proof that the Irish were nomads, hence barbarians. The English colonists thus developed a social theory that said the Irish had evolved to a level of cultural development analogous to the stage the ancient Britons existed at before they were civilized by the Romans. The Irish should therefore be made subservient to the colonizing English, (the true inheritors of Roman civilization) so that, through subjugation, they could come to appreciate civility and thus eventually achieve freedom as the former Britons had done.[7] This belief that meting out punishment to subordinated peoples and individuals "for their own good" will result in their eventual emancipation, while an enduring one, is belied by the historical record which offers more support for the theory that cruelty breeds brutality.

My point is straightforward: the boundaries separating categories of people, and, more importantly, the significance of differences between and among them, are, like culture itself, constructed by people—not given by nature or God—and they change over the course of history as contexts and social relations change. Being created by people, these fluid boundaries can also be challenged, changed and recreated by people over time, as indeed, historically, they often have been.

The story of Aboriginal and non-Aboriginal relations in British Columbia that I am telling here begins with England's sixteenth-century colonization of Ireland, rather than with Columbus' landing in the Caribbean, for a number of reasons. First, there is the obvious historical continuity: the British colonized British Columbia, the Spaniards did not, although they "discovered" the territory before the British. Second, the story of the colonization of Ireland tells of recurring hostilities among people of the same "race" and "cultural group." Rather than illustrating universal, ahistorical and immutable conflict based in "natural" racial or cultural difference, the history of England and Ireland is an example of contests for economic and political domination, and the historical process of "racialization" of the "other" so fundamental to colonial law and cultures.[8] The image I wish to evoke is easily recognizable in contemporary debates about *critical* multiculturalism and post-colonial politics: same-culture colonizers, and same-culture colonized.[9]

Finally, the appeal of Berger's choice of Valladolid as the preferred origin story for the history of Aboriginal legal rights in Canada may also be found in its acceptance of the historical inevitability, and hence justification, of European colonial conquest. Its insistence that colonial powers were and are motivated by good intentions and paternalistic—yet humanitarian—concerns for the best interests of the colonized, also reinforces familiar legitimations of colonial dominance.

"All this was done with the best intentions. We can only ask what would have happened had government's intentions *not* been good?" Phrases like this have become a common cliché used by the Canadian media to wrap up stories about how another government program, or lack thereof, has been implicated in some tragic chain of events in an Aboriginal community.

Assessing history solely on the basis of the intentions of the powerful, without reference to the consequences for the powerless, is a time-honoured tradition in western thought. Within this framework, the morality of a person's actions can only be judged on the basis of his or her intentions. This is based on the premise that people should not be held responsible for events beyond their control that contribute to their original actions having unintended consequences. At a very basic philosophical level, this is, of course, only fair. We as individuals are the only ones who know what our intentions are in the first place. Other people know our intentions only when we choose to communicate them. Our intentions motivate us to act in particular ways in relation to others, and our actions have consequences for ourselves and for those others. If our intentions, according to our own account, are honourable, but a person who experiences the consequences of our actions suffers, how is this to be resolved? The issue becomes more complex in real life where the questions "what ought you to know before you act?" and "whose intentions will be acted upon and thus enabled to have consequences?" must also be asked. "Judgment by intention" may be reasonable if "the individual" is considered as an isolated entity, but it becomes problematic when an individual is under-stood as a human being who lives in relationships with others in society.

The legal answer to this question in the liberal tradition is to grant rights to individuals, thereby hoping to ensure that the limit of one individual's rights is formed by the boundary at which another individual's liberty is inhibited.[10] In order for *groups* or *collectivities* or *peoples* to have similar protection within such a regime, they must be recognized in law as having legal rights. The history of Aboriginal/non-Aboriginal relations in Canada has been one in which courts and governments have repeatedly refused to recognize Aboriginal rights, while continuing to insist that their actions have been, and continue to be, guided by their "good intentions" in relation to First Nations. This "justification by intention" argument has been repeated by governments for hundreds of years now, despite the fact that the *consequences* of legally-sanctioned government policies have been, and continue to be, devastating for Aboriginal peoples. The federal government, in particular, has been repeatedly stymied by the unanticipated consequences of their good intentions. An option yet to be tried in the realization of governments' good intentions towards First Nations is the recognition of Aboriginal title to land, and rights to self-government.

Mutiny and Desertion as Common Sense

The initial conditions for theorizing and reflecting on property rights in America are of a European people who arrive on a continent of roughly five hundred established Aboriginal nations and systems of property...and who do not wish to become citizens of the existing Aboriginal nations, but wish to establish their own nations and systems of property in accordance with their European institutions and traditions.

—Philosopher James Tully, 1993, *An Approach to Political Philosophy: Locke in Contexts.*

Before the arrival of Europeans, approximately 500 Aboriginal nations existed in North America. These nations were diverse in modes of living, language, religion, social organization and relationships to land and resources. Therefore, the first rational option available to early European explorers and settlers was to behave as guests or immigrants, to recognize the sovereignty of already existing Indigenous nations, to live by their laws and to seek acceptance by their people.

But many deeply ingrained assumptions and widely held beliefs limit and constrain the possibility of contemporary people immersed in the dominant western culture imagining this as a practical or viable choice. European theories arising from psychoanalytic traditions have argued that fear and hostility are instinctive human responses to encounters with cultural "others." However, the weight of contemporary knowledge belies the proposition that such a reaction is either universal or natural. Oral historians and linguists have investigated the diverse ways in which non-Europeans have identified people other than themselves, including Europeans, at first contact. They found a variety of impressions and responses varying from adoration to repulsion, fear to amusement, hospitality to hostility and curiosity to indifference. Europeans have been represented in Indigenous thought by analogies as diverse as Gods, Devils, clowns and monkeys.[11]

European images of Indigenous peoples have varied across time and space as well. Early visitors to "new" worlds, like explorers and traders, frequently expressed both interest in and admiration for the peoples they met on their travels. Later visitors wishing to claim these lands as their own, such as colonial governors and settlers, portrayed Indigenous peoples as wild savages. Most influential in western thinking, however, have been various theories about social and cultural evolution that postulate a hierarchical series of stages through which it is claimed all human societies must proceed. "Primitive" societies, in which people live from hunting, fishing and gathering, represent the "first stage" in this scheme; while "civilized" industrial societies exemplify the "highest stage" of human development. In the field of jurisprudence, Sir

Henry S. Maine's 1861 volume, *Ancient Law*, sets out a conjectural history of the evolution of law from "primitive custom" that "mingled up religious, civil, and merely moral ordinances without any regard to differences in their essential character;" to "civilized law," which "severs law from morality, and religion from law." The purported independence of law from the social conditions of its emergence, and law's professed autonomy from the society in which it is practiced, were evidence, for Maine, that western law "belongs very distinctly to the later stages of mental progress."[12]

Another common idea that arises from the same social evolutionary premises is the analogy drawn between the stages of individual psychological development hypothesized by western developmental psychology, and the social organization of non-western societies. In this framework, adults are to children as Europeans are to Aboriginals. Within historical analyses, contemporary Indigenous societies, imagined as being "frozen" at "stages of development" believed to be "antecedent" to the present, are seen as resembling historical European ones. Dutch anthropologist Johannes Fabian calls this notion that "they" are now, as "we" were then, a "denial of coevalness" that he identifies as the most enduring obstacle to achieving mutually respectful dialogue between Europeans and "others."[13] Fabian uses the term "coeval" to describe how colonized and colonizer share both geographic space (land); and temporal space (time). Social inequality between peoples of different cultures, Fabian argues, is shaped by the historically-specific political and economic relationships between them. It does not emerge because they live at different hypothesized stages of evolutionary development. Power, not time, separates people of different cultures.

These social evolutionary premises support the common belief that, during the eighteenth century, when they came into substantial and sustained contact with each other, Europeans and members of British Columbia First Nations were so radically different from each other in terms of material living conditions, social organization, political structures, religion, intellectual development and individual freedom, that for British settlers to have integrated into the Aboriginal societies would have necessitated them stepping "backwards," both in historical time and in human psychological development. These beliefs are buttressed by images in paintings like those that decorate the Rotunda in the British Columbia Parliament buildings: luxuriously dressed and elaborately wigged British ship's captains benevolently bestowing gifts on scantily-clad and bewildered-looking Aboriginals.

But, consider what we know of the *real* conditions of life for the majority of people in eighteenth-century Britain: feudalism—dominated by the nobility, and the clergy living off the avails of peasant labour through tithing and maintaining power by force and threats of eternal spiritual damnation—was being replaced by industrial capitalism as the real source of power in the nation state.

Peasants, driven from the land, began to flock to the newly-emerging urban centres in search of subsistence from industry, rather than from hunting, gathering and agriculture. Accounts of factory conditions during early industrialization, and of the everyday life of ordinary citizens in cities like London, Manchester and Birmingham describe desperate urban poverty, squalor, alcoholism, prostitution and deprivation. It would be at least two centuries before women would be recognized as persons in British, and later Canadian, law, and we have yet to achieve mass literacy.

Compare this to what we now know of life during the same historical epoch among, for example, the Gitksan and Wet'suwet'en peoples. Their eighteenth-century societies were characterized by a hierarchical social structure dominated by chiefs and shamans; divisions of labour based in clan, gender and generation; an economy dependent on the accumulation and unequal redistribution of wealth derived from abundant natural resources among different categories of persons; spiritual beliefs linking ancestors, the living and the land that prescribed reciprocal obligations; social life, including marriage, divorce and inheritance controlled by elders. An oral, rather than written, tradition of recording history and administering law prevailed. That European and Indigenous cultures differed significantly is obvious. But was one "more advanced" or "less developed" than the other? This is not at all obvious. Answers are complicated first by the problem of criteria. As we know, technological complexity is not necessarily correlated with spiritual satisfaction or emotional well-being. Second, different categories of persons in both societies would likely evaluate their own cultures differently, depending on their position within it. Establishing universal criteria upon which to base such evaluations is an extraordinarily complex process, if it is to represent any authentic consensus. And, the question may be asked if universal criteria of what constitutes a "good society" are possible, or desirable.

What challenges the vision of unbridgeable cultural difference that has been codified in western law and in the popular imagination most fundamentally, however, are the actions of ordinary individuals in the everyday life of early colonial societies throughout history and around the world. Soldiers and sailors, who were often young unemployed men, were either pressed into service on trading and naval ships involuntarily ("shanghaied"), or signed on out of desperation in the absence of alternatives. Conditions at sea and in the armies were brutal, and troops frequently deserted their masters and escaped to live with the Aboriginal people they encountered on their voyages. Mutinies were common.[14] Historical accounts, and popular culture, often ignore the fact that, for Britain and other colonial powers, there were two problematic populations that had to be managed and controlled in order for imperial designs to be realized: Indigenous peoples, and colonial troops and settlers. Most telling, perhaps, are the histories of fragments of non-European populations, like Hawaiians,[15] and former African slaves who were fleeing the United States of

America.[16] Members of these groups, having no access to the protection of imperial power, frequently integrated into the Aboriginal societies whose acceptance their lives depended upon.

The belief reflected in law that Europeans arrived to lands without organized societies or laws is false. Legal scholar Brian Slattery has stated this flatly: "All national myths involve a certain amount of distortion," Slattery writes, "but some at least have the virtue of broad historical accuracy, roughly depicting the major forces at work. The myth that underlies much legal thinking about the history of Canada lacks that redeeming feature."[17]

To answer the question of why the option of recognizing the sovereignty of already existing Aboriginal nations, behaving as guests, and attempting to live by Aboriginal laws does not appear to have been taken up by early European jurists and settlers, we have to look to British and Euro-Canadian law and culture, rather than to Aboriginal beliefs and practices.

---

1. Said 1975: 1.

2. McEachern, Reasons 1991: 82. There are, however, debates about this date. Anthropologist Andrea Laforet commented: "Although McEachern sees this as a fixed date, receding relentlessly into the past, there is an alternative interpretation, i.e. that in 1275 the British defined 86 years as the measure of a very long time" (Laforet 1993:2). Lawyer William Henderson offers another correction, writing "...1189 is the date of the accession of Richard I (the 'Lionheart')" (Henderson, William B. 1991: 14 ftnt:45).

3. Hill 1958.

4. Canny 1973: 583, writes: "The questions that we must pose are how, at the mid-sixteenth century, the Irish, a people with whom the English had always had some familiarity, came to be regarded as uncivilized, and what justifications were used for indiscriminate slaying and expropriation?"

5. Ibid.,580.

6. "Transhumance" refers to the practice of owners and/or herders moving livestock on a seasonal basis between mountains and lowland pastures. It is contrasted to agricultural settlement where pasture lands remained fixed in one location.

7. Historically, when British settlers, first in Ireland, then in the American colonies, and later in British Columbia, looked to history and law for moral and political legitimization in their struggles for independence from the British Crown, they constructed a rhetoric recalling a "Golden Age" of "natural law" that, their story went, existed prior to the Norman invasion of Britain. See Andrews, Canny, Hair (eds.) 1973; and Knafla 1986(b). This local, or common, law has come to be known by the phrase "the fundamental laws of all Englishmen," which Robert Williams describes as "the opinion that the Anglo-Saxons of England lived as free and equal citizens under a form of representative government that was inspired by divine principles of natural law and the common rights of all individuals" (Williams, R. A. 1990:253).

8. "Racialization" refers to the ideological process whereby biological, genetic, or phenotypical characteristics are employed to classify categories of people. The most common example of the historically and socially constructed nature of racial categories is illustrated by the varying ways Jews have been classified throughout European history, where they have sometimes and in some places been classified as a distinct "race" of people, and at other times and in other places, not.

9. For an interesting examination of the process of racialization see Ignatiev, Noel 1995. The book examines the role played by identification with the dominant Caucasians and collusion in the oppression of Aboriginal and African-Americans in the historical ascendancy of Irish immigrants in the United States of America.

10. The notion that the morality of a person's actions can only be evaluated on the basis of their intentions is a central tenet of Kantian idealist philosophy. This privileges the subject's articulated interpretations and intentions, as compared to the interpretations and consequences experienced by others as a result of the subject's actions. This formulation assumes that individuals and their intentions and actions are not always already embedded in relationships, but can be decontextualized and considered independently. See Miles 1989 for a fuller discussion of "judging by intentions" in contexts of racial domination and subordination.

11. See Dauenhauer and Dauenhauer (eds.) 1994; Lips 1966; Wickwire 1994.

12. Maine (1861)1970: 15.

13. Fabian 1983.

14. For detailed discussions about mutinies in the early American colonies and the South Pacific, respectively, see Andrews et al (eds.)1973; and Obeysekere 1992.

15. See Koppel 1995.

16. See Alexander and Glaze 1996; Hudson 1997.

17. Slattery 1985: 114.

Chapter 4: Beginning at the Beginning

Aboriginal peoples, of course, did not go around talking about their rights; mostly, they spoke in a discourse of responsibilities and respect. But that discourse was circulated among themselves. When others came and established—or forced—dominance, it became relevant to speak of rights as a way of negotiating relations.
—Historian Peter Kulchyski, 1994, *Unjust Relations: Aboriginal Rights in Canadian Courts.*

Regardless of how the inhabitants themselves perceived their connections with the land, in every case a physical and economic relationship necessarily existed. Quite simply, when the English arrived, these people were already there, using lands in accordance with their own needs and their own ways of life, as people everywhere do.
—Legal scholar Kent McNeil, 1989, *Common Law Aboriginal Title.*

Aboriginal Peoples Were Here

When Britain became engaged in the colonization of the Americas, British legal rules were already in place that addressed several major questions which arose whenever British settlers established themselves in another territory. The "not-Christian enough" rationale, developed to cope with the Irish situation, became codified in law in *Calvin's Case* in 1608, when Britain's Chief Justice Coke articulated what has become known as the infidel rule: "if a Christian King should conquer a kingdom of an infidel, and bring them under his subjection, there ipso facto the laws of the infidels are abrogated, for that they be not only against Christianity, but against the law of God and of nature."[1]

A memorandum of the Privy Council of Great Britain in 1722 consolidated imperial law by setting out rules for establishing British sovereignty in two possible situations. The first option, alternatively referred to as the doctrine of discovery, or the doctrine of occupation, or the doctrine of settlement, was to be applied in circumstances where the land discovered was *terra nullius*—uninhabited by human beings.[2] The second option, the doctrine of conquest, was to be applied where Indigenous populations were encountered.

In the case of *terra nullius*, Britain simply proclaimed sovereignty by virtue of discovery and British law became, automatically, the law of the land. Where

Indigenous populations were found inhabiting the desired land, the law required that British sovereignty had first to be won by military conquest, or achieved through the negotiation of treaties, before colonial law could be superimposed.

Of course, Britain never had colonized and never would colonize an uninhabited land. Therefore, the doctrine of discovery/occupation/settlement based in the notion of *terra nullius* was never concretely applied "on the ground." Rather, already inhabited nations were simply legally *deemed to be uninhabited* if the people were not Christian, not agricultural, not commercial, not "sufficiently evolved" or simply in the way. In British Columbia, the doctrine of *terra nullius* has historically legitimized the colonial government's failure to enter into treaties with First Nations. The application of the doctrine of conquest to First Nations in British Columbia, which would have required recognition of the fact of their prior occupation, and their status as human beings, *was available within the confines of British imperial law* but was rejected by colonial governments in British Columbia. When Aboriginal people say today that they have had to go to court to prove they exist, they are speaking not just poetically, but also *literally*.

Oh, What a Tangled Web We Weave When First We Practice to Deceive...

> *Ordinarily, we think of language as describing a fact or a state of affairs...but a special capacity which is particularly inherent in the law makes things true simply by saying them.... This power is of course the attribute of judges and judicial decisions, among others. The texts of the law are thus quintessentially texts which produce their own effects.*
> —Sociologist Pierre Bourdieu, 1987, *The Force of Law: Towards a Sociology of the Juridical Field.*

The early history of British imperialism and its legal expressions constitute the beginning—"the first step in the intentional construction of meaning"—of the story which law itself tells about British and Canadian relations with First Nations in British Columbia. In law's imagination, a fundamental inequality was evident and established at the first moment of contact. This hierarchical relationship forms the cornerstone of the legal relations between Aboriginal peoples and Canadian governments, and is at the heart of each and every case of land rights litigation. It constitutes the foundational principles upon which the architecture of the Canadian state is built: the ultimate power of the British Crown to assert its will through simply *declaring* its sovereignty over foreign lands and peoples, supported, if necessary, by armed force; the fundamental relationship of Euro-Canadian domination and Aboriginal subordination;[3] and, the protection and advancement of the interests of the wealthy and the powerful classes of colonial society.

In these first moments in the story law tells us—in its assertion of *terra nullius*—we see the central role played by abstraction and theory in western law and culture: the world is conceived, *and acted upon*, as if reality can simply be conjured up in whatever form suits the desire of the powerful at the moment.[4] Within this ideology, human beings can be considered, legally, not to exist, and can be treated accordingly. At this most fundamental, common sense level, a study of British and Canadian law in relation to Aboriginal title and rights therefore begins not "on the ground," in concrete observations about different peoples' diverse ways of life, but rather "in the air," in abstract, imagined theory. Hovering, like the sovereign, who embodies this abstraction, over the land.

In the practices legitimized by this initiatory unleashing of the "will to power" we can see the antiquity of what continues to be a fundamental contradiction, paradox, or deceit in British and Canadian culture: an enduring abstract philosophical commitment to humanism—defined at the most elementary level as the fundamental equality of all human beings—co-exists with an enduring concrete material practice of inequality, and the domination of one group of people by another. It is within this space between the ideal and the real that ideologies of justification are constructed in law, government, imagination, and popular culture. This is the space wherein lies are legitimized and truths silenced. In the histories of colonial laws we can see both the mendacity and the crudeness of the original lie of European supremacy, and the shockingly unsophisticated nature of the edifice built upon it.

This same space between theory and practice, between avowed principles and lived experience, between the letter and the practice of the law, is one of the sites where Aboriginal peoples historically and contemporarily mount their resistance struggles. First Nations repeatedly expose both the failure of colonial law to obey itself in relation to Aboriginal peoples,[5] and the presence of systemic racial and cultural bias in the justice system.[6] When government policies and practices that systematically discriminate are juxtaposed with the Canadian state's formal commitment to democratic equality, hypocrisy is revealed.[7] In these ways, Aboriginal peoples strike repeated blows to the heart of Canada's liberal self-image and international personality.

So begins the long dance we call Aboriginal/nonAboriginal relations in Canada: a tango of domination and subordination, of resistance and repression, of compromise and intransigence, of accommodation and denial, of life and death.

Eclecticism

The English, in fact, were eclectic in their choice of aims and methods; at one time or another they tried almost everything.... Late-comers to the New World, they had an abundance of precedents from which to choose. No other colonial empire employed so wide a range of legal devices in establishing settlements, or allowed so many diverse forms of social, religious, and economic organization.

Many factors contributed to this diversity: a habit of eclectic borrowing; differences in time, place, and circumstance; differences in personality and purpose; and the absence of sustained interest and continuous effective control by the central government.

—Historian K. R. Andrews, 1973, in *The Westward Enterprise: English Activities in Ireland, the Atlantic and America, 1480-1650.*

In Canada, France preceded England in settlement, and entered into treaties with the Micmac, Maliseets, Montagnaix-Naskapi, Huron and Abenaki to secure them as allies against both the Iroquois and the English. Throughout the seventeenth century, numerous agreements were entered into between and among Aboriginal peoples and the French and English. Many of these treaties were verbal agreements, solemnized through assembly and gift exchange, and symbolized by, for example, wampum belts. Other treaties were written in French, and later, English, by colonial representatives, and signed by themselves and by Aboriginal representatives.

Before the arrival of Europeans, different Aboriginal Nations had political and economic agreements with each other regarding trade and commerce, war and peace. These initially served as models for the treaties they entered into with Europeans.[8] An important characteristic of early Indian-European treaty-making was that it conformed to Aboriginal political practices more than to European ones, reflecting the real balance of power that existed when Aboriginal peoples formed both the vast majority of the population, and possessed the necessary knowledge and skills to live in the North American environment.[9] Current legal and political conflicts revolve around issues of competing interpretations of the intentions of the original treaty-makers, the obligations of governments that arise out of the treaties, and whether these obligations have been honoured or not.

In some cases, Aboriginal peoples, relying primarily on oral histories, argue that their ancestors entered into "peace and friendship" agreements with Europeans that allowed the newcomers certain rights to travel and harvest resources. These treaties, they say, were never understood to be final surrenders of lands, rights or political sovereignty. Rather, they were agreements that would be renegotiated as needed to respond to changing conditions, and renewed regularly through deliberations and ceremonies like the ones from which they had originally emerged.

Against this, the Crown consistently argues that treaties should only be considered within the context of British law, without regard for Aboriginal legal practices at the time the treaties were made. It claims that the treaties are permanent and binding legal land cessions that also yield political sovereignty; and that the money paid to Indians constituted a trade of money for land, not lease or rental fees, or a toll, or a ceremonial exchange of gifts.

A significant challenge to the Crown's position also emerges from within British and Canadian law and centres on debates about the nature of informed consent. Contractual agreements like treaties are only valid if both parties were fully aware of the terms and the consequences of the contract they entered into. In some cases, Aboriginal representatives are asking courts to consider whether or not Crown representatives made their interpretation of the meaning of treaties clear, verbally, to the Aboriginal peoples they were negotiating with. If not, and if the Aboriginal signatories to the treaties were not English speakers, readers, or writers, what is the legality of those treaties signed with an "X" scrawled next to an anglicized Aboriginal name printed by the governments' treaty negotiators?

Imperialist Competitions in Terra Nullius

> Englishman, although you have conquered the French, you have not yet conquered us. We are not your slaves. These lakes, these woods and mountains, were left to us by our ancestors...they are our inheritance; and we will part with them to none. Your nation supposes that we, like the white people, cannot live without bread, and pork and beef! But, you ought to know, that He, the Great Spirit and Master of Life, has provided food for us, in these spacious lakes, and on these woody mountains.
> —Chippewa leader Minivavana, to an English trader, at Michilimackinac, Fall 1761.[10]

By the Treaty of Utrecht in 1713, France ceded control over the Canadian Maritime regions to England, while retaining Cape Breton Island, Ile St. Jean and miscellaneous islands in the Gulf of St. Lawrence. In 1759 the British captured Quebec after seven years of war, and the subsequent Peace of Paris, signed in 1760, temporarily sorted out disputes between France, England and Spain. France ceded all its remaining territories in Canada and its territories east of the Mississippi River. Spain ceded Florida to Britain, but retained its territories west of the Mississippi captured from France in 1759. As conflicts between colonial powers intensified, a pattern developed that would continue into the present: European powers, and later federal and provincial governments, engaged in disputes with each other over lands and resources, that excluded Aboriginal peoples. As if they didn't exist.

Imperialist Nostalgia[11] in Terra Nullius

"In the beginning all the world was America."
—Political philosopher John Locke, 1672.[12]

While the Treaty of Utrecht and the Peace of Paris were being negotiated and signed, eighteenth-century British society was undergoing rapid industrialization and urbanization. Members of the new middle and professional classes became concerned about the human costs of this process, represented by the plight of former peasants who increasingly formed impoverished rural and urban populations. Europeans increasingly looked to science for guidance in social policy at home, and for rationalizations of colonial policies abroad. Various treatises emerged that claimed to explain the whole history of all humankind in systematic and coherent ways, and that all began with theories about human origins. Although available information about Aboriginal ways of life was principally limited to explorers' and traders' idiosyncratic and unsystematic records, the authors of the "grand theories" of Enlightenment Europe usually began with an evocation of so-called "primitive life in the New World," meant to illustrate "raw human nature" and "original human society." For romantics like Jean Jacques Rousseau, the "state of nature" was to be found in a simple Garden of Eden, and Indigenous peoples in America, imagined as "noble savages," provided Europeans, steeped in the popular "common sense" of evolutionism, with appealing fantasies of their own primitive origins.

At the opposite extreme, for philosophers like Thomas Hobbes, the "state of nature" was an instinct-driven war of all against all. The establishment of society, and collective survival, depended upon the imposition of a sovereign's power and government to contain and control an essentially competitive and aggressive "human nature." The Hobbesian "state of nature" that he, too, claimed was being lived in eighteenth century Indigenous societies in the Americas, was one of constant warfare, an absence of law or government, and a life that was "nasty, brutish and short." Whatever the western rendition of "primitive life," Aboriginal peoples occupied one or another of these "savage slots" in the European imagination: noble child of harmonious nature, or dangerous child of animal instinct.[13] In whichever rendition, Aboriginal peoples were used as a *tabula rasa* upon which Europeans could project whatever theoretical or cultural fashion seized the fantasy of the day. In both renditions, the reality of the ways of life, lived experiences and self representations of Aboriginal peoples are sacrificed to the European imagination. These "grand theories" competed with each other for acceptance amongst professional and popular audiences.

Enough and As Good

John Locke is usually identified as the most significant political theorist of this imperial era in Britain. Locke gathered together arguments circulating during the early seventeenth century and set them out in theories that would serve many of the later legal and political justifications of European seizure of property in North America.[14] Locke, in the fashion of the times, argued that Aboriginal peoples lived in a pre-political state of nature representative of the first stage in universal human evolutionary development. Important characteristics of this early developmental phase included a hunting and gathering economy with no perception of established systems of property or government. Europe correspondingly represented the most advanced stage of evolutionary development. This was proven by the practice of agriculture; the existence of a legally codified system of property with written laws; a bureaucratic government; and a capitalist economy in which all exchanges of commodities in the market place between people are conducted through the common medium of money, the value of which is ultimately guaranteed by the state. The sovereign's image stamped on coinage symbolically represents the presence of the hovering sovereign mediating every monetary exchange between citizens.

Locke went on to theorize that Aboriginal peoples therefore had property rights only "in the products of their labour: the fruit they gather, the deer they catch and the corn they pick." In this they are governed by a "natural law," Locke mused, that says each individual may appropriate what nature offers up without consultation with, or consent by, anyone else "as long as there is enough and as good left in common for others." Locke reasoned that Europeans would increase the productivity of the land through agriculture and were therefore justified in appropriating Aboriginal lands without consent. Since this process was governed by the "natural law" of evolutionary development, if Aboriginal peoples inhibited European settlement, they would be in violation of natural law and could justifiably be eliminated. Philosopher James Tully concludes that, if Locke had recognized Aboriginal forms of property, and Aboriginal peoples as equal to Europeans, then "settlement in America would have been illegitimate by his own criteria of 'enough and as good,' and consent would have been required."[15]

Nation to Nation. Words to Paper.

> *And whereas it is just and reasonable, and essential to Our Interest and the Security of Our Colonies, that the several Nations or Tribes of Indians, with whom We are connected, and who live under Our Protection, should not be molested or disturbed in the Possession of such Parts of Our Dominions and Territories as, not having been ceded to, or purchased by Us, are reserved to them, or any of them, as their Hunting Grounds.*
> —"The Indian Provisions," *Royal Proclamation of 1763.*[16]

The prevailing conditions in eastern Canada during the early 1760s were very complex,[17] and formed the historical context in which the Royal Proclamation of 1763—a document that continues to be the subject of legal and political debates today—was issued. The British were faced with a number of problems. Their relationship with Indian nations who had been allies of the French was precarious. During the Seven Years War between Britain and France there had been active competition for Indian allies, and British army commanders in the field had been generous in their purchases of furs and exchanges of ammunition. After the war, London cut back these funds considerably and field commanders found themselves unable to honour commitments they had previously made. Entrepreneurial settlers and fur traders were making independent incursions on Indian lands and resources, impeding the development of the Crown monopoly. On the international front, Britain's hegemony in North America was still threatened by the Russians from the north, and the Spanish from the southwest. The Royal Proclamation of 1763 attempted to address all of these issues.

Competing interpretations of the historical, legal and political implications of the Royal Proclamation of 1763 have occupied a central place in Aboriginal title and rights discourse and litigation over the past two centuries. A key debate surrounds the question of whether or not the Royal Proclamation should be interpreted as having *recognized* already existing Aboriginal rights, or as having created these rights. The former, which has since come to be known as the "inherent rights" position, is based on the assumption that Aboriginal rights today flow continuously from the sovereignty of nations that pre-existed European colonization. The latter—the "delegated rights" position—argues that, in law, no rights can exist except those created by the will of the sovereign. Hence, contemporary Aboriginal rights could only be those that a sovereign, or a court, or a parliament chooses to assign. Such rights would always be based in the desires of these bodies, and not in Indigenous history. And what the sovereign creates, the sovereign can also destroy or dismiss, at his pleasure.

Analysts agree, however, on some points. The Royal Proclamation differentiated Indian title to land in North America from non-Indian title in five significant ways. First, it reflected the fact that, in 1763, the Crown understood that it must at least formally recognize the legitimacy of, and negotiate on equal political grounds with, "Indian *Nations*." The Royal Proclamation is guided by the doctrine of conquest set out in the Memorandum of the Privy Council in 1722.

Second, under the Proclamation, Indian title is defined as being collectively or communally, not individually, held. Furthermore, this title is limited to *use rights*, like hunting and fishing, that are comparable to perpetual leases rather than to ownership. The uses in question must be only those practiced before European arrival. The Royal Proclamation therefore acknowledges First Nations as having some form of interest in their lands and resources. Whether, by legal interpretations, or cultural assumptions, this "Indian title" is of equal value to "Crown title," or is some less valued form of property right that constitutes "a burden" on the Crown's title, is a subject of ongoing controversy.

Third, the Proclamation dictates that Indian title can be only be transferred to the Crown. A number of debates have arisen concerning both the intent and the consequences of this clause. Many historians have argued that the insertion of this clause was primarily motivated by a humanitarian, paternalistic concern to protect Indians from unscrupulous frontier land speculators. Others argue that this clause reflects a power struggle between the Crown as state, and corporate and private interests, for monopoly over lands and resources. Still others focus on competition between international imperial interests and those of the emerging local, colonial governments.

Fourth, the Proclamation identifies Indians as "Nations or Tribes"[18] and guarantees Indians the *protection* of the Crown. This would later come to be expressed as a "fiduciary duty." Ongoing debates involve whether or not this fiduciary duty and the obligations it entails should be interpreted as resulting from a negotiated, trust-like agreement between equal parties, or as reflecting a relationship of dependency analogous to the parent/child relationship which is also classified, in law, as a "fiduciary duty."

Fifth, the Royal Proclamation requires that Indigenous land rights can only be surrendered at a public assembly at which Indians give their consent. This issue comes up particularly in treaty litigation where some Aboriginal claimants argue that, whatever negotiations and agreements are claimed by the Crown to have been reached with their ancestors, the representatives who signed the treaties had not been mandated to do so by their constituencies, and there was insufficient knowledge of and/or participation by the required majority of the Indigenous land holders to render the treaty legal.

In these interpretations, the possibility that Aboriginal peoples may not have wanted to sell, cede or by treaty give sovereignty or lands to anyone is not provided for in the written words of the Royal Proclamation of 1763. Nor is the possibility entertained that Aboriginal sovereignty could remain dominant, or could co-exist with Crown sovereignty.

Another significant debate about the Royal Proclamation of 1763 centres on the degree to which both British and Aboriginal intentions and understandings should inform contemporary interpretations. United States Native American legal scholar Robert Williams Jr. argues that the proclamation's "two goals—facilitating the profitable Indian trade and protecting Indian lands to prevent costly hostilities—were viewed as complementary halves of a self-serving colonial policy put forward by mercantilist interests and their advocates in the British Ministry at Whitehall in the 1760s." "Its discourse," Williams continues, "was one of interest and expediency as articulated by armchair empire builders in the Old World, who viewed the honoring of promises made to savages in the New World as the cheapest, most 'expedient' means of containing both frontier defense costs and inland expansion by British American colonists."[19]

Canadian First Nations legal scholar, John Borrows, reiterates Williams' points about British intentions, but argues that interpretations of the Royal Proclamation limited to the words written in the document alone do not take into account the negotiations, gift-exchanges and other events that took place surrounding the production of the written text and recorded in First Nations oral traditions that reveal *their* intentions and interpretations. Ignoring the oral history of the Royal Proclamation, Borrows charges, "privileges one culture's practice over another." He goes on to argue that his inter-cultural interpretation of the Royal Proclamation suggests that "The Proclamation uncomfortably straddled the contradictory aspirations of the Crown and First Nations when its wording recognized Aboriginal rights to land by outlining a policy that was designed to extinguish these rights…. The different objectives that First Nations and the Crown had in the formulation of the principles surrounding the Proclamation is the reason for the different visions embedded within its text. Britain was attempting to secure territory and jurisdiction through the Proclamation, while First Nations were concerned with preserving their lands and sovereignty."[20]

---

1. Calvin's Case 1608 cited in Walters 1993: 360.

2. For a thorough, and very readable, account of the application of *terra nullius* in Canada, see Richardson 1993.

3. For a comprehensive analysis of this argument see Asch and Macklem 1991. The authors conclude: "We believe it abhorrent that Canada was constituted in part by

reliance on a belief in the inequality of peoples and that such a belief continues to inform political and legal practice in 1991" (510).

4. For a very thorough articulation of this argument see Derrida 1992. See also Hunt 1993; and Sayer 1987.

5. Aboriginal legal scholar James Youngblood Henderson, for example, explains that "Canadian law is not impersonal but racially biased; its legitimacy is threatened if not destroyed by its denial of order and freedom to Aboriginal people..." Henderson and Henderson 1985: 186.

6. See, for example, Hamilton and Sinclair (eds.) 1991; and Turpel 1991(c).

7. See Dyck 1991.

8. See Venne 1997; and Chamberlin 1997.

9. Dickason 1992.

10. Henry 1809 quoted in Jones 1982; and Slattery 1985: 119.

11. The phrase, "Imperialist Nostalgia," is taken from Rosaldo 1989, who defines it as the yearning for that which one has destroyed.

12. Laslett (ed.) 1964.

13. Francis 1992; and Trouhillot 1991.

14. Tully 1993(b).

15. Tully 1993(c): 10.

16. There have been a number of published versions of the Royal Proclamation of 1763, and wording varies in different publications. The quotation cited here is taken from Chief Justice Allan McEachern's 1991 *Reasons for Judgment*, in *Delgamuukw v. R.*, 313.

17. For a survey of debates about both the historical context in which the Royal Proclamation was negotiated and the legal consequences for Canadian Aboriginal peoples in the present see Borrows 1992, 1997; Slattery 1991; Walters 1993. For analysis from a Native American (U.S.A.) perspective, see Williams, R. A. 1990(b).

18. The intended meaning of this language has also been hotly contested, with some arguing that the British Crown thereby recognized the sovereignty of Indian Nations, and others asserting that the words were used rhetorically or insincerely by the British to appease the Indians.

19. Williams, R. A. 1990: 237.

20. Borrows 1997: 160-161.

PART III

TERRA INCOGNITA

(UNKNOWN LAND)

Chapter 5: The Great Chain of Precedent

Suddenly, even the most hardened land-market capitalist assumed the mantle of zealous advocate of the Indians' natural-law right to engage in unregulated real estate transactions. Neither the King, nor the landed colonies "owned" the lands on the frontier, argued these speculators. The Indian tribes occupied these lands as free and sovereign peoples. By natural law, the Indians could therefore sell their rights to the land to whomever they pleased, the Proclamation of 1763 and the landed colonies' charter claims notwithstanding.
—Legal scholar Robert A. Williams, Jr., 1990, *The American Indian in Western Legal Thought: Discourses of Conquest.*

Honour Among Thieves: South of the Border

In British law, one of the principal means that judges use to reach decisions about particular cases is through the use of precedent. Precedents are the decisions reached by previous judges in similar cases. A contemporary judge compares the facts before her or him, searches for cases that dealt with similar fact patterns, and interprets and applies the reasoning and findings of judges in those previous cases to the one at hand. This is referred to in legal parlance as the "doctrine of *stare decisis.*" It is based on the premise that fairness and equality before the law requires that like cases should be decided alike. Reliance on precedent is often pointed to as an inherently conservative characteristic of law, whereby justification must always be anchored in the past. However, contemporary critics argue that the notion that past precedents limit and determine present judgments is frequently overstated by representatives of the judiciary. Anthropologist Michael Asch and Law Professor Catherine Bell, for example, argue that "it is not precedent itself that binds, but judicial interpretation of the past and its relevance to the present.... Adopting interpretive strategies, a judge chooses one precedent in favour of another, appearing to find, rather than create law. The appearance of finding is important because it deflects charges of result-oriented reasoning and judicial legislation."[1] Legal scholars Gerald Torres and Kathryn Milun, point out that the rule of precedent serves more importantly to consolidate law's desire to define the future. They write, "Law, by drawing constantly on precedent to develop itself, strives to collapse linear temporal sequence by bringing the past forward and, by creating a new precedent, drawing the future into itself."[2] In a ritual practice judges call "citing the authorities," *Reasons for Judgment* are frequently written as narratives linking a chronology of precedents to the case at hand through descriptions of salient similarities of fact and argument. Contemporary Canadian judges ruling on Aboriginal title and rights cases usually begin their "precedents narratives" in eighteenth-century post-colonial U.S.A.

In 1776 the American colonies declared independence from Britain. In the ensuing years, three distinguishable factions emerged to dispute issues of land rights and lawful methods of acquisition of Indian lands. A faction of the American population that remained pro-British continued, after Independence, to argue for a literal interpretation of the Royal Proclamation of 1763, and asserted that the British Crown alone retained the prerogative to negotiate with and acquire land cessions from Indians. Another faction, consisting of legislators and political leaders of Virginia and the other colonies, argued that they held controlling rights to Indian lands on the basis of their Crown charters, having "inherited" the sovereign's prerogatives previously held by the British Crown and set out in the Royal Proclamation of 1763. Finally, a large group of frontier speculators claimed that, under natural law and natural right, the Indians themselves, as "sovereign princes of the soil," could sell their land to whomever they wished. Philosopher John Locke became involved in the management and exploitation of the British colonies on the eastern seaboard of America, and was an influential theorist in post-Revolutionary United States. Processes and events there codified Locke's theories into laws that formed the basis of precedents still employed today. This was the context in which three decisive legal judgments were rendered by Chief Justice Marshall of the United States Supreme Court.[3]

The first case, *Fletcher v. Peck*,[4] was heard in 1810. The State of Georgia had granted land to the New England Mississippi Land Company. The Company then divided and resold the land to a number of individuals, including the Plaintiff, Robert Fletcher. The Defendant, Peck, attempted to interfere with Fletcher's exercise of ownership, claiming to have acquired the same land directly from its original, Indigenous, owners. Chief Justice Marshall ruled, on the basis of the Royal Proclamation of 1763, that the State of Georgia's sale to Fletcher was illegal because the lands in question had never been surrendered by the Indians to either the British Crown, the government of the United States of America, or the State of Georgia. Marshall held that "Indian title" could only legitimately be extinguished by a European-derived sovereign, so neither Fletcher nor Peck had acquired lawful title. Another U.S. Supreme Court judge, Justice Johnson, dissented from Marshall's decision arguing that Indians "retained absolute proprietorship of their soil" which could be extinguished only by conquest or purchase. The significance of Chief Justice Marshall's ruling in *Fletcher v. Peck* has manifested itself as the decision has been used as a precedent by contemporary Canadian judges in decisions that uphold the Royal Proclamation of 1763's dictum that Aboriginal title may only be extinguished by the Crown, and not by lower levels of government, corporations, or private citizens.

The second case, *Johnson v. McIntosh*,[5] was heard in 1823. Johnson claimed that he had inherited title to a tract of land from his father who had purchased it from the Piankeshaw and Illinois Indians. McIntosh said he had purchased the same lot from the U.S. federal government, who claimed they had acquired the land from the same Indians at a later date; that is, after Johnson's father said he had purchased it. Chief Justice Marshall found in favour of McIntosh, ruling that the federal government alone had the exclusive right to acquire Indian title, therefore neither Johnson's father nor the Piankeshaw and Illinois Indians could legally buy or sell Indian land. Marshall argued that his ruling was based in law, and not necessarily in justice. He wrote that his decision was determined by, "History, and the decisions made and enforced by those Europeans who invaded America."[6] Marshall relied on the doctrine of discovery/occupation/settlement, and the assumption of *terra nullius* to defend his position, arguing that Crown title was grounded in the voyages of discovery made by the Cabots during the late fifteenth century. This second case in "the Marshall trilogy," *Johnson v. McIntosh*, is the decision most frequently selected as a precedent for application by contemporary Canadian judges to support judgments against Aboriginal claimants, on the basis that the Crown had an unfettered right to declare sovereignty over territories Britain deemed *terra nullius*.

The third and final case, *Worcester v. Georgia*,[7] was decided in 1832. The State of Georgia had attempted to enact jurisdiction over the Cherokee Nation by annexing its territory, annulling its constitution and laws, and requiring whites to obtain state permission before entering Cherokee territory. A white missionary, Samuel Worcester, after being arrested for refusing to comply with this statute, challenged the state's jurisdiction. These same lands, and jurisdictional arrangements, had been the subject of a treaty between the federal government and the Cherokee. Worcester argued therefore that the State of Georgia had no legal right to keep him off the Cherokee reservation.

Chief Justice Marshall ruled in favour of Worcester, saying that the doctrine of discovery/occupation/settlement was relevant only to governing relations between European nations, and not relations between states and the federal government. It yields to the Crown, Marshall wrote, only an exclusive right to acquire Aboriginal title as set out in the Royal Proclamation of 1763. It does not proscribe the terms of such acquisition, or what governmental powers may flow from the surrender of Aboriginal title to the Crown. In other words, Marshall ruled that the State of Georgia could not assume it had automatically inherited whatever powers the federal government may have acquired when it exercised its exclusive prerogative to extinguish Aboriginal title. More importantly, in his *Reasons for Judgment* in *Worcester v. Georgia*, Chief Justice

Marshall argued that the doctrine of discovery/occupation/settlement did not, in itself, necessarily rule out the possibility that some form of negotiations between Aboriginal title holders and Crown representatives may still be required in order for the extinguishment of Aboriginal title to be legitimate. This decision provides a precedent that *could* be interpreted to mean that Crown extinguishment of Native title and assumption of jurisdiction could require Aboriginal consent in order to take legal effect. Chief Justice Marshall's decision in *Worcester v. Georgia*, however, has not been selected by Canadian judges for use as a precedent.

None of the Indigenous peoples whose lands and rights were at issue in the litigation described above were represented in court. As if they didn't exist.

Honour Among Thieves: North of the Border

> By the treaty of 1873 the Indian inhabitants ceded and released the territory in dispute, in order that it might be opened up for settlement, immigration, and such other purpose as to Her Majesty might seem fit, to the Government of the Dominion of Canada, for the Queen and Her successors forever.... The treaty leaves the Indians no right whatever to the timber growing upon the land which they gave up, which is now fully vested in the Crown, all revenues derivable from the sale of such portions of it as are situated within the boundaries of Ontario being the property of that Province...[that] possesses exclusive power to regulate the Indians' privilege of hunting and fishing....
> —Lord Watson, Judicial Committee of the Privy Council of the British House of Lords, 1888.[8]

In 1888, the first significant legal decision involving issues of Aboriginal title and rights in Canada was heard by the Judicial Committee of the Privy Council of the British House of Lords, which was, until 1949, the highest court to which Canadian cases could be appealed. The *St. Catherine's Milling and Lumber* case provided a precedent that would be cited in every subsequent Aboriginal title case in Canada up to and including the present.[9]

The case involved a dispute between the federal government of Canada, the Province of Ontario, and a private corporation: St. Catherine's Milling and Lumber Co. The federal government had granted the company a permit to cut lumber on land they claimed had been surrendered to them by the Ojibway Nation under Treaty 3, signed in 1873. The Province of Ontario, however, charged St. Catherine's Milling and Lumber Co. with taking lumber without a valid permit. The federal government argued that the Ojibway had held full title to their lands until they surrendered their Aboriginal title to the Crown under the terms and conditions of Treaty 3, that included some monetary payments. To support their position, the federal government of Canada argued that Treaty 3 reflected the Royal Proclamation of 1763's recognition of full Aboriginal ownership and jurisdiction; which, having been surrendered to the Crown, now gave the federal government the right to issue permits to private companies like St. Catherine's Milling and Lumber. The Province of Ontario countered with the argument that, prior to the signing of Treaty 3, the underlying title to all the land at issue was not held by Aboriginal title, but was already owned by the hovering sovereign who acquired it by virtue of the doctrine of discovery/occupation/settlement set out in the Memorandum of the Privy Council in 1722. Treaty 3, according to the provincial argument, simply consolidated the extinguishment of whatever vague interests in the land the Ojibway *might* have had prior to contact with Britain, that might have remained a "burden on the Crown's title" after the Royal Proclamation of 1763 was issued, rendering the lands in question unencumbered Crown land. The *British North America Act* that consolidated Canadian Confederation in 1867, the Province of Ontario's argument continued, had transferred Crown land to provincial jurisdiction.

The Supreme Court of Canada agreed with the Province of Ontario, stating that "the tenure of the Indians was a personal and usufructuary[10] right dependent upon the goodwill of the sovereign." In other words, even if some form of Aboriginal title had pre-existed Britain's "discovery" of North America or survived the Royal Proclamation of 1763, it was a type of property ownership that was inferior to title in fee simple,[11] recognized as paramount by British law. Regardless, Aboriginal rights of any sort, the Supreme Court of Canada ruled, were only those created—not recognized—by the Crown. The federal government appealed the court's decision to the Judicial Committee of the Privy Council; which, in turn, upheld the Supreme Court of Canada's ruling. Lord Watson cited the precedent set by Chief Justice Marshall's 1823 decision in *Johnson v. McIntosh* upholding the doctrine of discovery/occupation/settlement based in the concept of *terra nullius*, as authority for the Lords' decision.

Much of the legal argument in the case of *St. Catherine's Milling and Lumber Co. v. R.* revolved around competing interpretations of what form of Aboriginal title or interest the Royal Proclamation of 1763 recognized or created. Lord Watson concluded that while "there was a great deal of learned discussion at the Bar with respect to the precise quality of the Indian right...their Lordships do not consider it necessary to express any opinion upon the point."[12] In effect, however, the Privy Council's decision affirmed that Aboriginal title was a mere "burden" on the hovering sovereign's underlying title to all the land.

Lord Watson's ruling that the only Aboriginal rights that could be recognized in law were those granted, or taken away, by the Crown, marked the rise to prominence of the theory of "legal positivism" in British and

Canadian jurisprudence. Legal positivism is a term used to describe the "tendency to treat jurisprudence as an exact science, a rational process that consists of identifiable data and rules,"13 modelled on the natural or physical sciences. Positivism in social theory is based on the assumption that human social life can be studied using the same methods as those employed by the natural and physical sciences. Its adherents claim that "objective" knowledge about social reality that is free of any and all bias can be obtained by trained researchers. According to positivist theory, social scientists should first use the five senses recognized by western culture—sight, sound, taste, touch and smell—to capture data on human behaviour. The next step is to organize the data according to prescribed categories. Finally, research findings should be explained by reference to theoretical frameworks developed by previous generations of social scientists. The sense of sight and the practice of systematic observation is the most privileged source of knowledge in positivist social research: "seeing is believing." Studies in behavioural psychology that place subjects in experimental environments and monitor how they respond to particular stimuli—say, for example, fear—represent the type of positivist social research that has been popularized, and that most people are familiar with. Conclusions are based on how a majority of research subjects respond to the particular stimuli. So, for example, positivist researchers conclude that "humans respond to fear by either fight or flight." Of course, this does not tell us anything about what frightens who, where, when, or why. Nor does it tell us who can fight and who cannot, or where anyone flees to. We will never know how people who were not research subjects responded, or whether there are third or fourth alternatives that have escaped the research design.

Legal positivism dispenses with the requirement that researchers must study phenomena that exist independently of the observer, *and substitutes law itself for "objective" reality*, and judicial decision-making for scientific methodology. Simply put, the law creates reality that is real because it has been created by the law. Hence, regardless of what might actually exist, "on the ground," under the doctrine of legal positivism, the Crown creates and extinguishes Aboriginal title and rights "at its pleasure."14 Critics of legal positivism argue that jurisprudence is better understood as resulting from the accumulation of judges' interpretations of evidence and arguments over time in specific social contexts, and that the arts, literature and humanities provide more useful models for understanding law than the hard sciences.15

The Ojibway, whose lands and histories were the subject of the dispute in the *St. Catherine's Milling and Lumber v. R.* case were neither consulted nor represented in court. As if they didn't exist.

Honour Among Thieves: in Africa

The estimation of the rights of aboriginal tribes is always inherently diffi-cult. Some tribes are so low in the scale of social organization that their usages and conceptions of rights and duties are not to be reconciled with the institutions or legal ideas of civilized society. Such a gulf cannot be bridged. It would be idle to impute such people some shadow of the rights known to our law and then to transmute it into the substance of transferable rights of property as we know them....

On the other hand, there are indigenous peoples whose legal conceptions, though differently developed, are hardly less precise than our own. When once they have been studied and understood they are no less enforceable than rights arising under English law. Between the two there is a wide tract of much ethnological interest, but the position of the natives of Southern Rhodesia within it is very uncertain; clearly they approximate rather to the lower than to the higher limit. [16]
—Lord Sumner, Judicial Committee of the Privy Council of the British House of Lords, 1919.

When deciding Aboriginal title and rights cases, Canadian judges have available to them a wide range of historic precedents, diverse interpretations of these precedents, and variously reasoned arguments to select from in construct-ing their own rulings. They may draw on arguments waged, and decisions made, throughout the history and geography of the British Empire-cum-Commonwealth. The ruling quoted above in an African case—*Re: Southern Rhodesia*—along with Chief Justice Marshall's American cases, and the Canadian *St. Catherine's Milling and Lumber* judgment, have come to constitute an unholy trinity of precedents repeatedly summoned by contemporary jurists.

The *Re: Southern Rhodesia* judgment sets out the principle that, in order to determine the legitimacy of Indigenous peoples' land rights claims, imperial courts should first assess the claimants' position on the ladder of evolutionary progress hypothesized by nineteenth-century evolutionary social theory. Lord Sumner's first option for those found to be "low on the scale," is a repetition of the Privy Council's Memorandum of 1722's doctrine of discovery/occupation/ settlement justified by the assumption of *terra nullius*, itself a repetition of Lord Coke's judgement in *Calvin's Case* in 1608. In 1722, whether or not British imperial law would classify Indigenous peoples as fully human beings was considered a religious question: were they Christians or infidels? In setting out his test in *Re: Southern Rhodesia*, Lord Sumner relied on secular social theory, re-articulating and re-legitimating the now archaic seeming assumptions of 1722 in the pseudo-scientific language of Social Darwinist evolutionism that had become entrenched by 1919. Social Darwinism was an attempt to apply Charles Darwin's theories of evolution in the plant and animal worlds to human history. Simply put, some Indigenous peoples could be classified, according to the Privy Council, as belonging to a lower order of human being than the British. On the basis of this abstract act of classification they could be deemed, in law, not to exist. Their lands and resources, and their rights to govern themselves, could be eliminated: through the force of law.

Lord Sumner's option for those Indigenous peoples deemed more "highly evolved" reflects the second clause in the Privy Council's Memorandum of 1722. Under the doctrine of conquest, since Indigenous peoples were recognized as existing human beings, British domination had to be achieved through military conquest and/or the negotiation of treaties. Indigenous legal codes could continue to be in force after the assertion of British sovereignty, until they were extinguished by the stroke of a pen, or by the cannons of the British navy. Following Sir Henry Maine, Lord Sumner elaborated evolutionary theory, applying its categories to legal codes and land tenure systems. He identified criteria by which courts could ascertain which Indigenous land tenure systems should be deemed worthy of being honoured by the British Crown. According to Lord Sumner, individual rather than tribal or communal ownership marked the difference between "civilized" and "savage" property law.

Not all judges think alike. In 1921 Lord Sumner's 1919 decision in *Re: Southern Rhodesia* was criticized and modified by Viscount Haldane, who issued a ruling in another African case before the Judicial Committee of the Privy Council. In *Amodu Tijani v. Southern Nigeria*,[17] Haldane argued that Indigenous land tenure systems should not be judged by British standards, but rather should be recognized and understood on their own terms: "In interpreting the native title to land, not only in Southern Nigeria, but other parts of the British Empire, much caution is essential," Haldane wrote. "There is a tendency, operating at times unconsciously, to render that title conceptually in terms which are appropriate only to systems which have grown up under English law. But this tendency has to be held in check closely."

The similarities and differences between Lord Sumner's ruling and Viscount Haldane's can be read as an historic illustration of the interconnections between law, history, anthropology and public opinion that have shaped Indigenous land rights litigation since the early days of British imperial expansion. Legal decisions in these cases, of necessity, rely on and reflect interpretations of history, culture, human nature and morality.

By the early years of the twentieth century, professional anthropologists for the most part had rejected the evolutionary theory of their nineteenth-century founding ancestors like Sir Henry Maine, Lewis Morgan, and Edward Tylor. The leading anthropologists of the 1900s-1930s, including Franz Boas, Bronislaw Malinowski, and H. R. Radcliffe-Brown, all argued for one version or another of positions based in cultural relativism, defined at its most essential level as respect for the fundamental equality of all human cultures, and the right of each culture to be judged on its own terms and not on the basis of another culture's evaluative criteria. This was not only a moral and a political stance, but reflected conclusions which had emerged as the discipline grew to include more professionally trained observers who spent longer periods of time living with non-European peoples.[18] The empirical data collected, and the lived experience of fieldworkers, challenged the abstractions of the "armchair academics," who, a generation before, had hypothesized the grand theories of universal human evolution from their ivory towers. Theories of scientific racism and Social Darwinist evolutionism could not sustain "on the ground" scrutiny.[19] Many Indigenous peoples' ways of life and histories simply didn't conform to the evolutionary models. Aboriginal Australians, for example, valued little in the way of technology and material goods, but lived within highly complex social structures governed by intricate kinship relations, led rich spiritual lives guided by complex and sophisticated cosmologies, and produced abstract art. Evolutionary theory had hypothesized incorrectly that they should be completely consumed by satisfying survival needs and be incapable of abstract thought. Northwest Coast peoples in North America were neither agricultural nor industrial, yet they lived in a hierarchical social structure, and accumulated and stored surplus wealth which, evolutionary theory claimed, people classified as hunters and fishers should not be doing. Anthropologist Marshall Sahlins has challenged the notion that non-industrial peoples' lives were taken up with the daily struggle of wresting subsistence from nature. He argues that industrial capitalism requires the average person to expend more hours of labour per day to meet basic subsistence needs than is demanded of participants in hunting, gathering and fishing economies.[20]

In his ruling in *Amodu Tijani v. Southern Nigeria* Viscount Haldane adopted a position of cultural relativism, launching an explicit critique of Lord Sumner's ethnocentric evolutionism. Haldane argued that Aboriginal title, "may not be that of the individual, as in this country it nearly always is in some form, but may be that of a community.... Such title...must be presumed to have continued to exist unless the contrary is established by the context or the circumstances," he concluded. While Haldane and Sumner differed on some points, neither questioned the fundamental premises that the British Crown had legitimate claims to sovereignty over the Americas; that the hovering sovereign held underlying title to all the land; and that colonial courts should determine what form of Aboriginal title could be recognized—or created—and by what criteria. The Royal Proclamation of 1763 defined Aboriginal title as communal and not individual. Lord Watson in *St. Catherine's Milling and Lumber* in 1888 had declared that Aboriginal title was created by the Crown in whatever image the Crown chose. Lord Sumner had, in 1919, defined legally recognizable Aboriginal title as individual and not communal. Viscount

Haldane in 1921 allowed that Aboriginal title could be communal and not individual. Both Sumner's and Haldane's rulings endorsed the dictum that legal recognition or non-recognition of Aboriginal title should be determined by the nature of Aboriginal societies and land tenure systems, *as these were understood by the court.* The microscope was resolutely trained on Aboriginal claimants who would be required to represent their cultures and laws in one or another framework determined by legal adaptations of European social theory. Questions about the moral, political or legal legitimacy of British colonialism were deemed by law to have been resolved and to not require further discussion. These issues were banished: silenced in legal conversations, and evicted from colonial courthouses. Their absence, however, continued to hover, over the sovereign.

In the legal disputes that followed Sumner's and Haldane's rulings, twentieth-century Canadian judges would select from any one of these precedents, or others, or some combination thereof, as their rationale of choice in rendering decisions in Aboriginal title and rights litigation. Various courts and judges would employ diverse and often contradictory understandings of a mélange of anthropological and historical theories for analyzing Indigenous societies,

It would not be until the closing decades of this century that the simple fact that "when the British arrived, these people were already there, using lands in accordance with their own needs and their own ways of life, as people everywhere do,"[21] would figure prominently in debates about the grounds for legal recognition of Aboriginal or Crown sovereignty in Canada.

---

1. Bell and Asch 1997:39-40. See also Postema 1991.

2. Torres and Milun 1990.

3. See Bell and Asch 1997; Doyle-Bedwell 1993; Macklem 1991; Slattery 1979; Williams R. A. 1990.

4. *Fletcher v. Peck*, 10 U.S. (6 Cranch) 87 (1810) at 146.

5. *Johnson v. M'Intosh* 21 U.S. (8 Wheat) 543 (1823) at 573.

6. Macklem 1991: 400.

7. *Worcester v. Georgia*, 31 U.S. (6 Pet.) 515 (1832) at 543.

8. quoted in Kulchyski 1994: 30.

9. *St. Catherine's Milling and Lumber Co. v. R.* (1885) 10 or 196 (Ont.Ch.); (1886) 13 OAR 148 (Ont.CAO); (1887) SCR 577(SCC); (1888) 14 AC 46 (PC).

10. A "usufructuary right" means the right to use property owned by another, as long as that use is permitted by the rightful owner, and does not interfere with the owner's rights or desires.

11. "Title in fee simple" refers to the most privileged form of individual ownership of private property protected by Canadian law. Most Canadian homeowners hold

"title in fee simple" to their property, subject of course to the good graces of their banks and mortgage companies.

12. quoted in Kulchyski 1994: 30.

13. Cotterrell 1984:10 quoted in Burtch 1992: 3.

14. For a more thorough discussion of the *St. Catherine's Milling and Lumber Company* case, see Slattery 1987; Macklem 1991.

15. White 1985, 1990.

16. *Re Southern Rhodesia* [1919] A.C. 211 at 233-4.

17. *Amodu Tijani v. Southern Nigeria* [1921] 2 A.C. 399(p.c.) at 403.

18. See Stocking 1987, 1991, 1992, 1995.

19. See Vincent 1990.

20. Sahlins 1972. See also Lee and DeVore 1966.

21. McNeil 1989.

Chapter 6: White Papers and Legal Tests

Legal orders may embody asymmetrical power relations, but power is always an interactional process. Dominant groups enjoy legally protected privileges, but they are also constrained by the law. And sub-ordinated groups that suffer under particular legal systems may find that law offers them, the less powerful, a measure of protection from the powerful, just as it sometimes offers them resources for action.
—Anthropologists June Starr and Jane Collier, 1989, *History and Power in the Study of Law: New Directions in Legal Anthropology.*

Law, Power and Resistance

Theoretical debates in the field of anthropology, politics and law center around questions of domination and resistance, justice and power: can marginalized groups, such as Aboriginal peoples, realize their aspirations for social change through legal processes?[1]

The most fundamental and traditional forms of legal critique in the western world are arguments and stories that expose the absence of neutrality or autonomy in law and legal processes. Feminists critique male dominance and sexist bias[2]; people of colour bring charges of systemic racism[3]; colonized and formerly colonized peoples reveal the legacy of imperialism;[4] advocates of labour and the poor unmask alliances between powerful business interests and members of the judiciary.[5] In response to the perennial question of how autonomous the law is from economic and political interests in "the last instance," the British theorist, E. P. Thompson, wrote: "Well, for most of the time when I was watching, law was running quite free of economy, doing its errands, defending its property, preparing the way for it, and so on.... But...on several occasions, while I was actually watching, the lonely hour of the last instance actually came. The last instance, like an unholy ghost, actually grabbed hold of law, throttled it, and forced it to change its language and to will into existence forms appropriate to the mode of production, such as enclosure acts and new case-law excluding customary common rights. But was law 'relatively autonomous'? Oh, yes. Sometimes. *Relatively*. Of course (emphasis in the original)."[6]

For Aboriginal peoples, as for other disempowered groups, the legal arena is a complex and often contradictory one in which to pursue social change.[7] On the one hand, entering into a legal battle requires that all parties accept the language and the rules of the court. Critics of this strategy argue that the extent of "translation" required, for example, to explain Aboriginal spiritual beliefs in the language of the law changes the meaning of those beliefs.[8] On the other hand, limited gains and protection of some historical rights have been achieved through legal struggles.

Many argue that Aboriginal peoples do not have the luxury of choosing *not* to engage in litigation to secure and protect rights.[9] As small minority communities—geographically dispersed and politically and economically marginalized and dispossessed—Aboriginal peoples in Canada have limited resources to draw upon in their struggles for economic justice, political rights, and cultural survival. There are many locations where resistance is mounted: maintaining and reproducing kinship-based communities and strong family bonds in everyday life; insuring personal and familial survival; continuing to hunt, fish, trap, and gather on the land; engaging in ritual and ceremony; negotiating with governments; litigating in the courts; and participating in civil disobedience. In British Columbia, struggles have been fought at each of these sites consistently and simultaneously since Europeans first arrived.

Certainly, law is not monolithic. This is demonstrated by appeal courts overturning lower court rulings, and by the publication of majority and dissenting opinions by panels of judges who fail to reach consensus among themselves on key points. The history of resistance through law waged by First Nations in B.C. illustrates the "use of law as a 'resource for action'" that Starr and Collier refer to. However, this history also raises questions about whether, looked at over the long term, the legal victories of Aboriginal peoples aren't short-lived and quickly co-opted, leaving exhausted human and financial resources behind in their wake. The history of legal struggles over Aboriginal title in B.C. raises the question of whether law, after all is said and done, inevitably turns out to be a servant of the rich and powerful.

Logic, Legal Hysteria, and Rifle Shots on Vancouver Island

There is no clear, evolutionary logic in the historical development of Aboriginal rights...(in the courts).... In spite of after-the-fact stories that have tried to imply a consistent logic...there was a basic incoherence, an instability and set of contradictions embodied in the original approach.... It is a history of sustained, often vicious struggle, a history of losses and gains, of shifting terrain, of strategic victories and defeats, a history where the losers often win and the winners often lose, where the rules of the game often change before the players can make their next move, where the players change while the logic remains the same, where the moves imply each other just as often as they cancel each other out. It is a complex history whose end has not been written and whose beginnings are multiple, fragmentary and undecidable.

—Historian Peter Kulchyski, 1994, *Unjust Relations: Aboriginal Rights in Canadian Courts.*

The questions that have been before the courts in British Columbia and Canada can be summarized briefly: (1) Did First Nations have legally recognizable title to their lands before the assertion of British sovereignty? (2) If they did have such title, does it continue today, or has it been extinguished? (3) If Aboriginal title and rights have not been extinguished, how can federal or provincial governments lawfully contravene or extinguish them?

During the years 1963-1991 a number of important cases were litigated in Canada concerning Aboriginal rights of various kinds. Those most relevant to the issues in dispute in the Gitksan and Wet'suwet'en case were: *R. v. White & Bob*; *Calder v. R*; *The Hamlet of Baker Lake v. Minister of Indian Affairs and Northern Development*; *Guerin v R.*; *R. v. Bear Island Foundation*; and *R. v. Sparrow*.[10] Together, these six cases represent the legal context in which *Delgamuukw v. R.* was initiated, heard, and ruled on.

In the process of ruling on the six cases listed above, and others, different answers were given by the courts to the key questions; a series of legal tests that set out the criteria through which Aboriginal title and rights could be recognized in Canadian law emerged; and Aboriginal Elders, anthropologists, and other expert witnesses became an integral part of contemporary legal processes. Aboriginal and non-Aboriginal plaintiffs and defendants, lawyers and judges, witnesses and researchers involved in Aboriginal title and rights litigation since the 1960s have studied, created, defended, and opposed the evidence, arguments and rulings that emerged in these cases. In order to understand the strategies adopted by the parties to *Delgamuukw v. R.*, it is necessary to comprehend, at least in skeletal form, this legal and historical context.

In British Columbia, the first of the modern Aboriginal rights cases was initiated in the spring of 1963 when Clifford White and David Bob,[11] two members of the Saalequn (Nanaimo) First Nation of central Vancouver Island in British Columbia, went deer hunting on the south slope of Mount Benson, a few miles inland from Nanaimo. They were arrested and charged under the *Game Act of British Columbia* (R.S.B.C. 1960) for being "in possession of deer during the closed season."[12] White and Bob argued that their right to hunt and fish for food on unoccupied Crown lands was guaranteed to them under the terms of a treaty signed between Saanich Chief Whut-Say-Mullett, and Governor James Douglas in Fort Victoria on February 7, 1852.[13] The case came to the attention of Thomas Berger, then leader of the British Columbia New Democratic Party and a practising lawyer in Vancouver. White and Bob's legal counsel argued that this treaty was protected by the *Indian Act* which, as federal legislation, was paramount over provincial legislation such as the *Game Act*.

The Province of B.C. argued that the treaty of 1852 did not constitute a treaty between the Crown and an Aboriginal nation but rather was a commercial conveyance between some individuals who were members of a group that were not a state and had no international personality, and a private enterprise, the Hudson's Bay Company, represented by its Chief Factor, James Douglas, who doubled as Governor of the Colony of Vancouver Island at the time. In other words, the Crown argued that the document was not a treaty but a private exchange of cash for land. The ancestors of White and Bob, the Crown claimed, had sold their land, and therefore their descendants had no rights on it, or to it.

The *White & Bob* case was the first to require a provincial government of British Columbia, and their lawyers, to develop legal arguments to defend their historical denial of Aboriginal title and rights. The province's solicitors adopted a position based in legal positivism and referred to the *St. Catherine's Milling* precedent, arguing first that Aboriginal title could only exist if it was created by a sovereign. The king had chosen not to create such rights because the Aboriginal peoples of British Columbia were "too primitive" according to the *Re: Southern Rhodesia* precedent. The province's legal argument relied on a particular interpretation of history that described the First Nations of British Columbia as minimally evolved nomads lacking law or government when Europeans first arrived. For the first time in court, the province articulated an interpretation of the Royal Proclamation of 1763 that was to become a hallmark of British Columbia's legal arguments in all subsequent cases. The province's lawyers claimed that, since British Columbia did not appear on most maps drawn by British cartographers (who had, in 1763, not yet travelled to the west coast), the Royal Proclamation of 1763 was not intended to apply to Aboriginal peoples here. What the sovereign (or, in this case, his mapmakers) did not see, did not exist.

Furthermore, they referred to the use of the present tense by the writers of the Proclamation in the phrase "the Indians with whom we are connected" as evidence that the authors' intentions were to exclude any Aboriginal groups with whom the Crown had not yet made contact. Berger argued that the present tense is the grammar of legal statutes, proclamations, and constitutions which are usually considered, legally, to "speak until they are repealed." The B.C. Crown's interpretation of the Royal Proclamation has been described by historians and legal scholars as "implausible," "indefensible" and "ridiculous."[14] It has, however, been argued repeatedly by prestigious lawyers, and declared "fact" by eminent judges, for 30 years.

The next line of legal attack developed by the Province of B.C. in the *White & Bob* case and in subsequent litigation, was that if there had, in fact, been some form of Aboriginal title before the arrival of Europeans in British Columbia, it was extinguished by the assertion of sovereignty by Britain, and by the enactment of land use legislation by the colonial legislature.

The absence of any First Nations consent to extinguishment of their land title was, within the framework of legal positivism, irrelevant: if Aboriginal rights are created and extinguished only by the sovereign, then Aboriginal consent is not required to do either. Anyway, concluded provincial lawyers, Indians "implicitly" consented to extinguishment of title. This, they argued, was "proven" by the fact that First Nations in British Columbia did not wage armed rebellions, appeared (according to non-Aboriginal interpretations) to acquiesce to colonial domination, were now believed to be assimilated into mainstream Canadian society, and were therefore no longer racially or culturally "pure." Crown lawyers pointed to Aboriginal "culture" measured by language, religion, clothing, food, weapons, modes of earning a living, housing, and means of transportation, for evidence. Any cultural change since contact with Europeans was presented as the natural outcome of a passive, inferior culture coming into contact with an active, superior one. Only those activities whose origins could be traced to pre-contact Aboriginal cultures *and which continued to be practiced*, could be classified under this rubric as "truly Aboriginal." This is referred to in law as the "frozen rights" theory, wherein Aboriginal cultures are "frozen" at the moment of "discovery," and any developments since that moment are interpreted as resulting from European influence. In other words, "ignoring Indian title was…seen as extinguishing it. Put another way, the argument asserted that the ordinary operation of a British colonial government had the effect of wiping out the legitimacy of any pre-existing aboriginal arrangements…. The argument of implicit extinguishment through ordinary legislation has not been raised in other parts of Canada."[15]

This represents one of many "double binds" in legal and popular discourses on Aboriginal rights. A double bind is a "damned if you do and damned if you don't" situation in which the outcome is always pre-determined, and in which explanations are arrived at by reasoning backwards from consequences to causes. From a social evolutionary perspective, to the extent that Aboriginal cultures are understood as not having changed after contact with Europeans, they are analyzed as being "arrested" at a "lower stage" of development, and incapable of "advancement." Such "primitive" peoples must not have had any concepts of property or law, and clearly cannot—today—be considered capable of being granted the same rights as those of "civilized" peoples. *They are too different to be considered equal.* To the extent, on the other hand, that Aboriginal cultures are understood as *having changed* and adapted some European ways to their own, then they are said to have voluntarily "assimilated" into the colonial culture, and clearly then have no grounds on which to claim "special" rights different from everyone else's. *They are too equal to be considered different.* Heads, the Crown wins. Tails, Indians lose.

When legal scholar, Patrick Macklem, tried to ascertain the way concepts of cultural similarity and cultural difference had impacted on "how the law has contributed to the current status of First Nations in Canada," he found that "Native difference is denied where its acceptance would result in the questioning of basic premises concerning the nature of property, contract, sovereignty or constitutional right. Native difference is acknowledged where its denial would achieve a similar result."[16] Macklem concluded that this discourse on cultural similarity and difference constituted a "rhetoric of justification" for legal judgements.

Anthropologists entered the legal fray in the *White & Bob* case, led by Wilson Duff.[17] Initially, anthropological research was principally concerned with documenting and describing various Aboriginal peoples' practices surrounding land and resource ownership and use, translating this data into language that lawyers and judges could understand, and considering whether or not these concepts of "Aboriginal title" were commensurable with concepts of property recognized by Canadian law. During the *R. v. White & Bob* trial, Wilson Duff responded to Berger's question concerning the meaning of the term "tribal territories" for the Saalequn as follows:

> Berger: When you say tribal territories, can you tell us what you mean by that? What use would the Indians have made of their tribal territories?
>
> Duff: This could be a very complicated statement, because they used different kinds of territories...with different intensity. They would use the rivers, of course, for fish with great intensity, and the beaches with great intensity, and the mountains and forest with somewhat less intensity, yet they would go at least that far back, not only to hunt the land mammal, deer, and also other land mammals, but to get bark and roots for basketry and matting and such things. These territories would be definitely used by them and would be recognized by other tribes as belonging to them.[18]

The lower court found both defendants guilty and fined Clifford White and David Bob $100.00 (or 40 days in jail in default) each. Berger was successful in obtaining a new trial for White and Bob and went on to win a decision by the County Court of Nanaimo, which was then upheld by the B.C. Court of Appeal and the Supreme Court of Canada. The document signed by Whut-Say-Mullett and Governor James Douglas was in fact a treaty. White and Bob indeed had the right to hunt and fish for food on unoccupied Crown land. Mr. Justice Tom Norris of the B.C. Court of Appeal further ruled that the treaty was, like other treaties signed between the Crown and Canadian Aboriginal peoples, consistent with the direction of the Royal Proclamation of 1763. He wrote: "the aboriginal rights as to hunting and fishing affirmed by the Proclamation of 1763 and recognized by the Treaty...still exist."[19]

The legal significance of this decision was that "for the first time a judge, and a well-respected British Columbia judge of conservative leanings at that, had presented a comprehensive opinion endorsing both the pre-existence and the continuing existence of aboriginal rights in British Columbia."[20]

Civilization and the Whimsical Destruction of Property

> *The assessment and interpretation of the historical documents and enactments tendered in evidence must be approached in the light of present-day research and knowledge disregarding ancient concepts formulated when understanding of the customs and culture of our original people was rudimentary and incomplete and when they were thought to be wholly without cohesion, laws or culture, in effect a subhuman species. This concept of the original inhabitants of America led Chief Justice Marshall in his otherwise enlightened judgment in Johnson v. McIntosh...to say 'the tribes of Indians inhabiting this country were fierce savages, whose occupation was war.... 'We now know that that assessment was ill-founded...Chief Justice Marshall was, of course, speaking with the knowledge available to him in 1823. Chief Justice Davey...[of the B.C. Court of Appeal] with all the historical research and material available since 1823 and notwithstanding the evidence in the record...said of the Indians of the mainland of British Columbia: '...they were undoubtedly at the time of settlement a very primitive people with few of the institutions of civilized society, and none at all of our notions of private property.' In so saying this in 1970, he was assessing the Indian culture of 1858 by the same standards the Europeans applied to the Indians of North America two or more centuries ago....*
> —Justice John Hall, Supreme Court of Canada, 1973, *Dissenting Opinion, Reasons for Judgment in Calder v. R.*

There is another aspect to the relationship between law, culture and power that is interwoven with the role law plays in enforcing particular rules in the interests of specific sectors of society. Law also "maintains power relations by defining categories and systems of meaning."[21] This defining and productive activity of law—setting the agenda, and constructing the parameters of what may be included and what must be excluded—is exemplified in the legal tests for Aboriginal title and rights. The tests are based on criteria the courts have established for evaluating claims brought before them by Aboriginal litigants.

Legal tests for Aboriginal rights reveal the power relations that are constitutive of legal encounters: judges construct the tests; claimants sit them; judges mark them: pass, fail or defer. Of course, the arguments and evidence presented by Aboriginal claimants, and political support for them from outside the courtroom, have also influenced the tests. That is to say, it is as a result of persistent Aboriginal resistance that these questions continue to be placed before the judiciary. To this extent, the evolution of the tests represents the outcome of contestation and negotiation. However, the Crown is the dominant partner in a hierarchical relationship with Aboriginal peoples in Canadian society; and this social inequality follows the parties into the courtroom in myriad ways. The Crown has greater access to more resources in every part of the legal process, and in every aspect of it. The playing field, as the popular expression goes, is not only theirs, it is far from level.

The history of legal tests for Aboriginal rights could start in 1550 with Valladolid. It could start in 1608 with Calvin's Case and the infidel rule. It could start with the memorandum of the British Privy Council in 1722 that set out the doctrine of conquest and the doctrine of discovery/occupation/settlement. It could start with Lord Sumner's dictum in *Re: Southern Rhodesia* based in an evolutionary framework. This is the history that followed First Nations, lawyers, and judges into court in British Columbia where the story of legal tests for Aboriginal title began in 1969 with what is now called "the *Calder* case," or "the Nishga case."[22] Chief Frank Calder, on behalf of the Nishga Tribal Council, asked the Supreme Court of British Columbia for a declaration that:

(1) the Nishga held title to their territory prior to the assertion of British sovereignty;

(2) that this title had never been lawfully extinguished; and,

(3) that this title is a legal right.

In support of their claim that their Aboriginal title had never been ceded, sold, surrendered or lost in war, the Nishga relied upon written archival evidence that showed they had begun petitioning the Queen and Colonial officials for recognition of their title since first contact with Europeans in the eighteenth century. Five Nishga hereditary chiefs, Frank Calder, James Gosnell, William McKay, Harry Nyce, and Anthony Robinson; one provincial archivist, Willard Ireland; and one anthropologist, Wilson Duff, testified as expert witnesses.[23] Both the chiefs and the expert witnesses focused on demonstrating extensive Nishga use and occupation of the Nass Valley.[24] Wilson Duff, acting as cultural translator, explained that the Nishga system of property ownership is different from, but analogous to, English common law property ownership. The skeleton of a legal test for Aboriginal title emerged in the following exchange between B.C. Supreme Court Judge Gould and Wilson Duff:

The Court: I want to discuss with you the short descriptive concept of your modern ownership of land in British Columbia, and I am going to suggest to you three characteristics (1) specific delineation of the land, we understand is the lot.

Duff: Yes.

The Court: Specifically delineated down to the lot, and the concept of the survey; (2) exclusive possession against the whole world, including your own family. Your own family, you know that, you want to keep them off or kick them off and one can do so; (3) to keep the fruits of the barter or to leave it or to have your heirs inherit it, which is the concept of wills. Now, those three characteristics...are you with me?

Duff: Yes

The Court: Specific delineation, exclusive possession, the right of alienation, have you found in your anthropological studies any evidence of that concept being in the consciousness of the Nishgas and having them executing such a concept?

Duff: My lord, there are three concepts.

The Court: Yes, or a combination of them.

Duff: Specific delineation...Physical landmarks, physical characteristics. The exclusive occupation did not reside in an individual. It rested in a group of people who were a sub-group of the tribe...The owners in this sense had certain rights of alienation. They could give up the tract of land, lose it in warfare, but in practice it would not go to anybody outside of the tribe, that is, a tract of Nishga land might change hands but it wouldn't go to other than a Nishga family.

The Court: So am I correct in assuming that there are similarities in the Nishga civilization in the first two characteristics, but not the third? All that alienation means, of course, is that you can sell it to anybody you like?

Duff: Yes

...

The Court: I will give two more characteristics of ownership, the right to destroy it at your own whim, if you like, and the other, that the exclusive possession should be of indeterminable time, that is, cannot be terminated by a person's life, that is, can be passed on to one's heirs. That makes five. Now, you have dealt with three. Now the right to destroy at whim, set fire to your own house; these matters you have been dealing with, would a group within the Nishga have the right, if the buildings at the mouth of a certain river had been in their exclusive use some time and they will say, 'Let's set fire to it,' would the tribe prohibit that?

Duff: I would think that they would have that right.

The Court: You would think they would have that right?

Duff: Yes.

The Court: Now, what about the duration of the right, not to destroy, but the right of exclusive ownership, would it go to their heirs?

Duff: Yes.

The Court: Or go back to the tribe for distribution?

Duff: In theory it belongs within that kinship group through time, with no duration in theory. It always remains with that same kinship group.

The Court: There is the matrilineal line?

Duff: Yes.[25]

The Supreme Court of British Columbia ruled that the Nishga were too "primitive" in the nineteenth century to have held concepts of property that could be considered on an evolutionary developmental par with the concept of property upheld by British law.

European colonial cultural beliefs, or ideologies, set up relationships between colonizer and colonized as a hierarchical set of binary oppositions in which one member of the pair is always symbolically superior to the other.[26] Colonizers are rational, the colonized are irrational. Colonizers are guided by reason, the colonized are driven by instinct. Colonizers are industrious, the colonized are lazy. Colonizers are active agents, the colonized are passive objects.[27] But binary oppositions are two-way streets: when colonizers describe the characteristics of the colonized, they are simultaneously describing themselves, through defining the differences between themselves and their "Other." Each description of the other is at the same time a description of self.[28] Interpreted from this perspective, Justice Gould's ruling can be read as defining Euro-Canadian property law, and presumably the more highly evolved cultural values reflected in that law as: individually owning land, building fences around it and kicking your family off it, and burning down your house on a whim.

When the Nishga case was appealed, the Justices of the B.C. Court of Appeal declared that if any form of Aboriginal title had existed it had been explicitly extinguished by Britain's assertion of sovereignty and "implicitly" extinguished by provincial land legislation prior to Confederation. The Nishga, on this basis, had no legal rights.

The Supreme Court of Canada, however, found differently when the case was appealed to them. In their 1973 decision, of the seven judges, one dismissed the case on a technicality and did not comment on the issues at trial. The remaining six found unanimously that Aboriginal title had existed prior to European arrival, based on long term occupancy. On the other important questions before them, the six judges split into two groups: Justices Ritchie and Martland supported the main judgment written by Justice Judson; while Justices Laskin and Spence supported the dissenting judgment written by Hall.[29] Judson, Ritchie and Martland agreed with the Province of British Columbia's argument that the Royal Proclamation of 1763 was not meant to apply to the then-undiscovered British Columbia. Relying on the *St. Catherine's Milling and Lumber Co.* precedent, they found that Aboriginal title was a "mere burden" on Crown title. From Chief Justice Marshall's ruling in *Johnson v. McIntosh* they drew the conclusion that the Crown had the exclusive right to extinguish Aboriginal title; and that whatever Aboriginal rights might have existed were lawfully extinguished by Britain's declaration of sovereignty. Judson, however, differed with the Crown on the nature of Aboriginal title. In what was to become an oft-quoted statement, he wrote: "...the fact is that when the settlers came, the Indians were there, organized in societies and occupying the land as their forefathers had done for centuries. This is what Indian title means and it does not help one in the solution of this problem to call it a 'personal or usufructuary right'."[30]

On the other hand, Justice Hall, supported by Laskin and Spence, argued that the Royal Proclamation was meant to apply to British Columbia; that while the Crown did have the right to extinguish Aboriginal title it must state its intention to do so in "clear and plain language," and it could not be concluded that "implicit" extinguishment had taken place by virtue of colonial authorities having simply ignored Aboriginal title. On the issue of the nature of Aboriginal title, Hall cited Lord Sumner's decision in *Re: Southern Rhodesia* stressing the possibility that some Indigenous property systems were sufficiently well developed to be recognized by British law, and Lord Haldane's caution in *Amodu Tijani v. Secretary of Southern Nigeria*, that non-British systems should be understood on their own terms and not only in relation to British law. Hall argued that, "to ascertain how far this latter development of right has progressed involves the study of the history of the particular community and its usages in each case. Abstract principles fashioned *a priori* are of but little assistance, and are as often as not misleading."[31] The Supreme Court of Canada appeal panel judges relied extensively on both the written historical record and the testimony of the expert witnesses, reserving their highest praise for the contribution of Wilson Duff. Hall wrote: "What emerges from the...evidence is the following: the Nishgas in fact are, and were from time immemorial a distinctive cultural entity with concepts of ownership indigenous to their culture and capable of articulation under the common law, having, in the words of Dr. Duff, 'developed their culture to higher peaks in many respects than in any other part of the continent north of Mexico.'"

The *Calder* decision therefore marks a significant departure from the positivist theory of Aboriginal rights which gave legal standing only to rights recognized by a sovereign. The Supreme Court of Canada's ruling in the *Calder* case was a victory for British Columbia First Nations and their supporters. Six Supreme Court of Canada judges agreed that Aboriginal title in fact existed, and three allowed that it may continue to exist.

Nevertheless, certain aspects of this landmark decision would haunt future Aboriginal land rights litigation in other parts of Canada. Justice Hall did not reject the test Lord Sumner set out in 1919 in *Re: Southern Rhodesia*, but affirmed it by using its criteria to distinguish the Nishga culture as qualifying for respect and recognition on the grounds of evolutionary theory. Hall's reasoning allowed for the possibility that other Aboriginal peoples might fail Sumner's and Haldane's tests. While both rejected crude and archaic concepts and language, neither Duff's anthropology, nor Hall's law, rejected the philosophical or theoretical premises of "neo-evolutionary" theory that in 1973 remained current in academic anthropology and embedded in popular culture. Various iterations of neo-evolutionary theory have emerged throughout this century.[32] Most recent versions eschew ethnocentric judgments, while still retaining beliefs in the determining role of the economy and technology in shaping culture. While rejecting the notion that all people progress through pre-determined "stages of development" from hunting and gathering to industrial capitalism, some *neo*-evolutionary theorists argue that European and European-derived cultures have brought most Indigenous peoples under western economic and cultural domination. This trajectory therefore now reflects historical experience, rather than theoretical hypotheses, they claim. Anthropologists like Wilson Duff, while they respected and supported First Nations peoples and were devoted to preserving their cultures, applied class-based western notions of "high" and "low" culture to their analyses of Indigenous cultures.[33] Peoples like the Nishga, therefore, with their abstract art, ornate carving, sophisticated architecture, and elaborate ceremonial life were judged within this framework to be "highly cultured." Like rural people and urban working classes whose cultures are classified as "low," some Aboriginal peoples without material cultural objects like totem poles, masks and carvings desired by Europeans, or elaborate ceremonial rituals like pot-latches, are classified as "simple." Unexamined evolutionary assumptions continue to incipiently and insidiously influence literature and the arts, and to inform "common sense" and popular culture.[34]

From Law to Politics and Back Again

I feel like a man who has been told he is going to die and is now being asked how he would like to be killed.
—First Nations leader George Manuel, responding to the *White Paper Policy*, Kamloops, 1969.

On August 8, 1969, at a press conference in Vancouver, B.C., newly-elected Canadian Prime Minister Pierre Elliot Trudeau was asked whether his government would recognize Aboriginal title and rights in British Columbia. He replied: "Our answer is no. We can't recognize aboriginal rights because no society can be built on historical 'might have beens'."[35] Trudeau's Minister of Indian and Northern Affairs, Jean Chretien, oversaw the drafting and publication of a new Canadian Indian Policy that was released later in 1969. The Liberal government's infamous "White Paper Policy" began with the statement, "...aboriginal claims to land...are so general and undefined that it is not realistic to think of them as specific claims capable of remedy except through a policy and program that will end injustice to Indians as members of the Canadian community."[36]

The White Paper Policy advocated the dissolution of any distinct legal or political status for Indigenous peoples, or their lands, and the rapid assimilation of Aboriginal peoples into the mainstream of Canadian society. Three B.C. provincial Indian organizations met in Kamloops, B.C. in 1969 to plan strategies for responding to the White Paper Policy. Unanimity was as elusive as ever, but, with equal consistency, was finally found in the fundamental premise that Aboriginal title had existed prior to European contact and still did. Several months later an "All Bands Assembly" in Vancouver agreed to have non-Aboriginal experts prepare an historical-legal argument in support of the recognition of Aboriginal title, to be presented to a parliamentary committee.[37] Opposition to the White Paper Policy's assimilationist goals was voiced by Aboriginal representatives across the country, and for the first time in Canadian history, First Nations organized themselves on a Canada-wide basis, mobilizing their members to present a united front in defence of their cultural and political survival.

Four years later, in 1973, when the Supreme Court of Canada handed down their decision in *Calder v. R.*, ruling that Aboriginal rights had in fact existed in British Columbia before contact with Europeans, and perhaps had not been extinguished, Prime Minister Trudeau was moved to allow that First Nations without treaties "May have more rights than we thought."[38] The federal government revisited its position and instituted the "Comprehensive Claims Policy" whose terms of reference mirrored the Supreme Court's judgment in *Calder*. Aboriginal nations were invited to bring forth claims to land that had been used and occupied by their ancestors, and that they themselves were still using. The story of the *Calder* decision and the Comprehensive Claims Policy is an archetype of the relationship between law and government policy in Aboriginal matters. The legal tail wags the political dog, and man's best friend rarely strays outside the yard the law fences in. Law is a force that politicians, bureaucrats, and Aboriginal peoples alike reckon with.

The Honour of the Crown Below Par

> ...Indians have a legal right to occupy and possess certain lands, the ultimate title to which is in the Crown.... The nature of the Indians' interest is therefore best characterized by its general inalienability, coupled with the fact that the Crown is under an obligation to deal with the land on the Indians' behalf when the interest is surrendered.... Any description of Indian title which goes beyond these two features is both unnecessary and potentially misleading.[39]
> —Chief Justice Dickson, 1984, *Reasons for Judgment, Guerin v. R.*

The next significant court case was fought in the 1970s in British Columbia by the Musqueam First Nation. In 1950, federal officials of the Department of Indian Affairs and Northern Development (DIAND) arranged for the Musqueam Indian Band—whose reserve forms a small enclave located in the elite urban neighbourhood of south-west Vancouver—to lease a portion of their land to the exclusive Shaughnessy Golf and Country Club. Land values were assessed, and a lease agreement was ratified by the Musqueam Chief and Council by way of a band referendum. Since, under the *Indian Act*, First Nations lands are held in trust for them as wards of the Crown who, like children, are not able to enter into legal contracts, representatives of the Department of Indian and Northern Affairs signed the final contract with the Shaughnessy Golf and Country Club on behalf of the Musqueam. In 1970, Musqueam Chief Delbert Guerin learned that before they had signed the final contract, DIAND officials had reduced the value of the land and agreed to terms significantly more favourable to the Shaughnessy Golf and Country Club than to the Musqueam First Nation. These were *not* the terms that the band membership had agreed to in their referendum, and DIAND officials did not advise the Chief and Council that they had renegotiated the contract before they signed it.

The Musqueam sued the federal government for breach of trust and the federal court awarded them $10 million in damages. The Federal Court of Appeal overturned this decision. The Musqueam then appealed to the Supreme Court of Canada who found that, indeed, the Crown and its agents have a fiduciary obligation to act in the best interests of Indians, and that this had not been done in the case before them. While "failing to uphold their fiduciary obligations" may seem an undeservedly polite way to describe the deceit and duplicity engaged in by government representatives in this case, the *Guerin* decision did mark a recognition by the courts of at least once instance of these all too common practices in the history of government relations with Aboriginal peoples.

It is the sections of the Supreme Court's decision that bear directly on the issue of Aboriginal title that are important to the story being told here. First, Chief Justice Brian Dickson's ruling in *Guerin* reiterates these fundamental points: that the Crown in the form of the hovering sovereign holds underlying title to all land, and that Aboriginal title is not proprietary and can only be surrendered to the Crown. However, the significance of Dickson's judgment is that he ruled that Aboriginal rights can apply to off-reserve lands. Second, the Supreme Court of Canada in *Guerin* ruled that the Crown's fiduciary duty is legally rooted in Aboriginal title, and not, as was argued by the Crown, in the discretionary benevolence of the Crown or the Department of Indian Affairs. Third, the *Guerin* decision provides a precedent that future judges could adopt to recognize that Aboriginal rights pre-existed European arrival and are inherent: recognized, and not created, by the British sovereign. Fourth, in the

Guerin decision the Supreme Court of Canada confirmed that Aboriginal title and rights are *sui generis*: "of their own kind; constituting a class alone; unique; peculiar."[40] The Courts, the ruling continued, have almost "inevitably found themselves applying somewhat inappropriate property law"[41] to the determination of Aboriginal title and rights. The characterization of the legal nature of Aboriginal title as *sui generis* provided Canadian courts with the opportunity to explore beyond the confines of English property law to determine the scope and content of Aboriginal title and its relationship with the Crown's interest."[42]

Finally, Madame Justice Bertha Wilson, the first woman to be appointed to the Supreme Court of Canada and one of the judges sitting on the bench when the case was heard, wrote in her contribution to the *Guerin* judgment that: "...the bands do not have the fee in the lands; their interest is a limited one. But it is an interest which cannot be derogated from or interfered with by the Crown's utilization of the land for purposes incompatible with the Indian title, *unless, of course, the Indians agree.*" (Emphasis added.)[43] This legitimated the position that Native consent should be required in order for Aboriginal title to be legally extinguished or contravened. Through this ruling, Justice Wilson created a precedent which was available to be adopted by judges when ascertaining whether or not particular Aboriginal peoples have consented to extinguishment of their Aboriginal title. Not only did the *Guerin* decision mark an instance of legal recognition that Aboriginal peoples in fact exist, but it suggested that it might be appropriate, morally just, *and legal* for their consent to be required before they could be "extinguished."

The Supreme Court of Canada's *Calder* decision marked a significant departure from the archaic legal positivism that had preceded it. And the *Guerin* decision went several steps further. However, in both cases, all the Supreme Court judges were unanimous in upholding the legitimacy of Britain's assertion of sovereignty, and the hovering sovereign's possession of the "underlying title to all the land." If extinguishment of Aboriginal title had not been properly effected historically, then the judges said it should be now, and they set out ways for extinguishment to be recognized and/or accomplished.

The final goal that courts and governments have shared—the desired outcome of litigation, as well as land claims and treaty negotiations—is the extinguishment of Aboriginal title, absolutely and forever; and the confirmation of the singular sovereignty of Crown title, absolutely and forever. Legal and political recognition of Aboriginal title and extinguishment of Aboriginal title have been inextricably interdependent and mutually defining. The assertion of dominance and the surrender of autonomy must occur at the same instant. This demand for a forced coupling of *recognition* of Aboriginal title with *extinguishment* of Aboriginal title was upheld by every legal decision up to

1997 in Canada, and is reflected in the Comprehensive Claims Policy's requirement that the settlement of any claim and the signing of any modern-day treaty is dependent on the Aboriginal peoples' surrender of Aboriginal title, and agreement to its extinguishment. To Aboriginal peoples this demand is unjust and humiliating. Those First Nations who have entered into modern-day treaties—often under tremendous pressures in the face of potential environmental crises—have agreed to legal extinguishment of Aboriginal title for the purposes of resolving contemporary claims. In each set of negotiations, however, compliance with the demand for extinguishment has been resisted by First Nations representatives to the last moment, and it has only been with tremendous reluctance that extinguishment has been agreed to. It is a question that divides Aboriginal communities, and many continue to refuse to take this final step.

The 1970s marked the beginning of the contemporary period of B.C. Aboriginal politics in which debates concerning the relative merits and effectiveness of civil disobedience, political negotiation, and litigation are ongoing. The preferred tactic, as evidenced by the resolutions of provincial and national Aboriginal conferences, has always been political negotiation. The strength of their legal position, and the refusal of successive British Columbia governments until 1990 to recognize the legal existence of Aboriginal peoples in the province, has led British Columbia First Nations into the courts primarily as a means to achieve a strong enough bargaining position to "bring the government to the table." First Nations have principally used the courts, not to *settle* the dispute, but to acknowledge its *validity*, after which nation-to-nation negotiations could honourably begin.

1. Clifford 1988(b); Just 1992; Lazarus-Black and Hirsch (eds.) 1994; Merry 1992; Mertz 1988. See also Danielson and Engle (eds.)1995; Hart and Bauman (eds.)1996; Leonard 1995.

2. The literature on this topic is vast. See, for a sample, Adelberg and Currie (eds.) 1993; Chunn, and Lacombe (eds.)1998; Smart 1989.

3. Turpel 1991(b); 1991(c); Williams, P. 1991.

4. Comaroff and Roberts 1981; Moore 1986.

5. There is a huge literature concerning the relationship between law and the economy, and questions about the role of law in class relations in western societies. For a survey see Hunt 1981; Snyder 1981.

6. Thompson 1978 quoted in Starr and Collier (eds.) 1989:25.

7. For a detailed explication of this issue see Coombe 1989.

8. For an articulation of this argument in the Canadian case see Turpel 1991(a).

9. For an articulation of this argument in the Canadian case see Henderson, J. Y. 1985; and Williams, R. A. 1987. The debate about the pitfalls and promises of

using the law to achieve radical social change has been most thoroughly developed by feminist legal scholars. See Cornell 1992; Young 1991. Razack 1991 describes a case study in which these questions were grappled with.

10. There have been other important cases tried during this period of time. I have selected for focus here only those *most* relevant to British Columbia in general, and the *Delgamuukw* case in particular. For detailed summaries of discussions surrounding arguments and judgments in these cases, and others, see Kulychyski, Peter (ed.)1994.

11. *R. v. White & Bob* (50 Dominion Law Reports (2d) [1965], 620.

12. Berger 1981:49.

13. Ibid.

14. See Tennant 1990:216-217. Tennant says: "This was a lawyer's argument contrived retrospectively. No one associated with any aspect of the Indian land question had previously read the Proclamation as not extending to the western edge of the continent(216)." Of the B.C. Crown's lawyers' analysis of the meaning of the use of the present tense, Tennant says: "Had the British monarch issued another proclamation stating that a royal biscuit was to be given to 'any person with whom We are having tea,' it would be ridiculous to argue that the provision applied only to persons at the table with the monarch at the moment of signing and that it did not apply to future tea parties. Today the Canadian Charter of Rights and Freedoms uses the present tense in expressing its guarantees: no sane person would maintain that its guarantees were intended to apply only at the moment the Charter was approved (216)."

15. Tennant 1990:217.

16. Macklem 1991:392.

17. For a survey of anthropologists' involvement in First Nations legal struggles during the last thirty years see Kew 1993-94.

18. Berger 1981:52-53.

19. *R. v. White & Bob* (50 Dominion Law Reports (2d) [1965], 620, cited in Berger 1981:53.

20. Tennant 1990:219.

21. Merry 1992. See also Danielson and Engle (eds.)1995; Hart and Bauman (eds.) 1996; Leonard, 1995.

22. *Calder et al v. A.G.B.C.* (1969), 8 Dominion Law Reports (3d), 59-83, [S.C.B.C.]. The "Nishga" now spell their name "Nisga'a."

23. Kulchyski 1994:61-126.

24. Berger 1981; Kulchyski 1994.

25. Kulchyski 1994:96-98.

26. Fanon 1963.

27. McGrane 1989.

28. Clifford 1988; Said 1992.

29. *Calder et al v. A.G.B.C.* (1973), 34 Dominion Law Reports (3d) [1973], 145-226. See also Sanders 1989.

30. *Calder et al v. A.G.B.C.* (1973), 34 Dominion Law Reports (3d) [1973], 145-226.

31. Calder:401.

32. See Durham 1990.

33. See Turner 1993.

34. Turner 1993.

35. Weaver 1981:3-4.

36. Canada, Government of, (1969) Department of Indian Affairs, Policy Statement:1.

37. Tennant 1990:171.

38. Tennant 1990:172.

39. *Guerin v. R.* (1984) 13 D.L.R. (4th) 321.

40. *Webster's New Collegiate Dictionary* (1981) Toronto, Ontario: Thomas Allen & Son Limited, 1156.

41. *Guerin v. R.* (1984) 13 D.L.R. (4th) 339.

42. Bell and Asch 1997:48.

43. *Guerin v. R.* (1984) 13 D.L.R. (4th).155.

Chapter 7: Conflicts and Constitutions: The 1980s

The federal government has a claims policy that they brought into place after the Calder case, and that claims policy was hollow. It was empty. It meant nothing. Still, the Gitksan and Wet'suwet'en entered into one of their phases of trying to resolve the land question in the mid-70s, and in 1977 qualified for federal funding to prepare negotiations…. Beginning in 1977, a tremendous amount of work was done, work that built on what was done before and took it even further. A base was built to prepare for negotiations.

—Medig'm Gyamk (Neil Sterritt), Gitksan, 1992, *It Doesn't Matter What the Judge Said.*[1]

The Master's Tools: The Comprehensive Claims Policy

Before a land claim could be considered for negotiation under the federal government's Comprehensive Claims Policy, Aboriginal "claimants" had to first "qualify" by presenting specific evidence to the federal government of Canada, and to the provincial governments. According to the terms and definitions set out in the Calder decision, to be eligible, a claimant group would have to prove that their ancestors were members of an organized society who had occupied and used specific lands and resources before Europeans arrived; and, that the present claimants continue to occupy these same lands, and to use these same resources today.

Aboriginal peoples and their supporters set about doing research to demonstrate that their territories had borders that could be delineated and transformed into lines on maps; and that their villages, their hunting, fishing and gathering spots, and their sacred sites, could be represented by Xs on those same maps. Feasting and potlatching, increasingly transmuted into nouns, appeared on administrative flow charts, representations of governments, complete with bureaucrats and pawns. Continually contested and negotiated processes for resolving disputes were written down and codified into written laws. Oral histories, songs, dances and prayers were documented and edited; tape recorded and word processed. Stories and memories were burned onto film.

Using the masters' tools to destroy the master's house,[2] reappropriating colonial schemes, converting them into resources for cultural survival, are strategies that oppressed people have honed for centuries. Mapping can be a profoundly powerful political act of naming, or re-naming what is yours, in your own language. Documenting hunting, fishing, gathering and food processing can be a way of seeing what television and schools have tried to render invisible. Graphing structures of government can reveal another potential for feasting systems that have been changing and adapting for thousands of years. Trying to understand the underlying philosophies of laws can help to create alternative visions of justice. Recording the knowledge of elderly people whose embodied histories may die with them is, in the contemporary world, an important part of safeguarding their unique experiences and wisdom for the benefit of all of humankind.

Aboriginal peoples in Canada in the 1970s, like Indigenous people around the world, were actively engaged in a decolonization movement that included efforts to liberate themselves politically and culturally from years of being told, and sometimes believing, that they had no right to dreams of self-determination, and no possibility of realizing them. They were digging out from under over 100 years of colonial domination, emerging sometimes from generations of institutionalization in residential schools, and prisons. For the Gitksan and Wet'suwet'en, and other Aboriginal peoples in Canada, having access to resources through the Comprehensive Claims Policy provided the necessary material resources that enabled people to become more deeply engaged in learning or re-learning their languages, their histories, their subsistence technologies and practices; and reflecting on their traditional and contemporary cultures. With the pragmatic determination of their ancestors, they tried to represent and translate themselves through images and languages that "others" might understand, without sacrificing their own dignity and integrity. As they sought to interrupt the historical monologue, and to initiate dialogue, these resources helped their voices to be heard, often for the first time, by non-Aboriginal Canadians.

The financial support provided by the federal government to prepare comprehensive claims submissions, and the implied promise that these claims would be taken seriously and responded to honourably, were integrated into the Aboriginal movement for decolonization: imperfectly and unevenly, and within the confines shaped by power relations, of course. But reappropriated they were.

The comprehensive claims process moved very slowly through the Office of Native Claims during the 1970s and 1980s.[3] The federal government's guidelines allowed it to negotiate only one claim at a time in each province or territory. In British Columbia, where the provincial government refused to participate on the grounds that no Aboriginal rights ever did or ever would exist in this province, the entire process was stalled. The Nishga claim, supported by the accumulated documentation of over 100 years of constant petitioning and preparing for litigation, had been filed first and lay dormant. All other First Nations knew that their claims would not even be considered until after the Nishga's was settled.

While the comprehensive claims process in B.C. was stuck in this logjam in front of the bottleneck built by the provincial and federal governments, the pace at which the exploitation of natural resources was proceeding accelerated, and profits from the forests and the seas flowed into corporate bank accounts unimpeded, except by political resistance. Many people feared that, by the time First Nations got to the table, there would be no resources left to negotiate. Throughout the 1980s, various B.C. First Nations mounted campaigns of civil disobedience. They and their supporters temporarily halted industry and transportation across their lands, and applied—sometimes successfully—to the courts for injunctions to halt development until their claims were heard and adjudicated.[4]

Title on the Baker Lake Tundra: Lower Peaks than Mexico

The exigencies of survival dictated a society composed of small, scattered groups. The band itself had no political hierarchy; that existed only at the camp level....

Major decisions all involved the hunt, conducted at the camp level, and were made by the oldest hunters. Neither individuals, camps nor bands claimed or recognized exclusive rights over a particular territory.... There is no evidence or reason to infer that the Inuit's nomadic ways, relationship to the land and social and political order changed from prehistoric (circa 1610) times until their settlement (circa 1950).

—Justice Mahoney, Federal Court of Canada, 1980, *Reasons for Judgment* in *The Hamlet of Baker Lake et al v. Minister of Indian Affairs and Northern Development.*[5]

Meanwhile, in northern Canada, a case that would establish important precedents in the area of Aboriginal law was winding its way through the maze of trials and appeals. The "Baker Lake case" had been launched in the Federal Court of Canada, Trial Division, in 1979. The Plaintiffs were the Hamlet of Baker Lake, the Baker Lake Hunters and Trappers Association, the Inuit Tapirisat of Canada, and individual Inuit living, hunting and fishing in the Baker Lake area of the Northwest Territories. The Defendants were the Attorney General of Canada and the Minister of Indian Affairs and Northern Development in Right of Her Majesty the Queen, and a consortium of mining companies. The plaintiffs asked the court for an order restraining the government from issuing land use and prospecting permits, granting mining leases and recording mining claims which would allow mining activities in the Baker Lake area, and for an order restraining the defendant mining companies from carrying on such activities there. They also asked for a declaration that the lands comprising the Baker Lake area are subject to the Aboriginal right and title of the Inuit residing in or near that area, to hunt and fish in these territories.

In their initial pleadings, the government defendants admitted that the Plaintiffs and their predecessors had occupied and used the Baker Lake area since time immemorial. They withdrew this admission during the trial. The mining companies denied that Aboriginal title had existed either before or after Europeans arrived in the region. Both the government and the mining companies argued that *if* Aboriginal title ever existed it was entirely extinguished by the Royal Charter of 1670 that granted the territory—then known as "Rupert's Land"—to Canada, or by subsequent legislation.

Judge Mahoney found the evidence of the Inuit elders about their ways of life and religious beliefs, and that of Superintendent Dent of the Royal Canadian Mounted Police "complementary," in so far as both described daily life within small hunting groups.[6] The principal conclusion the judge took from this evidence was that, prior to moving into settlements in the early 1950s, the Baker Lake Inuit were, in his words, "nomads." In his imagination, this meant they had no strong ties to specific, delineated tracts of land, or "civilized" concepts of private property.

Expert witnesses Dr. Elmer Harp Jr., Professor Emeritus of Archaeology at Dartmouth College, Hanover, New Hampshire, and Dr. J. V. Wright, head of the Scientific division of the Archaeological Survey of Canada, particularly impressed Justice Mahoney with their detailed and recognizably "scientific" evidence, and with the fact that they agreed with each other, as Mahoney did with them, on the fundamental issue of classification within the familiar social evolutionary framework: the Inuit were nomadic hunters, not settled horticulturists and therefore were low on the scale of evolutionary human development.[7] Justice Mahoney concluded that "those encampments of two or three families were the units described by the Inuit witnesses, encountered by Inspector Dent in the mid-1950s, by Norton in 1762, and discovered to have existed in the Thule period."[8]

Justice Mahoney was less impressed by the expert evidence of Dr. Milton Freeman, whom he described as "a social anthropologist, which is to say that he is neither an archaeologist nor a linguist; he studies the social behaviour of people in the context of their society or culture."[9] On the stand, Dr. Freeman elaborated on the nature of "band level societies," a term he had not used in his affidavit. The Crown and the mining companies objected to his testimony following his statement that the small hunting units described by both Inuit elders and local non-Inuit observers are "units of a much larger coherent organized society and very much interacting, interdependent, mutually dependent on interaction with other units within the society...this all constitutes a very coherent society which anthropologists have no problem in identifying...."[10] Freeman tried to explain that, while the Baker Lake Inuit may have hunted and camped in small family groupings during particular seasons, at other times they joined together with similar bands in large gatherings for the purposes of trade and exchange, ceremony, ritual, resolution of disputes, organization of government, and documentation of significant historical developments through oral history. The Baker Lake Inuit live sometimes in small bands; and at other times, in larger groupings. Freeman challenged simplistic classifications that rule out those concrete aspects of Indigenous life which do not fit neatly into abstract European theoretical categories.

Mahoney dismissed Freeman's evidence on a technical point: Rule 482 of the Rules of Evidence requires that an expert witness' testimony be laid out in an affidavit first, in order for the opposing lawyers to have adequate opportunity to review the expert opinion report and prepare for cross examination.[11] Freeman had stated in his affidavit that he would discuss the relationship between the Inuit and their environment. When Freeman described Inuit *culture*, Mahoney ruled that "this was not what was promised" in the affidavit, apparently understanding "environment" to include only the physical or natural landscape, but excluding human social, political and economic organization. Dr. Freeman was engaging in "persuasive arguments" on these issues, unbecoming to a scientist, the judge said.

Mahoney was similarly unimpressed by Dr. Peter Usher's evidence. Usher holds a Ph.D. in Geography. Quoting the *Shorter Oxford Dictionary* definition of geography as the "science that describes the earth's surface, its form and physical features, its natural and political divisions, its climates, productions etc.," Mahoney concluded that Dr. Usher's evidence didn't fall within his field of expertise. Mahoney wrote: "Dr. Usher's evidence had more the ring of a convinced advocate than a dispassionate professional.... Neither his formal training as a geographer nor his experience in and with the Arctic and Inuit qualify him to form opinions on political, sociological, behavioural, psychological and nutritional matters admissible as expert evidence in a court of law."[12]

More experts testified. Wildlife biologists, ethnologists, and experts on animal behaviour were called to the stand by both parties. Those called by the plaintiffs supported the Inuit hunters' claims that the caribou herds were declining and being driven away by mining activities. Those called by the government and mining companies discounted the Inuits' evidence, saying their knowledge reflected only their simple lived experiences and was therefore particular and limited, and should not be taken as seriously as the theories of "scientific experts." These non-Inuit experts claimed to base their knowledge on scientific surveys that reached far beyond the immediate area of Baker Lake, and produced results that could be generalized and tested against universal, law-like theories. They claimed the causes of the caribou herds' decline were multiple and complex.

Justice Mahoney ruled that "on the balance of probabilities...activities associated with mining exploration are not a significant factor in the caribou population decline."[13]

In summary, Mahoney, like judges before and after him, preferred to rely on his own "common sense" interpretation of Native testimony, supported by carefully chosen "factual" confirmation by "ordinary white people," and professionals selectively labelled "scientists" by a judge. Testimony by well educated and well respected—by the criteria of western scholarship—scholars of "softer sciences" like anthropology or social geography, was rejected.

Assessed from another perspective, it could be argued that evidence that supported the representation of Baker Lake Inuit societies as "high enough" on the scale of social development set by the *Re: Southern Rhodesia* test to have had "property usages and conceptions that could be continued under the British regime,"[14] was rejected in favour of images of small bands of nomads lacking political or social cohesion whom the same judgment had described as "so low on the scale of social organization that their usages and conceptions of rights and duties are not to be reconciled with the institutions or legal ideas of civilized society."[15] Expert witnesses whose testimony supported the former were dismissed as unprofessional "advocates" of Aboriginal political causes, while those whose interpretation supported the latter where respected as "scholarly experts." This evaluation was made by the court, and not by the standards of their respective professions.

On the legal source of Inuit Aboriginal title, Justice Mahoney set out a four-point test which he said the plaintiffs must prove to establish an Aboriginal title cognizable in common law:

(1) That they and their ancestors were members of an organized society.
(2) That the organized society occupied the specific territory over which they assert the Aboriginal title.
(3) That the occupation was to the exclusion of other organized societies.
(4) That the occupation was an established fact at the time sovereignty was asserted by England.[16]

The first criteria was drawn directly from the test in *Re: Southern Rhodesia*. Mahoney enforced this by referring as well to Haldane's decision in *Amodu Tijani v. Nigeria* about acknowledging differences between Indigenous property systems. Accordingly, Mahoney argued that different property regimes represented different stages of social evolutionary development. The Baker Lake Inuit passed Mahoney's test, but only just. Unlike the Nishga, who the Supreme Court of Canada found had "developed their cultures to higher peaks" than any other Indigenous peoples north of Mexico, Mahoney classified the Baker Lake Inuit as less advanced on the evolutionary scale. Mahoney wrote: "The fact is that the aboriginal Inuit had an organized society. It was not a society with very elaborate institutions but it was a society organized to exploit the resources available on the barrens and essential to sustain human life there. That was about all they could do: hunt and fish and survive."[17]

On the question of extinguishment, Mahoney ruled that neither the Royal Charter of the Hudson's Bay Company, nor admission of Rupert's Land into Canadian confederation had extinguished the common law Aboriginal title the Inuit held. Neither, he found, had legislation subsequent to 1870 had the effect of extinguishment. However, the unextinguished rights that Mahoney "found" were extremely limited. He argued that Aboriginal title could not have been proprietary because then the Crown *would* have formally extinguished it. His conclusion, in summary, was that the plaintiffs were entitled to a declaration that they have an Aboriginal right only to hunt and fish on the lands in question. "The aboriginal right asserted here encompasses only the right to hunt and fish as their ancestors did," Judge Mahoney wrote.

When the *Calder* case went to court in 1969 the trial took four days. No fully articulated "legal test" existed at the time and judges saw the question of Aboriginal title as a factual matter to be determined on the basis of empirical evidence of actual historic occupation and use of ancestral lands.[18] Such a test requires minimal evidentiary support, is relatively uncomplicated, and accessible to common sense reasoning and understanding. The straightforward arguments and the evidence required to prove historical use and occupation, in its simplicity, was also difficult for the Crown to dispute. However, only Aboriginal peoples, and not non-Aboriginals, are required to prove long term use and occupation, rather than pre-existing ownership and historical title, to establish legal ownership of land. And, the use and occupancy test suffered from being based on the demand that Aboriginal people demonstrate how their property systems were similar enough to be considered equal to British ones.

This is another double bind: if Aboriginal people emphasize the *similarities* between their land tenure systems and British ones, the courts may look more favourably on their claims because they appear familiar, but then the Aboriginal litigants sacrifice the opportunity to demonstrate the cultural uniqueness and ongoing validity of their own relationships to land, and surrender to the colonizer's language and legal concepts. If, on the other hand, Aboriginal peoples emphasize the *differences* between their relationships to land and those of British-derived cultures, they risk them being classified as too different to be understood as equal. Heads, the Crown wins. Tails, Indians lose.

Justice Mahoney's 1980 decision in *The Hamlet of Baker Lake v. Minister of Indian Affairs and Northern Development,* and his articulation of a precise, but complex, legal test for Aboriginal plaintiffs to meet, therefore marks an important turning point in this story: the recognition, and construction, of complexity around the legal Aboriginal title issue. The intricacies of diverse Indigenous relationships to land are complex and interesting. However, the historical/legal questions at stake remained the same: were Aboriginal peoples here when Europeans arrived? Did they live in organized societies with property laws? Were their rights lawfully extinguished according to British, Aboriginal or International law?

The Baker Lake test set the terms of legal and anthropological research questions for a decade to come.[19] The important knowledge required to understand and participate in the legal struggle for recognition of Aboriginal title and rights increasingly became the task of specialists like lawyers, consultants, Aboriginal Elders and a small coterie of First Nations leaders. Increasingly, ordinary people, Aboriginal and not, were ushered out of decision-making roles and into fund-raising and public education in support of litigation.

The Evolution of the Dedicated White People Band at Bear Island

> To conclude, in 1763, George III, with the advice of his United Kingdom Ministers, did not grant ownership of vast tracts of land to Indian bands...when a war had just been fought to acquire those lands....
>
> At that time, Europeans did not consider Indians to be equal to themselves and it is inconceivable that the King would have made such vast grants to undefined bands, thus restricting his European subjects from occupying these lands in the future except at great expense.
> —Justice Steele, Supreme Court of Ontario, 1989, *Reasons for Judgment*, in *Attorney-General of Ontario v. Bear Island Foundation et al.*

In the 1989 case of *The Attorney-General for the Province of Ontario* (the plaintiffs) vs. *the Bear Island Foundation and Gary Potts, William Twain and Maurice McKenzie Jr. on behalf of themselves and on behalf of all other members of the Teme-agama Anishnabay, and the Temagami Band of Indians* (the defendants),[20] referred to as "the Bear Island case," the Crown claimed unencumbered title to 4000 square miles of land in Northern Ontario. The defendants, *Bear Island et al*, argued that Crown title was burdened by Aboriginal title recognized by the Royal Proclamation of 1763, and by unfulfilled obligations under the Robinson-Huron Treaty signed in 1860. The Crown wanted the court to relieve them of this burden so that development could proceed unencumbered. The Bear Island trial remains the longest recorded civil hearing in Ontario history, lasting for 120 days.[21]

Like Judge Mahoney, Justice Steele was not impressed by the expert witnesses supplied by the Bear Island defendants, calling them "a small, dedicated and well meaning group of white people...[who]...in order to meet the aspirations of the current Indian defendants has pieced together a history from written documents, archaeology and analogy to other bands, and then added to that history a study of physical features and other times, together with limited pieces of oral tradition."[22]

Justice Steele ruled that the evidence presented did not, to his satisfaction, prove that the Teme-agama Anishnabay were members of an organized society in 1763.[23] He went on to conclude that, since neither the French nor the English considered Indians as equal to Europeans in the eighteenth century, the Crown's representatives who drafted and signed the written agreement could not have intended for the Royal Proclamation of 1763 to recognize Aboriginal title as the basis of any legitimate legal or political rights.

The Bear Island case illustrates an example of a conservative, archaic approach to the interpretation of history in the context of Aboriginal rights litigation. During the 1970s and 1980s, Canadian courts wrestled with the problem of how to interpret history in the context of Aboriginal rights litigation. The results varied, and were often contradictory. In 1973 when the decision in the *Calder* case was arrived at, Justice Hall had commented that historical documents "must be approached in the light of present-day research and knowledge disregarding ancient concepts formulated when understanding of the customs and culture of our original people was rudimentary and incomplete and when they were thought to be wholly without cohesion, laws or culture, in effect a subhuman species." Similarly, in 1977 in the case of *Kruger and Manuel v. The Queen*,[24] then Chief Justice Dickson of the Supreme Court of Canada argued that traditional legal approaches may not be adequate to the task at hand since "claims to aboriginal title are woven with history, legend, politics and moral obligations."[25] The idea that judges must be conscious of historical context when interpreting legal precedents, was offered again in 1985 in the *Simon v. R.*[26] case, when the Supreme Court of Canada overruled a decision by Justice Patterson in *R. v. Syliboy* made in 1929. In that case, Patterson had found that a particular agreement between the Crown and the Micmac in 1752 was not a treaty representing the "unconstrained Act of independent powers," but rather an agreement "between a civilized power and savages." The 1985 Supreme Court of Canada decision stated that "It should be noted that the language used by Patterson J...[27] reflects the biases and prejudices of another era in our history. Such language is no longer acceptable in Canadian law, and, indeed, is inconsistent with a growing sensitivity to native rights in Canada."[28]

However, in 1985, the very same year that Chief Justice Dickson of the Supreme Court of Canada issued this caution, in the Supreme Court of Ontario, Justice Steele handed down his decision in the Bear Island case using language and reasoning that resembled Patterson's 1929 ruling in both theory and substance. On appeal, in 1991, the Supreme Court of Canada rejected Steele's finding that the Teme-agama Anishnabay had "failed to prove that their ancestors were an organized band level society in 1763." However, they simultaneously ruled that they were unable to find any "palpable and overriding error" in Steele's findings of facts, although they did not necessarily agree "with all the legal findings based on those facts."[29]

Legal scholar Joel Fortune asked the obvious question: "How is it possible to distinguish Steele J.'s 'correct' determination of the facts from his 'incorrect' finding that the Teme-amaga Anishnabay did not constitute an organized society in 1763?"[30] Fortune answered his own question by concluding that the Supreme Court of Canada's Bear Island decision is an illustration of "the judicial reluctance to acknowledge openly that a legal outcome may rest on a question of historical interpretation."

The Bear Island judgment refashioned the Baker Lake test into a more complex three-part test, adding requirements for proof of the nature of Aboriginal rights enjoyed prior to the relevant date, as well as evidence of a system of land-holding and a system of social rules and customs. And, the Bear Island test added, this continuity of exclusive occupation must be evident up to the date of commencement of the court action. Therefore, the Bear Island claimants had to prove exclusive occupation from the eighteenth century until the time they started their claims action in the late twentieth century. This set a precedent whereby all Aboriginal claimants could be asked to show that they had excluded not only other Indigenous peoples from their territories from the time of European contact until the filing of their writ in a contemporary court, but that they had also kept well-armed European explorers, miners, traders, settlers and police off their lands.

In a practice that speaks to the uniquely autocratic prerogative of law, the legal tests for Aboriginal rights have been constructed and/or elaborated upon during the course of trials, and articulated by judges *post hoc*[31] in reasons for judgment, often in response to evidence and testimony presented for the first time in the particular trial being judged. Thus, claimants enter into a trial prepared to meet a test enunciated in a previous case, and find their arguments and evidence evaluated on the basis of criteria that emerge *in situ*. These criteria, in turn, influence the arguments lawyers advance and the kinds of evidence and expert witnesses they bring forward to support their arguments in a subsequent case. The tests have, therefore, shaped the research and testimony sought from anthropologists, archaeologists and other expert witnesses employed in the litigation process.

The evidentiary requirements for legal proof of Aboriginal title have correspondingly expanded exponentially, and, with them, the role and importance of anthropologists and other expert witnesses. The "land use and occupancy" studies that were previously required to establish long term, prior occupancy, now had to be supplemented by research into cosmology, language, spirituality, governance, law, family life, and world views. The increase in volume and complexity of evidence was generated by the court's responses to these cases, and the political context shaping both. Anthropologist Peter Elias concluded that "the tests set out by Mr. Justice Steele in Bear Island Foundation...may have crossed the line of social science comprehension...if the tests are elaborated much further, it won't be possible to meet them."[32]

The Master's House: The Repatriation of the Canadian Constitution

When the Constitutional process came along, in 1981 and 1982, the Gitksan and Wet'suwet'en asked themselves and talked to the elders and wondered: 'Can we create the political will on the part of the politicians in British Columbia and in the federal government to negotiate?'...

We have been consistent. You could see it based on the things that the elders were saying to the McKenna-McBride Commission between 1912 and 1913 and the points they were making when Indian reserves were being set up in the 1890s. We read and knew what they were saying, and there were elders in the 1970s and 1980s who were repeating those same comments and questions. They all wanted to resolve 'the land question'. They wanted recognition of who and what they were, and they wanted to have some dignity in their own land. The constitutional process provided an opportunity....So we entered that process. It didn't take long, however, to find out we were wasting our time in the constitutional process. It was clear nothing was likely to happen, because there was no political will or understanding at the time for anything substantial to happen.

The negotiation process wasn't available to us—it just wasn't working.

—Medig'm Gyamk (Neil Sterritt), 1992, It Doesn't Matter What the Judge Said.[33]

Another arena in which Aboriginal political struggles took place during the 1980s was created by the repatriation of the Canadian Constitution from Britain to Canada. As part of this process, Aboriginal peoples sought to have recognition of their inherent Aboriginal title and rights entrenched and given constitutional protection. Some British Columbia Indians, fearing that repatriation would jeopardize what they considered their direct relationship with the British Crown, recognized by the Royal Proclamation of 1763, mounted an international campaign to postpone repatriation of the Constitution until Aboriginal issues were dealt with. They were not successful in halting the repatriation process, but did succeed in wresting a commitment from the federal and provincial governments to include Aboriginal representatives in formal discussions concerning the formulation of the new *Constitution Act.* Negotiations took place during a series of five First Ministers'

Conferences held between 1983 and 1987, and resulted in the Meech Lake Accord[34] that, critics charged, failed to adequately protect the rights of Aboriginal peoples, Québecois and women.

The limited victory won by Aboriginal peoples in the Constitution debates was represented by Section 35(1) of the *Constitution Act, 1982* which states: "The existing aboriginal and treaty rights of the aboriginal peoples of Canada are hereby recognized and affirmed." This clause is described as an "empty box" which litigation and further negotiations must fill. In other words, it was left to the courts and to negotiations between federal, provincial and Aboriginal representatives to define what these "already existing" Aboriginal rights were: what is the content of these rights? What do they actually mean, to whom, in everyday life? Are these rights "inherent," arising from Aboriginal peoples' having been the prior occupants and rulers of the land now known as Canada; or are they "delegated," their legal and political source relying on recognition by the Crown? What would constitute legitimate extinguishment of Aboriginal title and rights: did such extinguishment have to be explicit, or could it be implicitly inferred? Was evidence of Aboriginal consent required to make extinguishment legal?

The case of *R. v. Sparrow*, launched in British Columbia in 1984, and finally ruled on by the Supreme Court of Canada in 1990, was the first to begin filling Section 35(1) of the *Constitution Act, 1987*'s "empty box."

Testing, Testing: From "Use and Occupancy" to "Culture" in the Sparrow Decision

> In the Court's view, the reason for concluding that the Musqueam Nation enjoys a right to fish lies not in the presence of state action conferring such a right, but instead arises from the fact that fishing is integral to Musqueam self-identity and self-preservation.... The nature and content of an aboriginal right is determined by asking what the organized aboriginal society regarded as "an integral part of their distinctive culture"....To be so regarded those practices must have been integral to the distinctive culture of the above society from which they are said to have arisen.
>
> ...The content of aboriginal rights thus is to be determined not by reference to whether executive or legislative action conferred such a right on the people in question, but rather by reference to that which is essential to or inherent in the unique relations that native people have with nature, each other, and other communities.
>
> —Chief Justice Dickson, Supreme Court of Canada, 1990, *Reasons for Judgment*, in *R. v. Sparrow*.[35]

The next, and final, important case that preceded *Delgamuukw v. R.*, was *R. v. Sparrow*. It began in the same year, 1984, that the Gitksan and Wet'suwet'en filed their Statement of Claim. On May 25, 1984, Reginald Sparrow, a member of the Musqueam band, was charged with fishing for salmon using a drift net that was longer than allowed by the Department of Fisheries-issued permit for Indian food fishing. Sparrow defended himself by saying he was practising an "existing Aboriginal right" protected under Section 35(1) of the *Constitution Act, 1982*. Sparrow was first found guilty in the Provincial Court of British Columbia. When the case was appealed to the British Columbia Court of Appeal, the appellate court agreed that Sparrow's Aboriginal right to fish had not been extinguished prior to 1982, but ruled that the mesh size regulations of the Department of Fisheries were still applicable. At issue when the appeal of the case went forward to the Supreme Court of Canada was whether the Musqueam First Nation could assert an Aboriginal right to fish that would override federal regulations which required a fishing permit and restricted the use of a drift net to a maximum length of 25 fathoms. The Musqueam asserted that their right to fish was an "existing aboriginal right...recognized and affirmed by s. 35(1) of the *Constitution Act, 1982*, and therefore paramount over federal law." To be regulated in the exercise of their right by Department of Fisheries and Oceans regulations was inappropriate and unconstitutional, they claimed.

The Supreme Court of Canada agreed with the Musqueam, and in their decision handed down on May 31, 1990 called for "a generous, liberal and purposive interpretation of s. 35(1)."[36] They found first that Aboriginal rights that exist in common law are recognized and affirmed by s. 35(1) of the Canadian Constitution that is paramount over all other laws. The Constitution, in other words, is the supreme law of the land.[37] As a result, laws that interfere with the exercise of constitutionally-protected Aboriginal rights must conform to constitutional standards of justification. For example, where a resource, like fish, is scarce, Aboriginal rights should take precedence over commercial and sports interests and be limited only by the requirements of conservation of the resource.

The *Sparrow* decision reiterated that the Crown must show a clear, plain and explicit intention to extinguish Aboriginal title, and that laws of general application applied to Indians should not be construed as having effected "implicit extinguishment." It is a common legal strategy in Aboriginal title litigation for lawyers for all parties to present judges with a number of possible interpretations: a kind of prioritized "wish list" of rulings their clients could live with. These various alternative arguments need not be logically consistent, and often begin from radically different premises. The Province of British Columbia's legal argument in support of "implicit extinguishment" constitutes such an alternative, or "fall back" position. Should a judge find that Aboriginal title and rights *did* exist at the time the British arrived, and therefore that some form of extinguishment of Aboriginal title *was* required, the Province of B.C. puts forward their argument that colonial governments in British Columbia have consistently demonstrated their *implicit* intention to extinguish Aboriginal title. To support this claim, the Crown presents evidence from the legal and historical record that documents how provincial courts and governments have denied and ignored First Nations' assertions of Aboriginal title since 1871. They argue, for example, that the fact that provincial wildlife acts were legislated without regard to Aboriginal rights constitutes support for the Crown's claim that Aboriginal rights were implicitly extinguished. This argument is an example of a common form of legal reasoning in which the law continually refers back to itself for justification and confirmation: contemporary irrationality and immorality is justified by its historic depth and breadth, and strengthened each time it is repeated.

These two positions—*implicit extinguishment* versus *explicit extinguishment*—has represented the boundaries and limitations of the Crown's legal position, and the Canadian government's political position, in relation to Aboriginal peoples. A third possibility, that Crown and Aboriginal titles might *co-exist*, is cast outside of this paradigm.

The Supreme Court, in *Sparrow*, affirmed the findings in *Guerin* in relation to the Crown's fiduciary obligations and noted that the relationship between Aboriginal peoples and the Crown should be "trust-like" rather than "adversarial." Native peoples do exist in a hierarchical relationship with the Crown, but this should be tempered by the Crown's fiduciary obligation to act as protector of Aboriginal people. Further, adequate consultation with Aboriginal peoples was clearly a pre-condition in determining whether laws that infringe on Aboriginal rights were constitutional. This interpretation of "existing Aboriginal rights" specifically allowed that the practice of such rights should be reasonably seen as necessarily evolving over time: "a modernized form of such a practice would be no less an aboriginal right."[38] That is, the fact that Reginald Sparrow now fished with high-tech gear rather than the implements his ancestors may have used two hundred years ago was not to be construed as evidence of his "assimilation" into Canadian society, or the transformation of his fishing practices into "non-Aboriginal" activities.

The Supreme Court of Canada's ruling in *Sparrow* acknowledged reliance on historical interpretation and expert evidence that contested interpretations presented by the Crown. The judges were particularly impressed by the testimony of anthropologist Dr. Wayne Suttles. The *Reasons for Judgment* in *R. v. Sparrow* state that "the anthropological evidence relied on to establish the existence of the right suggests that, for the Musqueam, the salmon fishery has always constituted an integral part of their distinctive culture. Its significant role involved not only consumption for subsistence purposes, but also consumption of salmon on ceremonial and social occasions. The Musqueam have always fished for reasons connected with their cultural and physical survival."[39]

On the central question of Aboriginal title, the *Sparrow* decision remained adamant on the fundamental, foundational issue. It stated: "It is worth recalling that while British policy toward the native population was based on respect for their right to occupy their traditional lands, a proposition to which the Royal Proclamation of 1763 bears witness, there was from the outset never any doubt that sovereign and legislative power, and indeed the underlying title, to such lands vested in the Crown."[40]

The Supreme Court of Canada judges were satisfied that the Musqueam had met all the requirements set out in the Bear Island test articulated by Justice Steele in 1985. In reconfiguring the legal test for Aboriginal title to require that an Aboriginal right be "integral to the distinctive culture" of the people in order to be legally recognized, the Supreme Court's ruling in the *Sparrow* case reflected emerging concerns at the forefront of western political culture as the twentieth century neared its end. "The category of 'culture' once and still endlessly debated by critics and ethnographers in mostly sequestered precincts," writes cultural critic Stanley Aronowitz, "has, over the past decade, become a major political issue.... The 1970s and 1980s were marked by the rise of 'new' cultural and political identities—gender, racial, sexual, national and ethnic—that manifested themselves as challenges to established powers," he concludes.[41] In Canada, public political debate during the 1970s and 1980s was dominated by campaigns, referenda and hysteria about Canadian unity and the possibility of Quebec separating and forming a sovereign nation state. "Sovereigntists" argued that the Québecois constitute what came to be called a "distinct society." Debates about whether this distinction should be defined on the basis of territory, language, or culture, raged. Questions about Aboriginal sovereignty or rights, and what could constitute distinctly Aboriginal cultures, were inevitably linked to, and often submerged by, the conflict between the two self-described "Founding Nations" as they sought to discover each other.

From a focus on materialist conceptions of technology and economic organization as the important determinants of social organization, and reflected in legal tests for Aboriginal title based in historic use and occupancy, western intellectual debates increasingly turned to a growing fascination with more idealist issues like spiritual beliefs, ceremony, ritual, language and the arts as the defining elements of people's political and social relationships with each other. "Culture" had become the principle marker of the difference between Aboriginal and non-Aboriginal people in Canada. It remained now for the law to define and codify "culture."

"A characteristic of law," writes French sociologist Pierre Bourdieu, "is its compulsion to capture and codify all that enters its field."[42] Visions, ideas, "cultures," and images of possible ways of being that dare to challenge the law are like butterflies who have flown into a collector's laboratory where they have been trapped and drained of life. Their wings pinned down and their bodies stretched out for maximum surveillance; they are encased in glass forever. A tag classifies and labels them, defining and identifying their place in the cosmos, as it has always been and always must be, forever fixed. The prospect of the Supreme Court of Canada determining what is and what is not "Aboriginal culture" is foreboding indeed.

Ping Pong

> *You have to go back to the mid-70s and the early 80s to understand why we did what we did. Because the provincial government refused to negotiate, and they said it, at least once a year, if not more often.*
> —Medig'm Gyamk (Neil Sterritt), 1992, *It Doesn't Matter What the Judge Said.*[43]

Several significant victories had been won by Aboriginal peoples in court during the 1980s, and the Supreme Court of Canada headed by Chief Justice Brian Dickson had shown itself to be relatively sympathetic to Aboriginal claims. Dickson had articulated the principle that interpretations of treaties, statutes, and the Constitution itself should be favourable towards Aboriginal peoples, and that, in judicial dealings with First Nations, the courts should endeavour to uphold "the honour of the Crown." The *Guerin* case in 1984 had resulted in a ruling that the Crown was bound by a legally enforceable fiduciary obligation to manage Aboriginal assets in the best interests of Aboriginal peoples, rather than in favour of non-Aboriginal public or private interests as the historical practice—illustrated by this case—had been. Dickson's court had insisted that Aboriginal or treaty rights could only be extinguished by governments expressing their intention to do so in "clear and plain language," and that colonial governments simply superimposing their law and government on Aboriginal peoples without their consent did not constitute legal extinguishment of pre-existing Aboriginal rights. If such unextinguished rights were shown to exist, so the thinking in the Supreme Court of Canada in the 1980s went, then interference with those rights by others—like provincial governments—would have to meet certain tests before it could be justified.[44]

When the Gitksan and Wet'suwet'en filed their Statement of Claim initiating *Delgamuukw v. R.* in 1984, the federal comprehensive claims policy, strangling itself and everyone involved in it in red tape, had almost ground to a halt across the country. The provincial government of British Columbia still refused to recognize the existence of First Nations, or to join in any negotiations on comprehensive claims with the federal government. The Constitution talks were at a standstill regarding the inclusion of clauses on Aboriginal rights. By the time the Gitksan and Wet'suwet'en trial began in

1987, litigation appeared as the only viable option left for First Nations in British Columbia to seek recognition and respect for their right to continue to exist as distinct peoples that they had been seeking for over 100 years.

1. Medig'm Gyamk 1992: 303.

2. Lorde 1984.

3. Coolichan 1985.

4. Tennant 1990(b).

5. *Hamlet of Baker Lake et al v. Minister of Indian Affairs and Northern Development et al* [1980] 5 WWR 193, 50 CCC (2d) 377 (FCTD).

6. Ibid., 202.

7. Ibid., 208.

8. Ibid., 213.

9. Ibid., 211.

10. Ibid., 212.

11. Ibid.

12. Ibid., 214.

13. Ibid., 210.

14. In *Re: Southern Rhodesia* (1919) A.C. 211.

15. Ibid.

16. *Hamlet of Baker Lake et al v. Minister of Indian Affairs and Northern Development et al* [1980] 5 WWR 193, 50 CCC (2d) 377 (FCTD), 219.

17. Ibid., 59-64.

18. Henderson W. B. 1991: 9-10.

19. Elias 1993.

20. *A.G. Ontario v. Bear Island Foundation* [1985], 49 O.R. (2d) 353, 15 D.L.R. (4th 321 (Ont. H.C.); *A.G. Ontario v. Bear Island Foundation* [1989] 68 O.R. (2d) 394, 38 D.L.R. (4th) 117 (Ont.C.A.); *A.G. Ontario v. Bear Island Foundation* [1991], 83 D.L.R. (4th), 381.

21. Bray and Thompson 1990; Clark 1990.

22. Steele, J. (1985) *Reasons for Judgment,* in *A.G. Ontario v. Bear Island Foundation* [1985], 49 O.R. (2d) 353, 15 D.L.R. (4th 321 (Ont. H.C.), 15.

23. Ibid., 21.

24. *Kruger and Manual v. The Queen* [1977] 4 WWR 300, [1978] 1 SCR 104, 75 DLR (3d) 434, 14 NR 495, 34 CCC (2d), 377.

25. Dickson, C.J., (1977) *Reasons for Judgment,* in *Kruger and Manual v. The Queen,* 377.

26. *Simon v. R.* (1985), 24 D.L.R. (4th), 390.

27. The use of "J" after a judge's name is a legal convention representing the title "Justice," i.e. writing "Patterson J." has the same meaning as the title "Justice Patterson."

28. Dickson, C.J. (1985) *Reasons for Judgment*, in *Simon v. R.*, 400.

29. *A.G. Ontario v. Bear Island Foundation* [1991], 83 D.L.R. (4th), 381.

30. Fortune 1993: 87-88.

31. *post hoc* is defined in *Webster's New Collegiate Dictionary* (1981) as "the fallacy of arguing from temporal sequence to a causal relation," 891. Simply put, rationalizing an action after the fact.

32. Elias 1993: 270.

33. Medig'm Gyamk 1992: 303.

34. For thorough discussions of Aboriginal issues and the Constitutional debates see Asch 1984. See Hawkes 1989 for discussion of the negotiation process. See Sanders 1983(a) for a cogent analysis of the legal issues involved. See Schwartz 1986 for a critique of Aboriginal positions and strategies.

35. *R. v. Sparrow* (1990), 70 D.L.R. (4th), 401-402.

36. *R. v. Sparrow* (1990), 70 D.L.R. (4th), 430.

37. "The common law doctrine of Aboriginal rights holds that the Crown's acquisition of North American territories was governed by a principle of continuity whereby the property rights, customary laws, and governmental institutions of the native people were presumed to survive, so far as this result was compatible with the Crown's ultimate title, and subject to lawful dispositions to the contrary." Slattery 1985:118.

38. *R. v. Sparrow* (1990), 70 D.L.R. (4th), 417.

39. *R. v. Sparrow* (1990), 70 D.L.R. (4th), 402.

40. *R. v. Sparrow* (1990), 70 D.L.R. (4th), 404.

41. Aronowitz 1993: 18.

42. Bourdieu 1987: 895.

43. Medig'm Gyamk 1992: 303.

44. Sanders 1992.

PART IV:

ECCE SIGNUM

(BEHOLD THE PROOF)

Chapter 8: Delgamuukw versus The Queen

Law is, of course, only one domain in which a culture may reveal itself. But like politics, marriage, and exchange, it is an arena in which people must act, and in doing so they must draw on their assumptions, connections, and beliefs to make their acts effective and comprehensible.... Like a single ritual, a network of exchange, or a contest for political leadership, one cannot hope to see all of a society through such a limited focus. But such an example can show us what it means to speak of law as culture and to trace out some of the implications this approach may have to offer...The world of formal courts offers a stage—as intense as ritual, as demonstrative as war—through which a society reveals itself to its own people as much as to the outside world.
—Anthropologist Lawrence Rosen, 1989, *Islamic Law and the Logic of Consequences.*

All the World's a Stage...

Trials have long served as ideal settings for writers of drama, satire and farce. The *Delgamuukw* trial could well be seen as living theatre at its best. 'Actors' representing all the key social categories of players in British Columbia history and contemporary life were there. The Aboriginal peoples, the Crown lawyers, the expert witnesses, and the Judge offered answers to the central question that has been in dispute in the Canadian west for two centuries: who owns the land? The Crown's legal representatives defended the "founding myth of White British Columbia," and their expert witnesses brought forward evidence unencumbered by the inclusion of Aboriginal or other critical voices. The Gitksan's and Wet'suwet'en's lawyers, well known for their work in labour, women's, prisoners' and human rights movements, represented "the new British Columbians," who do not see themselves in the original European settlers' official founding myths. The non-Aboriginal expert witnesses called by the Gitksan and Wet'suwet'en were part of a new generation of academics who came of age during the era of decolonization, and whose work was influenced by these experiences and intellectual discourses. For four years they faced each other and argued about who they were, where they came from, where they belonged, and how their children could live together in this geographical space called British Columbia, Canada. While their debates focused on the past, the real struggle was about the future: what would it look like, and who would shape it?

The narrative I recount in the following chapters chronicles the trial of *Delgamuukw v. R.* as it unfolded. The Gitksan and Wet'suwet'en, as the plaintiffs, presented their case first. The onus was on them to "prove" their claims. The Crown, as defendants, had principally to rebut the plaintiff's case, and only secondarily to demonstrate the merits of their counter-claim. For four years witnesses for both the plaintiffs and the defendants testified on behalf of one side, and were cross-examined by lawyers for the other. Their arguments and counter arguments revealed not only their respective stances on the issues before Chief Justice McEachern in this case, but also their visions of the past and aspirations for the future.

Do Aboriginal People Really Exist?

> *When they ask us what we feel our basis is in regard to our title, I don't think that there is any question. The title is very clear. The ownership has never changed. It is only the definition in the law in regard to ownership that has changed. When you're talking about justification and why we are and what we are, you're talking about history. It's amazing; when we become educated within your system, we're told that history is very important. Yet when you look at the history of Canada, where are we as aboriginal people? We're not included in this history. Yet our history is very rich.*
> —Miluulak (Alice Jeffrey), Gitksan Hereditary Chief, 1992, *Remove Not the Landmark.*

> *Like I said, our culture was on trial. We were told we didn't exist.... Ownership and jurisdiction is not something new for us. We have practised that. It is thousands of years old. We only want recognition.... We are right here before your very eyes.*
> —Yagalahl (Dora Wilson), Member, Gitksan-Wet'suwet'en Litigation Team, 1992, *It Will Always Be The Truth.*

The questions facing Chief Justice McEachern in the *Delgamuukw* case were the same ones every judge hearing an Aboriginal title and/or rights case in the British Empire-cum-Commonwealth, from the eighteenth century to the present, had addressed. They were:

(1) Did the Indigenous peoples in question own and manage their lands and resources before Europeans arrived?
(2) If so, have those property rights been extinguished by law at some time in history, or have they continued into the present?
(3) If unextinguished Aboriginal rights continue to exist, what are they?

(4) If unextinguished Aboriginal rights continue to exist, how can they be lawfully extinguished and/or justifiably contravened?

Fundamental moral, philosophical and political beliefs underlie the answer to the initial question: were the ancestors of contemporary Aboriginal peoples in Canada members of an organized society at the time Europeans first made contact with them?

Like many questions in law, if this is read literally, it is an oxymoron: a society, by definition, is organized. What could an unorganized society be? To understand what is really being asked, we have to step outside literal interpretations and common sense and enter into the historically and culturally specific universe of meaning that is British and Canadian colonial law. Just like anthropologists seeking to understand a foreign culture, we must try to interpret the question from within this perspective and seek to understand the culture of law from the inside.

An "organized society," according the rules of "law's culture," qualifies as such if it meets certain criteria specified by legal precedents, which themselves rely on various social theories for support and validation. The precedent that the first question in the legal test for Aboriginal rights refers to is Lord Sumner's 1919 decision in *Re: Southern Rhodesia*. The empirical information that an answer to this first question requires is knowledge of the ways particular Aboriginal peoples lived before contact with Europeans: the ways they managed their properties and resources; the ways they gathered, processed, stored and distributed food; the ways they celebrated births, and mourned deaths; the ways they marked marriages and divorces; the ways they traded and socialized with their neighbours, maintained social order, and worshipped their gods. Stepping back outside of "law's culture," the question appears as: will a British, or Canadian, court recognize these ways of life as those they have already defined as being representative of what they call "an organized society?" How will the law answer the questions it has posed for itself, by the criteria it has established for itself?

The Gitksan and Wet'suwet'en argued that they were here, living in a society that was by definition, description, and documentation, organized. In *Delgamuukw v. R.*, the provincial government of British Columbia argued for the application of Lord Sumner's test and the *Re: Southern Rhodesia* precedent, claiming that the Gitksan and Wet'suwet'en were so "low on the scale of social organization" that British Columbia was justified in declaring the territory in question *terra nullius* in the early nineteenth century.

The second question in the legal test for Aboriginal rights: "Did the ancestors of the Aboriginal claimants occupy a specific territory?" arises from the first. Only an organized society can occupy a specific territory. The third and fourth questions: "Did they exclude other organized societies?" and "Was occupation established at the time British sovereignty was established?" arise from the second. To answer these questions, evidence has to be produced that shows that Aboriginal peoples recognized identifiable borders that marked the lines between their territory and that of others. The Gitksan and Wet'suwet'en tried to demonstrate that both they and their neighbours knew the boundaries of their respective territories; although, like neighbours everywhere, they sometimes argued about exactly where lines should be drawn. The Crown argued that Aboriginal peoples in British Columbia were nomadic wanderers who lacked abstract concepts of property.

In the *Calder* case nearly twenty years earlier, the Nishga had asked the court only for a declaration that "...aboriginal title, otherwise known as the Indian title...has never been extinguished." The case did not address what such Aboriginal title might include. The Gitksan and Wet'suwet'en tried to push the question beyond these very general concepts. *Delgamuukw*'s claim was for legal recognition that Aboriginal title means ownership, jurisdiction, rights, interests, and financial compensation for resources exploited and destroyed between the arrival of Europeans and now. The Gitksan and Wet'suwet'en petition to the Supreme Court of British Columbia sought a declaration that:

> ...from time immemorial they and their ancestors have occupied and possessed approximately 22,000 square miles in north-west British Columbia ("the territory"), and that they or the Indian people they represent are entitled, as against the Province of British Columbia, to a legal judgment declaring: (a) that they own the territory; (b) that they are entitled to govern the territory by Aboriginal laws which are paramount to the laws of British Columbia; (c) alternatively, that they have unspecified Aboriginal rights to use the territory; (d) damages for the loss of all lands and resources transferred to third parties or for resources removed from the territory since the establishment of the colony; and, (e) costs.

The Nishga claim had been based on a model of collective or communal ownership. The Gitksan and Wet'suwet'en claim, however, was made by each of 35 Gitksan and 13 Wet'suwet'en chiefs, led by Delgamuukw (a.k.a. Ken Muldoe), representing themselves and all the members of their Houses, for ownership of specific territories. Their claim to jurisdiction, or self-government, was two-fold. First, the chiefs asserted their right to govern land-related activities on the 22,000 square miles that make up Gitksan and Wet'suwet'en territory, free of interference by provincial laws like the Wildlife Acts. This claim applied only to Crown lands and did not include fee simple private property owned by individuals who had purchased their land in good faith from the Crown. Second, they claimed the right for Gitksan and Wet'suwet'en laws to supersede the general laws of the Province of B.C. in Gitksan and Wet'suwet'en territory, particularly in relation to education;

health; family relations like marriages, divorces, adoptions and child welfare; justice and law enforcement.

Delgamuukw delivered his "Opening Address to the Court," on behalf of the Gitksan and Wet'suwet'en Hereditary Chiefs in Smithers, B.C., on May 11, 1987. He began: "The purpose of this case...is to find a process to place Gitksan and Wet'suwet'en ownership and jurisdiction within the context of Canada. We do not seek a decision as to whether our system might continue or not. It will continue."[1]

In seeking such a place within Canadian law, the Gitksan and Wet'suwet'en agreed that, for the purposes of entering into the legal process, they would not challenge the notion that what the courts call "the underlying title to the land" was held by the hovering sovereign symbolically represented by the Crown, (and embodied from time to time in judges, bureaucrats, soldiers, and Mounties.) They also agreed not to contest the requirement established by the Royal Proclamation of 1763 that Aboriginal land can only be sold to the Crown, and not to private corporations or non-Aboriginal individuals. Subject only to these two constraints, the Chiefs said, they, as representatives of their Houses and its members, own "and are absolutely entitled to occupy and possess" the 133 individual territories claimed, in a manner that is "for all purposes equivalent to ownership in fee simple."[2]

---

1. Gisday Wa and Delgam Uukw 1987: 1.

2. Ibid., 3.

Chapter 9: The Gitksan's and Wet'suwet'en's Case

So what we say is we have title and that is why we are talking to you about aboriginal rights, but we are not talking English Common Law definitions, international law definitions that have been interpreted and reinterpreted and sometimes extinguished by conquest and ceding treaties and other agreements like that. We are talking about the feeling that is inside all of us as Metis, Indian and Inuit people that this country belongs to us.... My whole point is that we must stop viewing aboriginal rights from the point of view of the dominant society if we are ever going to understand what the Indian people, the Inuit people, and the Metis want....

The question is whether there is a means of understanding this concept from the Native point of view.

—Aboriginal leader Bill Wilson, 1983, address to the First Ministers' Conference on Aboriginal Constitutional Matters, Ottawa.[1]

A Native Point of View

Each major Aboriginal title and rights case adjudicated during the nearly twenty years that elapsed between the *Calder* case and the *Delgamuukw* case had resulted in elaborations of the legal tests required to establish Aboriginal title and rights in law. An intricate configuration of abstract legal and anthropological arguments, expressed in increasingly obscure and mystifying language, was constructed through the litigation process from *Calder* onwards. Since the tests for Aboriginal title and rights had been developed *post hoc* by judges, litigants and their lawyers when preparing for and entering a trial could know what evidence previous courts had accepted or rejected, and been convinced or dissuaded by. They could only guess, however, at what issues might emerge during the course of their particular trial, and what an individual judge might decide to require in terms of evidence. It is often not until Reasons for Judgment are written that the reasoning used to evaluate the relative weight of evidence, and reach final conclusions, is revealed. The increasingly complex nature of the tests' questions required increasingly detailed and comprehensive research. This in turn necessitated the employment of an ever more varied range of professional consultants and legal advisors, thus driving the duration and costs of litigation higher and higher.

It bears remembering that the need for these expenditures from the public purse was created by judges and courts, and that few of the economic benefits generated flowed into Aboriginal coffers. It bears remembering, too, that the questions at the core of all this have been relatively simple and straightforward ones. Were Aboriginal people living here in "organized societies" before Europeans arrived? Answer: Yes. Has their ownership of the land ever been ceded, sold, treatied, or lost in war? Answer: No. Was this legal according to British imperial law? Answer: No, not unless Aboriginal people are categorized as insufficiently "evolved," or in some other way inferior to Europeans. Is this just according to historical or contemporary standards of morality or the letter of laws? Answer: No. It could be argued that continually rewriting the questions, redefining the qualifying tests, and reinterpreting what constitutes correct responses, has substituted for a just answer to these questions. What should be done in order for Canada and British Columbia to create "justice in our time" in relation to Aboriginal title, rights, and persons? This is the *real* question before the courts, the governments, and the Canadian population.

At the same time, however, moving away from the simplistic "common sense" logic of *Calder*'s "prior historical use and occupancy" test, and ultimately ethnocentric analogy with English common law principles as a basis for recognition of Aboriginal title and rights, has created a space for Aboriginal peoples to elaborate their unique understandings of their distinct cultures and relationships to the land. This has provided an opportunity for non-Aboriginal peoples to learn about, and begin to develop an understanding of, Aboriginal cultures on their own terms, rather than always in relation to, or in comparison with, Euro-Canadian cultures. The trap of common sense is that it resists and rejects what is not already known to it, and understands much about social life and history as being "natural" and "inevitable," rather than created by people themselves. Failing to move beyond "common sense" can limit the possibility of new visions of life and society emerging and being reflected upon.[2]

Stuart Rush, one of the lawyers for the Gitksan and Wet'suwet'en, explained the legal team's strategy in *Delgamuukw v. R.* "This Court," Rush said, "in hearing the evidence which will be presented in this case, will be faced with a series of legal and intellectual challenges and opportunities of a nature not normally found in matters that come before the bench."[3] Rush set out the first challenge to the Court as being to "reflect critically on European, or Euro-Canadian, ethnocentrism:... to understand and overcome the tendency to view aboriginal societies as existing at an earlier stage of evolutionary development.... We will be inviting this Court, through its rulings, to reject any legal theory of aboriginal rights which depends upon such evolutionist and supremacist assumptions."[4] The second challenge described by Rush was "the problem of communication between very different cultures."[5]

The Gitksan and Wet'suwet'en Hereditary Chiefs, in their opening address to the court, challenged Chief Justice McEachern to hear them on their own terms.

"Never before has a Canadian court been given the opportunity to hear Indian witnesses describe within their own structure the history and nature of their societies," Delgamuukw began. "The evidence will show that the Gitksan and Wet'suwet'en are and have always been properly counted amongst the civilized nations of the world; that their ownership of their territory and their authority over it has always existed; and that they have shaped a distinctive form of confederation between House and Clans. The challenge for this court is to hear this evidence, in all its complexity, in all its elaboration, as the articulation of a way of looking at the world which pre-dates the Canadian Constitution by many thousands of years," he continued.

A world view, as defined by anthropologists, is composed of two inter-related parts: a notion of how the world is structured and how its parts form a cohesive whole; and, a set of rules which set the structure in motion and control and direct it. The fundamental features of the Gitksan and Wet'suwet'en world view, and the central differences, or oppositions, between it and "the western world view" were described by the Chiefs in their opening statement. "The western world view," Delgamuukw explained, "sees the essential and primary interactions as being those between human beings." The Gitksan and Wet'suwet'en world view, on the other hand, understands human beings to be "part of an interacting continuum which includes animals and spirits." Secondly, in the Gitksan and Wet'suwet'en world view time is cyclical and past events "directly effect the present and the future," whereas in the western world view, time is linear and causality more direct. Thirdly, the Chiefs argued, westerners believe in accidents and coincidences, whereas Gitksan and Wet'suwet'en do not. The western world view makes fundamental distinctions between sacred and secular, spiritual and material, natural and supernatural, while the integration of these elements, "infuses the Gitksan and Wet'suwet'en thinking and major institutions," the Hereditary Chiefs' opening statement concluded.[6]

The answers to a number of the legal questions facing the court in *Delgamuukw v. R.* lie in descriptions of Gitksan and Wet'suwet'en ways of life as they were before European fur traders arrived in the late eighteenth century. The Gitksan and Wet'suwet'en, having made the decision to pursue their claims through the judicial system, endeavoured to both respect the terms and conditions of the court, and at the same time to maintain their own integrity and identity. They attempted to bring together the best of both worlds in areas of specialized knowledge, and present the most highly qualified people available—according to the criteria of both Aboriginal and mainstream Canadian cultures—as expert witnesses to the court. The Gitksan and

Wet'suwet'en litigation team studied previous cases and endeavoured to anticipate as many questions and challenges as possible. In addition to the testimony of Chiefs and Elders, the litigation team marshalled a tremendous amount of scholarly evidence to support their case, and attracted the support and participation of an impressive array of well-respected professional and academic witnesses.

The tradition of expert witnesses in British law dates back to the sixteenth century, when assemblies of neighbours and colleagues familiar with the events and persons entangled in a dispute were replaced by juries of presumably objective arbiters whose qualifications were that they knew nothing of the case, or the parties involved. Expert witnesses become necessary when judges and/or juries believe that the issues before the court require explanation and specialized knowledge beyond that which either a legal expert or an ordinary lay person can be expected to possess. Psychiatrists, asked to assess whether or not an accused person is sane enough to have planned and carried out the actions they are accused of, are the expert witnesses most familiar to the public through newspaper reports and television shows. In the *Delgamuukw* case, lawyers for the Gitksan and Wet'suwet'en argued that the Court had to try to gain understanding "across both a profound cultural divide, and from a distance of 200 years and more."[7] The expert knowledge referred to here consists in the unique understandings of life and cosmos embedded in different cultures over time. The best authorities on knowledge about Gitksan and Wet'suwet'en history and contemporary life were Elders, Chiefs, and members of Gitksan and Wet'suwet'en communities. They were the first expert witnesses to testify.

Experts in Living Memory

"It is very sad to say that some of the most powerful witnesses in the court case...have now died, but they saw within themselves the strength and the need to go and give their evidence in court."
—Medig'm Gyamk (Neil Sterritt), 1992, *It Doesn't Matter What the Judge Said.*[8]

The main evidence in support of the Gitksan and Wet'suwet'en claim to having lived in an organized society, with borders and laws, and of having owned, then and now, their territories, was to be presented by Chiefs and Elders through the telling of their two particular kinds of oral history: *adaawk* and *kungax.*[9] Before this testimony could be heard by the court, however, the Gitksan and Wet'suwet'en and their lawyers had to overcome a legal obstacle: the Crown argued that oral tradition should be considered inadmissible under what is known as the "Hearsay Rule." According to the law, the Crown claimed, oral histories constitute hearsay, since they purport to rely on the words and experiences of people who are deceased, and are not available for cross-examination.

The Gitksan and Wet'suwet'en chiefs and elders, and their lawyers and witnesses attempted to help the Chief Justice understand what he would be witnessing. In the opening address to the court, the Hereditary Chiefs instructed the judge that the *adaawk* and *kungax* should not be taken literally in a simplistic sense.[10] They drew analogies between distinctions made in both Aboriginal and western cultures between experience and hearsay, opinion and knowledge, lay people and experts. The Gitksan and Wet'suwet'en explained that their oral traditions describe the genealogies of various clans and families, and their relationships with their lands and resources. They explain cosmology and spiritual relationships and obligations. They document ownership of lands and resources, transactions, relations with neighbours, and historical events. *Adaawk* are Gitksan oral histories comprised of a collection of sacred reminiscences about ancestors, histories and territories that document House ownership of land and resources. The Wet'suwet'en *kungax* is a song, or songs, about trails between territories. The rights to perform particular *adaawk* and *kungax* are part of the privileges, like clan crests, that are inherited and stewarded by individuals and House groups when they take ownership and responsibility for the specific territories the oral histories tell about. Learning the content of the narratives, and the specific conventions of oratory and style with which they must be delivered, as well as coming to know how to properly perform the songs and dances that are, like the narratives, essential aspects of *adaawk* and *kungax*, takes many years. Chiefs and Elders are, therefore, the custodians of this specialized knowledge.

Gitksan and Wet'suwet'en oral tradition includes the feasting complex through which various oral accounts may be validated or contested by the people as a whole. When a host Chief and his House hold a feast to mark an important event, such as the transfer of property, the guests assembled serve as witnesses to the event or transaction being marked by the feast and they watch and listen to the performance of the *adaawk* or *kungax* at the feast gathering. If they are persuaded that the laws have been properly followed, the guests/witnesses validate the event or transaction by accepting the host's offers of food and gifts. If they disagree, they make their objections known by making a speech explaining their position and refraining from accepting anything from the host that might be construed as witnessing, validation or affirmation. Sometimes disputes are resolved within the framework of a single feast, and sometimes they remain contentious over longer periods of time. The Statement of Claim filed by the Gitksan and Wet'suwet'en said expressions of ownership come through the *adaawk*, *kungax*, songs and ceremonial regalia; confirmation of ownership comes through totem poles erected to give those expressions a material base; assertion of ownership is made through specific claims.[11] Before the Gitksan and Wet'suwet'en court case, neither *adaawk* or *kungax* had been performed outside of feast halls. "This was the first time our people brought forth what you call evidence. It isn't evidence to us. We call that our *Adaawk.*" Gitksan Elder Miluulak (Alice Jeffrey) explained.[12]

Anthropologists and ethnohistorians who submitted expert opinion reports on behalf of the Gitksan and Wet'suwet'en elaborated on the various methods social scientists use to analyze oral histories. Oral histories may be subjected to the familiar historical method of verifying when and where specific events took place by examining a variety of sources and comparing accounts of particular events.[13] This involves cross-referencing information from oral histories; ethnographies; historical documents; archaeological studies; and biophysical data on technology, resource and land use, and social organization to assess the degree to which "real events" or "literal truth" is reflected in the oral accounts. Richard Daly, an anthropologist who testified for the Gitksan and Wet'suwet'en, pointed out in his opinion report that "oral history is not the same as the individual reminiscences of an elder."[14] During his testimony, Daly reiterated in significant detail the section of his expert opinion report in which he explained the methodology he had employed in his analysis. "Oral tradition should be treated as a whole,…a corpus of linked and overlapping records of events that have been reiterated down through the generations. Individual tellings of one Chief's history must be compared with one another, and then with the accounts of the same or related events from the viewpoint of other Chiefs. When this is done carefully, the oral tradition can be treated as a valid historical source," Daly wrote.[15]

Scholars who employ the methodology outlined by Daly classify the oral histories of some traditions as more factually reliable by these criteria than others. Expert witnesses repeatedly referred to the particular richness of Gitksan and Wet'suwet'en oral histories, and to the rigorous demands for validation through feasting that have resulted in the *adaawk* and *kungax* being ranked as valid and dependable historical sources by generations of anthropologists and ethnohistorians.

Second, a rigorous analysis of oral history involves the even more complex task of interpreting the many layers of meaning revealed by oral tradition when it is understood within the cultural context of its performance.[16] Such an analysis requires the interpreter to describe and explain the different historical and local contexts in which oral tradition is transmitted, including the political dynamics involved in various forums, the reputations of different speakers, and the uses of various rhetorical strategies and performance techniques.

Finally, the background knowledge and prejudices that members of audiences bring to the performance of any recitation of oral histories contributes to the interpretation of the meaning of the verbal text. Of course, written history can be critically evaluated in much the same way: documents are written by particular people in particular contexts for particular purposes, and each generation of readers brings to their reading of historical texts new ideas and experiences that would have been unknown to the original scribes. "Oral tradition differs from western science and history," Anthropologist Julie Cruikshank writes. "But both are organized systems of knowledge that take many years to learn, and both are perpetually open and incomplete."[17]

Chief Justice McEachern determined that he was satisfied that the *adaawk* and *kungax* had gone through a "sifting process" through their having been told and retold and witnessed repeatedly, and that lent them an "enhanced trustworthiness" in his eyes. But, he added, "historical facts sought to be adduced must be truly historical and not anecdotal."[18] McEachern decided to admit the oral history evidence and testimony, saying he would "weigh" it at the end of the trial. He expressed his willingness, however, as the judge of first instance in a case of such importance, to "lean towards admissibility" and to "harken to the evidence."[19] The judge said he would use two principal criteria to determine what weight to give the oral histories in relation to other evidence. First, he would try to distinguish between what "a deceased elder said he or his elders did, and what they believed," and allow only the former to stand as evidence. Second, he said he would accept the plaintiff's culturally specific definition and identification of the distinction between folklore ("antimahlaswx" in Gitksan), and laws or traditions, allowing only the latter to stand as evidence.[20]

Chief Justice McEachern also promised to rely on precedents set in cases where the issue of oral tradition testimony had been dealt with. First, he said, he would take from *Kruger v. R.* the direction that evaluation should be based on "facts pertinent to that Band and to that land, and not on any global basis."[21] Second, Allan McEachern referred to another of Brian Dickson's rulings in the case of *R. v. Simon,*[22] where the former Chief Justice of the Supreme Court of Canada found that to demand written support where oral tradition was the only source of evidence available, would be to "impose an impossible burden of proof." Chief Justice McEachern's decision, early in the trial, to admit oral tradition evidence as an exemption to the Hearsay Rule, gave the Gitksan and Wet'suwet'en and their supporters cause for optimism.

Eighteen chiefs testified in person at the trial, beginning with Gyolugyet (Mary McKenzie) in Smithers on May 13, 1987. An additional ten Gitksan and Wet'suwet'en, who were not chiefs, testified, and a further thirty-eight witnesses tendered, and were cross-examined on, territorial affidavits. Thirty of these were chiefs. The Chiefs and Elders hold the responsibility for learning and transmitting the oral tradition—including laws, legends, and histories—of their Houses and clans. These witnesses have earned their credibility, and the respect of their communities, over the course of their lifetimes. They represent an Indigenous aristocracy, gerontocracy and intelligentsia. They are also people who, through their life histories, embody the experiences of Aboriginal-White relations in British Columbia over many decades. In previous land rights litigation, the employment of Elders testifying in their own languages as expert witnesses had been minimal. The more common practice had been to employ, as witnesses, anthropologists who had interviewed Elders, and who, having thus become experts, would translate, represent, and analyze for the court what Elders had told them about their histories. The Gitksan and Wet'suwet'en strategy attempted to replicate this ethnographic process in the courtroom. The Chiefs and Elders testified directly to the judge, with Chief Justice McEachern assuming the role, in the first instance, of the white anthropologist hearing these oral histories for the first time.

In evaluating the oral histories during the course of the trial, Chief Justice McEachern remained particularly concerned about maintaining a clear distinction between "historical facts" and "beliefs." As he later reflected in his *Reasons for Judgment*, "At an early stage of the trial I expressed the hope that I could make a convenient but simplistic distinction between what European-based culture would call mythology and "real" matters.... I have concluded that it would be overly simplistic to attempt such a distinction, and I must accordingly reject mythology as a valid distinction between what is and what is not part of an *adaawk* or *kungax*."[23] However, as the Chiefs' testimonies proceeded, the judge became increasingly impatient about having to actually listen to the oral histories. He took exception, particularly, to witnesses singing in court. "This is a trial," he reproached an Elder at one point, "not a perfor-mance."[24] Besides, he added, the significance of the music was lost on him as he had "a tin ear."

The Gitksan and Wet'suwet'en offered the court, in some instances— notably the Gitksan *adaawk* of Medeek, and the Wet'suwet'en *kungax* of the House of Goohlaht—archaeological and geological evidence that supported events and places noted in the oral histories in order to link these with conventional scientific proof. The *adaawk* of Seeley Lake Medeek tells about a massive landslide accompanied by the presence of a supernatural grizzly bear. Rolf Mathewes, a paleobotanist, testified that his research showed that a massive landslide had occurred in the area around 3,380 years ago. Alan Gottesfeld, a geomorphologist, added his support for the *adaawk* based on results of research conducted in accordance with the scientific methodology required by his discipline.

Since the Gitksan and Wet'suwet'en were the plaintiffs in the case of *Delgamuukw v. R.*, it was their case that was presented first, and the onus was on them to present convincing evidence to prove their claims. The Crown, as the defendants, were required only to protect themselves by refuting and rebutting the plaintiffs' testimonies. Crown lawyers cross-examined the Gitksan and Wet'suwet'en Elders in the antagonistic manner characteristic of the adversarial Canadian legal system. Yagalahl (Dora Wilson), a member of the Gitksan-Wet'suwet'en Litigation Team, recounted how she felt observing this part of the trial: "There were lots of times where I just felt like screaming: 'Hey, you're wrong. How dare you say this? How dare you do this? How dare you be disrespectful to my elder sitting in that witness stand? How dare you speak to her that way? How dare you speak to him that way?"[25] "But," Yagalahl remembered, "one of our witnesses had a lot of fun with one of the lawyers. She is an elderly person. She is in her eighties. She had been to the hunting area, berry-picking area, you name it, on the territories most of her life. So in her evidence, she was talking about times when they went out berry-picking. The lawyer was trying to say that she didn't really know her territory. He was trying to confuse her by using the place names.... Here he was questioning, questioning, and what he was doing—and didn't realize—was he was going up and down, up and down, this mountain that she was describing. Finally she got annoyed, and...she says to the interpreter, 'What's the matter with this lawyer? Is he crazy? We've been up and down that hill a lot of times now.' So sometimes it was funny."[26]

In presenting their case, the Gitksan and Wet'suwet'en asked the court to hear and understand them on their own terms, within the context of the Gitksan and Wet'suwet'en "world view." Chief Justice Allan McEachern, at several points during the trial, cautioned that this evidence was "subject to objection and weight which would be adduced at the end of the trial." He said any evidence could be disregarded "if it is contradicted, or if its value as evidence is destroyed or lessened either internally or by other admissible evidence, or by common sense."[27] In anticipation of such skepticism, the Elders' testimony was augmented by testimony by expert witnesses in cartography, paleobotany, geomorphology, forest ecology, fishery biology, ethnoarchaeology, linguistics, historical geography, anthropology, and history.

The Ancestors are Watching

Sitting in the courtroom, I felt this heavy burden like all of my ancestors were sitting on my shoulders, and anything that was said on the witness stand had to be the truth as we were taught, because the truth, I remember my grandmother saying, is something that you don't forget. Because if you tell a lie, at some point in the future, you always get tripped up and it comes out. The politicians have proven that out.
—Yagalahl (Dora Wilson), 1992, *It Will Always Be The Truth.*[28]

Lay people, also recognized as expert witnesses by the Court, included members of Gitksan and Wet'suwet'en Houses who had received training through Indigenous forums, and/or who had obtained professional and academic credentials in relevant fields. After the Elders finished testifying, these younger—mostly middle-aged—Gitksan and Wet'suwet'en took the stand as expert witnesses. These people are apprentices to the Elders in the "traditional" system, as well as being members of their own generations with their particular experiences and acquired knowledge. Many work within their own communities and within the institutions of the majority Canadian society in the fields of political negotiation, law, education, health, welfare, and community administration. They represent an emerging Aboriginal professional class, political leadership, and intelligentsia.

In order of appearance, the first expert witness to testify on behalf of the Gitksan and Wet'suwet'en after the Elders was Neil Sterritt, hereditary chief and cartographer. He described how the Gitksan and Wet'suwet'en delineated boundaries and how these had been translated for mapping purposes. Sterritt's evidence focused on explicating the subject of internal boundaries between the 133 territories, and between the Gitksan and Wet'suwet'en and their Aboriginal neighbours. He explained how ownership was and is established and property transferred, and through what processes boundaries and ownership could change. He provided numerous illustrations of complex deliberations over territories.

To be acknowledged as an expert in court requires that the judge recognize the witness as such. Therefore, in a dispute, lawyers for each side attempt at the outset to disqualify or cast doubt on the expertise of each other's witnesses. Expert witnesses are often subjected to aggressive cross examination in which their credentials, their methodologies, and often their personal characters can be challenged. Heather Harris, a non-Aboriginal woman who had married into a Gitksan family and been adopted into a House and clan, and who also held a degree in Anthropology, testified about the genealogies she had collected that described the matrilineal kinship system that forms the basis of Gitksan and Wet'suwet'en social structure. The lawyer for Canada, Marvyn Koenigsberg, suggested to Harris under cross-examination that she may have "gone native," a derogatory accusation historically used to discredit anthropologists who were seen to have crossed the great divide between Aboriginal and European cultures, and hence to have lost their capacity for scholarly—defined as "objective"—research and analysis. The phrase, "going native" is also frequently used as a sexist and racist slur against white women who marry Indians.

The Gitksan and Wet'suwet'en witnesses were followed on the stand by anthropologists who also testified as expert witnesses.

---

1. Canada 1983 cited in Asch 1989: 123-124.

2. Bourdieu 1990. See also, Miller 1992: 55-65.

3. Gisday Wa and Delgam Uukw 1987: 22.

4. Ibid., 23.

5. Ibid., 24.

6. Ibid., 38-40.

7. *Delgamuukw v. R.* (1987), 40 D.L.R. (4th) 685 (judgment on admissibility of oral tradition as an exception to the "hearsay rule," hereinafter referred to as "*Delgamuukw,* oral tradition").

8. Medig'm Gyamk 1992: 303.

9. For excerpts from this testimony see Gisday Wa and Delgamuukw 1992.

10. Gisday Wa and Delgam Uukw (1987), 38-42.

11. Gisday Wa and Delgam Uukw 1987.

12. Miluulak 1992: 59.

13. See Vansina 1965, 1985.

14. Daly 1988.

15. Daly 1988: 60-61.

16. See Cruikshank 1990, 1992, 1994.

17. Cruikshank 1992: 26.

18. *Delgamuukw,* oral tradition: 698.

19. Ibid., 697.

20. Ibid., 655.

21. Ibid., 653.

22. *R. v. Simon* (1985) 24 D.L.R. (4 th) 390 (S.C.C.)

23. McEachern 1991 *Reasons for Judgment, Delgamuukw v. R.*: 46-47.

24. Quoted in Monet and Skanu'u 1992: 42.

25. Yagalahl 1992: 201.

26. Ibid., 201.

27. *Delgamuukw,* oral tradition: 172.

28. Yagalahl 1992: 199.

Chapter 10: Experts on Behalf of the Plaintiffs

In the end, if anthropologists help the rest of the citizenry understand the First Nations discourse, then we will have made an invaluable contribution to the necessary dialogue. The Chiefs' voices will not be silenced. The crisis of anthropologists over how they are perceived, and what their role should be pales before the larger issue of working out just land claims.

—Anthropologist Antonia Mills, 1996, *Problems of Establishing Authority in Testifying on Behalf of the Witsuwit'en.*

Anthropology: Interpretation and Understanding?

Anthropologists first began to work in the capacity of expert witnesses on Aboriginal history in the United States when the Indian Claims Commission was established in 1946 to adjudicate land rights claims. From this starting point, almost half a century ago, certain enduring problems have confronted anthropologists who have become involved in these proceedings.[1] Courts, governments, and colleagues in the hard sciences disparage anthropologists for ceasing to be loyal academics and becoming too sympathetic to the people they work with. Indigenous people accuse anthropologists of being agents of colonialism, of appropriating their cultures, and of representing them from the perspectives, and in the interests, of the dominating society. Judges trained in dualistic and positivistic legal traditions have tended to consider "objective research" and "subjective interpretation" as polar opposites, and as synonymous with truth and falsehood, respectively. The differences between an adversarial legal forum, where simple true or false answers are demanded; and an academic forum, where detachment and absence of intellectual commitment are rewarded, have made marriages between law and anthropology rocky.[2]

Criticisms from all these parties focuses on the central methodology of cultural anthropology: participant observation and fieldwork.[3] Ethnographic research requires anthropologists to immerse themselves in the daily lives of the people they are studying, and to record and analyze their own observations. Fieldwork also involves extensive interviewing of research subjects in an effort to understand what the people who are members of the culture being studied say about themselves, and perhaps about colonial cultures and anthropologists. Field research is usually supplemented by studies of archival and other documents, and by canvassing academic literature on the same topic and/or area to glean what other researchers have learned and reported on. Quantitative methods, like statistical analysis, are also often incorporated into anthropological research. Issues concerning the impact of the context in which research is carried out, and of the anthropologists' own background and attitudes, on her or his research are legion. These questions are the subject of an ongoing and exhaustive critique within the discipline.[4] Anthropologists who have endeavoured to respond to these criticisms espouse "reflexive anthropology,"[5] "collaborative methodologies,"[6] and "experimental ethnographies."[7]

Reflexivity in anthropology refers to the acknowledgment that a human researcher studying other human beings will bring with them to the research endeavour attitudes and ideas about themselves, about the people they are studying, and about their relationship to each other. Taking seriously the problem that most anthropologists have historically been citizens of the nation states engaged in the colonization of Indigenous peoples, reflexive anthropology has paid particular attention to examining the influence of power relations located in race, gender and class structures, on ethnographic research. Rather than pretending that these issues can simply be eradicated by striving for "researcher objectivity" and the mimicking of natural science research models—as they accuse positivists of doing—reflexive anthropologists argue that recognition and acknowledgment of "biases," and accounting for their influence on their research findings, is both intellectually honest and politically responsible. Reflexive anthropology is not restricted to examining the ideas and attitudes of researchers but also addresses issues such as the impact of funding, and of processes like litigation, on anthropological research. Neither is it restricted to the study of "other" cultures. Rather, contemporary anthropology has encouraged more and more attention to critical studies of colonial settler cultures.[8]

Collaborative research methodologies include research subjects as participants in the research process: as consultants in the design, implementation and analysis of research in an effort to transform the traditional power relationship between researcher and researched. Adherents of collaborative methodologies argue that their approach simply recognizes and acknowledges what really goes on during the creation of what becomes an ethnographic text. That is, social knowledge in general, and anthropological knowledge in particular, in practice, emerges in large part from conversations between researchers and research subjects, and it is the product of these inter-cultural and inter-personal interactions, where the research subject is often the teacher and the researcher the student, that constitutes the essence of ethnographic knowledge.

To more transparently describe and communicate the way this knowledge has been created and produced, some contemporary anthropologists have rejected the traditional single-authored, authoritative monogram of historical anthropology, and are experimenting with new forms of writing and representation that attempt both to share authority and royalties with research subjects, and to use plain language to reach a wider audience than the academic one alone.

"Telling the truth" in reflexive, collaborative ethnographies takes the form of considering the influence of context and researcher/researched relationships to begin with, and trying to achieve a more comprehensive ethnographic description by including a broad representation of research subjects describing and analyzing their various experiences, and expressing their diverse views, in their own words. Locating, or "grounding," research in the needs of particular communities, as well as in the demands of academia, is another hallmark of much contemporary anthropology. The goal of "the new ethnography" is not the discovery of immutable facts or the refinement of more abstract theories, but rather the encouragement of understanding and mutual respect. Pretenses to unattainable "scientific objectivity," the "new" anthropologists charge, simply ignore the inherently interpersonal nature of the human study of human society, and mask unreflected upon and unaccounted for biases under a cloak of value neutrality.

The post World War II growth in Aboriginal political strength has had a significant impact on anthropology. The contemporary generation of anthropologists, having come of age in the same era, have had to come to terms with Indigenous critiques that have charged, and often proven by their own ethnographic endeavours, that many of the descriptions written by previous generations of ethnographers were at best limited and partial, and at worst inaccurate and insulting. Feminist anthropologists, for example, have produced a body of literature showing that the voices of Indigenous women have either been absent from, or misrepresented in, the classic ethnographies written by both male and female anthropologists.[9] The emerging recognition of the "native point of view" in anthropology and other disciplines, and of the right of Aboriginal people to represent themselves, is primarily a consequence of the ongoing struggle Aboriginal peoples have engaged in since the advent of colonialism. Many Aboriginal groups now demand significant participation in and control of ethnographic research conducted among them, a process they identify as "the decolonization of anthropology."[10] The presentation of the plaintiff's anthropological evidence in *Delgamuukw v. R.* reflected the contemporary conditions of, and approaches to, research with First Nations in Canada in the 1980s.

Of course, these new approaches in contemporary anthropology present important problems, to which there are no easy answers. No communities, including Aboriginal ones, are homogeneous. They are divided by gender, class, internalized racism, and local axes of inequality. There is not one "native point of view"; there are many. Local Indigenous power relations can shape the outcome of collaborative anthropological research, as can research funding from private and public agencies. Evaluating how an anthropologist can develop analyses that simultaneously respect indigenous representations, and also employ the tools of the discipline to critique these explanations is difficult, to say the least. Ethical considerations present individuals with increasingly complex choices, in anthropology no less than in most other disciplines, and no less, for that matter, than in everyday life in the contemporary world. A significant aspect of any contemporary anthropologist's training focuses on these issues, and on how to conduct valid, reliable, rigorous research in such contexts.

Here Come the Anthros

> The anthropologists' role in the trial was to take out of the bulk of undigested evidence the relevant and significant evidence in order to create a picture of a viable, functioning and current society... Secondly, the anthropological evidence was intended to translate the evidence of the people to combat the ethnocentrism in the judicial consideration of their society....
> We knew that the Judge shared the cultural perceptions of the governments and therefore the anthropologists had to break through his vision and to introduce him to the native world view.
> —Lawyer Stuart Rush, 1991, *The Role of Anthropological Evidence in Land Claims Litigation: The Gitksan Wet'suwet'en Case as an Illustration.*[11]

The issues in dispute between the parties in the courtroom at the *Delgamuukw* trial rested on the description and analysis of Gitksan and Wet'suwet'en society before European arrival. More concretely, the question that the plaintiffs and the defendants offered competing responses to was whether or not the approximately 9000 Aboriginal people living in northwestern British Columbia during the early nineteenth century constituted an organized society as defined by colonial law. According to the Gitksan's and Wet'suwet'en's witnesses, at the time in question they supported themselves by hunting, fishing and gathering natural resources. Their principal means of subsistence was salmon fishing. They harvested, preserved and stored food. They traded surpluses with their neighbours. They were matrilineal people, who reckoned descent and inheritance through their mothers. They were organized into clans and Houses led by chiefs. They engaged in various rituals, ceremonies and public assemblies, accompanied by feasting. Some feasts, and the system of reciprocal feasting between and among Houses, clans and villages, constituted an institutionalized process governed by laws and protocol for conducting the affairs of government and law.

The first professional anthropologist to testify for the Gitksan and Wet'suwet'en in *Delgamuukw v. R.* was Dr. Richard Daly, who took the stand for three weeks in February and March, 1989. Daly had received his Masters degree in Anthropology from Manchester University in 1975, and since that time had been employed in various professional positions. Daly's 700-page expert opinion report, entitled "Anthropological Opinion On The Nature of the Gitksan and Wet'suwet'en Economy," was largely based on research he conducted with the Gitksan and Wet'suwet'en during 1986 and 1987 while he was also preparing his doctoral dissertation under the supervision of Dr. Richard Lee at the University of Toronto. Daly's report contained eight chapters: theory and methodology in anthropology; kinship economy; ownership and management in a kinship economy; the natural environment, nutrition and production strategies; the seasonal round of economic activities; storage, the accumulation of values and social hierarchy; the question of trade; and the feast: paradigm for social interaction and the circulation of values. Daly's methodology included extensive archival research as well as interviewing of elders and participant observation. He listed the following specific sources for his opinion report:

(1) the transcripts of witness' statements and commissioned evidence of witnesses in the trial;

(2) formal interview data he collected during his research in the form of written fieldnotes that had been submitted to the court;

(3) knowledge he obtained through informal discussions, not recorded in writing;

(4) ethnographic monographs, including the Barbeau-Beynon papers, oral histories and fieldnotes collected by John Cove, Father Morice, Diamond Jenness, Franz Boas, Wilson Duff, John Adams, and Marjorie Halpin;

(5) articles and books on general history and economic history.

Daly described his research activities as follows: "Anthropologists seek to determine the truth through their work, seeking validation or invalidation of propositions by cross-referencing data and seeking to place the phenomena studied in as fully rounded a context as possible."[12]

Crown lawyers challenged Daly's qualification as an expert witness on the grounds of Section 11 of the Evidence Act which says that an expert should disclose the facts upon which his opinion is based. They argued that Daly's failure to turn over notes relevant to two years of participant observation was a breach of this requirement. Further, they charged that his report was "opinion thinly disguised as argument"; that he had interwoven oral histories with other information, "the foundation of which is highly questionable"; and, that his report duplicated evidence already given by other witnesses. Finally, the Crown argued that, since Daly's participant observation had been conducted after the commencement of the trial, and could not be replicated because precisely the same conditions would never again exist, his methodology was "unscientific" and his report should not be admitted as expert evidence.[13] Chief Justice McEachern qualified Daly as an expert and agreed to hear his testimony and determine its value by weighing it at the end of the trial in the context of the entirety of evidence presented.

Dr. Antonia Mills followed Daly in March, 1989. Mills had graduated with a doctorate in cultural anthropology from Harvard University in 1969. Since that time she has lived, worked, and taught in British Columbia and has conducted participant observation and archival research among the Dunneza-Cree (Beaver) First Nations and the Wet'suwet'en, primarily. Her 216-page opinion report, entitled "The Feasts, Institutions and Laws of the Wet'suwet'en," focused on Wet'suwet'en cultural history, and emphasized religion and cosmology.[14] Mills' particular research interest for several years has been reincarnation beliefs and practices among the Wet'suwet'en. Crown lawyers argued that Mills' training and work emphasized psychology, symbolism and religion and was therefore "not of interest to this case."[15] Like Daly, she had conducted participant observation following commencement of the court action. Like Daly, she was accused by the Crown of being an advocate who lacked objectivity, and who duplicated the evidence of the lay witnesses. Chief Justice McEachern, however, allowed her testimony, subject to his evaluation of its weight at the end of the trial.

Crown lawyers focused their cross-examination of Mills on the question of warfare. They took umbrage to a statement she made in her 20-year old Ph.D. thesis on the nature of warfare in western society:

Crown Counsel: On page 60, you set out your description of western society. I'm not going to read it out, but I just ask you to read over the first couple of paragraphs down to the line "Normal men have killed perhaps 100,000,000 of their fellow normal men in the last 50 years." Was that your view in 1969?

Mills: Yes.

Crown Counsel: And is that your view today?

Mills: I think I probably am a bit more sophisticated than that, but people certainly continue to kill their normal men. It's not as if I'm saying that other people don't do it as well. It's not as if I'm claiming that the Wet'suwet'en didn't kill one another.[16]

Chief Justice McEachern intervened in the Crown's cross-examination of Mills on the subject of her alleged romantic biases:

> Court: Are you surprised to find so many like Ogden[17] writing that the masses came out of their huts naked? Had their level of civilization not progressed beyond that at or just after the time of contact?

Mills replied that the Wet'suwet'en normally wore clothes.

> Court: I've heard...I have an impression that I am hearing perhaps the best side of these people, which is understandable, but you haven't said anything about wars.... Would you call them war-like?...the people generally?

Mills answered that she found it difficult to respond to a question that required her to make sweeping generalizations that characterized an entire people as either "war-like" or not. The Chief Justice continued:

> Court: There is a suggestion of slaves. Did the Wet'suwet'en take slaves?

Mills explained at length the similarities and differences between "slaves" and hostages taken in war.

> Court: There is even a suggestion in one of the pieces about cannibalism. Was that a feature of the Wet'suwet'en in any way?

> Mills: No.[18]

The Chief Justice apparently suspected Mills, the plaintiff's only female anthropologist, of presenting a romantic picture of the Wet'suwet'en.

Romanticism is a valid criticism often levelled at the discipline of anthropology. There is an extensive literature on the subject, including much by anthropologists themselves,[19] and by Indigenous critics who complain that anthropological romanticism camouflages the devastation wreaked on Indigenous cultures by colonial domination.[20] Aboriginal intellectuals charge that romanticized descriptions of their cultures are as one-dimensional and inaccurate as those that depict Aboriginal cultures as barbarous and cruel. Romanticism, they argue, is one projection of the European imagination, and savagery another. The Crown's "critique of romanticism," however, seems to be based on the simplistic idea that any evidence that the Gitksan and Wet'suwet'en peoples were NOT war-like, naked, slave-owning cannibals at the time Europeans arrived in the late eighteenth century, is romantic, and therefore not believable. End of conversation: facts are a nuisance in this monologue.

Law and Masculine Hysteria

In Western Europe, since the period of the Enlightenment in the 17th century, men have assumed a strong connection between their rationality and their sense of masculine identity. They have learned to appropriate rationality as if it were an exclusively male quality denied to "others": women and colonized people in particular....

Since 'rationality' is identified with knowledge, it is similarly denied to these same "others." Emotions and feelings are likewise denied as genuine sources of knowledge within the culture. Rather, they are associated predominantly with weakness and femininity, and so as antithetical to the 'strengths' with which boys learn their sense of masculine identity. Men could only assert their humanity by mastery over the physical world, and by learning to dominate their passions and desires. It is this inherited notion of self-control as dominance that has been so closely identified with modern forms of masculinity.

Such a view also begins to explain the depths to which men can feel threatened by emotions and feelings.

—Psychologist Lawrence Seidler, 1987, *Reason, Desire, and Male Sexuality.*[21]

On day 210 of the trial, anthropologist and film-maker Hugh Brody took the stand on behalf of the Gitksan and Wet'suwet'en. Brody's opinion report was based on participant observation, interviews, and archival research that included perusing the Barbeau-Beynon archives, Indian Agents' letters and reports, documents from the MacKenna-McBride Royal Commission of 1913-1916, trapline registration forms from the 1920s, and records of territorial disputes documented by white settlers.[22] Brody's report went on to summarize the history of research into Aboriginal title and rights over the past twenty years, noting the trend away from assimilation studies popular in the 1960s, through the land use and occupancy studies of the 1970s, and into the ownership and jurisdiction studies of the 1980s. He wrote: "The assumption that rights of ownership are established on criteria of land use or occupation now appears naive. We do not apply these criteria to our own rights. We do not draw boundaries around our territories by using and occupying them." Brody also reviewed anthropological theory, arguing that, until very recently, anthropology had ignored "how people regard themselves."[23]

Brody described the purpose of his report as being "...to bring some part of another people's world view into ours."[24] But, "the heart" of his endeavour, Brody wrote, was "to recognize and then break free from Euro-Canadian ethnocentricity."[25] One of the first steps in that process was to recognize that European intellectual thought, as expressed through language, was abstract and conceptualizing. "Hunting peoples," Brody wrote, "dislike generic categorizing language and prefer specific and concrete vocalization...hunting and gathering societies might be said to believe above all in facts."[26] Brody's focus on European ethnocentrism was what Chief Justice McEachern and the Crown's lawyers objected to most strongly. The Crown selected four passages from Brody's opinion report as evidence that "his report has nothing to contribute to the issues before this court."[27]

First, the Crown objected to the following statement on page 2 of Brody's report:

> ...our society has occupied the lands of other societies, and is committed to a particular kind of historical process. This means that settlers and governments have tended to see native peoples through unclear or distorting lenses.

Chief Justice McEachern entered the fray to dispute this statement, saying:

> Court: I have expressed the view for some time that courts of law are troubled on a daily basis with this question of feelings. Feelings are what make people function the way they do in many cases, but it's not something that laws and judges can manage very well. And if somebody wants to tell me what somebody else's feelings are, I have to discount it very substantially, because firstly he may have misconstrued the feelings, and secondly, the feelings may not be rationally founded.[28]

> ...

> Jackson:[29] My Lord, perhaps I might be permitted, in response to Mr. Goldie's point in reading that particular part which you just read and the whole relevance of how native society is perceived.

> Court: Does it matter...in any real sense, does it matter?

> Jackson: Well, My Lord, my point was to deal with these issues, and the relevance of a social scientific analysis to the appropriate legal conclusions, which of course are for Your Lordship to decide...

> Court: Let's assume for the purpose of this argument...they are going to...they are going to be found to have the rights that are claimed in the Statement of Claim. Does it matter if, from the time of contact, circa 1800 A.D., that they have been treated badly or they have been treated well? Does it make any difference?

> Jackson: I think the way Your Lordship has framed it, no. It does not. But it is our submission that understanding the cultural context in which that took place will enable Your Lordship to make a conclusion, a legal conclusion.

> Court: The fact is that a reserve was established, or an area was logged, or a mine was found and exploited or something of that kind. Those are facts that may speak to all sorts of issues relevant to this case, but if—does it

make any difference if settlers and governments have had an attitude or have viewed things in a particular way? The more I hear of this case, the more it comes back to the old question, 'what are the facts?' As the detective used to say, 'what are the facts, ma'am?

Jackson: …just the facts…

Court: Yes. 'Just the facts, ma'am.' I know that it's late in the day to try and boil things down. I know it's late in the day to change the rules, and I don't want to change the rules upon which we have been functioning, but that sort of a passage, "This means that settlers and governments have tended to see native peoples through unclear or distorting lenses"…seems to me to be of highly questionable relevance. You might just as well say what happened indicated that Indians have tended to see governments through unclear or distorted lenses and that probably the answer would…what is…what difference does it make? Of course…do they have rights and what are they? …not how the people view each other….

Jackson: My Lord…

Court: As I said a moment ago, they may view each other from completely irrational bases. They probably do. Most people do view each other from an irrational basis. Again, what difference does it make?

Jackson: I think it does make a difference, My Lord, in terms of understanding events which have taken place which are relied upon by my friends as evidence of loss or acquiescence in the loss of rights. And I will….

Court: I have grave misgivings about the conspiratorial theory of history, but that's perhaps a cultural impediment that I am going to have to try and avoid as we proceed. Go ahead, please, Mr. Jackson….[30]

Next, the Crown pointed to a statement on page 49 of Brody's report, that read:

Gitksan and Wet'suwet'en reserve lands amount of some 45 square miles. According to white interpretations of events, the villages that make up most of the 45 square miles represent the conclusion of a historical process.

Mr. Goldie, lawyer for the Province of British Columbia, objected strongly to this passage.

Goldie: My Lord…. I check my assumptions at the door, and I don't think it's appropriate for a witness to talk about "we." If he is talking about some other culture, let him talk about it…but I leave my assumptions at the door, and I don't want to deal with cross examination on the basis that I am depending on some particular point of view that is ascribed to me or to my client for that matter.

It would be a very interesting and perhaps educational process if Mr. Brody told us about ourselves and held up a mirror to us, but what has that got to do with this litigation?

Chief Justice McEachern agreed with the Crown.

Court: "According to white interpretations...." What white interpretations? All white interpretations? It doesn't say some. I don't know if it means some, but...isn't that just so wide and sweeping and so extensive that it's not keeping to deal with it? That's what every white person thinks? And then again we still have the problem. If he does, so what? We are still talking about rights that arose at the time of contact, as I read the authorities. I mean, I just have difficulty with the nature of this evidence. It seems to me it's way beyond what any court has ever been asked to look at before. I suppose there have been things as broad as that...isn't this...hasn't this perhaps gone over the line?

I must say I find that statement to be terribly, terribly exaggerated, and when you get into that area, you know that you are having a terrible time coming to grips with anything that's going to be useful. I mean, I think if the witness wants to say that's his view, I suppose that's all right. He doesn't say that. He says this is what everybody thinks. I don't think that is even close to being right. And if...well, maybe that's his view. Maybe he thinks every white person thinks that.

Brody: There is...and I said I am dealing at a high level of generality here self-evidently...there is a core to the intellectual assumptions that are made within our intellectual heritage, and these assumptions say a lot about what is expected to happen to tribal and aboriginal peoples.

Court: Well, I can understand the approach, Mr. Jackson, when we are talking about the culture of the Indian people, and one has to be generous, which is not really the word I am looking for, but quite relaxed about the extent to which evidence can go, because it's a very ill-defined kind of a study. But when you are talking hard facts, such as the McKenna McBride,[31] you have got terms of reference, you have got a transcript, you know it was said, then it seems to me that there isn't much that can be said about that. It speaks for itself...Truly, there must be limits, and I am just having trouble finding what they are here. I have a terrible feeling that I am way beyond them, and you are asking me to go way beyond them...It's like when you are in a contest or a game and they suddenly say we are not going to play it according to the rules. I just have the sense that I am asked to listen to material that is not something that a judge should be hearing.[32]

Brody's critique of "frontier culture" incurred the wrath of the Crown lawyers and the Judge as well, and the following statement from page 69 of his report was presented as another reason to disqualify him as an expert witness:

The encounter between native culture and frontier whites may be said to constitute a meeting of culture and anti-culture. Whites who are roaming, often alone, far from their own land, encounter those who are absolutely at home. The whites have thus in a way shed society. The native people they deal with are absolutely at home....

Finally, Crown lawyers pointed out the following statement about settler history, claiming it revealed Brody's inappropriate biases most strongly:

Newcomers, sure of their superior knowledge, understanding and rights, do as they think fit, encourage others to do likewise and call upon the forces of Canadian law and order if too directly thwarted and opposed.[33]

The lawyer for the Government of Canada summed up the Crown's objections to Brody's qualifications as an expert witness:

Crown Counsel: It is my submission what Mr. Brody is doing is describing attitudes of white people...how they feel about what's going on, and how to a certain extent the Indians feel from his point of view in response. And it is my submission that inquiry is irrelevant to the issues in this lawsuit. The issues that are being put forward by the plaintiffs for Your Lordship to decide is 'did the government, the white government impose jurisdiction?' Questions like were reserves created and what were they? How the whites felt and how the Indians felt is beyond the purview of this inquiry.

It's an interesting question. I am sure it is one which has probably concerned many a graduate thesis. But to determine—to go into detail about what was happening is in my submission irrelevant. It is, of course, in my submission, also in the nature of argument and speculative in the extreme.... If this kind of evidence is allowed it's tantamount to allowing experts to act as counsel and it's as if all the 45 or 50 witnesses that Your Lordship has heard for over a year...that Your Lordship cannot evaluate and interpret that evidence, but that you require the assistance of an expert to do so.[34]

Chief Justice McEachern asked this question of Crown counsel regarding Brody's admissibility:

Court: Well, let me pose this scenario...That an expert in the sense of a person highly trained and experienced in the discipline who has strongly held and widely publicized views on the question, is nevertheless called as an expert witness and he's qualified in the sense that he has shown that he has all the experience-related requirements of an expert. Can the court say...I won't hear this witness because he has a well known and admitted point of view? Is that not a matter that goes to weight?[35]

Mr. Goldie, lawyer for the Province of B.C., responded and summed up his objections as follows:

Goldie: Normally speaking, the experts every day are called who are—who are known as the proponents of a point of view. That is to say, they favour a particular theory. But this is not a case of favouring a particular scientific theory.

Court: He favours a party.

Goldie: He is favouring a party. That's the thrust of my submission, My Lord, and if he favours a party that takes him out of the category of the expert who says, well, I believe in the such and such theory of relativity.

Court. Yes.

Goldie: And I will stand up and be counted on that point, but there is no such suggestion of that here.

Court: And then proceeds to try and persuade the court that his theory is right.

Goldie: That's correct.... That's correct...but his theory....

Court: What's the point of this?

Goldie: His theory has got nothing to do with the particular parties to the case. There is no theory being advanced here in my submission.... My principal objection is that he says his report is an overview.... The word overview means that he cherry-picks from the evidence of others.... I don't mind his saying that every other anthropologist except himself is wrong and he's right.... That's his privilege....

Court: You can't get ready for a case like this without being closely associated with the people...but the question is does it go beyond that when he says, as he said before, he likes Indians and he has an—or aboriginals—and he has a favourable disposition towards them. Does that disqualify him?

...In a perfect world I would hope that parties would confine their expert testimony to persons whose objectivity is not open to question. That may not always be possible. And, indeed, it might be a dangerous test to apply, because the person who hides his biases is no more credible than the person who makes it known. The former may be more dangerous than the latter.[36]

The Crown's, and the Chief Justice's, response to Brody's testimony are indicative of the fundamental challenge to the court's self-image and legitimacy that a critique of ethnocentrism raises. "Judicial neutrality," the linchpin of the British and Canadian legal systems' claims to legitimacy, depends on maintaining the public perception that law is the expression of universal reason, that judges are without racial, gender or class bias, and that everyone is equal before the law. As his "tin ear" prevented him from hearing the oral histories, so Allan McEachern's myopia blinded him to his own biases.

Academic Freedom

I agreed to do the research with the understanding that I would be free to draw my own conclusions from the materials I examined. We also decided that it would be best to have me work independently of other researchers...so that my interpretations could stand alone. Accordingly, I did not read any of the other reports before submitting my final opinion and appearing on the witness stand, nor did I attend the trial before that time.
—Historian Arthur Ray, 1991, *Creating the Image of the Save in Defence of the Crown: The Ethnohistorian in Court.*

The presentation of evidence in *Delgamuukw v. R.* followed a chronological historical narrative. Following testimony that focused on Gitksan and Wet'suwet'en ways of life before the arrival of Europeans—labelled by historians the "prehistoric" era—witnesses described the arrival in the territories of fur traders and then settlers. The years during which Europeans initially made contact with Aboriginal peoples and became involved in first sporadic, and then regularized, trading relations with them, but before European settlement began in earnest, have been dubbed by academics the "protohistoric" era. With European settlement came written record keeping, which ushered in the "historic" period.

The legal questions that relied for answers on descriptions and analyses of the protohistoric period spanned those relevant to the prehistoric—or pre-European settlement—era, and the historic—or post-European settlement—era. First, an analysis of the nature of Aboriginal societies before contact was required to determine whether or not an organized society existed at the moment of contact, and when Britain declared sovereignty. Another legal question was what changes took place in Gitksan and Wet'suwet'en society and culture, and particularly in their property ownership and management systems, during the protohistoric years? This issue was crucial to the Crown's argument that the development of delineated borders and property law was not a feature of pre-contact Aboriginal societies but rather had emerged as a response to the European-Aboriginal fur trade. They claimed that, by the time Hudson's Bay Company trader William Brown arrived in 1822 and brought them into "history" by writing about them in his journals, the Gitksan and Wet'suwet'en had already undergone such significant social change as a result of their contact with European trade goods during the protohistoric period that Brown's journals could not be read as describing "aboriginal practices."[37] Chief Justice McEachern, in his *Reasons for Judgment*, would later explain the legal significance of firm boundaries between historical periods: "The difference between the pre-historic, proto- and historic periods is relevant to the question of determining what are aboriginal as opposed to non-aboriginal practices," he wrote.[38]

Oral history, linguistics, archaeology, ethnography and historical records are the usual sources of knowledge relied upon to provide information about the protohistoric and historic periods. Oral histories, in particular, offer Aboriginal reflections on these encounters, and some classical ethnographies augment this knowledge base. Europeans' experiences of the protohistoric era are represented in fur trading company's books and reports; ships' logs; traders' accounts, journals and diaries; and government records. Before evidence concerning the protohistoric and fur trade periods of history could be heard, the court had to determine how to classify these sources of evidence in legal terms.

In 1989, midway through the trial and two years after his 1987 ruling on the admissibility of oral history testimony, Chief Justice McEachern made a second ruling on evidence. This gave direction on how the court would interpret historical documents recognized as such within the academic study of history.[39] McEachern divided this material into two categories. Category 1 included documents written by contemporaries; that is, first hand observations made by historical actors such as fur traders, missionaries, and government agents of their own environments, experiences, and opinions. Category 2 was reserved for historians' interpretations and opinions of these primary documents.[40]

Documents written by contemporaries are called in law—as a term of art—"ancient documents." According to common law rules, ancient documents are admissible if they are "more than thirty years old, produced from proper custody and otherwise free from suspicion."[41] The point is that the documents must be in their original state, and it must be shown that they could not have been tampered with or changed since they were first written and secreted away. Although he did allow, theoretically, that it was possible such documents may contain mixtures of "fact and hearsay," Chief Justice McEachern ruled that "ancient documents admitted into evidence are, subject to weight, *prima facie*[42] proof of the truth of the facts stated in them."[43] That is, ancient documents are assumed to have been produced through a process whereby brute facts, existing independently of cultural or any other form of interpretation, were observed and recorded by unbiased writers in a similarly objective fashion. The records of early explorers, fur traders, and colonial officials, that had been housed in archives, were classified as "ancient documents."

On the question of the role of interpretation of historical documents, the Gitksan and Wet'suwet'en argued that each document should be accompanied by an historian to provide a context for interpretation. The Crown argued that all documents should be admitted and then weighed by the judge in the context of the evidence as a whole. Chief Justice McEachern ruled that historians may express their opinions "based upon inferences from the documents about the recorded facts of history."[44] They would not be permitted, however, to "construe a written document...or generalize upon the broad sweep of history which is so often subject to learned disagreement and revision."[45] His assumption appeared to be that the original written document represented a form of "pure" knowledge, the singular truth of which would be discoverable forever by future generations of rational thinkers. There is no consideration in this theory of the way that different generations of readers, living in different contexts, and reading these ancient documents for different purposes, may interpret their meanings differently. That is to say, the possibility that *both* written and oral histories begin as human creations, and that their meanings are interpreted and reinterpreted over time, challenges the law's desire to classify history in discrete periods, and to codify historical knowledge into simple true and false categories.

As he had done in regard to the distinction between history and mythology in oral histories, the Chief Justice asserted that, in the case of historical documents, fact and opinion could be clearly differentiated within them. In keeping with law's self image as "a site where universal reason actualizes itself, owing nothing to the social conditions under which it is manifested,"[46] the judge declared that he could and would make the final determination of what was fact or truth, and what was not. He wrote: "Impermissible opinions and the conclusions [historians] wish me to reach in connection with the subject matters of their opinions will undoubtedly be interwoven with permissible opinion, and it will be my responsibility to disregard the former while profiting from the latter."[47]

The Chief Justice made a third evidentiary ruling on the admissibility of "treatises," defined as written materials including published books and articles, and unpublished theses, essays and studies."[48] The Crown argued that "only totally unbiased, non-controversial, generally accepted works that have endured and survived expert public review such as standard texts, qualify as learned treatises."[49] Chief Justice McEachern disagreed with the Crown, and concluded that such an orthodox approach was not practical in this case. He decided to admit all such material subject to weight, and to objections by counsel that particular items may be untrustworthy because of "disabling bias or a demonstrated lack of competence or for other reasons."[50]

Following the Chief Justice's decision to admit this evidence, one of Canada's foremost authorities on fur trade history, Dr. Arthur Ray of the University of British Columbia, took the stand on behalf of the Gitksan and Wet'suwet'en. Ray began his report with a description of the task he was asked to perform by the plaintiffs. The Gitksan and Wet'suwet'en Hereditary Chiefs commissioned Ray "...to examine the economic history of the Middle Skeena River-Lake Babine region in order to (a) search for evidence of the native exercise of title in the area; and, (b) to examine the way the Gitksan, Wet'suwet'en and Babine responded to economic developments following European contact."[51] Ray's evidence began with a description of the years beginning around 1800, and continued with discussions of two time periods: (1) The Transitional Years, 1830–1860; and (2) Competition and Economic Diversity, 1860-1915. The sources Ray examined for this study were Hudson's Bay Company records, ethnographies, and interviews with contemporary key informants. The details of his research and report have subsequently been published in peer-reviewed academic journals.[52]

Dr. Ray began his testimony with a brief overview of the 9000 strong pre-contact Gitksan and Wet'suwet'en population. He described villages, locations of fishing sites, and Indigenous social structure. Ray described how the Coastal Tsimshian peoples began trading sea otter pelts for European goods around 1778. They brought these new items along with them on their regular excursions to trade with their Gitksan neighbours who lived inland. The Gitksan then traded these goods with their Wet'suwet'en neighbours, and with their Athabaskan trading partners further to the east, as they had been doing for centuries. Gitksan and Wet'suwet'en participation in the maritime phase of the European-Aboriginal fur trade was minimal, and had little impact on Gitksan and Wet'suwet'en ways of life, Ray testified. During the 1800s the sea otter was overharvested to near extinction, and the maritime phase of the European-Aboriginal fur trade gradually came to a close as British and Canadian trading companies established forts and began to trade with interior peoples for beaver, mink, muskrat, bear and other land mammal furs. Gitksan and Wet'suwet'en involvement in the land-based phase of the fur trade was more active, and effected some changes in relations with neighbouring peoples, in ownership and management of territories and in the economic organization of hunting and trapping.

William Brown—the author of the first written descriptions of Gitksan and Wet'suwet'en ways of life—arrived in 1822 to establish Fort Kilmaurs on Babine Lake. Based on his research in the Hudson's Bay archives, Ray argued that: "What is abundantly clear from Brown is that you have a fully-articulated feasting system with house territories, family heads. In other words, the system—the very system that the ethnographers...begin to describe with Morice some 60 years later is a system that essentially Brown has just given us the bone outline for in 1822...."[53] The Hudson's Bay Company records and the oral histories, as well as ethnographic, archaeological and linguistic evidence all document extensive trade in the region as a whole in both primary and manufactured goods. Harmon[54] and Brown described well-organized and managed trade in furs, dressed skins, leather, fish, fish oil, blankets, shell beads, berry cakes, nets and dogs.[55]

Quoting from Brown's journals, Ray testified that "Brown discovered that the regional economy was a delicately balanced system in which villages were linked together by kinship ties, trade, gambling and potlatching activities."[56] Brown described the people as living in four major villages between which were scattered territories of the constituent Houses. He recorded that "access to Babine and Wet'suwet'en house territories was tightly controlled by 42 'nobles' and 'men of property'."[57] The immediate problem this presented to fur trader Brown was that "lineage heads gave only a few of their fellow kinsmen the right to hunt and trap" and most of their produce was "tithed" to the Chiefs. It was only the Chiefs who the Hudson's Bay Company could deal with. "These elders," Brown wrote, "generally had well-established trading connections already" and were interested in trading with the Hudson's Bay Company only if it was to their advantage.[58]

Brown described how frustrated Hudson's Bay Company men trading with the Gitksan and Wet'suwet'en during the early years of the fur trade became when they had to compete with other Aboriginal traders who could, simply put, offer better prices and better trade goods than the Hudson's Bay Company could. A similar problem arose regarding Brown's dependence on Aboriginal people for transportation. Ray wrote that "Even at rates the Hudson's Bay Company considered to be unreasonable, it was difficult to persuade Indians to transport goods at the times the company wanted. The Indians were said to be willing to do the work only when it suited them because they had a variety of alternative work that was easier and more lucrative."[59]

Brown resorted to acting as a middleman between the Athabaskans and the Gitksan and Wet'suwet'en, importing the moose hides they so highly valued from Company trading posts east of the Rockies and trading these for furs. Ray quoted an excerpt from Brown's journals to illustrate this. Brown wrote: "I made then [1823] what I considered very handsome presents consisting of cloth blankets, shirts, etc... But the following day they brought back the whole and informed me that it was not to receive such articles as these that they had given me their furs. One of them, Snuggletrun [the second highest ranked Hot-set leader] from whom I had received about twenty skins I had given two yds Red Strouds, one flanal shirt, one awl, one firesteel, one gun flint, two needles, two hanks thread, two yards gartering, ten ball, one half point powder, one point shot and one sixth point tobacco, requested I take back the whole and give him a dressed skin in the place."[60]

In analyzing the records of William Brown, Ray introduced new historical research that had been inaccessible until the late 1960s, and had subsequently been ignored by previous researchers working in the area.[61] Brown's journals challenged many assumptions held by earlier historians and anthropologists about the pre-contact nature of Gitksan and Wet'suwet'en society. Ray noted that, in the course of his research, he "...discovered that all the important ethnographic studies of the region, such as those of A. G. Morice, Diamond Jenness, Irving Goldman and Julian Steward had not used this material because it was unavailable to them. More recent writers, most notably Vernon

Kobrinksi and Charles Bishop, draw heavily on these earlier published ethnographies, but ignored the critical Brown material."[62]

The legal significance of Ray's report and testimony was that it supported the claim that the Gitksan and Wet'suwet'en "did occupy the territory in dispute at the time of initial European contact."[63] "Of considerable importance to the Wet'suwet'en," Ray noted, "Brown outlined a feasting and house territory system that was very similar to the one the hereditary Chiefs described in their opening statement 170 years later."[64] Further, Ray's testimony provided documentary evidence in the form of reports written by an Englishman that the Gitksan and Wet'suwet'en did manage and conserve their lands and resources through a House (lineage) territory system, before the local commencement of the European-Aboriginal fur trade that focused on beaver. Brown's documentation of Gitksan and Wet'suwet'en "men of property" owning trapping sites and controlling access to beaver—whose meat they disdained but whose pelts they valued for trade—contradicted the Crown's argument that the only resources that Aboriginal peoples regulated at all were those they relied upon for subsistence, and that they had not engaged in production of surpluses for trade before Europeans arrived.

Both federal and provincial Crown lawyers emphasized pre-contact intra-Indian violence in their cross-examination of the Gitksan's and Wet'suwet'en's witnesses, a strategy that reached its peak in the cross-examination of Arthur Ray who titled an article he later wrote about his experiences in the *Delgamuukw* case "Creating the Image of the Savage in Defence of the Crown."[65] In it he wrote: "It was apparent to me that the Counsels for the Crown had two major objectives in mind when they pursued this line of questioning. They hoped to raise doubts about the reliability of Brown as an observer and they tried to suggest that the area was in a state of turmoil at the time of first contact. I think this line of inquiry also reflected an underlying and disturbing attitude of Crown Counsel toward Native people—that they were revengeful and violence-prone before the 'civilizing' influences of European missionaries and government officials modified their behaviour."[66]

Counsel for the government of Canada, James Macaulay, concentrated on challenging Dr. Ray with anecdotes drawn from the reports of early traders and explorers that depicted violent confrontations. The essence of the federal cross-examination of Arthur Ray is illustrated by the following exchange:

> Macaulay: I put it to you, Dr. Ray, that's really the point of the cross-examination, or one of the points any how, that this is a very fragile system and it was interrupted by such things as a single killing.... Do you agree that the reciprocal killing system had that effect?

> Ray: My point would be that societies generally value peace, that's both within groups and between groups; that their systems for sustaining peace

break down from time to time are easy enough to prove. And if you wanted to use the European example, just remember the period we're talking about is close to the Napoleonic Wars, right?

Macaulay: Yes.

Ray: A lot more people got killed in those. And would you not say that those European societies valued peace as well?

Macaulay: I'm not saying European societies valued peace, Dr. Ray—

Ray: Well, would you say that the European societies had equally fragile systems? No human society has been able to sustain peace both in itself and between itself....

Macaulay allowed that this might be the case. However, it was the presumably spontaneous and unpredictable—unorganized—nature of Aboriginal violence that he was referring to:

Macaulay: Isn't that the source of the violence...that the endemic violence was based on a fair degree of truculence...that there was a certain excitability and ferocity that led to the whole village becoming involved....

Late on the second day of Ray's cross examination by the Crown, Chief Justice McEachern intervened:

Court: Maybe I can ask you this, Dr. Ray: Mr. Macaulay has been suggesting a tendency toward violence and you have been resisting that and you are saying that wasn't the state of things, or at least it wasn't the normal diet for the period you are talking about. Yet, there seems to be some pretty strong suggestions that there was warfare on the Skeena, and I take it you are saying that was at some later time?

Ray later wrote: "I replied by saying that I thought the portrayal of Indian society as being a violence-prone one was an ethnocentric point of view. I noted that I did discuss violence in my opinion, but I also made it clear that feasting provided one way of dealing with the problem. Murders did not always lead to revenge killings by the offended relatives."[67] Ray explained that: "My only point was I do not subscribe to the bloodthirsty savagery of Native people, nor the noble savage. I don't subscribe to either. I see Native people as people. They have the same problems that other peoples have around the world and in different points in time. That was the main point of my report. Nothing more; nothing less."[68]

Like many academics who have testified as expert witnesses in court, Arthur Ray concluded upon reflection that the adversarial courtroom is an inappropriate forum in which to hold scholarly debates. Lawyers are rarely familiar with historical methodology, he charged, and they "take extreme positions" and "champion points of view" chosen for their strategic value in bolstering their clients' cases, rather than their historical validity.[69]

1. See Beals 1985; Campisi 1991; Clifford 1988; Dobyns 1978; Dreyfus and Dreyfus 1979; Dyck 1993(b); Feldman 1980; Foster and Groves 1993; Harries-Jones 1985; Hedican 1986; Hedley 1986; Kousser 1983; LaRusic 1985; Lurie 1956; Maddock 1989; Manners 1956; Paine 1985; Rosen 1977; Salisbury 1976; Sansom 1985; Tremblay 1983; Waldram 1993; Wright 1988.

2. Geertz 1983(b); Van Esterik 1985; See also *POLAR: Political and Legal Anthropology Review*, Volume 10(2), November 1996, Special Issue: Anthropology Engaging Law, Washington, D.C.: American Anthropology Association.

3. Hammersley and Atkinson 1983.

4. Behar and Gordon (eds.) 1996; Clifford and Marcus (eds.) 1986; Fox 1991; Marcus and Fischer 1986; Rosaldo 1989.

5. See Ruby 1982; and Rosaldo 1989.

6. See Ryan 1990, 1992; Warry 1990.

7. See Behar and Gordon 1996; Brody 1985; Clifford and Marcus (eds.) 1986; Marcus and Fisher 1986.

8. Thomas 1994.

9. This is a vast literature. But see for summaries: Behar and Gordon 1996; di Leonardo 1991(ed); Moore 1988.

10. Ryan 1985.

11. Rush 1991: 13-14.

12. Daly 1988: 26-28.

13. Transcripts, Vol. 184: 11822.

14. Mills 1987. Mills has also published a book presenting her opinion report and her experiences as an expert witness. See Mills 1995.

15. Transcripts, Vol. 196: 12860.

16. Transcripts, Vol. 196: 12869.

17. Peter Ogden was a fur trader and explorer who traveled from the Oregon Territory to northern British Columbia in the early 1800s. Although he did not directly encounter either the Gitksan or Wet'suwet'en on his travels, he recorded in his journals anecdotes he had heard about them and other First Nations in the region. Subsequent documentation by fur traders like William Brown who worked directly with the Gitksan and Wet'suwet'en, and ethnohistorical and archaeological research, have shown Ogden's descriptions to be unreliable.

18. Transcripts, Vol. 201: 13319-13321.

19. See Stocking 1987.

20. See Deloria 1969.

21. Seidler 1987.

22. Brody 1987(b).

23. Ibid., 6.

24. Ibid., 2.

25. Ibid., 7.

26. Ibid., 5.

27. Transcripts, Vol. 210: 14217.

28. Transcripts, Vol. 211: 14254.

29. University of British Columbia Professor of Law, and Lawyer for the Gitksan and Wet'suwet'en, Michael Jackson.

30. Transcripts, Vol. 211: 14254.

31. The judge is referring to the Report of the McKenna-McBride Commission that was charged with examining the allocation of Indian reserves throughout British Columbia from 1913-1916.

32. Transcripts, Vol. 212: 15381-15389.

33. Brody 1987(b): 71.

34. Transcripts, Vol. 211: 14253.

35. Transcripts, Vol. 211: 14257.

36. Transcripts, Vol. 210: 14215-14258.

37. Hudson's Bay trader William Brown was the first European to keep systematic written records describing his dealings with the Gitksan and Wet'suwet'en, and their social organization from his point of view. The North West Company had operated Fort St. James on nearby Stuart Lake from 1806-1822 and their traders had obtained "second-hand information about the Babine, Gitksan and Wet'suwet'en. Subsequently, William Brown discovered that some of this intelligence was not accurate." (Ray, 1991(b): 302).

38. McEachern, *Reasons* 1991: 35.

39. *Delgamuukw v. B.C.* (1989) 38 B.C.L.R. (2d) 165 (judgment on the admissibility of historical documents), referenced as "*Delgamuukw* 1989 documents."

40. Fortune 1993.

41. Delgamuukw 1989 documents, ftnt 55: 169.

42. "1. true, valid or sufficient at first impression; 2. self-evident; 3. legally sufficient to establish a fact or a case unless disproved." *Webster's New Collegiate Dictionary.*

43. *Delgamuukw* 1989 documents:ftnt 55: 171.

44. Ibid., 175.

45. Ibid., 175-176.

46. Bourdieu 1987: 820.

47. *Delgamuukw* 1989: 176.

48. *Delgamuukw v. B.C.* (1989) 38 B.C.L.R. (2d) 176, referenced as *Delgamuukw*, 1989, treatises.

49. *Delgamuukw*, 1989, treatises: 187.

50. Ibid., 187-188.

51. Ray 1987: 1.

52. Ray 1991(a); 1991(b).

53. Ray 1991(b): 304.

54. Harmon was a Northwest Company trader who made contact with the Carrier, neighbors of the Gitksan and Wet'suwet'en, during the early 1800s.

55. Transcripts, Vol. 203: 13478.

56. Ray 1987: 46.

57. Ray 1991(b): 303 (quoting Brown, Fort Babine [Kilmaurs] District Report, 1822-23, B. 11/e/1).

58. Ray 1991(b): 304.

59. Ray 1987: 76.

60. Ray 1991(b): 308 quoting Brown, Fort Babine [Kilmaurs] District Report, 1822-23, PAMHBC B.11/e/2, footnote 13.

61. Ray 1991(b): 310.

62. Ray, 1991(a): 15. Ray is referring to the following works of these authors: Bishop 1979; Goldman, Irving 1940, 1941, 1975; Jenness 1943; Kobrinski 1977; Morice 1970; Steward 1961.

63. Ray 1991(b): 309.

64. Ray 1991(a): 16.

65. Ray 1991(a).

66. Ray 1991(a): 19.

67. Ray 1991(a): 25.

68. Ray 1991(a): 23.

69. Ray 1991(a): 26.

Chapter 11: The Crown's Case

We are a poor people with rich resources. That is why the province and the federal government are running scared. And that is why they wouldn't deal with us. If it was a barren land, do you think they would bother with us? The taxes that are generated from our resources are what is paying for all of the things that they are doing against us.

They had huge mounds of money to pay their lawyers, and they had a lot of lawyers.... And the office staffs. It was unbelievable, the amount of people that they had working with them.... They had money like it was going out of style. They had the staff behind them that could run and fetch whatever it was that they needed on a moment's notice—and we were criticized because of our miserable little amounts. I don't feel one bit ashamed of where that money comes from. It is a mere pittance of what is owed to us. A pittance...because over a hundred years the resources have been just raped out of our territories....

That's our money paying for all of this. Why? Because the resources and the taxes that are generated from those resources are what those people are afraid of losing.

—Yagalahl (Dora Wilson), 1992.[1]

The Political Economy of Litigation

The defendants in *Delgamuukw v. R.* were *Her Majesty the Queen in Right of the Province of British Columbia and the Attorney General of Canada*: "the Crown." They asked the court for "a declaration that the Plaintiffs have no right, title or interest in and to the Claim Area, and the resources thereon, thereunder or thereover."[2] The Province of British Columbia argued that, although the Gitksan and Wet'suwet'en had no rightful claims at all, in the event that the court found that they did, and there were any damages to be paid or compensation due, it was the federal government's responsibility to pay. The federal government argued that some of the costs should be borne by the province.

The Province of British Columbia's argument in the *Delgamuukw* case was constructed on the basis of four building blocks. First, they argued that Gitksan and Wet'suwet'en societies were only minimally organized during what the Crown called "pre-historic" times. The Crown claimed that no system of government or property law existed among Aboriginal peoples prior to European contact that could be recognized as equal to, or deserving of respect by, British or Canadian law. The Crown also had a fall back position in the event that the judge might reject *terra nullius* and find that some form of legally recognizable Aboriginal rights were being practised when Europeans arrived in northern British Columbia during the eighteenth century. They argued that the only locations that could possibly have been used and occupied to any extent, and therefore could possibly be recognized as subject to an Aboriginal claim, were the village sites next to rivers with large salmon runs. According to the Province of B.C., the ancestors of the Aboriginal peoples appeared to have used and occupied only those spaces which were later designated by the federal government as reserves, and for which the federal government is responsible. The only resource the Gitksan and Wet'suwet'en may have any claim to, said the Province, were salmon, also a federal responsibility.

The second building block of the Crown's argument was the claim that the hunting territories and access routes outside the major villages were used only incidentally, sporadically, and arbitrarily by anyone who wished to wander about. Their position was that no consistent use, or occupation, or ownership, or management was ever exercised in these territories. Although the Gitksan's and Wet'suwet'en's maps showed 133 distinct and bounded territories that included identified village and camp sites, and precise locations where resources and game were located in each, the Province of B.C. argued that no one ever travelled far from a riverfront village-cum-reserve to hunt or gather on these territories. According to the Province of B.C., the ancestors of the Gitksan and Wet'suwet'en peoples appear *not* to have used and occupied those spaces that are now under lease to multinational forestry companies, and from which 3 million cubic metres of timber were harvested during the four years of the *Delgamuukw* trial.[3]

Third, the Crown argued that elementary concepts and systems of property rights emerged among the Gitksan and Wet'suwet'en following the commencement of European-Aboriginal trade: during a period they referred to as "protohistoric times." Captain James Cook's meeting with Ahousat Chief Maquinna on the west coast of Vancouver Island in 1774 marks the first recorded European contact with First Nations in what is now British Columbia. The key time period for the Crown's case, therefore, encompassed the 48 years between 1774 and 1822 when Hudson's Bay Company trader William Brown established a fort in Gitksan and Wet'suwet'en territory and began recording the first significant British observations of the Gitksan and Wet'suwet'en. Since Brown's journals described social organization that closely resembled the House and clan social structure and the land tenure system that the Gitksan and Wet'suwet'en witnesses described, the Crown argued that Brown was writing about a society that had already been significantly assimilated into British culture between the time of Captain Cook's 1774 landing several hundred miles away on the west coast of Vancouver Island, and Brown's arrival in Gitksan and Wet'suwet'en territory in 1822. Therefore, the Crown posited, Brown was not describing a "truly aboriginal society." This rationale for invalidating Brown's observations was the cement that held the Crown's edifice together. Prior to the advent of the European-Aboriginal fur trade, so the Crown's story goes, the Gitksan and Wet'suwet'en lived in nomadic, unorganized, unstable groupings. As a result of becoming involved in the fur trade, Aboriginal peoples took the first necessary step to assimilating into civilized European society by developing ranked societies based on social inequality, the Crown concluded.

Finally, the Crown argued that, even if some form of Aboriginal title or rights had been held by the Gitksan and Wet'suwet'en, they had been extinguished by the simple assertion of British sovereignty, or by the assumed acquiescence of Aboriginal peoples to the superimposition of British and Canadian law.

In summary, these four arguments constituted the Crown's case: (1) Ultimately, the British Crown had the right to assert sovereignty and extinguish Aboriginal title and right. (2) Anyway, Gitksan and Wet'suwet'en societies were "unorganized" before contact with Europeans: hierarchal social organization and property law was absent. (3) These developed in response to the European-Aboriginal fur trade through a process of assimilation of Aboriginal ways of life to those of the European settlers. (4) The Gitksan and Wet'suwet'en had acquiesced to British and Canadian rule.

Anthropology: The Science of "Man"?

It is clear that theories do much more than explain social life; they also define the understandings that underpin different forms of social practice, and they help to orient us in the social world...Naturally, granted what is at stake, human beings will always be tempted to espouse theories that give them a sense of moral orientation, and even more theories which support the practices they find advantageous....
—Philosopher Charles Taylor,1985, *Social Theory As Practice.*

Behind and supporting...the understandable prestige of the natural science model, stands an attachment to a certain picture of the human agent. This picture is deeply attractive to moderns...it shows us as capable of achieving a kind of disengagement from our world by objectifying it....
—Philosopher Charles Taylor, 1985, *Philosophy and the Human Sciences.*

The Crown's lawyers argued that their critique of the evidence presented by the Aboriginal plaintiffs and their expert witnesses was based on principles of a scientific research methodology. They entered an article entitled "The Expert in Court," written by Anthony Kenny and published in a 1983 edition of the *Law Quarterly Review*[4] as an exhibit. In this paper, Kenny set out four criteria for determining whether a discipline is sufficiently scientific in its methodology to justify the admission of expert opinion evidence in a court of law: "First," Kenny wrote, "the discipline must be consistent. That is to say, different experts must not regularly give conflicting answers to questions which are central to their discipline.... Second, the discipline must be methodical. A procedure carried out by one expert to reach a particular conclusion is one which must be capable of duplication by any other expert.... Thirdly, the discipline must be cumulative. The findings of one generation of workers in the discipline are not called in question by the workers of the next...research, once done, does not need doing again; if you have to repeat someone else's experiments, or re-sample his population, on the very same issue, that shows you there was something wrong with his experiment, or something faulty in his sampling.... Fourthly, the discipline must be predictive, and therefore falsifiable...it must predict the not yet known from the already known (as the doctor's diagnosis of the nature of a terminal illness predicts what will be found at the post mortem), and is falsified if it proves otherwise."[5]

Kenny's first and third criteria are particularly problematic, from any methodological perspective. If experts cannot disagree and debate without discrediting their areas of study, and if the findings of one generation cannot be called into question by the next, then neither scientific nor democratic progress can be made. All four of Kenny's criteria—but particularly two and four, in their demand for the replication of research contexts and procedures, and the ability of studies to reliably predict outcomes—are the criteria of positivist science, modelled on the methodology employed by natural scientists. Inclusion of disciplines whose knowledge bases arise from people-studying-people (anthropology, sociology, political science, history, literature) within this paradigm rests on the assumption that human beings are like water, and their behaviour can be predicted in the same way that we can predict water will always boil when it reaches a certain temperature. This is a proposition that generations of social scientists have contested, arguing that humans are social beings: meaning-makers whose lives are lived, and whose decisions and actions are taken within networks of relationships with their environment and with other human beings. The "research environment" of life, differs in its essence from the controlled laboratories of experimental science. The systematic study of human beings requires methodologies that take account of the dynamic particularities of human social life as it is lived and experienced by human beings, including the researchers themselves.[6]

People's own accounts and analyses of their lived experience have no legitimate place in the framework Kenny provides for determining what knowledge is valid. Ethnographic fieldwork and participant observation research, where anthropologists live with, and extensively observe ordinary people going about the course of their daily lives, cannot possibly meet the criteria set out by Kenny. Disciplines like history and anthropology that have undergone significant changes in recent years in response to the inclusion and consideration of the scholarship of previously excluded categories of persons— like women and Indigenous peoples—are rendered unreliable and inconsistent by a positivist approach.[7]

It is not only professionals in the "human sciences" who encounter difficulty in meeting Kenny's criteria for qualification as "expert witnesses." In the realm of European physical sciences, neither Copernicus, Galileo, Newton nor Einstein would have passed the first test of their expertise in their day. Neither have any of these astronomers and physicists passed the third test, since all of their findings have been questioned and modified by other astronomers, physicists and mathematicians in subsequent generations. Most significant in this context, however, is the fact that Charles Darwin, on whose theories of biological evolution nineteenth century anthropologists, historians and jurists based their hypothetical formulations of social evolution, could not have passed any of Kenny's four criteria.

Kenny's criteria are fundamentally anti-scientific in their devaluing of criticism, reflection, accumulation of knowledge, and change in response to new information. The Crown's tenacious advocacy of positivist social theory, scientific methodology, and empiricism is particularly ironic in light of the mystical foundation of Crown title: the phantasmic apparition of an ethereal sovereign hovering over the land.

---

1. Yagalahl 1992: 203.

2. McEachern 1991, *Reasons for Judgment* in *Delgamuukw v. R.*, Vancouver, British Columbia: 43.

3. Glavin 1990: 179.

4. Kenny 1983.

5. Ibid., 113.

6. There is a huge literature on this debate within the social sciences. For an accessible entry to the debate see Rosaldo 1989.

7. See Behar and Gordon (eds.) 1996.

Chapter 12: Experts on Behalf of the Defendants

Court performances introduce the cultural practices of the dominant group to the subordinate group as they impose new regulations and conceptions of social relationships. In their public ritual performances, courts operating in situations of cultural diversity and unequal power tend to apply the rules of one group to other groups. These performances demonstrate the procedures of the dominant order, demand compliance with it, and illustrate through both the imposition of laws and their enactment in the daily life of subordinate peoples, the ways it applies to everyday life. Thus, court performances are one way of expanding the hegemony of the law. Not only are ideas articulated but they are superimposed on everyday life in front of an audience of relatives, neighbours, and friends.
—Anthropologist Sally Merry Engle, 1994, *Courts as Performances*.

Her Majesty's Loyal Anthropologist

The Crown claimed that their critique of the plaintiffs' evidence was based on objective, neutral, scientific criteria of evaluation and research methodology, and that these principles were what guided them in *their* selection of expert evidence. In order to support their arguments, lawyers for the Crown turned to social science. They were particularly attracted to those branches of the social sciences that continue to give credence to theories of universal laws of social and cultural evolution, and that posit that all societies follow western Europe, over time, on the climb up the developmental ladder from hunting and gathering to modern industrial capitalism. The Crown called experts in historical cartography, history and anthropology. Most of the Crown's witnesses were professionals and government employees rather than academics or scholars. These included: a physician, several guide outfitters, a retired local politician and self-described pioneer, a popular historian, fisheries officers and a retired federal Indian Agent. No Gitksan or Wet'suwet'en, or member of any other First Nation, testified on behalf of the Crown.

The centrepiece of the expert evidence for *Her Majesty the Queen In Right Of The Province Of British Columbia And The Attorney General of Canada*, and, specifically, for the prestigious Vancouver law firm of Russell & DuMoulin who represented Her In Right Of Them, took the form of an opinion report prepared under Russell & DuMoulin's direction by Sheila Patricia Robinson, Ph.D., a cultural geographer by training, who was accepted by Chief Justice McEachern as an expert witness in anthropology. Robinson had never held an academic position, nor has she published her expert opinion reports so they can be scrutinized by either her colleagues or the public. She is a professional witness, hired by law firms on short-term contracts to testify for the Crown in numerous Aboriginal rights cases.[1] Robinson's tasks in this capacity are twofold. First, she assists Crown lawyers in their attempts to discredit Aboriginal people and the expert witnesses who testify for them. Second, she provides academic research to support the Crown's legal arguments.

Sheila Robinson's report, entitled "Protohistoric Developments in Gitksan and Wet'suwet'en Territories," consisted of an introduction and five sections, covering 29 pages; and an additional 67 pages of supporting notes and references were appended to the main body of the report. The central narrative in Robinson's story is about social change caused by the arrival of manufactured commodities during the European-Aboriginal fur trade. In order to understand how, when, why, and what change took place she had to first describe Gitksan and Wet'suwet'en societies as they were before Europeans and their commodities appeared.

As befits the role of the defendant's expert witness, Robinson began her report by casting doubt on the credibility of the plaintiffs' primary source of knowledge on the matters in dispute: Gitksan and Wet'suwet'en oral histories. Although the Crown's witness had not studied Gitksan and Wet'suwet'en oral traditions, she dismissed oral history as a invalid source of knowledge out of hand, supporting the Crown's contention that they should be treated as "hearsay" rather than "history." She wrote: "It is important to emphasize the limitations inherent in any theory of aboriginal land use which attempts to reconstruct a 'reality' that existed long before any relevant written records were kept and long before the memory of living man...." Taken by itself this may be a perfectly reasonable statement. However, without further specification of what those limitations are—such as Richard Daly's review of methodological problems in the study of oral traditions in general, and Gitksan and Wet'suwet'en oral traditions in particular, had provided—Robinson's point is simply a rhetorical statement of the obvious. Her critique of oral history appears even less plausible when the scholarly sources she relied on to describe Gitksan and Wet'suwet'en social organization before European contact are scrutinized: 47 of her 82 bibliographic references on this subject were based substantially on oral histories collected from Aboriginal elders by anthropologists. The Crown's witness rejected oral tradition on theoretical and methodological grounds, and then selectively relied on oral tradition to support the descriptions of pre-contact Aboriginal cultures that form the basis of her report. When lawyers for the Gitksan and Wet'suwet'en questioned Robinson about how she rationalized drawing conclusions from data whose validity she denied by definition, she replied that she had described pre-contact Aboriginal society "to the extent that that can't be done."[2]

Robinson's report continued: "I am generally suspicious of writers who tend towards a static or structural treatment of any society…. The ideal models may outline rules of behaviour, but do not adequately account for ongoing adjustments—in population distribution and density, in resource distribution, in alliance formations, and so on. Gitksan and Wet'suwet'en societies were never static…. Reconstructions of traditional native socioeconomies which fail to account for indirect European influence deny the dynamic dimensions of ongoing cultural adaptations and resign their subjects to an untenable— however romantic—'snapshot' stasis," she wrote.

Under cross examination Dr. Robinson was able to name only one text that fit the description she set out of "static or structural treatments," and that study referred not to the Gitksan and Wet'suwet'en but to a different Northwest Coast Nation, the Kwa'kwak'wakw. This text has since been substantially revised by the authors themselves, based on later research.[3] Robinson could not name any sources that described the Gitksan and Wet'suwet'en in the "romantic" fashion her report referred to, nor could she identify any sources that claimed no changes had occurred in Gitksan and Wet'suwet'en society and culture during the eighteenth and nineteenth centuries—or before or since, for that matter. Under cross-examination by Peter Grant, lawyer for the Gitksan and Wet'suwet'en, the Crown's witness insisted that she was not referring to the opinion reports submitted by the plaintiff's anthropologists when she made these statements. Taking her at her word, then, and as there is no empirical evidence to support her critique, it is fair to conclude that the importance of these introductory sentences in her report does not lie in their literal meaning but in their connotations: in the images they evoke, rather than in the facts they reveal.[4]

In a rhetorical sense, Robinson's introductory paragraph alludes to two popular stereotypes of anthropology as idealistic and romantic, and/or as abstract and intellectually elitist. It repeats the well-known charges that anthropology idealizes non-western cultures, "freezes" Indigenous peoples in time before contact, and denies post-contact change. These are legitimate critiques of some "old" ethnographies that, ironically, are over-represented in Dr. Robinson's own bibliography.

In the context of the *Delgamuukw* trial, Robinson's references to "romantic," "idealized" and "unchanging" descriptions of Aboriginal societies serve to represent her, in contrast to the "straw anthropologists" she set up in her report, as a reasonable, scholarly woman who deals in objective facts, rather than romantic ideals. This helped establish common ground—emphatic communion—between Dr. Robinson and Chief Justice McEachern: we are people of like mind; we are educated; we are objective; we are intelligent; we are on the same side.

Robinson went on to dismiss the evidence presented by other expert witnesses who had testified for the Gitksan and Wet'suwet'en. Sylvia Albright, an Ethnoarchaeologist, had cited archaeologist Gary Coupland's recent research in north-western British Columbia in her testimony for the plaintiffs. Coupland found ample archaeological evidence of land mammal hunting having been carried on in the Gitksan and Wet'suwet'en territories circa 500 B.C., and argued that cultures with hierarchically ranked social structures had emerged by that time.[5] In her initial proposal to Russell & DuMoulin, Sheila Robinson had suggested that "archaeological reports could be quite worthwhile," and she had referred to archaeologists MacDonald, Allaire and Coupland as "usually forming sound opinions." By the time she testified at the *Delgamuukw v. R.* trial Robinson had changed her mind about the validity of archaeological data in general, and the reliability of Gary Coupland's findings in particular. She dismissed Coupland's work—which did not support the Crown's argument that social ranking among the Gitksan and Wet'suwet'en emerged in response to the eighteenth-century European-Aboriginal fur trade—claiming that there had been too little archaeological research in the Gitksan and Wet'suwet'en territories for any data to yield conclusive evidence.[6]

There is little dispute in the archaeological literature about whether or not Coupland's findings are valid.[7] Where debate does arise within the discipline is on the question of migrations during the period under study. That is, archaeological evidence neither proves nor disproves the question of whether the present Aboriginal inhabitants are the biological descendants of the people who lived in the region 5000 years ago. Some archaeologists argue that other Aboriginal people may have migrated into the region between 3000 B.C. and 1744 A.D. and killed off, or otherwise displaced, the people they found occupying the land. It is these "migrants," they argue, who may be the ancestors of contemporary Aboriginal peoples. The Crown favours this theory as it challenges Gitksan and Wet'suwet'en oral histories that assert that their ancestors have occupied their territories since "time immemorial." The insistence on proof of "pure" *biological* descent to be considered as "legitimate" heirs with inheritance rights is an artefact of European patriarchal cultures, reflected in British property and estate law.

Unlike the Gitksan's and Wet'suwet'en's anthropologists, Sheila Robinson conducted no fieldwork with them, or with any other Aboriginal peoples. Hence, she was not subjected to the same criticisms of "favouring a party" that were levelled at Mills, Daly and Brody. Since Robinson had not conducted fieldwork, she was presented by the Crown as not having been "contaminated" by the thinking of any "others;" or by any of her own potentially irrational sentiments, that may be triggered by empathy or any other emotion. No one would accuse Sheila Robinson, as Crown Counsel had Heather Harris, of having "gone native." No one would disparage her, as the Chief Justice had Hugh Brody, for "liking Indians." No one would even ask her if she "liked white people."

Having cast doubt on the credibility of the plaintiff's witnesses and on the reliability of their evidence, Robinson proceeded to set out the methodology she had employed in researching her expert opinion report: "This report is based on a review and interpretation of existing information, largely contained in secondary sources, both published and unpublished, concerning the Gitksan and Carrier,[8] as well as other Northwest coast and interior native groups. I have not carried out fieldwork.... Nor have I conducted archival research.... My general understanding...is shaped by the research I carried out for my doctoral dissertation. In connection with this study of Indian agriculture on the northern Northwest Coast.... I investigated ethnographic and early historic records pertaining to the Tlingit, Haida, Coast Tsimshian and neighbouring native populations.... Although my analysis in the present report borrows from the work of others, the conclusions are my own."

There are, however, several important contradictions between Robinson's Ph.D. thesis and her testimony as an expert witness, beginning with her reliance on theoretical speculation and comparative data drawn from studies of the Gitksan's and Wet'suwet'en's neighbours. In her 1983 doctoral dissertation—after quoting and criticizing two other scholars for relying on "inference or speculation"—Robinson argued that, although "piecemeal reconstruction of particular developments is perhaps a tedious route to scholarly enlightenment...[it] eventually leads to more easily substantiated and probably more appropriate hypotheses. And it is in keeping with the works of scholars who stress that the analysis of cultural processes is not always amenable to rigid theoretical treatment because historical records may yield unanticipated yet illuminating data."[9]

Contemporary ethnohistorians have, indeed, been engaged in work that focuses on the particularities of local variation, rather than on the construction of theoretical generalizations.[10] When Robinson took the stand as an expert witness in *Delgamuukw v. R.* she was asked to substantiate her claim that the theoretical framework presented in her expert opinion report was "innovative, credible, and in keeping with recent ethnohistoric, cultural-ecological and cultural-evolutionary research."[11] She testified that she had been guided by a 1986 volume of the journal *Anthropologica*, edited by Dr. Edward S. Rogers of the Royal Ontario Museum in which he summarized his recommendations for future ethnohistorical research. Rogers urged scholars to develop more precise descriptions of locally distinct pre-contact cultures, take greater account of regional variation, and exercise more caution in asserting comparative generalizations. He listed the following factors that should be taken into account in future studies: climatic changes, game cycles, spatial distribution of resources, production of trade items, resource productivity, size of fish, demographic patterns, technology, sociopolitical organization and the influence of religious beliefs and behaviour patterns.[12] Peter Grant asked Sheila Robinson whether she agreed with Dr. Rogers' recommendations.

Grant: You would agree that these are factors that should be considered in analyzing the pre-contact society? Do you agree that in a study of the Gitksan or the Wet'suwet'en the climatic changes should be taken into account?

Robinson: Oh, I would think so.

Grant: Game cycles should be taken into account?

Robinson: Yes.

Grant: Spatial distribution of resources should be taken into account?

Robinson: Yes.

Grant: Production of trade items should be taken into account?

Robinson: Well...I would say yes.

Grant: Resource productivity should be taken into account?

Robinson: To the extent that it can be.

Grant: And the...size of fish?

....

Robinson: I would say that fish, characteristics of fish perhaps rather than just size might be important for this area.

Grant: For the Gitksan and Wet'suwet'en area?

Robinson: Yes.

Grant: Good. I agree. So characteristics of fish should be taken into account for Gitksan and Wet'suwet'en?

Robinson: Perhaps.

Grant: And...cultural considerations?

....

Robinson: To the extent that they can be.

Grant: The technology...the technology of the Gitksan and Wet'suwet'en should be taken into account?

Robinson: Yes.

....

Grant: And sociopolitical organization should be taken into account?

Robinson: Yes.

Grant: And the influence of spiritual beliefs and behaviour patterns—

Robinson: Yes.

Grant: Now, in your research and preparation of your report you did not take into account climate, did you?

Robinson: Not specifically.

Grant: Game cycles?

Robinson: Not specifically.

Grant: Spatial distribution of resources?

Robinson: Yes, to some extent.

Grant: Did you refer to that—describe that in your report?

Robinson: I don't know. I'm sure you've had a more thorough review of the paragraphs in recent days than I have. But, yes, it has got a spatial component to it in its description of the changes in hunting territories and so on.

Grant: But I am talking about spatial distribution of resources, that would be game and where they are located?

Robinson: Did I take it into account? Yes, to some extent.

Grant: But you have indicated before you weren't sure where these resources were located within the Gitksan and Wet'suwet'en territory?

Robinson: I'm not sure what level of detail you were asking for, then or now.

Grant: And did you deal with the production of trade items?

Robinson: Yes, to some extent.

Grant: And to the extent it is reflected in your report?

Robinson: Yes. Not necessarily.

Grant: Well, we have nothing—

Robinson: Not necessarily expressed in the report directly all the consideration I made of the exchange of trade items.

Grant: Well, what sources did you rely on for your analysis of the spatial distribution of resources? If you want you can look at the bibliography of your report.

Robinson: Oh, can I?

Grant: Yes.

Robinson: Well, that's great. Perhaps we can go and list all the writers again who have dealt with spatial distribution in the territories.

Grant: No, no, no.

Robinson: No, no, no. Please don't shake your head at me.

Grant: I want to ask you this, what sources did you deal with with respect to spatial distribution of resources among the Gitksan and Wet'suwet'en?

Robinson: Kobrinsky and Bishop, among others.

Grant: Okay. Thank you. Which sources did you rely on in your consideration of production of trade items with respect to the Gitksan and Wet'suwet'en?

Robinson: Any of those sources which are referred to in chapter three of my dissertation which pertain to trade and the discussions of production and exchange, the circulation of wealth and so on. And also to those scholars that I have listed several times now who are included in the bibliography. I can either go alphabetical if you go through the footnote list again, or I can recite them probably from memory going from north to south.

....

Grant: You may have misheard me again.

Robinson: No, I didn't mishear you.

Grant: I asked what sources did you rely on in support of your analysis of the production of trade items *among the Gitksan and Wet'suwet'en?*

Robinson: Well, I relied on more than those sources that pertain directly to the Gitksan and Wet'suwet'en.

Grant: I understand that.

Robinson: Well, I'm glad.

Grant: I want to know specifically which ones relate to the Gitksan and Wet'suwet'en?

....

Robinson: Specific information on the Gitksan and Wet'suwet'en...is expressed in the Brown reports...

Grant: But the Brown reports that I have been discussing with you...are not cited in your report?

Robinson: No, they are not cited in the report.[13]

Contrary to the argument in support of locally-specific research that she had articulated in her doctoral dissertation, and that is endorsed by leading ethno-historians, Robinson proceeded to reconstruct a description of Gitksan and Wet'suwet'en cultural history based on theoretical speculation and analogies to other First Nations' histories.[14] The Crown's witness described Gitksan and Wet'suwet'en society as a "segmentary" one that lacked "mechanisms to create and sustain centralized political and economic authority," but admitted that this was based on theoretical generalizations about the nature of "segmentary societies" and not on data about the Gitksan and Wet'suwet'en.

The final sentence of Robinson's introductory paragraph expresses the central legal point of the exercise: "In this context, Gitksan and Wet'suwet'en claims about 'traditionally' having owned and managed certain territories are questionable."

Robinson's analysis of pre-contact Gitksan and Wet'suwet'en society is built on a framework that organizes each section of her report, and is characterized by three features. First, the Crown's legal argument is faithfully supported. Second, data drawn from historical studies of other First Nations are frequently substituted for specific information about the Gitksan and Wet'suwet'en, even when this is available in the research literature. This is analogous to substituting French history for German history: there are parallels at high levels of generalization, but significant differences are well recognized. Third, Robinson's argumentation is often internally contradictory resulting in statements described by logicians as oxymorons: "combinations of contradictory or incongruous words."[15]

Malignant Mythology

Every self-respecting people has its own founding myths; British Columbia whites, were, and are, no exception. The traditional White views were fully formed by the 1880s and remained little changed until the 1950s. These views belittled the worth and the claims of Indians while legitimizing the land ownership and political jurisdiction of the colonial authorities and their successors...only occasionally, and especially during the last quarter century, when the provincial government has had to defend its views in court, were attempts made to construct coherent legal or philosophic arguments in support.... The province's arguments in the Delgamuukw case provide the most comprehensive example of such an attempt.

—Political scientist Tennant, 1992, *The Place of Delgamuukw in British Columbia History and Politics—and Vice Versa.*

The Crown witness' expert opinion report was presented in the form of a historical narrative. Sheila Robinson's description of the pre-contact period, which her report began with, supported several key points in the Crown's argument. It provided a baseline description of Gitksan and Wet'suwet'en society as minimally organized and unstable. Further, Robinson tried to demonstrate that the most highly valued lands were the main villages, and not the territories that surrounded them; and that all territories changed hands frequently and easily, there having been little if any law or regulation in the society as a whole, particularly with regard to property.

Robinson described the pre-contact period as "pre-historic," "pristine," "traditional," and when a "truly aboriginal way of life" existed. "Pristine" is defined in the dictionary as: "(1) belonging to the earliest period or state. (2) a: uncorrupted by civilization; b: free from soil or decay: being fresh and clean." Most anthropologists have long since jettisoned the term "pristine" as an inappropriate description of pre-contact Aboriginal societies. The term and the concept are now interpreted as reflecting the worst forms of evolutionism and romanticism practiced by the discipline in its earliest days. The term "pristine" harkens back to European philosophers like Jean Jacques Rousseau, who, horrified by the social and environmental effects of industrialization, projected their nostalgic desires for an imagined Garden of Eden in their own imagined rural past onto contemporary Aboriginal cultures.

Robinson began with a description of pre-contact Gitksan and Wet'suwet'en society that covered, by her own admission, an unspecified period of time prior to the arrival of European commodities. Under cross examination, lawyer for the Gitksan and Wet'suwet'en, Peter Grant, asked Robinson to delineate the length of time referred to in her cavalier sweep though history: Perhaps 100 years? Perhaps 10,000 years?

Grant: You have no sense of the time depth of which is being discussed there?

Robinson: No, I don't.

Collapsing thousands of years of Aboriginal history into one vaguely-worded paragraph infers that Aboriginal cultures were static for thousands of years before European arrival, implying that they were incapable of change by themselves, but required the beneficent stimulus of colonial invasion in order to "evolve."

Robinson's report continued: "Oral traditions describe groups of *settlers* wandering about until they *discovered unoccupied lands*. According to the narratives, the *pioneers established villages* and *laid claim to fishing sites, hunting territories*, and other *resource-producing areas by using them*. The act of discovery, often reinforced by *supernatural occurrences*, constituted the *basis of claim* in many myths. However, *repeated use* seems to have maintained *rights to resources*." (Emphasis added.)

Grant asked Robinson for sources of facts to support the statements made in this paragraph:

> Grant: I would ask you if you can give one example of where the Gitksan have acquired territory by seizure of unclaimed land?
>
> Robinson: No, I cannot.
>
> Grant: Can you give one example of where the Gitksan have acquired land by discovery?
>
> Robinson: No, I cannot.
>
> Grant: Can you give one example of where the Gitksan have acquired land by occupying and using unclaimed territory?
>
> Robinson: I've read examples of these, but I don't know if they apply to the Gitksan in the historical or the modern.
>
> Grant: Can you give me one example of where the Gitksan acquired land by gift?
>
> Robinson: Not specifically, no.[16]

Again, given the absence of any empirical support for her descriptions of pre-contact Gitksan and Wet'suwet'en cultures, the significance of this section of Robinson's report also appears to be rhetorical. Her use of language evokes a parallel between the British settlers' founding myth, and that of the ancestors of the Gitksan and Wet'suwet'en. This is a common theme in B.C.'s populist political culture, and appears repeatedly in arguments against the legitimacy of Aboriginal claims in British Columbia. In this part of "White British Columbians' founding myth," the ancestors of contemporary Aboriginal peoples were simply the first ones to arrive on the continent, and they laid claim to "empty" land by using it and occupying it in the way of migrants everywhere, always. Europeans simply did the same thing when they came a few thousand years later. Its all very natural and inevitable, and non-Aboriginal people therefore have as strong a claim to the land as Aboriginal people do: the only difference between them being a few thousand years of use and occupation.

The introduction to Section IV of Robinson's opinion report is entitled "Gitksan Territorial Ownership: Traditional." It reads: "Section IV...[theorizes]...about the dynamics of territorial acquisitions and control in traditional Gitksan societies prior to the protohistoric period. Emphasis is placed on the fact that traditional Gitksan societies were never stable and that rights to certain territories probably changed hands frequently. A scenario where the most highly valued territories were those close to the relatively stable village bases in prehistoric times is developed to contrast with the description of protohistoric and early historic patterns of Gitksan land holdings presented in Section V."[17] She described a number of processes to substantiate her contention that "territorial rights changed hands frequently," drawn either from material on other Northwest coast groups or from anthropologist John Adams' study of the contemporary Gitksan potlatch.[18]

The Crown's witness continued, summarizing her position on pre-contact land and resource management: "Speaking generally, one may expect that *some form of organized control* would have been exercised over *access* to the fisheries and other *resources* which were *necessary for survival* and over the *local trails and bridges* which facilitated *prehistoric trade networks*.... In my opinion, outlying *borders were 'probably hazy'* because there was little need to define them precisely...." (Emphasis added.)

A number of points were made in this paragraph that were fundamental to the Crown's argument. There is "some form of *organized control*" (read: NOT ownership), "exercised over *access*" (read: NOT ownership), "to the *fisheries*" (read: NOT trees and game), "and other *resources*" (read: NOT property), "which were *necessary for survival*" (read: meet the basic survival needs of humans as organisms), "and over the *local trails and bridges* which facilitated prehistoric trade networks" (read: NOT borders or boundaries).

The Crown's case was based on the theory that scarcity of resources produces competition between people who depend on these same resources, and that such competition leads to concepts of property and the establishment of borders and boundaries to protect one group's access to resources against the incursions of another group. This argument had both a theoretical and an empirical aspect. Empirically, the questions that required answers were: what game and other resources—like trees—were in the territories? How abundant or scarce were they? What demands did the Gitksan and Wet'suwet'en place on these resources? How did they obtain and use them?

The Crown began by trying to establish that there were few game or other resources in the territories outside major village sites, and that the Gitksan and Wet'suwet'en did not significantly utilize or value the resources that were there. Scholars who specialize in this field have developed ways of calculating population to resources ratios, and analyzing different forms of social organization to hypothesize how resources were allocated and distributed, and if competition between people for access to these resources was present and contributed to pressures on the resource supply.

The Gitksan and Wet'suwet'en Chiefs' oral histories had been replete with references to the locations and uses of the resources in question.[19] Arthur Ray, testifying for the Gitksan and Wet'suwet'en, had argued that: "Before contact, the Gitksan and Wet'suwet'en were highly dependent on their salmon fisheries. They located their semi-permanent villages beside the most reliable fishing sites and tapped the adjacent countryside for a variety of other resources. Local population pressure would have made it necessary for them to conserve these other resources, particularly game. The house-territory system was well-suited for that purpose."[20] Other expert witnesses in paleobotany, ecology, forestry, and wildlife management had provided detailed evidence of the location and extent of game and other resources in the territories.

The Crown's witness admitted, under cross-examination, that her knowledge of the ecology of this area was limited. Robinson could not answer questions about where various game were located or what their habits were. When confronted with evidence about their use she equivocated in the extreme, going so far as to suggest the possibility that, not only were fish the primary source of subsistence, but that fish *skins*, rather than animal furs or hides, supplied a significant part of Gitksan and Wet'suwet'en clothing.

Robinson: ...We have to think in terms of the used resources rather than what's out there in terms of the natural environment. So the environment as it is used is different than the environment as it exists.

Grant: Well, the coastal Tsimshian use the sea-based resources, the interior Gitksan use the rivereen resources, at least as far as the fish is concerned, right?

Robinson: Yes.

Grant: You don't know what they wore, the interior Gitksan and Wet'suwet'en. You have already told us that?

Robinson: For which time period, sir?

Grant: Pre-contact?

Robinson: No. I don't think anyone knows what they wore pre-contact.

Grant: But we can assume that they wore something in the winter months?

Robinson: Yes, I think so.

Grant: And we can assume that it wasn't from fish?

Robinson: Not necessarily. I have seen references to the use of fish skin.

...

Grant: This is Harmon. You remember Harmon? You referred to him earlier, Dr. Robinson?

Robinson: Yes.

...

Grant: Where he refers to "The Native of New Caledonia, we denominate Carriers..." You see that?

Robinson: Yes, I do.

Grant: Okay. Now, turn the page over. And then he gets into a description of them: "...Their clothing consists of a covering made of...the skins of the beaver, badger, muskrat, cat or hare. The last they cut into strips, about one inch broad, and then weave or lace them together, until they become of a sufficient size to cover their bodies, and to reach their knees. This garment they put over their shoulders and tie about their waistes. Instead of the above named skins, when they can obtain them from us, they greatly prefer, and make use of blankets, capots, or Canadian coats, cloth or moose and red deer skin. They seldom use...either leggins or shoes, in the summer." Now, that description by Harmon is of the eastern Carrier. You would agree that that is some indication of what the aboriginal people of the interior, the north central interior of B.C. was wearing by a contemporary historical account?

Robinson: Well, in the historic period for the Carrier or the eastern Carrier.... And I am gratified to see the reference of using the skin of fish for clothing is mentioned at the bottom of that paragraph.

Grant: Yes. Well I knew you would find that.

Robinson: Well, good.

...

Grant: Well, let's read what is there since you pointed it out. "The women, however, in addition to the robe of beaver or dressed moose skins, wear an apron, twelve or eighteen inches broad, which reaches nearly down to their knees. These aprons are made of a piece of deer skin, or of salmon skins, sewed together. Of the skin of this fish, they sometimes make leggins, shoes, bags, etc. but they are not durable; and therefore they prefer deer skins and cloth, which are more pliable and soft. The roughness of salmon skins, renders them particularly unpleasant for aprons."

You have to—in any of the analysis of Gitksan and Wet'suwet'en pre-contact you have to take into account that there was some resources that they relied on for clothing?

Robinson: Locally. Some resources that they relied on for clothing, yes, I would think so.

Grant: Yes. And you are not suggesting that you assumed that they wore fish skins in the winter months in the central interior of B.C.?

Robinson: I don't know. Harmon has given us a comment about the use of fish skins as part of the clothing. But there is no reference here to what seasons of year they wore the fish skins and whether or not they comprised part or all of their clothing.

...

Grant: But would it not be fair to assume that the Gitksan and Wet'suwet'en would rely upon furs from within their area for clothing pre-contact?

Robinson: I imagine that they relied on them to some extent. We have here a description of the use of other species of animals for clothing, or fish.[21]

So the resources were there and the people used them. The next question relevant to the Crown's case was, was there sufficient pressure on the resources that people may have been led to compete for them? Peter Grant referred Robinson to paragraph 28 of her opinion report and the supporting footnote on page 68 of part 2.

Grant: You state, and this is your statement, and I think we've already established that this is conjectural on your part: "My reasoning is that it is only when there is pressure on a certain resource, when competition draws attention to a certain resource, then there is need to define it specifically." Accepting that reasoning, you must analyze all potential sources of pressure on the resource to come to a conclusion; do you not agree?

Robinson: Not necessarily. And I do not believe there is information about all possible pressures coming to bear on resources.

Grant: You would—to come to a conclusion about pressure on a certain resource, it would be relevant to determine the utilization of that resource for clothing needs, would it not?

Robinson: Not necessarily.

...

Grant: Would it not be necessary to determine the utilization of that resource for feasting purposes?

Robinson: Not necessarily.

...

Grant: Would it not be relevant to determine the necessity or the utilization of that resource for trade purposes?

Robinson: Not necessarily.

Grant: You say not necessarily?

Robinson: Yes.

Grant: So ?—

Robinson: You're talking about resources generically, and I wouldn't say that any of those criteria you've just put to me are applicable for all situations. I'm not quite sure what situation you're referring to, Mr. Grant.

Grant: Well, what situation are you referring to in your footnote; do you know?

Robinson: I'm not sure what you're referring to, sir.

Grant: I'm referring to the second sentence in…footnote 28a: 'My reasoning'…. 'My reasoning' being Sheila Robinson's reasoning?

Robinson: Yes.

Grant: 'Is that only when there is pressure on a certain resource when competition draws attention to a certain resource, then there is a need to define it specifically'?

Robinson: Yes.

Grant: What resource are you talking about?

Robinson: I'm talking about a general principle as is expressed with regards to cultural ecological theory, and I did draw attention earlier to a reference, Robert Netting, and his very basic book called 'Cultural Ecology,' and you'll find there's reference to these general principles there. Your list of questions that had to do with specific characteristics or attributes associated with each resource, each or any resource, I said not necessarily, because I didn't think they were applicable criteria.

Grant: You applied this reasoning in this statement to the Gitksan and the Wet'suwet'en?

Robinson: Yes, I have.

Grant: In fact, …there is no evidentiary basis for the utilization of this approach and its applicability to the Gitksan, is there; the approach starting 'My reasoning is…'?

Robinson: Well, that may be your opinion, it's not mine.

Grant: Is there an evidentiary basis for applicability to the Gitksan?

Robinson: Yes. I think the basic premise in anthropology is that comparative examples are of extreme use, are of usefulness in identifying situations from one area to another. Anthropology is imperative.

Grant: When there's not sufficient data about the specific society you're studying?

Robinson: When there is some specific data it's also useful to use comparative approaches, because it tends to lessen the entrapment one can fall into by treating any society in isolation or as a unique example. These general principles and cultural ecology have brought application...

Grant: Are you finished?

Robinson: For the time being, yes.

Grant: Thank you. Maybe I'll ask you a question.

Robinson: Oh, good.

Grant: You're stating that with respect to that sentence that it is irrelevant whether the Gitksan rely on any specific resource for clothing, feasting, trade goods, it's irrelevant to determine whether or not there is pressure on that specific resource?

Robinson: I think you're putting words in my mouth. These are not quite the questions you asked me earlier in—you're summarizing them in a slightly different manner. It's difficult for me to put the kind of words you're putting to me now against the list of questions you've just asked me. You were asking me whether or not these factors are necessary or necessarily taken into consideration in looking at pressure on any resource, or that's how I understood those questions to be.

Grant: Well, let me rephrase them. In determining whether or not there is pressure on a certain resource among the Gitksan, it would be relevant to determine whether the Gitksan would utilize that specific resource for clothing, would it not?

Robinson: Only if it was the kind of resource that was ever used with clothing.

Grant: Yes or no?

Robinson: If it was ochre it wouldn't be.

Grant: Maybe. Of course, I'm talking about a resource used for clothing?

Robinson: To the extent that that could be determined, yes, it would be relevant.

Grant: To the extent that it can be determined if the Gitksan used a specific resource for feasting, it would be relevant to determine that so as to determine the pressure on that resource?

Robinson: To the extent that that could be known, yes.

Grant: Yes, you agree. And similarly, with respect to the utilization of a specific resource with respect to trade or exchange, as you've phrased it, it would be relevant to determine the pressure on that resource by the Gitksan?

Robinson: To the extent that that could be known, yes.[22]

The acquisition and production of goods for trade among the Gitksan and Wet'suwet'en, and between them and their neighbours was another source of possible demand, or pressure, on the resources in the hunting territories.

In the first draft of the report that she had submitted to her employers, Russell & DuMoulin, Robinson had written: "In late pre-historic times Gitksan and Wet'suwet'en people were already involved in extensive aboriginal exchange networks, were already increasingly being influenced by coastal dwellers with whom they exchanged locally-produced and exotic commodities, were already developing ways to more effectively exploit local resources to satisfy subsistence and exchange related needs, and so on."

Peter Grant questioned her on the absence of this opinion from her final report.

Grant: And that was your opinion at that time based on your sources?

Robinson: Yes.

Grant: And that's your opinion today? You didn't change your opinion?

Robinson: No, I didn't.

Grant: But you did not include that opinion in your report, did you?

Robinson: Oh, gee, I would think that I had, but it would perhaps...

Grant: I would ask you to take a chance over the evening to look at that.

Robinson: Because I certainly think that it's stated in my report that coast-interior trade or exchange did not spring up as a result of the European induced fur trade, but that there was an extension of, an expansion of and intensification of that after contact.

Grant: Okay...I know you make reference to coastal-interior trade...before contact in the pre-historic time.... But here you're saying more than that....

Robinson: I may have expanded it there, but I don't think that the idea was left out of the report.

Grant: You can look at the report, and if I stand to be corrected, I will ask you first thing in the morning.

Robinson: I may have changed phrasing. I don't think the content was ignored.

Grant: I couldn't track this, doctor. I couldn't track this into your report, and you may direct me to where I should have looked to track it.[23]

Finally, Grant showed Robinson a map on which the location of various game species and other resources like berry patches had been marked out. The map shows these resources as being distributed throughout the territory and not simply immediately surrounding the village sites.

Grant: And mountain goat you've referred to as one of the trade goods. And in this case we see that there are mountain goat both inside and outside the black outlined area. But if the Gitksan and the Wet'suwet'en were involved in using or trading mountain goat furs or mountain goat skins then they would require access to these territories?

Robinson: Not necessarily. And I might say that knowing some things about the environment is only one of the several factors that have to be taken into consideration. Without knowing about the density, the distribution of those animals that are being exploited, without knowing what their recovery rate is after exploitation or during exploitation, and without having some idea of the demands on those natural resources by the local population, the natural distribution makes little sense by itself. It doesn't tell me anything.

Grant: It does tell you something, doesn't it?

Robinson: It tells me that the animals were present or not present.

Grant: It tells you that if the Gitksan required those animals for their own use or for trade they would have to have access to places where those animals were located?

Robinson: Yes, they would.

Grant: Thank you, doctor.

When none of the empirical requirements to support their arguments could be met, Crown counsel opted to focus on the issue of defining "the economy" as a discrete sphere within a social structure, limited to transactions mediated through exchanges in a capitalist market place. This is a euphemism, from an historically-specific point of view, for saying that an "economy" that could be recognized by the court as such came into being only after Europeans arrived. This debate was most clearly illustrated during the cross-examination of the Gitksan's and Wet'suwet'en's witness, Hugh Brody, by one of the Province of British Columbia's lawyers, William Goldie. Goldie had been trying to make Brody agree with his statement that the Gitksan and Wet'suwet'en had "no reason to travel" more than twenty miles away from their riverfront villages "for economic reasons." Brody had been resisting, arguing that they travelled to hunt animals in the territories for subsistence food, used hides for clothing and trees for housing, and accumulated surpluses for trade.

> Goldie: …Let us restate the assumptions that I am asking you to make. One, the primary food source is at the door-step of the home in Hagwilet. You accept that? The second assumption is that the territory in which the hunting is carried out is 90 miles away from that home. Number 3, that subsistence is not an economic activity in the question I am about to ask you. Number 4, that extended time is a period in the winter time of up to 7 months. You understand these assumptions?

> Brody: Yes.

> Goldie: Now, on those assumptions I suggest to you that the only logical reason for somebody being away from his home 90 miles for an extended period in the winter time would be to carry on an economic activity other than subsistence?

> Brody: Well, your assumptions logically compel the conclusion, because you have defined economic activity to exclude subsistence in your assumptions.

> Goldie: Yes.

> Brody: So, it follows logically, not as a matter of any empirical interest, but as a matter of logic that they are not out there pursuing an economic activity.

> Goldie: Yes.[24]

The *facts* establish that there were many reasons to want the resources one had to travel to get to. The *theory* asserts that none of those reasons were "economic," and further, that this means there could be no reason for any borders or rules to exist to regulate access to or use of these resources.

The third premise of the Crown's argument was that there was little competition among the Gitksan and Wet'suwet'en for access to the resources in the outlying territories. Robinson's depiction of pre-contact Gitksan and Wet'suwet'en society included a description of the social and political structure with a particular emphasis on economy, trade and land tenure. In this regard she wished to show that there was nothing we would recognize as a system of property ownership, that these societies were "never stable," and that "rights changed hands frequently." She wrote: "Where conflict over resources was minimal, boundaries were probably vague and faded away from the village cores. I envision a patchwork configuration where controlled resource-producing areas away from village bases were linked up by a system of trails. But prior to the intensification of pressure on interior fur resources sparked by European demands for furs there would appear to have been no need for a sophisticated and elaborate body of rules governing access to resources or for extensive and defined areas of land for their exploitation."[25]

However, at the same time, in order to convey an image of pre-contact society as unstable, and continually rocked by warfare, Robinson contradicted herself by describing a situation of intense, and organized, competition surrounding property rights. She wrote: "House rank was not fixed through time, and chiefs of the same side competed to recruit members and to amass wealth for potlatching. Wealth was derived in part from resources taken from house-controlled territories. Households within a side did not have equal access to 'shared' resources: higher-ranking chiefs were evidently able to lay claim to the more productive areas."[26]

Finally, Robinson concluded her analysis of pre-contact Gitksan and Wet'suwet'en cultures by proclaiming the Crown's legal argument. She wrote:

"In my research I have discovered no conclusive evidence that suggests that, prior to the advent of European influence in the claims area, the Gitksan and Wet'suwet'en lineages and families identified ownership rights to large and precisely defined tracts of hunting territories."

It is tempting to simply dismiss the Crown's witness. But that would ignore the important rhetorical impact of Robinson's courtroom style. When judges, lawyers, and lay people listen to weeks and weeks of testimony, some of it highly technical and specialized in nature, the details and logic of argument easily become lost in a maze of "technobabble." Robinson succeeds in reinforcing a sense that the subject matter being dealt with is of a highly technical and complex nature that only well-educated specialists can possibly comprehend.[27] In fact, what is being discussed is quite straightforward: were there game and other resources in the specific geographical locale in question, that is, the hunting territories shown on maps? The overwhelming bulk of evidence says yes, there were resources there. Did the people who lived on that specific piece of land during these specific times, the late eighteenth and early nineteenth centuries, use these resources? Again, the answer to this question is yes. These conclusions are drawn from empirical data. Was there competition and conflict between groups of Gitksan and Wet'suwet'en over property and resource rights, and were there laws that regulated how these conflicts were to be resolved? Substantial evidence was presented to the court to support affirmative answers to these questions. As well as oral histories and ethnographies, this evidence included a variety of research sources, including studies based in the kind of "scientific" methodology the Crown claimed to support.

However, was this socially organized use of resources one that a British or Canadian court would classify as being what Lord Sumner described as "differently developed...but...hardly less precise than our own," and that Viscount Haldane allowed "could continue to be honoured within the framework of British sovereignty"? These are theoretical—and political—questions whose answers are determined not by empirical observation but by ideological assessment. And that is the prerogative of judges.

Hegemonic Moments

Antonio Gramsci coined the term hegemony to refer to power that maintains certain structures of domination but that is ordinarily invisible.... Hegemony refers to power that 'naturalizes' a social order, an institution, or even an everyday practice so that 'how things are' seems inevitable and not the consequence of particular historical actors, classes and events. It tends to sustain the interests of a society's dominant groups, while generally obscuring these interests in the eyes of subordinates.
—Anthropologists Susan Hirsch and Mindie Lazarus-Black, 1994, *Introduction: Performance and Paradox: Exploring Law's Role in Hegemony and Resistance.*

My premise is that the structure and dynamics of a ceremonial performance event serve to orient those who participate in it (and no doubt its spectators as well) toward distinctions of class and rank that subsequently become inscribed in administrative regulations and codes of practice—even, under some circumstances, in the black letter of the statutory law.... I focus on one such hegemonic moment when it was possible to look 'behind the law' at legal categories in the making.
—Anthropologist Joan Vincent, 1994, *On Law and Hegemonic Moments: Looking Behind the Law in Early Modern Uganda.*

The Crown's case against the Gitksan and Wet'suwet'en offers a window onto a "hegemonic moment" when abstract speculations and simplistic assumptions were transformed by the power of law into truth and facts. The Crown imagines that the core of legally significant cultural difference lies in the contrasts that they hypothesize exist between Aboriginal peoples' and Europeans' relationships to property and to commerce: private property defines European culture, and the absence of private property defines Aboriginality. By deconstructing the Crown's arguments and Robinson's testimony building block by building block we can see the legal categories of "Aboriginal" and "non-Aboriginal" in the making: the process and reasoning by which the Crown constructs legal subjects in its own image and creates truth in its own interests.

It is not necessary to accept, nor would be it be reasonable to consider, the Gitksan's and Wet'suwet'en's and their witnesses' evidence about pre-contact Aboriginal society as beyond doubt, question, challenge, or critique.[28] Oral history is, like written history, a product of particular authors working in particular networks of power relations, at particular historical times, and for particular purposes. Anthropological theories and findings should always be contested and debated. However, even within a conservative framework of analysis, within the Crown's own professed criteria for legitimately "scientific" empirical research, it is obvious that the Crown's evidence and arguments about the nature of Gitksan and Wet'suwet'en social organization before European arrival were, at best, weakly supported by arcane and archaic academic research, and furthermore frequently defied a broad consensus in Canadian society at large of what constitutes "common sense" and "truth." The average person, for example, would consider it reasonable to assume that people living in the intemperate climate of north-western British Columbia would more likely have dressed themselves in the hides and furs of minks and muskrats, than in fish skins. This is my first critique: on the basis of the best evidence by the Crown's own criteria, the difference between the Gitksan's and Wet'suwet'en's case, and the Crown's case, as presented to Court, was not the difference between two equally valid interpretations arising from different cultural premises; nor was it the difference between opposing but equally legitimate positions in academic debates about historical interpretation: it was the difference between sense and nonsense.

The Crown's legal argument that pre-contact Gitksan and Wet'suwet'en cultures lacked property law, and Robinson's supporting testimony, was summed up in this sentence from her report: "In the absence of competition over scarce resources, there is no reason for the rules to exist." Under cross-examination Robinson explained that this statement was based on her reading of certain social theories:

> Robinson: …from my own reading and cultural ecology, I would say that a general rule of thumb that many anthropologists or cultural geographers go by is that people seldom assert exclusive or limiting control over any kind of specific or general resource unless there is a need to do so.[29]
>
> Grant: And here you are speculating, are you not?
>
> Robinson: Yes. And my speculation is based on a very extensive reading of cultural ecology as a source of comparative examples and from comparative examples from the northern northwest coast region and adjacent interior region, among other sources.[30]

What underlying assumptions are necessary to accept as a universal fact that: "in the absence of competition over scarce resources, there is no reason for the rules to exist"? And to infer that the social organization of eighteenth-century Gitksan and Wet'suwet'en peoples could not have generated institutions and rules akin to what contemporary Canadians call property law and resource management?

The Crown's argument resonates with a conservative form of naturalism: theories of human nature that posit the universal and ahistorical existence of an individual who is first and foremost an autonomous, atomistic, biological organism. In order to survive and achieve their nature-driven imperative to reproduce the species, the needs of human organisms must be met. These needs can be reduced, for all important purposes, to food, clothing, shelter and sexual reproduction. Human beings, in this way of thinking, are instinct-driven animals to whose brains a capacity for rationality has been added, to varying degrees. The degree to which rationality and culture have been added on to different organisms is measured by the degree to which an individual or group manifests narrowly-defined "economic rationalism" in acts of "rational decision-making" which qualify as such if their end result is profit and/or the ability to increase one's power over other individuals, thus gaining access to *their* resources.[31] Rationality, within this belief system, is demonstrated by an individual's, or group of individual's, success, in competition with others, in securing the necessary material goods required to meet their needs: survival of the fittest. The Crown's argument relies on acceptance of the hypothesis that the "natural" motivation for people to develop an intense relationship of identity with land and resources is the imperative to meet one's "needs" as individual organisms and aggregates of organisms as against the needs of other individuals and organisms. In the dominant western culture, identity with land reaches its peak of expression in individual private ownership in fee simple. This is the core concept of western "possessive individualism," characterized by the slogan "I own therefore I am."[32]

But what if, despite facts presented to the contrary, the animals located in the Gitksan's and Wet'suwet'en's territories were not only *needed* for subsistence and clothing, or trade and commerce? What if they were also *desired* for feasting, gift-giving, prestige, sociality, joy, spiritual sustenance and renewal? What if the land is not a passive object awaiting human labour to transform it? What if the land is alive itself? What if the animals and resources are not awaiting human dispensation at all? What if they are sentient beings, part of a circle of life, an ecosystem? What if they are reincarnations of ancestors? Why then could there be reasons for agreements to be made between people about rules of access and "ownership" rights? Why then might a poet, a shaman, a carver, an artist, a mother, a father, a sister, a brother, a lover, a friend have a "logical reason for being away from his home 90 miles for an extended period in the winter time?" Why then could there be many "reasons to travel?"

Psychiatrist Cisco Lassiter argues that: "The world of the modern European self is located in a Euclidean-Newtonian space, homogeneous, uniform, and continuous: a space without sacred places, where all places are essentially interchangeable, and where geometry forgets the spiritual meaning of the earth, the land, and the human need for home...."

The identity and well-being of the aboriginal self, on the other hand, Lassiter continues, "depends on earth, ground, and place for an essential relationship to departed ancestors, cultural traditions, the world of the dead, gods, and time itself...this self cannot survive without access to the traditional sacred places, orientation by tribal landmarks, rootedness in the earth and in kinship relations."[33] Clearly, the Crown's position did not recognize or respect the equality or integrity of such an Aboriginal relationship to land. This is my second critique: the philosophical premises of the Crown's argument were ethnocentric.

It is hardly surprising that the Crown's arguments reflected the dominant ideology glorifying private property and profit, and the ideal of an individualistic, unencumbered self. But there is a further puzzle in the Crown's case: an apparent paradox arises from the fact that the best evidence from all sources strongly supports the conclusion that the Gitksan and Wet'suwet'en met all the conditions required, by the criteria of conservative European political theory, to have had concepts of, and laws regulating, private-like property: they identified boundaries between territories, they produced for subsistence and exchange, they accumulated and stored surplus, and they engaged in conflicts with each other over resources. They had property, laws to protect it, and the will to defend it. These were the criteria required by the Crown's theory for people to "qualify" as "rational economic men." Given that, officially, Canadian courts are governed by principles of human equality that direct them to assess people on the basis of their behaviour and not their race, how could the Crown still *logically*, in their own terms, argue that the Gitksan and Wet'suwet'en systems were "too primitive"—that is, too different and inferior in comparison to "civilized" systems—to be recognized by the law?

The paradox is resolved by considering another assumption that underlies the way of thinking and being that the Crown's argument represented that goes beyond ethnocentrism. The liberal critique of ethnocentrism chastises anyone who thinks that their own cultural practices are the only, and the best, in the world. The resolutions to problems defined as rooted in ethnocentrism are education and tolerance: we should all learn to appreciate and respect the particular values of *all* cultures on their own terms, and we should not judge others by our own culturally-specific criteria. However, this liberal position begs a number of questions.

First, the liberal critique of ethnocentrism rests on a definition of "culture" as beliefs and values that can be isolated from political and economic organization; and the premise that "cultural differences" are the main cause of strife between peoples. Relationships between members of diverse cultures take place within the context of power relations, and differential access to resources. Therefore, the ethnocentrism of the dominant has consequences for the subordinate that simple changes in beliefs and values will not ameliorate. In other words, "cultural" differences may not be the main problem: unequal distribution of wealth and power and property may be. Second, the liberal critique of ethnocentrism does not address the thorny problem presented by the fact that a foundation stone of conservative European theory has been that European culture is *not* one local and historically-specific way of life among many, but represents a *universally superior* one. Therefore, it is not theoretically possible for the dominant western culture to enter into dialogue with any others on an equal footing without first forfeiting its self concept of universality and supremacy. Were its leaders to reject these foundational assumptions, how could the political and economic domination of colonial peoples be justified?

Historically, British colonial thought was based on the particular extrapolation of possessive individualism most influential in theories of Social Darwinism that ranked and compared people: civilized as superior, primitive as inferior. "Primitive" human organisms were characterized as animal-like beings driven by base survival instincts only minimally mediated by rationality or culture. The "needs" of primitives were strictly limited to the survival and reproduction of the human organism. Therefore, within this framework of analysis, even if the Gitksan and Wet'suwet'en appeared to be behaving much like property-owning European economic rationalists, their classification as "primitives" supports a conclusion that whatever their *observed behaviour* in fact consisted in, eurocentric theories claim they were driven by instinct, and not by rationality, a characteristic that, by definition, "primitives" lack.

To understand the Crown's argument we must, again, enter Law's culture: we must leave tangible evidence behind on "the ground" and take flight into the abstract, imagined world of the hovering sovereign. If, and only if, we accept a theory of human nature and human social life as being naturally and inevitably acquisitive and competitive, and we accept that Europeans and Aboriginals are different and unequal human beings, then—and only then—can the Crown's argument make logical sense, within their own framework of analysis and within a dominant ideology that claims all human beings are equal. This is my third critique: the Crown's argument was not simply ethnocentric eurocentric, but racist. I use the term "racist" in this context to denote an explanation of human behaviour based principally on the presumably inherent, naturalized habits and characteristics of a group of people who have been classified as belonging to a particular "race" or cultural group. My conclusion that the Crown's argument was racist rests on the fact that such a categorization is necessary to make their argument logical and coherent.

Logical gymnastics aside, the basic story remains the same: Aboriginal people were here and they had laws governing relations with strangers. They obeyed their own laws. The British arrived, and they had laws governing relations with strangers, but the colonists neither respected Aboriginal laws nor obeyed their own laws. Since first contact, Aboriginal peoples have insisted that the newcomers negotiate a mutually respectful, lawful relationship with them. Successive colonial governments have refused to do so, opting instead to assert their dominion by whatever means necessary, including armed force and the subversion of their own law. The original questions, too, still remain: why are Aboriginal peoples forced to present a defense of their histories and cultures to the courts, by the rules of the courts, in the language of the courts, within the theoretical frameworks of the courts, to begin with? Who is responsible for this never-ending, unresolved dispute?

---

1. Robinson 1987(b); 1990; 1991. See also, Pryce 1992.

2. Transcripts, Vol. 292: 21668.

3. Under cross-examination Robinson explained that she was referring here to Rosman and Rubel 1971. Transcripts, Vol. 293: 22157.

4. See Mertz 1992, 1994; O'Barr 1982.

5. Coupland 1986: 18.

6. Transcripts Vol. 289, 21727-21730.

7. Ives 1990.

8. "Carrier" is a name applied to some First Nations, including some Wet'suwet'en, in northern British Columbia by fur traders and later adopted by anthropologists.

9. Robinson 1983: 409.

10. Kretch 1991.

11. *Delgamuukw v. R.*, Exhibit 1191-5.

12. Rogers 1986: 207-210.

13. Transcripts, Vol. 293: 22165-22171.

14. This section of Robinson's opinion report covered six pages and encompassed 12 paragraphs. What appears at first as an impressive 10 pages of supporting notes is revealed upon closer examination as repetitions of eight sources, summarized as follows: Adams 1969; Boas 1916; Davidson 1955; Duff 1959; Garfield 1951; Inglis and MacDonald 1979; Jenness 1943; Tobey 1981. All of these sources rely, to some extent, on oral tradition. Of these eight references, only Adams deals specifically with the Gitksan. Adams conducted fieldwork among the Gitksan during the mid to late 1960s.

15. *Merriam-Webster Dictionary* 814.

16. Transcripts, Vol. 292: 22191-22195.

17. Robinson 1987(a):17.

18. Adams 1969.

19. Gisday Wa and Delgam Uukw 1992.

20. Ray 1991(b): 311-312.

21. Transcripts Vol. 293: 22177-22179.

22. Transcripts Vol. 293: 22151–22205.

23. Transcripts Vol. 289: 21798.

24. Transcripts Vol. 214: 15494.

25. Robinson 1987(a): 19.

26. Robinson 1987(a): 20.

27. See Mertz 1992, 1994; O'Barr 1982.

28. See Cove 1996; Paine 1996 for critiques of the anthropological evidence.

29. Transcripts Vol. 189: 21644.

30. Transcripts Vol.192: 22175.

31. For a classic critique of these social theories, known as "theories of economism" see Dumont 1977; Dreyfus and Dreyfus 1979; Klamer 1987.

32. Macpherson 1962.

33. Lassiter 1987: 220. These statements about identity assume and reproduce the notion of homogenous identities. This is the subject of significant critique by those who claim the assertion of a singular identity blurs important differences, such as gender and class, within cultural groups. These "modernist" concepts of culture and identity are the terms of the legal discourse in court. It is within this context that I cite Lassiter. See Crosby 1996 for a critique of this formulation of contemporary Aboriginal identity.

CHAPTER 13: Jewels in the Crown

The time of which the Chief Justice speaks to arrive at his decision could be looked upon as just one inch.... It is only a short period of time in comparison to the length of time that the Gitksan and Wet'suwet'en people have been on their land.... If we were to look at a time line, the time that we have been on our lands could be measured in several feet.
—Satsan (Herb George), Speaker, Office of the Hereditary Chiefs of the Gitksan and Wet'suwet'en People, 1992.[1]

Temporal Purgatory: The Protohistoric Period

Having constructed to their own satisfaction the image of an "unorganized" pre-contact society, the Crown put forward their rendition of what happened to the Gitksan and Wet'suwet'en when European commodities joined Aboriginally-produced items among their trade goods. Sheila Robinson's expert opinion report focused on the protohistoric period and she offered a succinct definition of her subject matter: "By 'protohistoric,'" she wrote, "I mean the time prior to European presence in the area claimed by the plaintiffs but when European influence was felt through native intermediaries.... 'Historic' refers to times when Europeans were present—even if intermittently. 'Prehistoric' applies to all time prior to the protohistoric era."

This periodization scheme (prehistoric, protohistoric, historic) represents traditional academic categories of analysis. Conceptualizing history in these terms highlights the arrival of European commodities, and then persons, and their subsequent activities as the decisive motor force in Aboriginal history, and follows logically from the widely-held assumption that Aboriginal societies had been static and unchanging for tens of thousands of years before engaging in contact with Europeans for the past two hundred and fifty or so years. This is, of course, a logical framework for an analysis whose purpose is to establish the determinacy of European activity and the supremacy of European culture. This periodization scheme therefore serves the interpretative purpose of defining the relevant categories of the discussion in eurocentric terms, super-imposes this categorization on the Gitksan and Wet'suwet'en, and concludes that this was a crucial and transforming turning point in their history, rather than, perhaps, a significant period in a very long, continuous historical process. It stresses universal and externally-determined change only, rather than a dynamic relationship between the latter and internally-determined change and continuity. Most importantly, however, it is a *model*, an abstract construct developed by academics to facilitate comparison and theoretical speculation. A temporal classification scheme like this is not a fact. In ordinary, everyday life, time period categorizations serve as heuristic devices: shorthand flags that facilitate communication between people with shared languages and experiences. Law seeks to transform such time period categorizations into locked, airtight repositories that incarcerate lived histories in time-bound cells, as if processes and relationships do not traverse the boundaries between historical epochs.

The first question to be asked regarding the specific history of any particular group's experience of the protohistoric era, is when did this period begin and end for them? Two primary sources are usually consulted on this question: archaeological data that establishes the dates of the first items of European manufacture unearthed in a given area; and historical documents in the form of records and observations kept by European traders. Oral tradition is also studied for references to the arrival of these new things, and how they impacted the Indigenous peoples concerned.

The first and second building blocks of the Crown's argument were that Gitksan and Wet'suwet'en societies had been unorganized at the time they were "discovered" by Europeans, and that they lacked property law. Their third building block was the argument that the delineation of property and borders, and a territorially-based social organization emerged among the Gitksan and Wet'suwet'en in response to the European-Aboriginal fur trade. Given the extent of social change that the Crown wished to prove took place during the protohistoric period, it was important for their argument that this period be as long as possible. A long protohistoric period was also important to Sheila Robinson to justify her methodological decision not to consult archival records like William Brown's because, she argued, they were written long after a "truly aboriginal" way of life had ceased to be lived. Sheila Robinson explained the importance of her argument to the Crown's legal case: "Recognition that protohistoric European-influenced developments took place and were significant has one very important implication. It casts suspicion on any portrayal of a "pristine" or truly aboriginal way of life based on contemporary knowledge," she wrote.

The Crown's witness took on the task of establishing the date at which the protohistoric period began. In her opinion report Robinson wrote: "Vitus Bering's voyage to north-western Alaska from Siberia was in 1641. There is no doubt that trade in European commodities from Siberia into North America began some time earlier. The protohistoric period perhaps extends back as early as the mid-sixteenth century, when Russians first began to settle into the Kamchatkan peninsula." Bering's voyage actually took place in 1741. Robinson claimed under cross-examination that *"1641"* represented a typographical error. Undaunted, Robinson stretched the point even further when the Judge intervened and asked for more details about early foreign influences.

Court: What Euro-Canadian influences would extend back four centuries?

Robinson: Coming from the east coast of North America and also up through the Mississippi drainage there is some—there's some thought that indirect European influence was having its effect on Indian groups quite removed from the direct sources of contact. Some of those influences included diseases spreading through, and perhaps extracting considerable tolls on some populations before there was ever any real historic record of it. There seems to be—and even such—such things as the introduction of horses from Spanish sources, for instance, seems to have had tremendous effect on the settlement patterns and economic behaviour and social relations of Indian groups through the plains and prairies, for instance. So something as minor as the horse coming in caused tremendous dislocations through the prairies.

Court: That would go back to the 16th century?

Robinson: Yes. So the post-contact period or protohistoric period has been traced to the first arrival of Europeans in the New World. Some scholars take it back that far. From the north northwest American direction and the Siberian connections some people are saying that if we lift the notion that only Europeans can affect North American cultures then we are dealing with an Asiatic influence; Chinese, Japanese and so on. That seems to have stimulated trade and trade economies. That's much more conjectural as you push it back into the past, but there are certainly scholars who agree that indirect influences were important.

Court: Thank you.[2]

Peter Grant asked Robinson what factual evidence she relied on to support her statement that "there is no doubt that trade in European commodities...began sometime earlier" than Captain Cook's 1774 landing. Grant confronted her with the fact that, upon reviewing the sources listed in her bibliography in support of this statement, he was unable to find any references to European-manufactured goods having been found in the territory prior to 1780.

Grant: What I suggest to you, with all due respect, Dr.Robinson, is there isn't a scintilla of evidence...that there was European trade goods moving into the Gitksan or Wet'suwet'en area before 1786...[yet] here you say there is no doubt....

Robinson: I have no doubt at all that there wasn't a considerable amount of protohistoric influence coming from Asiatic sources or Northern Russian sources in the protohistoric period, as I have defined it mid-17th century onward.

Grant: Into the Gitksan and Wet'suwet'en area, doctor?

Robinson: I have absolutely no reason to think that they were isolated from what are otherwise described in several places as broad trade patterns, broad developments occurring.

…

Grant: Well, doctor, look, you have explained what you meant by there is no conclusive evidence…. 'More likely than not,' I think you said. But here you say there is no doubt. That's pretty conclusive…isn't it?

Robinson: Yes, and I'll stand by that. I will say that there is no doubt. We may not have material items representing that in that claims area yet. I would say that further archaeological research will no doubt turn them up.

Grant: And that is speculative?

Robinson: Yes, it is, but it's based on my opinion.[3]

On the key issue of duration of the protohistorical period, Robinson eventually vacillated under cross-examination.

Grant: …when are you referring to as "prior to the advent of European influence?"

Robinson: Well, we've discussed this, and I think we're going to leave it as the mid-eighteenth century and Chirikov's arrival on to the northern coast.[4]

According to the Crown's framework of analysis, the arrival Captain Cook in 1774 marks the beginning of the protohistoric period in British Columbia. The arrival of a second European man, Hudson's Bay Company trader William Brown in 1822, heralds the end of the protohistoric period and the beginning of the historic period in Gitksan and Wet'suwet'en territory. Accepting these broad parameters, the protohistoric period shrinks from Robinson's initial suggestion of a 400-year duration to one lasting only 72 years. According to evidence subsequently accepted by the Judge, the proto-historic period for the Gitksan and Wet'suwet'en in effect began in 1778 and ended in 1822, therefore encompassing only 44 years.

Robinson's excesses in attempting to stretch the protohistoric period back to the arrival of the horse on the Prairies, and thus suggesting, given the context in which her statements were made, that this was relevant to the Gitksan and Wet'suwet'en, was tantamount to saying that from the moment the first Toyota hit a Canadian road, we all began to adopt Japanese socio-economic, political, and cultural characteristics. This Crown argument illustrates the absurd conclusions to which legal argument and abstract logic can lead.

Who Created Private Property?

By the late 1950s or early 1960s, I assumed that the issue of land tenure...had been resolved once and for all and that 'hunting territories' came into existence after the arrival of Europeans. This assumption was challenged by investigators...who convinced me that after several decades of my previous viewpoint, it was time to reexamine the complex topic.... In spite of the extensive literature on the land occupied by the original inhabitants of North America, we still know very little about Indian relationships to land and its resources.... Fortunately, there are scholars who continue to labor very hard at understanding the wisdom of Indian elders and the remarks of traders and other Europeans that have been preserved.

—Anthropologist Dr. Edward Rogers, 1986, *Epilogue: Reevaluations and Future Considerations.*

The issues being debated in the courtroom during *Delgamuukw v. R.* about the impact of the "protohistoric" period on Indigenous societies have occupied academics in this field for many generations. The key question they have addressed is whether or not conceptions of private-like property, and laws codifying and defending such land ownership, existed among Aboriginal peoples prior to their involvement with Europeans. Sheila Robinson notes in her 1983 Ph.D. thesis that the question of the impact of the European-Aboriginal fur trade on Indigenous societies is far from settled among anthropologists and ethnohistorians.[5] Chapter VII of her doctoral thesis, entitled "Assessing the Impact of Early Contact With Europeans on Northern Northwest Coast Indian Socioeconomies," which encompasses 77 pages, began with the following paragraph: "How scholars have viewed the impact of early contact with representatives of Western civilization on Northwest Coast Indian cultures has varied considerably.... Their interpretations of the cultural contact situations during the maritime fur trade period fall into three distinct categories. The first claim that contact with the earliest explorers and fur traders provoked essentially no changes in the traditional social and economic organizations of the Northwest Coast Indians (the minimal cultural change hypotheses); the second argue that this early period of intercultural interactions wrought devastating changes in the traditional native socio-economic organizations (the negative impact hypotheses); while the third identifies a series of progressive developments in the early historic period which triggered the efflorescence of Northwest Coast cultural organization to levels which were unattainable before the Europeans arrived (the positive impact hypotheses.)[6] Robinson was most critical of the "minimal cultural change hypotheses," that she attributed to authors like Joan Wike and Robin Fisher who, she claimed, argue that the fur trade brought "essentially no changes in the traditional social and economic organization" of First Nations.[7] This is an oversimplification:

what these researchers argue is that, while cultural *changes* took place, cultural *transformation* did not. However, Robinson is correct in her observation that a good deal of debate about the impact of the fur trade on First Nations remains unresolved. Her thesis also accurately describes the current state of the art in fur trade studies when she argues that: "If theoretical emphases are shifted away from tracing developments in structural processes towards understanding the nature of particular historical developments which can be documented, we will achieve a clearer understanding of early post-contact adaptations."[8] Robinson's 1983 suggestion that, "given the variations in Indian-European interactions during the early historic period, it may be profitable to break the records down to a point where separate communities' involvements with the foreigners and their native trading partners can be examined more closely," also finds widespread support in the literature.[9]

In the introduction to her 1987 expert opinion report, Sheila Robinson located her analysis within the discipline of ethnohistory. She wrote: "Most modern scholars engaged in North American ethnohistoric research agree that indigenous populations were profoundly affected by indirect contact with Europeans before they experienced direct contact with them. Although the nature, timing, intensity and repercussions of protohistoric European influence varied considerably from region to region, research indicates that no native groups in what is now known as British Columbia were isolated from stimulus stemming from the European presence in the New World."

When Robinson was asked by lawyers for the Gitksan and Wet'suwet'en to substantiate her claim that her expert opinion report reflected contemporary ethnohistorical theory and research, she referred to the recent work—not cited in the bibliography of her report—of scholars like Colin Yerbury, Stacey Krech, Toby Morantz, Arthur Ray and Charles Bishop.[10] The *current* work of each of these scholars, however, challenges the Crown's central theses. Charles Bishop, writing in 1987, summarized the thinking of "most modern fur trade scholars" when he wrote: "...It became orthodoxy to view the European fur trade as giving rise to...[an] individualized and privatized form of territoriality. Beginning in the 1960s, more intensive regional, ethnographic, and historical studies began to undermine some of the specific tenets of the general theory. By the 1970s, it was becoming evident to a small core of specialists that an accumulation of data pertaining to a variety of times and areas, combined with theoretical and conceptual refinement, was challenging the applicability of the general theory itself."[11]

The Gitksan and Wet'suwet'en and their witnesses presented an analysis of the impact of the fur trade based primarily on local knowledge. Their narrative explained how, following his 1774 arrival at Ahousat, Captain Cook initiated a trading relationship with Chief Maquinna in which First Nations supplied sea otter pelts destined for a burgeoning European fashion market. Most fur trade scholars agree—based largely on analyses of written records kept by European traders—that the goods demanded by the First Nations traders were largely luxury items as opposed to essentials. Joan Wike, who analyzed the logs kept by trading ships' captains, says that, during the initial stages of the maritime fur-trade iron, copper, guns and ammunition were traded. By the end of the period, the demand was for rum, molasses, pilot biscuits and luxury items.[12]

Fur trade scholars also agree that the Aboriginal peoples of the northwest coast whom the Europeans encountered were shrewd and experienced traders who exerted a good deal of control over transactions by employing strategies such as withholding furs to drive up prices, placing "advance orders" for future trade goods and refusing to trade unless they were satisfied.[13] They have concluded that the Aboriginals' interest in trade was for the purposes of elaborating their ceremonial systems as opposed to improving the sufficiency of their subsistence exploitation for which Indigenous technology continued to be used well after guns and ammunition were acquired and used for warfare and social control.

The "on the ground" practice of the west coast fur trade, like that of early treaty-making in eastern Canada, conformed to Aboriginal business etiquette, requiring long preliminary discussions, feasting and performances, and exchanges of gifts and other formalities, before transactions were made. And, as was the case throughout the colonial world, other relations developed between the European visitors and their Aboriginal hosts. Some sailors were taken captive when negotiations failed and conflict developed, some were killed, some deserted their ships and remained on shore. The many unions between European fur traders and Aboriginal women are still represented in too many Canadian history books as "desperate" choices made by European men who, "needing women," had no other options. Referred to in HBC records as "country marriages," these were often, in fact, solemn and binding legal arrangements conducted according to Aboriginal marriage laws.[14] These were not "inferior" forms of European marriage, but rather matrimonial commitments made between members of groups of visitors and hosts. As would be expected in such a situation, the customs of the hosts prevailed. These unions were sometimes arranged between chiefs and ships' captains or trading company executives in order to consolidate trading relationships. This practice followed both European and Aboriginal protocols regarding arranged marriages between royal families and powerful business interests. Contemporary scholars, re-examining legal history from a perspective of gender and racial equality, have found numerous examples where early colonial courts recognized the legitimacy of these marriages, and upheld the authority of Aboriginal law as against European laws, demonstrating both the uneven application of legal principles in practice, and the importance of context in shaping local power relations.[15] As is the case always and everywhere, not all unions between European men and Aboriginal women were sanctified by anyone's laws, or entered into from positions of equality.

The Crown's arguments in *Delgamuukw v. R.* reflected popular B.C. mythology about the fur trade era. Simple Aboriginal peoples, so the settler's founding stories go, were humbled by the obvious superiority of European men, awed by their technology, and dazzled by their flashy commodities. These accounts tell of Aboriginals who were easily tricked by the clever commercial chicanery of the Europeans, and eagerly abandoned their own ways in a desperate pursuit of European trade goods. Their lust for beads and trinkets was fatal, and sounded the death knell for Indigenous cultures, these settlers' narrations conclude.

The land tenure system and the social and political structures that the Gitksan and Wet'suwet'en claimed were in place before Europeans—or their commodities—arrived, *really* arose, according to the Crown, as a direct response to the European fur trade. The Crown's case therefore required evidence that, in the course of the protohistoric period, a system of property ownership and resource management, based in Houses ranked in a hierarchical manner and articulated with other Houses and clans throughout the region, emerged, stimulated by the desire for European things. Robinson's central thesis in relation to the impact of the fur trade was summed up in the following paragraph of her opinion report: "Gitksan and Wet'suwet'en claims of traditional ownership and occupation of certain territories can be challenged on the basis that they do not account for developments which occurred during the protohistoric period. These changes include adjustments in boundaries between the Gitksan and Wet'suwet'en and their neighbours as well as more precise delineation of boundaries within and at the margins of Gitksan and Wet'suwet'en territories. Both processes of territorial demarcation are linked to and were stimulated by indirect contact with Europeans through the eighteenth and early nineteenth centuries."

The Crown specifically argued that desires for, and competition over, these new commodities stimulated the Gitksan and Wet'suwet'en to trap hitherto unexploited, or under-exploited fur-bearing species on territories outside of their villages, and at a distance from the main subsistence source of salmon in the rivers. Initially, the Crown claimed, the Gitksan and Wet'suwet'en were drawn into subordinate relations with their coastal neighbours, and, later on, with Europeans directly. Subordination, the Crown claimed, led them to mimic those who dominated them. Finally, reasoning backwards from the point of consumption to the point of production, the Crown argued that, because the furs Aboriginal people traded would ultimately be sold in a capitalist commodity economy, Aboriginal trappers were now members of a new culture and lived in a new form of social organization, whether they knew it or not.

During the first phase of the European-Aboriginal fur trade on the northwest coast—from 1774 to 1800 approximately—ships stopped at coastal ports only long enough to trade with Aboriginal representatives for furs, food and other supplies. These coastal Aboriginals became brokers and middlemen, trading European goods with their inland neighbours. Two sections of Robinson's report dealt primarily with this first half, or maritime phase, of the fur trade that spanned approximately 20 years. "Section 11: Protohistoric Developments in Gitksan and Carrier land use" consists of ten paragraphs with 27 pages of supporting notes. As was the case in the previous section of her report that dealt with pre-contact social organization, most of Robinson's sources of information on the protohistoric period were not based in studies of the Gitksan and Wet'suwet'en. Section III of Robinson's report was entitled "The Expansion of Coast-Interior Trade." Robinson began by saying that she was really just expanding on the points made in the previous section but emphasizing how "new European wealth stimulated northern coastal societies and economies to the point where a different kind of social and economic organization began to emerge." According to Robinson's narrative, the coastal Tsimshian became aggressive middlemen and three superchiefs arose, among them a Legaik. Twenty paragraphs long, this section of Robinson's report was devoted primarily to a retelling of a story about the rise of Legaik's dynasty. The Legaik story takes up the better part of seven pages, and is based almost entirely on an unpublished undergraduate honours thesis completed at the University of British Columbia in 1978.

This section of Robinson's report supported the Crown's argument that the Gitksan and Wet'suwet'en land tenure system and social structure was "borrowed" by them from the Coast Tsimshian people during the protohistoric period. Robinson wrote: "It was less a matter of what goods they acquired than who furnished them, and how they were used. There was considerably more status to be gained through relations with the 'superior' coast people than through exchange with 'inferior' Athabaskans."[16]

Peter Grant confronted Robinson on cross-examination, presenting William Brown's descriptions of Gitksan trading relations with their coastal neighbours, with the interior Athabaskans, and with the Hudson's Bay Company:

> Grant: Well, let's look at page 11 (of Brown's report) then: 'It does not appear to me that we are able to cope with these people by making derouines into the country they are in the habit of visiting unless we sell our property so cheap as to prove prejudicial to the trade of Western Caledonia, and even then we will not be able to secure one half of the trade, for we do not meet on an equal footing as they receive goods at a low rate from the vessels which frequent the coast.' Now, would you agree with me that that's

consistent with logic, that the trade—the goods that Brown had to get would have been over land, that is coming into New Caledonia right?

Robinson: It's consistent with a Eurocentric logic….

Grant: I'll rephrase my question so you understand it. Brown got his trade goods…over land, right?

Robinson: Yes.

Grant: And the vessels got their trade by sea?

Robinson: Yes.

Grant: It was cheaper to get the trade goods up by sea at that time than over land?

Robinson: Was it? I don't know that.

Grant: You don't know that, okay. Assume that it was cheaper to get them by sea, or let's not even assume that, let's just say that what Brown says here is true, they received goods at a low rate from the vessels which frequented the coast. And Brown is saying: "We will not be able to meet on an equal footing." For whatever reason, Brown says they could not compete giving the goods to the Indians at the same rates as the vessels.[17]

There were repeated references in Brown's journals to the importance of deer and moose hides traded with the east. Arthur Ray had argued that, by the time Brown arrived in 1822, the trade was one where the scarcer furs were traded for moose and deer hides with the Athabaskans; and the plentiful fish, with Europeans for manufactured commodities. Under cross examination, Robinson admitted that the sentence in her report that read: "There was considerably more status to be gained through relations with the 'superior' coast people than through exchange with 'inferior' Athabaskans" was "speculative" and based on Kobrinsky, Steward and Goldman, who did not have access to Brown's journals.[18] Finally, she said she relied "on a considerable understanding of cultural ecological theory which suggests that, in all likelihood, that's what occurred…." An archaic interpretation of cultural ecology mirrors crude evolutionism and supports the assumption that "simple" societies always assimilate the characteristics of "complex" societies when they come into contact. The underlying logic of this formulation that serves the Crown's interests tells a story about how, just as the Wet'suwet'en "naturally" copied the Gitksan, and the Gitksan "naturally" modelled themselves on the Coast Tsimshian, so "naturally" the Gitksan and Wet'suwet'en emulated Europeans after contact.

This section of Robinson's report supported two points in the Crown's case. First, the Crown argued that, in having to defend themselves against Legaik's aggression—itself motivated by participation in the European-

Aboriginal fur trade—the Gitksan and Wet'suwet'en consolidated the external boundaries of their territories which had been "hazy" during the pre-contact period. Second, this brought the Gitksan and Wet'suwet'en into subordinate trading relations with the coastal Tsimshian peoples.

The other major source Robinson relied upon in this section was an account by anthropologist George MacDonald. MacDonald argues, on the basis of data he acknowledges to be conjectural, that competition over European trade goods, particularly metals, stimulated increased warfare for control of trade routes during the protohistoric period.[19] Robinson relied extensively on MacDonald's rendition of the "Epic Of Nekt," a "warrior's saga," that told the stories of great battles between the Gitksan and their Tsimshian neighbours during this era. Robinson quoted MacDonald as saying that, in the Indigenous accounts, "Motives are stated in terms of revenge rather than economics," (that is, motivation based on issues not determined by European influence. (ed.)) MacDonald concluded, however, that while the wars were fought over "important oolachen fishing grounds," he *believes* "it was the pursuit of metals and improved weapons, rather than control of the oolachen trade, that prompted this aggression."[20] It is interesting to note that what MacDonald and Robinson accepted as "true" in the oral history was that wars were fought. What they rejected as "untrue," however, was Aboriginal peoples' *explanation* of what the wars were about. Even MacDonald, however, acknowledged that the objects of battle were transportation routes and that "territories were sacrosanct." While in theory oral tradition is rejected, in practice it is selectively relied upon for "data," and European social theory is superimposed as explanation.

As sea otter stocks declined on the coast, the Hudson's Bay Company continued to expand across what was to become the province of British Columbia, building forts and engaging in trade with Aboriginal peoples throughout the first half of the nineteenth century. The land-based fur trade period of the protohistoric era encompassed, roughly, the years 1800-1850 in the province as a whole. However, local areas experienced these incursions at different times and to different degrees. Even if we consider the first sporadic contacts between European and Gitksan and Wet'suwet'en *human beings*, rather than contact between people and commodities, a reasonable time to commence the dating of the protohistoric period in this *particular* area, then the "protohistoric period" before William Brown arrived and during which the Crown argued that dramatic social change occurred, encompassed only about 15-20 years, a considerably shortened time frame compared to Robinson's original suggestion of over 400 years of European-induced cultural assimilation. In fact, regularized Gitksan and Wet'suwet'en participation in the land-based fur trade did not begin in earnest in their territories until the 1820s, when William Brown arrived.

Robinson's opinion report was based primarily on her doctoral dissertation on coastal history, and the differences between the experiences of the interior Gitksan and Wet'suwet'en and those of the coastal peoples in relation to the maritime fur trade were significant. Her haphazard substitution of coastal Tsimshian, Haida and Tlingit historical data for specific documentation of Gitksan and Wet'suwet'en experiences is particularly problematic in relation to this period of time that is crucial to the Crown's argument.

Section V of Robinson's report, entitled "Gitksan Territorial Ownership: Protohistoric/Early Historic," consisted of four paragraphs and spoke to the issue of the Gitksan's internal boundaries during the later half of the protohistoric period: the time the land-based fur trade commenced. Robinson argued that potlatching increased substantially during this period as a result of competition between Chiefs, and that land holdings changed hands frequently through potlatching. Section VI, the final section of Robinson's report, is entitled "Protohistoric Changes in Wet'suwet'en Social and Economic Organization, after Kobrinsky." It is a five and a half page regurgitation of a ten page discussion paper written by anthropologist Vernon Kobrinksy in 1977. In this paper, Kobrinsky outlined an admittedly conjectural three-stage history of social development for the Northwestern Carrier that Robinson, on behalf of the Crown, adopted as a framework for her rendition of Gitksan and Wet'suwet'en history. Kobrinksy suggested that structural changes in Carrier society—supposedly having 'evolved' from simple bands to more complex clan social organization—could have been a direct response to the changing economic conditions initiated by participation in the European-Aboriginal fur trade. In the second paragraph of this section Robinson explained her choice of Kobrinsky as an authority, writing: "Kobrinsky's viewpoint is important for two reasons. First, his assertion that significant socio-economic changes occurred during the proto-historic period supports claims that European influence was a major factor in disrupting 'traditional' native lifestyles before direct contact between Indians and Europeans occurred. Second, much of the ethnographic evidence he assembles related to changes in styles of resource control. Specifically, Kobrinsky asserts that precise delineation of territorial boundaries relating to the allocation of rights to fine-fur species was a by-product of the fur trade."[21] Kobrinksy, like Adams, Bishop, Kretch and many other researchers in this field, has subsequently revised his thesis.

In her proposal to Russell & DuMoulin, Robinson had explained the limitations of her opinion report, writing: "This will not be a comprehensive overview but will legitimize the positions taken by Kobrinsky and MacDonald in the terms of theoretical traditions in the social sciences."

Peter Grant questioned her about this:

Grant: You saw your role here as legitimizing Kobrinsky and MacDonald, not determining whether or not they could stand up under careful scrutiny of those in support and in opposition to them; isn't that right?

Robinson: Well, no.

Grant: Then why did you use the word legitimize in your proposal?

Robinson: It's one of my favourite words. But in the context of this paragraph, and in the way that cultural ecologists often do their work, is that they do use comparative examples from all over the world that investigate similar kinds of relationships or aspects of relationships between people and their environments, and what I intended to do there, not realizing that when I submitted this report in May that that would be the end of it, but what I would have liked to have done, and what I intended to do there, is put this in the context of some general ecological theories, which showed that this is not an unusual situation, that this kind of scenario occurs all over the world and it's consistent with models in ecological anthropology and cultural geography which show—explain how these relationships work. So basically what I was going to do there, rather than, as I say, not a comprehensive overview but say let's pull together perhaps a set of cultural ecological works that put this in the context and explain that this is not an unusual way of looking at the world.

Grant: I do not want to look, and I will not refer to those views that oppose or challenge Kobrinsky and MacDonald on this point. I will look and find those that support them, that was what you set out as your approach and that's what you mean by legitimize, you would buttress their theory?

Robinson: Oh, yes. And I don't see that that's objectionable at all.[22]

One of the few sources based on Gitksan-specific research that the Crown's witness relied on quite extensively was John Adams' 1969 unpublished doctoral dissertation. Adams conducted participant observation research among the Gitksan during the 1960s, before Brown's documents were available and working with the assumption that the first written records pertaining to the area began in 1867, 45 years after Brown's journal had been written. Adams' central thesis was that: "The traplines as we know them today were drawn up to regulate the fur trade which is post-contact.... How much the territories may have changed since the coming of the Whites is unknown.... The actual rate of change seems quite rapid, though Gitksan informants often deny that there are any changes at all. They assert that 'things have always been just as they are now for thousands and thousands of years.'"[23] By 1987, however, Adams, like most northwest coast scholars, was in the process of rethinking some of his earlier assumptions about the impact of the fur trade on property law among First Nations on the northwest coast. He asked, in the introduction to an issue of the academic journal, *Arctic Anthropology*, "What could possibly account for Northwest Coast stratification prior to the coming of Europeans? Unfortunately, political ideology has played a major role in this matter for at least 50 years."[24]

Robinson argued that when the earliest fur traders arrived in Gitksan and Wet'suwet'en territories, the Aboriginal population was sparse and much of the land that may have previously been used for hunting had already been "abandoned." Robinson's report described protohistoric Gitksan and Wet'suwet'en property management: "The protohistoric and early historic shift in economic emphases towards the production of furs for exchange · probably also resulted in some resource-producing areas being abandoned. In other words, new gaps emerged in the village 'patchworks.' These new gaps were probably closer to villages than the prime peripheral hunting territories. Although several of the examples cited consider European diseases a major factor contributing to the abandonment of certain territories, it can also be suggested that some territories were simply abandoned if they had few fine fur-bearers to begin with, or as their fur stocks were depleted. I envision what can be described as a centrifugal shift in territorial holdings throughout the protohistoric and historic periods, with mid-range territories being increasingly abandoned in favour of outlying ones." She went on to lay the groundwork for arguments that would emerge later that, once fur-bearing species were depleted in a given locale, the territory was simply abandoned and therefore could be "discovered," and "claimed by migrants." Of course, given that the Crown's and Robinson's argument began with the assumption that land had no meaning except what the Crown defined as an "economic" value, and therefore was not desired by Aboriginal peoples before the European-Aboriginal fur trade, it proceeds logically that there would be no value remaining after the fur trade's purposes were served.

The debate that Robinson refers to about whether changes in Gitksan and Wet'suwet'en relationships to land were primarily stimulated by their participation in the European-Aboriginal fur trade, or were the result of population loss due to smallpox epidemics is a familiar one in academic northwest coast studies and in British Columbian political culture. An outbreak of smallpox was first recorded among the Gitksan and Wet'suwet'en during the 1770s, and subsequent epidemics of measles, influenza, whooping cough, tuberculosis, and scarlet fever took a heavy toll in 1837-1838, and 1862-1863.[25] Alongside these epidemics, "lingering diseases, such as influenza, scrofula, and syphilis, observed among later native populations, can also be inferred for the early contact period" researcher Steven Acheson writes.[26]

This rapid decline in population, and the decimation and demoralization that accompanied it served to reinforce theories that Aboriginal peoples constituted a "vanishing race." This was, and is, a popular notion that both historically and contemporarily helps to rationalize the expropriation of lands and the exploitation of peoples already considered doomed to extinction. The debate about which had more impact on Indigenous societies, the arrival of commodities or the arrival of diseases, is an important one. If the Crown wanted only to prove the "facts" that changes in boundaries and borders took place during the fur trade, the cause of these changes would seem irrelevant, in a strictly "legal" sense. However, the moral and ideological differences between claiming that the lust for European commodities prompted change, rather than arguing that Aboriginal peoples were innocent victims of diseases brought by Europeans, speaks to one of western cultures' solutions to the problem of political responsibility.[27] If Indigenous peoples changed because they wanted material things, then they may be considered somehow responsible and guilty at the same time: they are responsible because they displayed rational choice behaviour in pursuing the accumulation of goods; but they are thus guilty of losing their "pristine" Aboriginality and are no longer attractive to westerners. Furthermore, this line of reasoning goes, they were compensated, in that they did receive the things they wanted; and why should they get "our" things if they don't want to become like us? There is something fundamentally "unfair" about that to a conservative, or neo-conservative imagination. It parallels the way many people feel about welfare recipients "getting something for nothing" and not suffering sufficiently to "deserve" assistance. Wealth and its pursuit are extraordinarily contradictory and confusing questions for westerners.[28] Not having it shows you to be an undeserving failure, but possibly of a kindly disposition. Having it shows you to be deserving of success, but possibly of an unkindly disposition. The accumulation of wealth is western capitalist culture's most viciously enforced imperative, while it is one of Judeo-Christianity's greatest sins.

On the other hand, if native people changed their behaviour because many of their numbers were eliminated by disease, they were not responsible. According to western biomedicine, the body is a passive victim randomly attacked by germs that do not discriminate on the basis of race, gender or social class. It would not be as morally acceptable, or politically legitimate, for Crown representatives to say out loud, "we nearly wiped you out with smallpox, so tough luck," as it is for them to say "you went for the goodies, so tough luck."

The Magic of Commodity Fetishism

The wealth of those societies in which the capitalist mode of production prevails, presents itself as an immense accumulation of commodities...

A commodity is in the first place, an object outside us, a thing that by its properties satisfied human wants of some sort or another. The nature of such wants, whether they spring from the stomach or from fancy, makes no difference...

The utility of a thing makes it a use-value.... But so soon as it steps forth as a commodity, it is changed into something transcendent...The mystical value of commodities does not originate...in their use value
—Philosopher Karl Marx, 1867, *Capital Volume 1.*

Fetishism denotes the attribution of life, autonomy, power, and even dominance to otherwise inanimate objects.... Thus, in the case of commodity fetishism, social relationships are dismembered and appear to dissolve into relationships between mere things...man has become the slave of the commodities he himself has produced but which now appear before him as objects imbued with the power to render him their tool....
—Anthropologist Michael Taussig, 1980, *The Devil and Commodity Fetishism in South America.*

Another important legal question whose answer was located in the protohistoric period was what kind of social organization existed among Aboriginal peoples at the time Britain asserted sovereignty? The Crown's case was necessarily inconsistent since they wanted to establish two contradictory arguments. First, they wanted to demonstrate that Aboriginal society was sufficiently "primitive" to legitimate the application of the doctrine of discovery/occupation/settlement, and the principle of *terra nullius*. Second, they wanted to prove that, at precisely the same moment in time—the early nineteenth century—in precisely the same place, precisely the same people were sufficiently "evolved" to have begun organizing themselves into a House and clan social structure with matrilineal descent systems and established and protected private-like property. The Crown's and Robinson's argument was that all this took place within a period of at most 78 years (1744-1822), dated from the moment Captain Cook landed at Ahousat; or perhaps over the course of 22 years (1800-1822), dated from the commencement of the land-based fur trade, and fully developed by the time William Brown described it in his 1822 journal. The Crown claimed that the sophisticated land and resource ownership system Brown documented was a response to European influences, which would render hunting and trapping for the European-Aboriginal fur trade not "aboriginal practices," according to the law. This argument also assumes that any social and cultural changes that took place after contact necessarily resulted in "European" and "not Aboriginal" practices. However, Gitksan and Wet'suwet'en involvement as active participants in the land-based fur trade began around the early 1820s: *after* William Brown's arrival. In 1803-1806, when, according to the Crown, British sovereignty was established in the area, the Gitksan's and Wet'suwet'en's lived experience of British "culture" was of having acquired a smattering of items of European manufacture, and of having met a handful of fur traders wandering through their territories.

The last gasp of the Crown's argument was to claim that the desire for, and competition over, new commodities brought by European fur traders stimulated the Gitksan and Wet'suwet'en to exploit the territories outside of their villages and at a distance from the main subsistence source of salmon in the rivers. Given the relatively few European trade goods actually present in Gitksan and Wet'suwet'en territories at the time, and the minimal actual contact that had taken place between Aboriginal and non-Aboriginal persons in the region, the Crown relied heavily on the theoretical assumption that even such minimal lived experience with things manufactured by Europeans, in a capitalist mode of production, could dramatically transform an Aboriginal society. It is not necessary to dismiss the importance of economic power and technological sophistication, or the lure of commodities and consumption, to recognize that human history and social relations are shaped by far more complex a web of interacting forces than any unicausal theory can support. Most contemporary social scientists agree that the causes of social and cultural change are multiple, the processes complex, and explanation cannot be reduced to a single, determining, causal factor like economic, or technological, or ideological change. Rather, current thinking on this subject focuses on the interactions and interrelationships between many forces and factors that produce changes in societies and cultures over time.

The Crown's argument, however, relied on archaic notions of simplistic determinism and on concepts of human nature as driven by a passion to compete with each other in a race to accumulate material goods: commodities or "things." Tracing the crucial argument about the actual impact of European goods on Aboriginal social organization from its first statement in Robinson's doctoral dissertation, to her initial proposal to Russell & DuMoulin, and then through subsequent iterations in evolving drafts of her expert opinion report written under their direction, and finally to the interrogation of her argument under cross-examination, reveals the necessary ambivalence inherent in her hypothesis. In her doctoral dissertation, Robinson had been firm about the need to avoid simplistic unicausal theories of social change. In her initial proposal to Russell & DuMoulin, Robinson suggested that the European-Aboriginal fur trade may have accelerated *already existing* trends, but did not *cause* new forms of social organization.

Peter Grant explored the question of causal theory under cross-examination, referring Robinson to her early correspondence with Russell & DuMoulin:

Grant: That's a fair statement of the state of the art in the field?

Robinson: Yes, and I would say that cultural ecologists, and that's people that deal with cultural geography, cultural anthropology and archaeology who share a common interest in the relationship between people and land and changes in those relationships, do indeed recognize that sometimes profound socioeconomic changes are triggered by relatively small or what appear to be small factors. And that often direct cause is obscured by the subsequent consequences. And this is something that I think is generally recognized as a theoretical orientation in other scholarly fields.

Grant: But there is some legitimacy to the criticism within the field that relatively minor external stimuli can trigger profound changes and patterns of socioeconomic behaviour, there is some legitimacy to the concern that this is often undemonstrable speculation?

Robinson: Not within the field, I would say that criticism is levelled at it. I think the criticism comes more from people that are outside the fields of anthropology and cultural geography who don't know where the theories of explanation are derived....[29]

In a subsequent draft proposal to Russell & DuMoulin, Robinson promised that in her report, "particular attention will also be paid to theories which regard relatively minor external stimuli as catalysts or 'triggering' factors which can provoke significant internal adjustments in socioeconomic configurations."

Robinson's final report, while employing vague and inconclusive wording, is emphatic on the question of European commodities being the 'prime-mover' or "triggering" factor causing change. And, finally, under cross examination, Robinson moved quite definitely from her initial position, reflecting the state of the art in the field—that "assumptions that relatively minor external stimuli can 'trigger' profound changes in patterns in socioeconomic behaviour are often dismissed as un-demonstrable speculation"—to the following:

Grant: Even if you accept the proposition that in 1805 some metal comes inland through the Gitksan area, are you saying that that would lead to the change to a territorially-based society from a nonterritorially-based society?

Robinson: Yes. I think that the influx of European wealth was a major triggering factor...

In the late nineteenth century, Karl Marx described a bizarre characteristic of capitalist cultures that he called a belief in "the magic of commodity fetishism." Marx claimed that, in the western European culture of his time, people behaved as if they believed that commodities, although they are inanimate objects, were endowed with a form of magical power that seduces people into believing that they need these commodities to survive. Members of capitalist cultures, Marx wrote, find themselves wanting desperately to possess many "things" and to harness the mystical power they believe the "things" possess. People begin to believe that, in order to be happy, whole persons and live a good life, they must possess these "things" by exchanging money and consuming them in the market place.

The Crown's argument about the impact of the arrival of a few European-manufactured commodities relied on the assumption that the magic of commodity fetishism was powerfully at work among the Gitksan and Wet'suwet'en peoples in north-central British Columbia during the early nineteenth century, when, according to the Crown, they were *not* organized as a capitalist society. Given this, the Crown's argument must then rest either on the assumption that commodity fetishism is a universal characteristic of human nature and not specific to capitalist cultures; or, that the Gitksan and Wet'suwet'en, as "primitive" peoples, were simplistic and easily swayed by the need for instant gratification of their desires for new "things." Once again, the foundations of the Crown's case were eurocentric at best, and racist at worse. Once again, the Crown's image of human life as driven by acquisitive desires to accumulate "things" is an impoverished one that does not represent a consensus of European thought, or non-Aboriginal "cultural values," or a desirable vision of the future.

While the Crown's arguments reflect outdated social theory, they also reinforce the very contemporary values of consumer capitalism. In asserting these theories as universally applicable and representative of "human nature," rather than as an illustration of an historically and culturally specific "belief system" of a sector of the dominant western European society, the Crown attempted to codify into law its image of the ideal self and a model of society driven by the "rationality" of individual economic accumulation and self-aggrandizement. By attributing "scientific" status to these theories of human behaviour, the Crown could dispense with the experience and analyses of the actual people involved in living these processes, since their behaviour could now be explained as being determined by "natural" forces outside themselves, over which they had neither control nor necessarily awareness. The minimal contact with European social or economic organization that the Gitksan and Wet'suwet'en had actually experienced when, according to the law, they were transformed without their knowledge into something "not truly aboriginal," was of no concern to the Crown's theories.

These theories can be traced through several centuries of European thought, and they are currently enjoying a resurgence in contemporary neo-conservatist ideologies, whose adherents can recognize only two forms of human behaviour: "either bargaining gambits—the approved behaviour of the 'successful;' or madness—the discredited behaviour of the 'failures.'"[30] If industrial capitalism's motif was represented by the slogan "I own, therefore I am," consumer capitalism's raison d'être can be expressed as "I buy, therefore I am." Our world is increasingly driven by the creation of insatiable desires for things we don't need, while our needs for what we have forgotten to desire go unmet.

The Crown's case, therefore, was empirically unsupported; scholastically archaic; logically confused; ethnocentric, eurocentric, and racist. Ultimately, it defends and enforces an image of human beings and a vision of human society that many people, Aboriginal and non-Aboriginal, including myself, reject as oppressive to the best in human potentiality.

1. Satsan 1992: 53.

2. Transcripts Vol. 291: 21865-21867.

3. Transcripts Vol. 291: 21865-21867.

4. Transcripts Vol. 291: 21966.

5. Robinson 1983.

6. Robinson 1983: 423.

7. See Wike 1951; Fisher 1977.

8. Robinson 1983: 408.

9. Robinson 1983: 425.

10. Rogers 1986: 1.

11. Bishop 1987: 7-9.

12. Wike 1951.

13. Fisher 1977.

14. See Canada, Royal Commission on Aboriginal Peoples 1993. But see also Backhouse 1991 for a feminist critique of the Royal Commission's analysis of this case.

15. Foster 1992.

16. Robinson 1987(a): 16.

17. Transcripts Vol. 293: 22157-58.

18. Transcripts Vol. 292: 22126-27.

19. MacDonald 1984.

20. MacDonald 1984: 73, quoted in Robinson 1987(a): 34.

21. Robinson, 1987(a): 24.

22. Transcripts, Vol. 289: 21747-21751.

23. Adams 1969:14; 1973.

24. Adams 1987: 69.

25. Acheson 1995: 13, Table 1.1.

26. Acheson, 1995:11. See also Boyd 1990: 137.

27. Foucault 1975; Tesh 1988.

28. See Simmel 1978.

29. Transcripts, Vol. 289: 11145.

30. Gordon 1988: 54.

Chapter 14: From a Fur Trading Frontier to a White Man's Province

The settler came to re-create an alien civilization on the frontier, while the fur traders had to operate largely within the context of the indigenous culture.... That is, generally traders reacted to what they saw, while settlers tended to react to what they expected to see.
—Historian Robin Fisher, 1977.

Believing What You See. Seeing What You Believe.

Although most of the key legal questions relevant to the "tests" for Aboriginal title and rights rested on interpretations of the pre-contact and fur trade periods, subsequent events in the history of First Nations relations with British Columbia governments and populations were also relevant. During the four-year trial of *Delgamuukw v. R.* Chief Justice McEachern was presented with evidence and arguments by the Gitksan and Wet'suwet'en, and by both the federal and provincial governments that took the form of contested historical narratives that stretched from first contact to the present

Following the fur trade, British Columbia moved into what historians call "the settlement period." The establishment of the Colony of Vancouver Island, granted to the Hudson's Bay Company by Royal Charter on January 13, 1849, marked the end of the fur trade period and the beginning of the settlement period, although significant numbers of British settlers did not begin arriving before the 1860s. The political, economic, cultural and legal implications of the transition from the fur trade to settlement are significant, since they involved a marked difference in the value—broadly defined—of land to non-Aboriginals, and created the positions of governor, members of the provincial assembly and justices of the peace. The legal practice of settlement was expressed in a rapid proliferation of laws regarding ownership of land, access to resources, and political relations between Indigenous peoples and settlers, and within and between settler populations.

The first Governor of the new colony of Vancouver Island was a lawyer, Richard Blanchard, appointed in 1849. He proved unequal to the task at hand, and was replaced in 1851 by James Douglas, Chief Factor of the Hudson's Bay Company at Fort Victoria, who assumed the additional position of governor. Douglas was the son of a Scots trader and a "free coloured woman" of British

Guyana. His wife was the child of a Hudson's' Bay Company factor and a Cree woman. Fisher describes Douglas' attitudes as "a mixture in which the knowledge of the fur trader was accompanied by the paternalistic concerns of the nineteenth-century humanitarian."[1] In this way, Douglas embodied and personified the transitional historical period he governed.

Fourteen agreements were made between Governor Douglas and various Aboriginal nations on Vancouver Island between 1850 and 1854; that have become known as the "Douglas Treaties."[2] The questions about Douglas and, particularly, "the Douglas treaties," that are legally important today can be summarized as follows: First, were these agreements treaties, or merely private purchases made by the Hudson's Bay Company? Second, did Douglas recognize Aboriginal title in a proprietary sense, or merely in the use and occupancy sense? Third, did Douglas recognize an Aboriginal interest in all lands, or only those "under cultivation, village sites or fenced fields?" Fourth, did Douglas take a consistent stand throughout his period as governor, or did he change his mind, or did the instructions he received from London change over time?

While scholars concur that these agreements should be interpreted as treaties that clearly recognized some form of Aboriginal interest in the land and that required explicit cession and/or extinguishment, there are debates about what the scope of the Aboriginal title Douglas recognized was. Fisher, for example, argues that the treaties were based on current British opinion about the nature of Aboriginal land tenure.[3] He concluded that Douglas was authorized only to confirm a right of occupancy of lands under cultivation, village sites and fenced fields, but not to recognize Aboriginal title as equivalent to ownership or sovereignty in a European sense. Indians would have hunting and gathering rights over other lands as long as these were "waste" and not allocated to settlers. Political scientist Paul Tennant disagrees with Fisher. He argues that: "The most important fact about the Douglas treaties is that they stand as unequivocal recognition of aboriginal title. It was with this initial acknowledgement that the British established their rule in British Columbia."[4]

It has been argued—and here we encounter the beginning of another dominant theme in Aboriginal/state relations—that one reason for Douglas having ceased to address the question of Indian title was that, as the costs of administering the colony increased, neither the Hudson's Bay Company nor London allocated a sufficient increase of funds to accomplish the task.[5]

The colonial office in London, and the legislative assembly in Victoria, were both concerned not only, or even principally, with Indian matters. Rather, they were consumed with planning a very culturally-specific and homogenous colony. An early instruction to the governor of the colony of British Columbia was to insure the transfer of "a cross section of British society to the colony," and a process whereby "a just proportion of labour and capital" would be achieved, and "paupers, squatters and land speculators" would be prevented from settling.[6] Their ambition to create a civilized "whiteman's province" would be expressed in immigration and settlement policies, state ideology, popular sentiment and sporadic outbursts of hostility and violence towards Asians as well as Aboriginal peoples throughout the province's history.[7]

Douglas initially respected Aboriginal law to the extent that he regularly ordered Europeans to pay compensation to the families of victims injured by them. During the course of the 1850s, however, Douglas increasingly invoked British law to settle both European-Native disputes and intra-Native disputes. In 1855 he wrote optimistically that he thought the Indians were beginning to have a clearer idea of the nature of British law which, he said, was "the first step in the progress of civilization."[8] Governor Douglas appointed his brother-in-law, David Cameron, a linen-draper from the West Indies, as Supreme court Justice in 1853, and as Chief Justice in 1856.

The Gold Rush of 1857-58 brought the Pacific northwest to the forefront of Britain's interests in North America.[9] The summer of 1858 began with the arrival of 400 miners in Victoria, and by September there were thousands.[10] With the influx of miners and increasing numbers of settlers, Douglas gave up his former practice of "legal pluralism" and insisted that Indians and Whites alike seek redress through representatives of British law rather than through traditional modes or individual retaliation.[11]

In 1858, the British established direct rule on the mainland, creating British Columbia. Douglas resigned as Chief Factor of the Hudson's Bay Company and retained the position of Governor only. In 1861, the House of Assembly passed a petition in which they stated their belief that "the extinction of Aboriginal title is obligatory on the Imperial Government,"[12] and sent it to the Duke of Newcastle, seeking funds to extinguish Aboriginal title. The requested funds never arrived. Instead, the Duke of Newcastle wrote back acknowledging, "...the great importance of purchasing without loss of time the native title to the soil of Vancouver Island...but the acquisition of the title is a purely Colonial Interest and the Legislature must not entertain any expectation that the British Taxpayer will be burthened to supply the funds or British Credit pledged for the purpose."[13]

This correspondence has become important in contemporary litigation. If it can be shown that the British Crown, and/or the Parliament of Canada, recognized Aboriginal title in British Columbia, then the more recent story constructed by the Province of British Columbia's lawyers that posits an uninterrupted and uncontradicted history of *non-recognition* by the Crown of Aboriginal title from the moment of contact is significantly challenged.

As always, politicians and jurists engaged in rationalizing colonial rule drew in various ways from the intellectual climate of their times. Charles Darwin had published *Origin of the Species* in 1859. His theories hardened into doctrine, and the fiction that the British represented a superior race, and the Aboriginals an inferior one, was rapidly transformed from speculative hypotheses, into pseudo-scientific dogma, popular mythology, and ideological justifications for colonization. John Locke's theories were increasingly drawn upon and popularized as scientific and moral justifications for colonization. Fundamental to this social evolutionary ideology is the notion of an absolute and unbridgeable difference between races. In the absence of recognition of cultural similarities, negatively valued difference ruled the day. Increasingly, Aboriginal peoples were represented in local provincial, Canadian and British literature and propaganda as "wild savages," rather than "noble savages." Historian Robin Fisher explains: "The British colonist established a line of cleavage based on race and could not permit any crossing of that barrier by admitting that the Indian was in any way comparable to western man."[14]

When, in 1864, local legislative assemblies replaced direct rule by London, James Douglas retired as governor and was replaced by Frederick Seymour in British Columbia and Arthur Kennedy on Vancouver Island. Neither Seymour nor Kennedy were actively concerned with Indian land rights and they left the responsibility for policy-making in this area to their newly-appointed Chief Commissioner of Lands, Joseph Trutch. Trutch "personified settler interests and attitudes, considering Indians 'as bestial rather than human,' 'uncivilized savages,' 'ugly and lazy,' 'lawless and violent.'"[15]

Trutch turned to Social Darwinism for justification of his policies. He argued that Indians had not evolved to the stage where they could conceptualize ideas of property. Furthermore, following Locke, he reasoned that hunting, fishing and gathering did not involve the application of human labour to the transformation or cultivation of the land, and therefore, he claimed, the Indians were not using the land efficiently. Trutch disposed of the Douglas Treaties, claiming that, since there had been neither civilization nor law among the First Nations, no treaties had been required. He argued that the monies given to Indians during negotiations were to purchase short-term peace and not to purchase or extinguish title, which was not necessary. He invented a rule that a maximum of ten acres should be allotted to each adult Indian male, and then reduced the allocations of reserve lands that Douglas had laid out accordingly.

Douglas, in an effort to encourage Indian assimilation, had guaranteed Indians the right to acquire land under the same conditions as those offered to settlers; that is, by cultivating it and building on it. His vision was that Indians would move off the reserves after having been cared for, civilized, and Christianized by missionaries, and would then become equal citizens of the colony. Trutch passed an ordinance that prohibited Indians from pre-empting land without the written permission of the Governor. By 1875, there was only one, single case of an Indian pre-empting land under this condition.[16]

Vancouver Island and the mainland were united into one colony, British Columbia, in 1866. By this time the Aboriginal population had been reduced to approximately 40,000 people, although there were still less than 100 non-Aboriginal residents in the Gitksan and Wet'suwet'en territory and the "whites depended on Indian participation for the success of most economic activity."[17]

Smallpox and other diseases continued to decimate the Aboriginal population throughout the latter half of the nineteenth century. However, as was the pattern in British Columbia, the Gitksan and Wet'suwet'en continued, during the settlement period, to fish, hunt, gather and trade with each other, with other Aboriginal groups, and now, with non-Aboriginals. In fact, they furnished the Hudson's Bay Company staff with most of their requirements.[18] The economic interests of the non-Indians at the time were limited to the extraction and transportation of resources, particularly furs and gold.

Missionaries joined fur traders and settlers at what had now become a European frontier. The interests and ideologies of these diverse groups were not always identical. Settlers, for the most part, assumed that Indians were "primitive" peoples destined by natural selection to vanish. Aboriginal claims could therefore be ignored, and certainly need not be considered serious obstacles to settlement. Missionaries, however, were intent on saving heathen souls, and many believed that Indians need not vanish, but could survive if they ceased to be Indians and assimilated into the dominant white society.[19] Hence, missionaries often placed themselves in the position of protectors of the Indians against the rapacious disregard shown by settlers and the calculated manipulations of traders; and as advocates on behalf of Aboriginal peoples in representations to governments. Into their pre-existing life ways and institutions First Nations incorporated: near annihilation by relentless epidemics of infectious diseases; Christianity; wage labour in guiding, packing, canoeing, and mining; and, later on in the century, employment in fish canneries.

To the settlers, Aboriginals were wild, wicked children. To the missionaries, Aboriginals were noble, innocent children. To the governments, Aboriginals were a potentially expensive legal and social problem. To the merchants, Aboriginals were suppliers and consumers of commodities. To some non-Aboriginal individuals, Aboriginal individuals were friends, lovers, co-workers, spouses and relatives.

On the One Hand, and On the Other...

Federal jurisdiction is derived from s. 91(24) of the Constitution Act, 1867, which has been read to permit Parliament to single out native people and treat them differently than non-native people. Parliament is also entitled to treat native people the same as non-native people under laws passed pursuant to other heads of federal power...for example, The Fisheries Act. Provincial legislatures are not entitled to treat native people differently than non-native people, but can pass laws regulating native forms of life so long as such laws are of general application and do not touch on matters which are inherently Indian....

In the end all this means that Parliament and provincial legislatures pass laws regulating the life and culture of native people without native consent.

—Legal scholar Patrick Macklem, 1991.

Canadian Confederation under the *British North America Act* (*B.N.A. Act*) took place in 1867. Consistent with the theory articulated in the Royal Proclamation of 1763, the Crown's underlying title and sovereignty were confirmed. Section 91(24) of the *B.N.A. Act* conferred on the federal Parliament jurisdiction over "Indians and Lands reserved for Indians." Provincial governments were given jurisdiction over wildlife and game, education, health, social services and some justice and corrections areas. Provincial authority in these areas encompasses the entire population, including Aboriginal peoples, but the province may not pass legislation specifically addressed to Indians. Hence the legal and legislative basis for the historic provincial government policy of refusing to recognize Aboriginal people as distinct populations.

British Columbia did not join Confederation until 1871. Negotiations between London, Ottawa and Victoria began two years earlier in 1869. Both London and Ottawa expressed concerns about the fact that British Columbia did not appear to have a process in place for legally extinguishing Aboriginal title and releasing land for settlement. The Colonial Office queried the absence of treaties based on the Royal Proclamation of 1763. The British Columbia delegation, represented by Joseph Trutch as chief negotiator, spent June and July of 1870 in Ottawa negotiating the Terms of Union which were passed by Order-in-Council in July 1870. Clause 13 refers to Indians:

> The charge of the Indians, and the trusteeship and management of the lands reserved for their use and benefit, shall be assumed by the Dominion Government, and a policy as liberal as that hitherto pursued by the British Columbia Government shall be continued by the Dominion Government after the Union.

To carry out such a policy, tracts of land of such extent as it has hitherto been the practice of the British Columbia Government to appropriate for that purpose, shall from time to time be conveyed by the local government to the dominion government in trust for the use and benefit of the Indians on application of the dominion government; and in case of disagreement between the governments respecting the quantity of such tracts of land to be so granted, the matter shall be referred for the decision of the Secretary of State for the Colonies.

In effect, the Terms of Union gave the province of B.C. direct title to all public lands. Confident that the "Indian title question" was resolved, the province now lumped Indians together with non-white immigrants as ineligible for even the most basic civil rights, including the vote. By 1871, a theory of Aboriginal title in British Columbia, legitimized by Lockean political theory and nineteenth-century evolutionism, had been formalized in colonial policy and articulated in popular ideology as the "founding myth of White British Columbia." It remained yet to be codified into law to become "the truth." No Aboriginal representatives were involved in the negotiations or agreements that led up to the passing of either the *British North America Act* or the Terms of Union.

It was not until after 1870 that the Gold Rush brought large numbers of whites, including surveyors, miners, merchants, missionaries and government administrators to the Gitksan and Wet'suwet'en territory. A permanent white settlement was established at Hazelton, but whites remained a numerical minority, who continued to buy large quantities of dried salmon and other foodstuffs from the local Indians."[20]

Joseph Trutch wrote to the Prime Minister of Canada, Sir John A. MacDonald, in 1872, offering his analysis of the situation: "We have here in B.C. a population numbering from 40,000 to 50,000, by far the larger portion of whom are utter savages living along the coast, frequently committing murder and robbery among themselves...and only restrained from more outrageous crime by being always treated with firmness and by the consistent enforcement of the law...."

The negotiations surrounding Indian policy in the Terms of Union of 1871 are of considerable contemporary legal and political significance since arguments have been made by historians that Trutch intentionally allowed a mistaken impression to remain with federal officials that the Indian policy in British Columbia, like that in the rest of the country, had dealt with Indian title by treaty before opening land for settlement. In the rest of Canada, major treaties with Indians west of Ontario had been signed during the 1870s; and reserve lands were being allocated on the basis of the national 80 acres per family standard, and not the 10 acres per adult male actually being allocated in B.C. If Trutch did, in fact, intentionally deceive federal officials, this evidence would support the Aboriginal argument that the federal government has consistently recognized their interests, whereas the provincial government has not. More to the point, such a finding of fraudulent action would place in doubt the legal status of *all* land title throughout the province, and would cast a shadow on British Columbian settlers' history and self-image. Former Governor James Douglas wrote to federal Superintendent of Indian Affairs Powell to protest Trutch's allocations, and stated that his intention and practice as Governor had been to allocate whatever lands the Indians themselves identified as being required.[21] In 1873, Sir John A. MacDonald, having realized that Trutch was allocating only 10 acres to adult males, officially requested the Province of B.C. adopt the 80 acre per family national standard for allocation of reserve lands.

In 1874 the B.C. legislature passed the B.C. Lands Act aimed at consolidating previous laws affecting Crown lands. The following year the federal government took an extraordinary action when the Dominion Deputy Minister of Justice ordered the provincial law disallowed, in part because it did not take into account Aboriginal title, and prevented Indians from pre-empting land without written permission from the government. The federal Deputy Minister cited the Royal Proclamation of 1763 in support of his position, arguing that British Columbia, by being the only province not to follow British policy in this regard, jeopardized the "honour of the Crown."[22]

Following the federal government's disallowal of the B.C. Lands Act in 1875, the federal and provincial governments agreed to constitute a joint federal-provincial reserve commission to examine the land question. Three Commissioners were appointed to the Indian Reserve Commission: former Hudson's Bay Company men, Anderson and McKinlay, for the federal government and provincial government respectively; and Gilbert Sproat, a settler and self-taught ethnographer who had lived among the Nuu'chah'nulth of Vancouver Island, as a third. No Aboriginal people were consulted or involved either in the formation of the Commission, or in the development of its terms of reference. Some First Nations, when advised that they would not be permitted to discuss Aboriginal title but would be limited to pleading for reserve allocations, boycotted the process. Some attended the hearings, defied the agenda, and spoke about their land rights. Others set out detailed arguments for specific reserve allocations.

In order to assist the Commission, the provincial legislature moved to have the *Papers Connected with the Indian Land Question in British Columbia, 1850-1875* ("The Papers") published. Joseph Trutch, however, managed to withhold the collected papers from the legislative assembly, and, more importantly, from the Indian Reserve Commission.[23] The withholding of this publication from public, particularly Aboriginal, access would play an important part in future relations between Aboriginal peoples and the British Columbia provincial government. *The Papers* contain correspondence between the British Colonial Office and, first Douglas, and then Trutch. That is, *The Papers* constitute the official documentary record of the critical period in British Columbia history when the Crown consolidated its title to the province's lands.

A reading of *The Papers* leaves little doubt about a few key legal and historical points. For one thing, it is clear that the British Crown was initially cognizant of, and anxious to settle, Aboriginal interests in land. For another, the British Crown clearly wanted this accomplished in as "legal" and "humanitarian" a way as possible, reflecting the principles of British colonial law and policy. That the British Crown had consistently assumed that the Royal Proclamation of 1763 applied to British Columbia, and that its terms should provide a framework for negotiating treaties with First Nations in British Columbia is also plainly and repeatedly stated in *The Papers*. On the other hand, the Crown did not wish to pay the costs effected by these policies, nor did they want any problems to arise that might impede settlement. The balance between humanitarian concern and economic efficiency shifts repeatedly throughout, but by the end of the twenty-five year period covered by *The Papers*, settlement—and settlers'—interests are clearly at the forefront. When choices had to be made between spending money or dispensing justice, Aboriginal interests were consistently sacrificed. Correspondence from first colonial, and then provincial officials, follows a similar pattern and conclusion. The shift in attitude and position from Douglas to Trutch is plainly represented. The documents tell neither a humanitarian, nor a heroic, nor a law-abiding story. Greed, dishonesty, petty corruption and a lust for power sporadically justified by racism, crude even for its time, are what the *Papers Connected with the Indian Land Question in British Columbia, 1850-1875* reveal.

---

1. Fisher 1977: 68.

2. See Fisher 1977; Madill 1981; Tennant 1990(a).

3. See Fisher 1977; Duff 1969.

4. Tennant 1990(a): 20.

5. Fisher, 1977: 150.

6. Fisher, 1977: 60.

7. The literature on race relations in British Columbia has grown substantially in recent years. An entry into this literature can be obtained through the following: Adachi 1976; Hudson (ed.) 1997; Johnston 1989; Li 1988; Roy 1989; Ward 1978.

8. Fisher, 1977: 65.

9. See Knafla 1986(b); McLaren, Foster, and Orloff (eds.) 1992.

10. Fisher 1977: 95.

11. Galois 1992. See also Foster 1981, 1992(b); McLaren, Foster and Orloff (eds.) 1992.

12. Public Archives, Ottawa, C.O. 305/17, 133-34.

13. Newcastle to Douglas, 19 October 1861, *Papers*, 214.

14. Fisher, 1977: 93.

15. Tennant 1990(a): 39.

16. Fisher 1977: 165.

17. Galois 1987: 21.

18. Ray 1987: 83.

19. Fisher 1977: 143.

20. Ray, 1987: 83.

21. Douglas to Powell, 14 October, 1874, *Papers* p. 53. British Columbia officially agreed to 20 acres, but never honoured the agreement in practice (Tennant 1990: 46).

21. Province of British Columbia, Papers of the Legislative Assembly, 37th, Victoria 1873-74: 1027-28.

22. See Fisher 1977: 187; Tennant 1990: 47.

Chapter 15: Old Questions. New Century.

From time immemorial the limits of the district in which our hunting grounds are have been well defined. This district extends from a rocky point called "Andemane," some two and a half or three miles above our village on the Skeena River to a creek called "She-quin-khaat," which empties into the Skeena about two miles below Lorne Creek.

We claim the ground on both sides of the river, as well as the river within these limits, and as all our hunting, fruit gathering and fishing operations are carried on in this district, we can truly say we are occupying it.

—Gitksan Chiefs of Gitwangak, 1884.[1]

The First Definite Hint...

This claim was presented to the Provincial Government of British Columbia in 1884. Witness for the Crown in *Delgamuukw v. R.* and popular historian, David Ricardo Williams described this petition presented by the Gitwangak Chief as "the first definite hint by natives that they possessed proprietary rights."[2]

The *Indian Act* had been passed in 1876, bringing every aspect of Aboriginal life under the scrutiny and administration of the federal government.[3] In 1884 clauses were added that outlawed the carrying out of, or assisting in, or purchasing or supplying goods for, or communicating about, potlatching, sundancing, and other Aboriginal cultural practices. Since these ceremonies were also the means by which vital events like births, marriages and deaths were recorded in the oral tradition, and where transfers of lands and rights through inheritance or alliance were witnessed and effected, this ban constituted a criminalization of Aboriginal cultural, political, legal and economic institutions and practices. The *Indian Act* also delegitimated traditional chiefs and systems of law. These further incursions on their ways of life increased resentment on the part of First Nations towards the governments, and led to more and varied forms of protest against, and resistance to, the colonial regime.

Native resistance took on a number of forms during this period. Individual confrontations decreased, nativist and syncretist religious movements[4] began, and organized public protests and petitions became common place. In 1872 a large crowd of Coast Salish people assembled outside the New Westminster Land Registry office to protest the illegal seizure of their lands. Throughout the 1870s various groups sent petitions and delegations to state their grievances to government. Four issues preoccupied them: (i) recognition of Aboriginal title; (ii) insufficient and arbitrary reserve land allocations; (iii) encroachment on lands and resources by whites; (iv) lack of support from governments for developing agriculture and animal husbandry.[5]

In 1885 three Coast Tsimshian chiefs, accompanied by missionary William Duncan, became the first of many delegations to travel to Ottawa "to tell them our troubles about our land."[6] Among the Chiefs' principle demands was that a public inquiry be held into the land question. By way of response, Provincial Premier Smithe agreed to a meeting between federal, provincial and Nishga and Tsimshian leaders. He insisted, however, that missionaries, who he alleged had put the idea of land title into the minds of Aboriginal peoples to begin with, not be allowed to attend. The federal and provincial governments did, however, agree to a public inquiry that began in the winter months of 1887. Nishga Chief David Mackay addressed the hearings. He said:

> What we don't like about the Government is their saying this: "We will give you this much land."

> How can they give it when it is our own? We cannot understand it. They have never bought it from us or our forefathers. They have never fought and conquered our people and taken the land in that way, and yet they say now that they will give us so much land—our own land.

> These chiefs do not talk foolishly, they know the land is their own; our forefathers for generations and generations past had their land here all around us; chiefs have had their own hunting grounds, their salmon streams, and places where they got their berries; it has always been so. It is not only during the last four or five years that we have seen the land; we have always seen and owned it; it is not new thing, it has been ours for generations.

> If we had only seen it for twenty years and claimed it as our own, it would have been foolish, but it has been ours for thousands of years. If any strange person came here and saw the land for twenty years and claimed it, he would be foolish. We have always got our living from the land; we are not like white people who live in towns and have their stores and other business, getting their living in that way, but we have always depended on the land for our food and clothes; we get our salmon, berries, and furs from the land.[7]

British Columbia Premier Smithe dismissed the First Nations' claims, telling them:

When the whites first came among you, you were little better than the wild beasts of the field.... The land all belongs to the Queen.... A reserve is given to each tribe, and they are not required to pay for it. It is the Queen's land just the same, but the Queen gives it to her Indian children because they do not know so well how to make their own living the same as a white man, and special indulgence is extended to them, and special care shown.

Thus, instead of being treated as a white man, the Indian is treated better. But it is the hope of everybody that in a little while the Indians will be so far advanced as to be the same as a white man in every respect. Do you understand what I say?[8]

The Crown's legal arguments in *Delgamuukw v. R.*, whose answers lie in what took place during this historical period, centred on questions of "abandonment" of land and "acquiescence" to colonial rule. The Crown continued and expanded their claims that Aboriginal lands were frequently "abandoned." The Crown alleged that, being anxious to assimilate and participate in the new—superior—economy and culture, Aboriginal peoples voluntarily abandoned their traditional territories and outlying villages, along with fishing, hunting, gathering and trapping activities, and became wage labourers. They settled into villages that the government then "gave" them as reserves, and eagerly converted to Christianity. Their lands—never really "owned" in European terms in the first place, and now abandoned and unused by previous claimants anyway—became available for pre-emption and settlement by settlers.

The Crown argued that Aboriginal people complied with colonial rule and did not mount important or serious resistance. Not only did the Crown have the absolute right to "implicitly" extinguish Aboriginal title by simply declaring sovereignty and imposing British law; but, the Crown argued, First Nations "implicitly" consented to extinguishment, and to other assimilation policies, both legally and culturally. When federal and provincial laws were enacted and Indians obeyed them, so the interpretation goes, they were effecting legal extinguishment of title, whether they knew it, or intended to, or not.

The Gitksan and Wet'suwet'en argued that they had never consented to extinguishment of their Aboriginal title and rights. When they complied, sometimes, with various laws, they did so, they testified, either because they agreed with them in spirit, or because they were coerced by force of arms and/or numbers, to accommodate the settlers and governments. As to abandoning their lands—again, they argued that they had not abandoned hunting and trapping and fishing practices or territories, but continue to use them for purposes other than permanently residing on them or gaining *all* of their subsistence and livelihood from them. Furthermore, they argued, to the extent that people have ceased earning their living from the land, it has not necessarily been by choice, but rather because they have been prohibited by laws and regulations from accessing their lands and resources, and from trading and selling the products of their territories. Therefore, by force of necessity, many have had to earn their living in the Euro-Canadian controlled economy.

In 1888 the first significant legal case involving issues of Aboriginal title and the effect of the Royal Proclamation of 1763 in Canada was heard in Ontario. In *St. Catherine's Milling and Lumber Co. v. R.*[9] the issue in dispute was the legality of a logging permit issued by the federal government to the private St. Catherine's Milling and Lumber Co. Lord Watson, of the Judicial Committee of the Privy Council of the House of Lords in Britain, ruled that only the federal government had the right to enter into treaties and extinguish Aboriginal title, and that Aboriginal title had no pre-existence, but was created by the British Crown through its recognition in the Royal Proclamation. Aboriginal title, as a creation of the British Crown, could remain in effect only "at the pleasure of the Crown" and could be eliminated by any contrary action by the Crown, however implicit, Watson's ruling concluded. Lawyers for the Province of British Columbia in the *Delgamuukw* case cited the *St. Catherine's Milling and Lumber Co.* decision as a precedent in support of their arguments.

It was by reading newspaper reports about the *St. Catherine's Milling and Lumber Co.* case that British Columbia Indians became aware for the first time of the Royal Proclamation of 1763, and seized upon it as evidence that the British Crown should in fact, by their own law, recognize and guarantee Aboriginal rights. "The idea that there could be imperial intervention in indigenous policy in Canada was no Indian invention. The Royal Proclamation of 1763 represented imperial recognition of Indian political and territorial rights against local 'frauds and abuses'," legal scholar Douglas Sanders explains. "As this became known among British Columbia Indians, they began to discuss the possibility of taking their case directly to London."[10] British Columbia Aboriginal peoples, then and now, interpreted the Royal Proclamation's words to mean what they said: that the Crown recognized Indian nations and land rights and pledged to protect them. What Aboriginal peoples didn't anticipate was that sovereigns, and representatives of sovereigns, could and would interpret this Proclamation in various abstract ways, including the interpretation that, since B.C. First Nations did not exist "in the eyes of the Sovereign" in 1763, they could be excluded from consideration under the terms of the Proclamation. They appear to have failed to understand the magic land ownership possessed by the omnipotent hovering sovereign.[11]

The Crown arguments described above, however, are *post hoc* rationalizations developed in the 1960s. It would be a mistake to assume that law is monolithic and cannot or did not adapt to local contingencies if opportunity demanded. When, in 1898, Beaver Indians assembled at Fort St. John demanding a treaty before they would allow gold seekers into their territory, the federal government complied. At the time there were few white settlers in the region, and, once the provincial government was assured that they would not be financially responsible for treaty annuities, they did not oppose the process. Treaty 8, signed in 1899 and covering a corner of north-eastern British Columbia, acknowledged the pre-existence of Aboriginal title and the applicability of the terms of the Royal Proclamation of 1763 to British Columbia, including the requirement that consent must be obtained before extinguishment of title can be legally valid. However, rather than being recognized as a precedent supporting the application of the Royal Proclamation of 1763 to British Columbia, succeeding British Columbia jurists have relegated Treaty 8 to the category of an anomaly, and ignored it.

The late nineteenth century witnessed the beginning of an important theme in British Columbia Aboriginal history. Some First Nations, like, for example, the Nishga, began early on in their contact with Europeans to successfully articulate their pre-existing economic and political structures to those of the Europeans. An Indigenous elite, well schooled in English language and law, developed under the tutelage of Anglican missionaries. Participation in the commercial fishing industry has formed the economic basis of a network of wealthy families on the coast, who have succeeded very well for generations, by anyone's standards. Had the predictions of European anthropological and social theories been realized, the expected outcome should have been the rapid assimilation of these successful individuals into Canadian society. In British Columbia, however, these families have formed the backbone of the anti-colonial resistance struggle and the movement for recognition of Aboriginal title. Money earned in fishing and logging has been churned back into communities and nativistic movements through continued feasting and potlatching—despite legal prohibition—and has funded the development of political organizations, the employment of lawyers, and the sending of delegations to Ottawa and London. During the 1890s the Nishga led a province-wide protest movement among Aboriginal peoples. They established their own newspaper and used it as a vehicle for organizing and educating Indians all over the province.

A census was taken in British Columbia in 1880 that listed First Nations as a majority of the total population of 49,459. The census of 1891 counted 98,173 persons in the provincial population, of which only one third—around 35,000—were Indians. During the 1870s and 1880s a sudden and large influx of miners had poured into British Columbia; a colonial administration had been established and an array of laws governing lands, resources and policing were enacted. Intensive white settlement began, missionaries arrived, and smallpox decreased the Aboriginal population substantially. Aboriginal people took employment in the new industries and continued working on their lands, and mounted a wide range of resistance activities at local, provincial, national and international levels aimed at maintaining control over lands and resources.

During the early years of the nineteenth century, British colonial policy had been strongly influenced by humanitarian sentiment in Britain that conceptualized the mission of Britain to be to "take the evils of slavery, ignorance and paganism at source, to extend to the simpler people the benefits of steam, free trade and revealed religion, and to establish not a world empire in the Napoleonic sense but a moral empire of loftier interest."[12] This is known in legal terminology as the "trusteeship theory of colonialism," and in anthropological literature as colonization through "tutelage."[13] Benevolent white colonial parent; innocent brown Indigenous child.

By the latter half of the nineteenth century, however, racial attitudes in Britain began to harden and move away from the previous humanitarian approach. Armed rebellions like the Indian mutiny, wars in South Africa, Maori-European wars, and rebellion in the West Indies were once again fuelling the "wild savage" image, always the other side of the same coin on which the "noble savage" is stamped. Land-hungry settlers rationalized that the "wild savages" were incapable of using their lands productively, but could be disciplined as agricultural labourers on White-owned farms. Strict white colonial parent; incorrigible brown Indigenous child.

Debates about this period engaged in by the parties in dispute during the *Delgamuukw* trial consisted in the Gitksan and Wet'suwet'en and their witnesses arguing that First Nations' resistance to colonial rule had been firm and consistent since contact, had employed a range of strategies, and had taken place in diverse forums according to circumstances. The Crown countered that, throughout the era in question, Aboriginal peoples had been abandoning life on the land, acquiescing to colonial rule, and rapidly and voluntarily assimilating into Euro-Canadian society. Evidence of protests was dismissed by the Crown as either the work of "outside agitators" like missionaries or as the unfounded complaints of a dissident minority of Indians. The Crown interpreted any First Nation compliance with colonial law and policy, or any participation in the Euro-Canadian controlled economy as proof of voluntary assimilation.

The early years of the twentieth century saw increasing agricultural settlement and the beginnings of serious land speculation in Gitksan and Wet'suwet'en territory in anticipation of railroad construction. The Boer War that ended in 1905 ushered in an era of large scale expropriation of Gitksan and Wet'suwet'en lands to provide veterans with "unoccupied farmlands." Crown witness David Williams described a number of incidents in this period where "Indians took up arms against whites pre-empting land." But, Williams concluded, these episodes "did not seem to have been provoked by aboriginal claims."[14]

The Era Of Permanent Penetration

Any person who without the consent of the Superintendent General
expressed in writing receives, obtains, solicits, or requests from any
Indian any payment or contribution, or promise of any payment or
contribution, for the purpose of raising a fund or providing money for
the prosecution of any claim which, the tribe or band of Indians to
which such Indian belongs, or of which he is a member, has or is
represented to have, for the recovery of any claim or money for the
benefit of the said tribe or band, shall be guilty of an offence and liable
upon summary conviction for each such offence to a penalty not
exceeding two hundred dollars and not less than fifty dollars, or to
imprisonment for any term not exceeding two months.
—*Indian Act*, Section 141, amended 1927.

Dr. Arthur Ray's opinion report on economic history concluded that, during the period 1860-1915, the Gitksan's and Wet'suwet'en's traditions were not incompatible with "progress" or "development." Ray discussed numerous attempts made by local Indians to farm, log and become involved in the commercial fishery. A few succeeded, but many were thwarted by lack of support from government, and hostility by settlers. Because Indians were then, and still are, legally wards of the Crown, their lands are "held in trust for them by the Queen." They could not use their lands or resources as collateral to obtain loans, or to capitalize development of their lands, or become involved in commercial ventures. Although interested in pursuing new forms of economic activity, the Gitksan and Wet'suwet'en did not equate this with either assimilation or acquiescence, seeing wage labour and business as ways to enhance and supplement their already existing economy.

Ray documented the persistent, and largely successful, resistance to external domination of their economy practised by the Gitksan and Wet'suwet'en during this period. He argued that their efforts were impeded when "federal and provincial governments passed conservation legislation which curtailed their economic flexibility and weakened their subsistence base. The economic activities of the Gitksan, Wet'suwet'en and Babine in the Upper Skeena River area had not created the problems that this legislation was intended to resolve. Rather, the laws were needed to protect resource-based industries, particularly the salmon canning industry that had been developed by Euro-Canadians outside of the region."[15]

Both the Gitksan and Wet'suwet'en, and the Crown called additional expert witnesses to testify before Chief Justice McEachern during the trial of *Delgamuukw v. R.* on settlement history and the impact this had on Aboriginal cultures. Dr. Robert Galois, an historical geographer, testified for the Gitksan and the Wet'suwet'en. Galois described the 1890s as the years of the Klondike

Gold Rush and the building of the Dominion telegraph line over Gitksan territory. He noted that, while new opportunities and sources of wealth in some ways enhanced and elaborated pre-existing Aboriginal practices, they also produced adjustments in the internal division of labour and changes in the "seasonal round" of activities. And, with Europeans came, as always, disease and Christianity. Significant population decline brought about by diseases led to changes in settlement patterns, and some elements of Christian practices and beliefs modified the feasting system.[16]

David Ricardo Williams was called by the Crown to counter Galois' testimony. Referring to the early years of the twentieth century in British Columbia as the "era of permanent penetration," Williams painted a picture of Gitksan and Wet'suwet'en peoples eagerly complying with the colonial government's assertion of jurisdiction over them, and with the arrival of Euro-Canadian-owned resource extraction companies. To support his arguments he relied on evidence that First Nations did not engage in large-scale armed rebellions and worked in white-owned resource extraction industries. They engaged in very little vandalism, and were generally considered good workers by their non Aboriginal employers.[17]

Damned if they do and damned if they don't: had Aboriginal peoples organized armed rebellions, committed acts of vandalism, refused to participate in the new economy, or failed to succeed as workers and producers, they would have been deemed backward, culturally underdeveloped, and unworthy of equal legal, political and property rights. Not having chosen these strategies, they are analyzed as having surrendered their lands and rights, are deemed assimilated, and unworthy of distinct legal, political and property rights. Heads the Crown wins. Tails, Indians lose.

In 1906, the Coast and Interior Salish peoples sent a delegation of chiefs to London where they were told that their grievances could only be dealt with by the Canadian federal government.[18] In 1907, the Nishga Land Committee was organized within the framework of Aboriginal social structure: the sixteen members represented each of the four clans in the four Nishga villages. Wealthy and worldly wise aristocrats and successful fishermen, photographs of the Nishga Land Committee taken during this era show sixteen solemn men, well-dressed in tailored three-piece suits, silver and gold watch chains, and polished leather shoes.

It was at this time that a new partner joined the dance: lawyer and advocate Arthur O'Meara. O'Meara had practised law in Ontario for twenty years before moving to British Columbia, where he became an Anglican missionary. He served as sole legal advisor to the Indian Rights Association and the Nishga Land Committee, and formed the Society of Friends of the Indians of B.C. to raise money and sponsor public talks. O'Meara and the Nishga Land Committee prepared a lengthy petition to the Crown that included a declaration of traditional Nishga ownership, reiterated the terms and conditions set out in the Royal Proclamation of 1763, and explained that these terms had not yet been met in British Columbia.

The following year, 1908, a delegation of Gitksan chiefs travelled to Ottawa to present a petition protesting the wrongful expropriation of their territory. In the summer of 1909, Interior Nations gathered and formed an organization named the Interior Tribes of British Columbia that then amalgamated with the Nishga and other First Nations on the north coast to form the Indian Rights Association. A delegation of chiefs met with Prime Minister Wilfred Laurier during his 1910 tour of British Columbia and articulated their case. Laurier assured them he would look into it; and, if he found the facts warranted it, would not hesitate to forward the Indian Rights Association's petition to the Judicial Committee of the Privy Council in London for adjudication.

During the first decade of this century, land speculation and settlement in various parts of British Columbia was proceeding at an accelerated rate. Meanwhile, the Indian Reserve Commission continued its work, now headed by A. W. Vowell. However, in 1911, the Province of British Columbia announced a new policy that terminated the "granting" of any further Indian reserves. The federal government responded that no further alienation of Crown lands to non-Indians in B.C. could occur until two outstanding issues between the federal and provincial governments had been dealt with: First, how Aboriginal title had been, or remained to be, extinguished in British Columbia would have to be clarified. Second, the provincial government must adopt the federal standard of allocating 80 acres of land per family to Indians, rather than the 10 acres per adult Indian male that the British Columbia government had been in the practice of allocating. An impasse between the federal and provincial governments had been reached. They resolved it by jointly establishing a Royal Commission on Indian Affairs in British Columbia, known as the McKenna-McBride Commission.

Through a process of negotiation that included the two levels of government, but excluded Aboriginal representation, the terms of reference for the commission were determined: the question of legal land title was not to be entertained. The Royal Commission's mandate was simply to adjust the size of reserve land. However, knowing that Aboriginal title was the single issue the First Nations wanted to discuss, official documents preceding and following the McKenna-McBride Commission state unequivocally that the land title question would be dealt with separately, and most likely by a court. Some Aboriginal nations boycotted the hearings because of the exclusion of land title from the terms of reference, while others participated in various ways, as their forebears had a generation before in response to the Indian Reserve Commission established by Joseph Trutch.

White settlement was consolidated, and mining and agricultural development increased during the period from 1914-1921. While local level Aboriginal protest continued in the form of confrontation, and petitions and meetings concerning land and resource use were organized at regional levels, the Gitksan also participated in province-wide lobbying efforts, including making a presentation to the McKenna-McBride Royal Commission that completed its work in 1916. The schedule of reserves which was the product of its efforts was given to yet another body, the Ditchburn-Clark Commission, who cut off and further "amended" the reserves set aside by McKenna and McBride—without Aboriginal consent. Orders-in-Council conveyed these reserves from the Province to the Federal Government. When the McKenna-McBride Royal Commission completed its work in 1916, Indian reserve land had been reduced by 47,058 acres valued at $1,522,704.00 and new reserves totalling 87,292 acres valued at $444,853.00 had been added.[19] Many First Nations refused to accept the findings of the Royal Commission and turned their attention to preparing their case for the Judicial Committee of the Privy Council in London.

From 1910 to 1927, British Columbia Indians believed that their case was in the process of coming before the Privy Council in London. Their belief was based on Prime Minister Laurier's promise made in 1910 to look into their claims; on the terms of reference for the Royal Commission having excluded the land title issue claiming it could only be resolved in court; and on Commissioners McKenna's and McBride's recommendation that this case be heard. In fact, the federal government was not preparing any case for the Privy Council, nor did they advise the many Aboriginal representatives they met with during these years that they were not pursuing the promised hearing before the Judicial Committee, but were, in fact stalling such a claim from proceeding.

Since 1763 the Judicial Committee of the Privy Council had recognized the "pre-existence" of Aboriginal rights and their continuity throughout the empire unless explicitly extinguished according to the letter of British colonial law. However, technically speaking, the Judicial Committee of the Privy Council could normally only act on a Canadian matter if it came to them by way of an appeal of a Canadian court decision. Aboriginal people, being wards of the Crown, required permission from the Crown before they could file a writ in court. Therefore, as long as neither the First Nations, nor a government had initiated a court action and been allowed to appeal the decision, Canadian officials could legally refrain from forwarding the Indians' petitions to London: no court case, no judgment, no appeal.

Finally, in 1914 the federal cabinet passed an order-in-council stipulating that the federal government would refer the claim of the British Columbia First Nations to the Exchequer Court of Canada "with the right of appeal to the Privy Council" providing three conditions were accepted by the First Nations: (1) if the court found in favour of the Aboriginal title, the Indians would surrender this title to be extinguished completely in return for the same sorts of treaty benefits negotiated elsewhere in Canada, and would accept the recommendations of the McKenna-McBride Royal Commission; (2) any obligations of the province would be fulfilled by its granting the land for the reserves; (3) the province would take part in the court case represented by legal counsel of its own choosing, while the Indians would be represented by counsel nominated and paid by the Dominion government. O'Meara was detested by government officials, and this provision was specifically meant to exclude him. The Allied Tribes of B.C. rejected all three conditions, and continued their lobbying efforts, stressing their preference for negotiations with governments rather than litigation.

Meanwhile, in another corner of the British Empire, the Judicial Committee of the Privy Council issued the infamous 1919 ruling in *Re: Southern Rhodesia*, classifying the Indigenous Africans as "too low on the scale of social organization" for their rights to be recognized under the British regime. Perhaps buoyed by this decision, Duncan Campbell Scott, Superintendent of Indian Affairs, ordered the recommendations of the McKenna-McBride Commission to be implemented without Aboriginal consent. However, in 1921 Lord Sumner's decision in *Re: Southern Rhodesia* was criticized and rejected by Viscount Haldane's ruling in *Amodu Tijani v. Southern Nigeria* that argued that Indigenous land tenure systems should not be judged by British standards, but rather recognized on their own terms.

The Allied Tribes of British Columbia recognized the Haldane decision as favourable to their cause and sent a formal petition to the Canadian Parliament in 1925 asking that a committee be struck to initiate the process of bringing their claim to the Judicial Committee of the Privy Council. A Special Joint Committee of the Senate and House of Commons was appointed by the government of Canada in 1926 to enquire into the Petition of the Allied Tribes. Although invited, the provincial government of British Columbia declined to participate or to send observers. The committee included H. H. Stevens, Conservative MP for Vancouver Centre; Minister of Indian Affairs Charles Stewart; future prime minister of Canada, R. B. Bennett; and four Senators from British Columbia. The majority-Liberal committee began hearings in March 1927.[20]

The question of documentation was contentious. O'Meara presented quotations from instructions sent by the Colonial office to Douglas that demonstrated that the British Crown recognized Aboriginal title in B.C. The Chairman of the Committee intervened, saying that O'Meara could not quote from documents not in evidence. Aboriginal representative Andrew Paull interrupted and explained that Duncan Campbell Scott had refused to give him access to the *Papers Connected with the Indian Land Question*, the same documents Trutch had withheld from the Indian Reserve Commission, in which could be found all the evidence referred to. Stevens had with him in the room that day *The Papers*, but refused to allow them to be entered into evidence. The collection was his private property, he argued, and he feared losing it. Scott said the Department of Indian Affairs had only one copy and also would not risk entering it into evidence for fear the court would misplace it. Finally, O'Meara was allowed to read sections of *The Papers* into the record.

The Committee interpreted the testimony of two traditional Chiefs from the interior of B.C. who, being neither English speakers nor knowledgeable in the language of legal disputes, had not used the words "aboriginal title" in their presentation, as evidence that these Chiefs did not believe they held title. Simultaneously, the Committee reasoned that, because the articulate, English-speaking, Aboriginal representatives had not presented proof of the antiquity of their title through their own oral tradition, their claim was obviously of recent invention and unduly influenced by whites, as evidenced by the use of legal language like the term "Aboriginal title."[21] The Committee concluded that: "Tradition forms so large a part of Indian mentality that if, in pre-Confederation days, the Indians considered they had an aboriginal title to the lands of the Province, there would have been tribal records of such being transmitted from father to son, either by word of mouth or in some other customary way. But nothing of the kind was shown to exist."[22]

The Committee rejected all the claims of the Allied Tribes, and set out seven arguments in support of their position. First, without commenting on pre-existing title, they argued that the assertion of British sovereignty was itself evidence that no prior title had been acknowledged or could continue. Second, the Committee claimed that the Hudson's Bay Company had achieved the "conquest" of B.C. Third, they pointed out that all Indians were not in agreement with the claim since all did not belong to the Allied Tribes organization. Fourth, the committee declared that the Aboriginal title claim was only fifteen years old, since that was when it was first articulated as a legal claim. The committee ignored, therefore, the ample documentation of resistance through civil disobedience, violent and non-violent confrontation, petitioning, letter-writing and Indian appearances before various committees of inquiry. Fifth, they found that Indians had implicitly consented to the denial of Aboriginal title by their acceptance of government reserve policies, which the committee said "they accepted for years without demur." Sixth, the committee blamed "mischievous white agitators" for Aboriginal discontent. Seventh, they chastised the Indians for rejecting the findings of the Indian Reserve Commission and the McKenna-McBride Commission and for continuing to "take up the time of the government and Parliament with irrelevant issues."[23]

The Parliamentary Committee did not recommend that the Allied Tribes claim be forwarded to the Judicial Committee of the Privy Council. Instead, they made two alternative proposals. First, that an annual allotment of $100,000.00 should be made to British Columbia Indians in lieu of treaty payments. Second, they recommended an amendment to the *Indian Act*, Section 141, that would criminalize organizing for political or legal recognition of Aboriginal title in B.C. The official explanation, and the one accepted by both federal and provincial governments, was that this clause was necessary to protect "simple," impressionable Indians from exploitation by cunning white lawyers like O'Meara. However, the language of Section 141 did not specify that it was applicable to non-Indians only, and, in effect, the amendment made it illegal for any organization to exist if pursuing recognition of British Columbia First Nations' Aboriginal title and rights was one of its objectives. Paternalistic rationales have served to exclude Section 141 of the *Indian Act*, and Canada, from inclusion in the usual list of totalitarian colonial regimes who outlaw opposition, and to thus perpetuate the image of Canada as a liberal, democratic, humanitarian colonial power.

Among British Columbia First Nations the amendment is remembered bitterly, and mention is often made of it in discussions of First Nations' political history. In Indian memories, section 141 is usually linked with the potlatch prohibition, and the combination of the two produces the still common belief, which presumably existed from 1927 until 1951 as well, that any gathering of Indians or any discussion of land claims was illegal without the permission of a missionary, Indian agent, or police official. Until this section was amended in 1951, no such public, legal activity did take place. First Nations throughout British Columbia, however, continued to feast and potlatch clandestinely, and to talk about Aboriginal title and rights.

Resistance versus Assimilation

> *Where there is resistance, there is power.*
> —Anthropologist Lila Abu-Lughod, 1990, *The Romance of Resistance.*

The decline of the British Columbia First Nations' population reached its lowest point of 22,000 in 1929.[24] Throughout the 1930s and 1940s numbers grew slowly, and Aboriginal peoples continued to organize politically in various ways in an attempt to better their lot, achieve the right to vote, and survive such travesties as the advent of residential schools administered by various churches and the Department of Indian Affairs. The *Indian Act* made failing to attend residential schools a criminal act, and provided for legalized punishment of Native parents who refused to comply with church and government officials who demanded they turn their children over to their care.[25] The explicit goal of the residential school policy was to break the bonds between generations, thus "freeing" the young from the shackles of tradition and the influence of their families. For the most part, graduates of the residential schools did not assimilate into Canadian society as the policy predicted they would. Many had no desire to, and others who tried found the doors closed to them. At the same time, when they returned to their home villages they often found they had lost both the ability to communicate fluently with parents and grandparents and the practical, as well as social, skills necessary to live from the land and to fit into village life.

The post-World War II era is noted by many analysts as a turning point in Aboriginal/non-Aboriginal relations. Following the defeat of Hitler and the revelations of Nazi atrocities, the western world entered a period of racial liberalism. Canada's image of itself, both nationally and internationally, as a free, democratic country where all citizens are equal regardless of race, religion or origin, was marred by the existence within its borders of a category of people whose legal, political and social identity had been racialized by the *Indian Act* and the *Constitution Act* (1867). The poverty and marginalization of Indians became a source of public embarrassment and efforts began to be made to improve living conditions on reserves and, once again, to assimilate Indians into mainstream Canadian society.

In 1947 British Columbia Indians were allowed to vote in provincial elections, and in 1949 Nishga Hereditary Chief Frank Calder, who would some twenty years later become "the Plaintiff" in *Calder v. R.*, was elected as Canadian Commonwealth Federation (CCF) Member of the Legislative Assembly for Atlin, British Columbia, becoming the first Indian elected to any post-Confederation Canadian legislature. The federal vote was not extended to registered Indians until 1961.

In 1949 the Judicial Committee of the Privy Council was replaced by the Supreme Court of Canada as Canada's highest court of appeal. Although Canadian judges were still free to use decisions of the Judicial Committee as precedents, "conventional wisdom among judges, lawyers, academics and government officials held that aboriginal rights were both insignificant and irrelevant."[26] Since Indians, publicly complied with the legislated banning of land claims activity imposed in 1927, the powers that be assumed that they, too, had forgotten about it. In a positivistic world, what a man cannot see does not exist.

Amendments to the *Indian Act* in 1951 dropped from the books—but did not repeal or acknowledge as wrong—both Section 140 prohibiting potlatching, and Section 141, prohibiting the pursuit of legal recognition of Aboriginal title and rights. Further changes to the *Act* allowed Indians, for the first time since 1884, to consume alcohol in public places, but not in their own homes. This circumscribed, but did not undermine, the lucrative "informal economy" of bootlegging alcohol to Indians which constituted a launching pad for many a settler family's climb up British Columbia's social ladder. The alcohol amendments to the *Indian Act* in 1951, like the ending of prohibition in Canada in the 1930s, moved some of the profits of the liquor trade from the unregulated, untaxed, illegal sphere into the regulated, taxable coffers of hotel and bar owners. In 1960, all restrictions on Indian purchase and consumption of alcohol were lifted, and provincial government-owned liquor stores opened adjacent to many reserves, further centralizing both profit, taxes and policing. The revised *Indian Act* that emerged after 1951 also revoked the provision that stipulated that any registered Indian who received a university degree would automatically lose their legal Indian status, reflecting a disavowal of the evolutionist notion that education and Indianness were necessarily incompatible. And, the 1951 amendments allowed First Nations women to participate in band council elections for the first time.

Potlatches, feasts and traditional dances were held again, in public, in numerous villages beginning in 1953. Paul Tennant marks the 1959 Native Brotherhood of British Columbia (NBBC) Convention as the first significant occasion since the 1927 banning of political activity on the land question where B.C. Aboriginal peoples had the opportunity to gather and openly discuss pursuing legal actions once again. He argues that the leaders who organized this convention had two goals in mind: a short term objective focused on consolidating the NBBC as a provincial organization to represent all status Indians in B.C. to a parliamentary committee; and a long term objective of pursuing the legal recognition of Aboriginal title.[27]

On the political front, the provincial government of British Columbia continued to refuse to recognize the existence of any Aboriginal rights or title, while simultaneously denying health, education and social services to registered Indians, arguing that they were a federal responsibility for which the province received no financial support or taxes. They advocated the elimination of "special status," and the legal, political, social and cultural assimilation of Aboriginal peoples—and their lands and resources—into Canadian society. In the mid 1960s, the federal government began a series of consultations with selected Aboriginal leaders. Despite the consistent stand taken by these representatives at these consultations—that is, that the recognition of Aboriginal title and rights must be justly dealt with before any honourable negotiations could take place— Prime Minister Trudeau and Indian Affairs Minister Chretien produced the 1969 White Paper Policy that brushed aside the issue of land and resource ownership and provided a blueprint for assimilation.

Evidence about the period between 1927 and 1984 was heard during the trial. Gitksan and Wet'suwet'en and academic, expert witnesses, recounted a narrative of resistance and survival. They discussed the impact of various plans, like the residential school policy, on everyday life, family relations and individual psyches. They talked about the legacy of alcoholism, drug abuse and violence in their communities. They talked about economic marginalization resulting from increased restrictions on their access to their lands and resources, about their experiences of expropriation and dislocation as more and more of their land was turned over to settlers and corporations, and about the daily struggle to survive and to defend their rights to exist as distinct peoples. They argued that they had changed, but that they had neither vanished, assimilated, nor "evolved" into "not truly aboriginal" peoples.

The Crown presented a counter narrative of acquiescence and assimilation. Their strategy began with efforts to show that the witnesses were unreliable and lacking in knowledge. Geoff Plant, lawyer for the Province of British Columbia, and currently a Liberal Member of the Legislative Assembly in British Columbia, cross-examined an elderly woman about the number of residents in her home village, trying to challenge the accuracy of her testimony, and her credibility as a witness:

Plant: Do you know how many members there are on the band list?

Gwaans: No.

Plant: Do you know how many people live on the reserve?

Gwaans: No.

Plant: Do you have an approximate idea of how many people live on the reserve?

Gwaans: No.

Plant: Is it in the order of hundreds of thousands, tens of thousands of people?

Gwaans: No.[28]

Plant continued his interrogation, raising the issue of assimilation and relying on a version of what has come to be called the "pizza test" for evidence.[29] The "pizza test" refers to what has become Crown Counsels' stock in trade argument in land rights trials that "proof" of assimilation—and hence ineligibility for consideration of distinct rights—can be achieved by showing that Aboriginal people often work for wages, are members of Christian congregations, use "western" technology, attend public schools and consume "white food." Following this line of reasoning, it has become commonplace for Aboriginal witnesses to be questioned about how many times they have eaten Kentucky Fried Chicken, Big Macs and pizzas, for example.[30] Geoff Plant pursued this line of questioning in his cross-examination of Gwaans:

Plant: Is there electric lights on the reserve?

Gwaans: Are you going to pay the bill?

Plant: Do you pay the bill, Mrs. Ryan?

Gwaans: Yes, I did....

...

Plant: So far as you know, do the members of the Band who live on the Reserve, do some of them own automobiles and trucks?

Gwaans: Well, I seen some cars there, but I didn't ask.

Plant: You have seen some cars on the reserve?

Gwaans: Well, they will call me nosey if I ask them, the people there.

Plant: You have seen people who live on the reserve drive cars?

Gwaans: Oh, yes.[31]

...

Plant: And there is a school on the reserve?

Gwaans: Yes.

Plant: Is there a church on the reserve?

Gwaans: Yes, two churches. Salvation Army and United Church.

Plant: Which church do you go to?

Gwaans: Salvation Army.[32]

Having shown, to their satisfaction, that the Gitksan and Wet'suwet'en have assimilated into mainstream Canadian society, the Crown called further witnesses to testify to the beneficial achievements of government assimilation policies. Former Department of Indian and Northern Affairs official Mr. McIntyre was called by the Crown as an expert witness. Chief Justice McEachern himself intervened in McIntyre's testimony. Although McIntyre was not a social scientist of any description, the Chief Justice asked him to evaluate the social consequences of the policies McIntyre himself designed and administered, and to analyze their value in the context of other variables:

McIntyre: ...in my opinion I would say that the biggest—that the biggest problem facing these people today is one of lack of economic opportunity, and I think if they had a—if they had an improved economic circumstance that many of their—of their social problems might be lessened.

Court: I have heard in this evidence—in this case evidence about employment, which I gather would be included within your category of economic opportunity. I have heard about education, housing, alcohol and drugs, health, gambling. I dare say there are others. Could you rate them as degrees of seriousness, or is that a reasonable request to make?

McIntyre: ...I observe what appears to be considerable improvement of that. For instance, I see a number of good quality homes that have sprung up. I see—I see community halls and recreation facilities that have come into existence. I am aware that band councils are apparently taking on greater responsibility.[34]

Of course, widespread poverty and unemployment are serious impediments to health and happiness and community well-being. However, the Crown's argument is that assimilation into the existing economy on terms dictated by the dominant society, and not on the basis of recognition of Aboriginal title and self-government rights, is the most desirable route for First Nations to take.

Finally, in June 1990, the proceedings in *Delgamuukw v. R.* drew to a close. Plaintiffs, defendants, lawyers, and witnesses made their closing arguments, filed the last of their exhibits, packed up their briefcases, and settled in to await Chief Justice McEachern's decision. What would the judge make of all he had heard, read, seen and felt over the preceding four years?

---

1. Gisday Wa and Delgamuukw 1987: 11.

2. Williams 1987.

3. See Dyck 1991.

4. "Nativist" religious movements were those, like the Ghost Dance, that sought to maintain, revive or revitalize religious beliefs rooted in pre-contact Indigenous cosmologies. "Syncretist" religious movements were those that sought to incorporate elements of Christianity into Indigenous belief systems that resulted in various fusions and combinations of religious beliefs.

5. Tennant 1990: 53.

6. Tennant 1990: 55.

7. Cited in Berger, 1981: 58.

8. Provincial Premier Smithe Province of British Columbia, *Session Papers*, 1887: 264; quoted in Tennant, 1990: 58.

9. *St. Catherine's Milling and Lumber Co. v. R.* (1885) 10 OR or 196 (Ont.Ch.); (1886) 13 OAR 148 (ont.CA0); (1887) 13 SCR 577 (SCC); (1888) 14 AC 46 (PC).

10. Sanders 1986; Tennant 1990.

11. Sanders, Douglas 1992: 295.

12. Morris 1973:39, quoted in Asch 1984: 62.

13. Dyck 1991; Paine 1977.

14. Williams D. R. 1987: 48.

15. Ray 1987: 93-94.

16. Galois 1987: 22.

17. Williams D. R.1987: 7.

18. The historical account in the remainder of this chapter relies substantially on Tennant 1990.

19. Tennant 1990: 105-107.

20. Tennant 1990: 106-108.

21. Tennant 1990.

22. Canada (1927): viii, quoted in Tennant 1990: 110.

23. Ibid., 109-113.

24. Acheson 1995: 11.

25. Brody 1983; Haig-Brown 1988; LaViolette 1973; Tennant 1990.

26. Tennant 1990: 218.

27. Tennant 1990: 129.

28. Quoted in Monet and Wilson 1992: 45.

29. Williamson 1989.

30. See Richardson 1975 for an early example of this argument in the James Bay Cree and Hydro Quebec trials.

31. These responses reflect the meticulous concern with the accuracy and truth of spoken statements, with a speaker's responsibility to only say what they know, and not to overstep their authority, that is characteristic of Elders in cultures based in oral tradition. The response of a Cree hunter in 1974, while being sworn in as a witness to the court, has become famous as the quintessential statement of Aboriginal concepts of truth-telling. The hunter said he couldn't swear to "tell the truth, the whole truth, and nothing but the truth," but could only promise to tell what he knew. (See Richardson 1975.) Many people, Aboriginal and non-Aboriginal, do not own their cars outright but are buying them gradually through payments. Therefore, Gwaans truly does not know whether the cars are owned or not, and does not think she has the authority to inquire. Her responses also evidence a different approach to the issue of property. Ownership is an important question that must be appropriately investigated, precisely proven, and therefore cannot simply be assumed. Gwaans appears to be saying that, just because people *occupy* and *use* these cars, they don't necessarily own them. Possession does not appear to be nine-tenths of Gitksan or Wet'suwet'en property law.

32. Ibid., 46.

33. Quoted in *Reasons* 1991: 185.

PART V:

DIES IRAE

(JUDGMENT DAY)

Chapter 16: Reasons for Judgment

Nasty, British (Columbian), and Long

A beginning, as Edward Said said, "is the first step in the intentional construction of meaning."[1] The Chief Justice's 394-page, single-spaced *Reasons for Judgment* began:

This has been a long trial.

After numerous pre-trial proceedings, including taking the commission evidence of many elderly plaintiffs, interlocutory applications and appeals, the trail began in Smithers on May 11, 1987.

After 318 days of evidence, mainly at Vancouver but partly at Smithers, the evidence was substantially completed on February 7, 1990.

Legal argument began in Smithers on April 2, 1990 and continued there for 18 days. Argument continued in Vancouver for a further 38 days, and the trial ended there on June 30, 1990.

A total of 61 witnesses gave evidence at trial, many using translators from their native Gitksan or Wet'suwet'en language; "Word Spellers" to assist the Official Reporters were required for many witnesses; a further 15 witnesses gave their evidence on Commission; 53 Territorial Affidavits were filed; 30 deponents were cross-examined out of Court; there are 23,503 pages of transcript evidence at trial; 5,898 pages of transcript of arguments; 3,039 pages of commission evidence and 2,553 pages of cross examination on affidavits (all evidence and oral arguments are conveniently preserved in hard copy and on diskettes); about 9,200 exhibits were filed at trial compiling, I estimate, well over 50,000 pages; the plaintiffs' draft outline of arguments comprises 3,250 pages, the province's 1,975 pages, and Canada's over 1,000 pages; there are 5,977 pages of transcript of argument in hard copy and on diskettes. All parties filed some excerpts from the exhibits they referred to in argument. The province alone submitted 28 huge binders of such documents. At least 15 binders of Reply Argument were left with me during that stage of the trial.

The Plaintiffs filed 23 large binders of authorities. The province supplemented this with 8 additional volumes, and Canada added 1 volume along with several other recent authorities which had not then been reported....[2]

Needless to say, this judgment has been a difficult one to prepare....

The plaintiffs, the aboriginal people who now live in parts of the territory I shall describe, sincerely believe that they own and have a legal right to govern this vast territory by reason of long use and possession. They harbour a great sense of injustice and resentment that they have waited so long for their aboriginal interests in the territory to be decided while non-natives have acquired title to much of this land, and while its resources have been exploited by others. The plaintiffs believe, passionately, that their claims are just.

It is common, when one thinks of Indian land claims, to think of Indians living off the land in pristine wilderness. Such would not be an accurate representation of the present life-style of the great majority of the Gitksan and Wet'suwet'en people who, while possibly maintaining minimal contact with individual territories, have largely moved into the villages. Many of the few who still trap are usually able to drive to their traplines, and return home each night.

Similarly, it would not be accurate to assume that even pre-contact existence in the territory was in the least bit idyllic...there is no doubt, to quote Hobbs, that aboriginal life in the territory was, at best, 'nasty, brutish and short.'[3]

The Chief Justice misspelled the eighteenth-century British philosopher's name, Hobbes. McEachern is referring to Hobbes' speculation that there was a time in human history when people lived "in a state of nature," that he described as a "war of all against all" in which life was "nasty, brutish and short." As was the fashion of his times, Hobbes hypothesized that contemporaneous Indigenous peoples of the Americas lived at this "stage of development." Given that, at the time he was writing, little information or knowledge about Indigenous peoples was available, even the most conservative contemporary "Hobbesian" political philosophers do not interpret Hobbes' description of Indigenous life literally. Rather, it is understood as a metaphor for what a society ruled by brute force and unmitigated individual ambition, rather than law and reason, might be like.

The Vast Emptiness

The Chief Justice then proceeded to identify and describe what had been in dispute at the trial, and what was at stake in his judgment. He wrote:

This action is mainly about land, 22,000 square miles of it (58,000 square kilometres), which I shall call 'the territory'....[4] The total territory is a vast, almost empty area except in the Highway 16-C.N.R. corridor where most of the plaintiffs' villages are located.... In addition to about 5,000 to 7,000

Gitksan and Wet'suwet'en persons…there are upwards of 30,000 others (mostly of European extraction), who are living within the territory….[5]

The territory is a rich agricultural area…and there are vast forestry resources throughout much of the territory. Equally important are the salmon and other fisheries of the Bulkley, Nass, Skeena and Babine Rivers. Most of the invaluable and irreplaceable Skeena salmon stock pass through the territory by way of the Skeena and Babine Rivers to their destiny in the spawning grounds of Babine Lake.[6]

Although some game animals may not be as plentiful in the transportation corridor as they were at the time of European contact, or before the railway was built, I am not persuaded there is either a shortage or an excessive abundance of wildlife in the territory…. I do not suggest that clear cut logging has been an ecological advantage to the territory. That is for other disciplines to ponder and to weigh against economics. Aesthetically, Dr. Hatler's description of 'moonscape' is appropriate. I was encouraged to notice on my travels through the territory that areas logged as recently as 3 to 6 years ago are starting to show signs of regeneration….[7]

There are some mining resources in the territory, including the Equity Silver Mine which is reported to have limited remaining ore reserves, but mining is not currently significant when compared with agriculture and forestry which are the economic mainstays of the region. There are, unquestionably, immense forestry reserves throughout the territory which are of great economic value.[8]

The trees, fish, game and minerals constituted only inanimate things defined by their potential economic value. The Chief Justice relived in his *Reasons for Judgment* the visionary moment that generations of his judicial ancestors had experienced before him: Chief Justice McEachern looked and saw before him in British Columbia, *terra nullius*:

The most striking thing that one notices in the territory away from the Skeena-Bulkley corridor is its emptiness. I generally accept the evidence of…[Crown] witnesses such as Dr. Steciw and Mrs. Peden and others that very few Indians are to be seen anywhere except in the large river corridors. As I have mentioned, the territory is, indeed, a vast emptiness….[9]

Might Makes Right

Having beheld *terra nullius*, the Chief Justice continued his textual re-enactment of law's narrative:

I have heard much at this trial about beliefs, feelings, and justice. I must again say, as I endeavoured to say during the trial, that Courts of law are frequently unable to respond to these subjective considerations. When plaintiffs bring legal proceedings, as these plaintiffs have, they must understand (as I believe they do), that our Courts are Courts of law which labour under disciplines which do not always permit judges to do what they might subjectively think (or feel) might be the right or just thing to do in a particular case. Nor can judges impose politically sensitive non-legal solutions on the parties. That is what Legislatures do, and judges should leave such matters to them.

Instead, cases must be decided on admissible evidence, according to law. The plaintiffs carry the burden of proving by a balance of probabilities not what they believe, although that is sometimes a relevant consideration, but rather facts which permit the application of the legal principles which they assert. The Court is not free to do whatever it wishes. Judges, like everyone else, must follow the law as they understand it....

I am sure that the plaintiffs understand that although the aboriginal laws which they recognize could be relevant on some issues, I must decide this case only according to what they call 'the white man's law.'[10]

I now propose to discuss the law relating to the question of extinguishment of aboriginal interests.... I must start with the proposition that the plaintiff's aboriginal rights in the territory at the time of sovereignty existed at the 'pleasure of the crown.'[11]

As the mortal embodiment of the hovering sovereign, Allan McEachern affirmed Britain's declaration of sovereignty and simultaneously extinguished Aboriginal title. His decision on how extinguishment was legally effected was, ultimately, the single, significant finding in his entire judgment in *Delgamuukw v. R.* McEachern ruled that the simple assertion of British sovereignty was sufficient to extinguish any Aboriginal title or rights that may have existed. It was simply common sense, the judge argued, to acknowledge the impossibility of coexistence between the "civilized" British, and the "primitive" First Nations. Chief Justice McEachern cited U.S. Chief Justice Marshall's early nineteenth-century precedent in support of his ruling:

The underlying purpose of exploration, discovery and occupation of the new world, and of sovereignty, was the spread of European civilization through settlement. For that reason the law never recognized that the settlement of new lands depended upon the consent of the Indians. So early as the year 1496, her monarch granted a commission to the Cabots, to discover countries then unknown to Christian people, and to take possession of them in the name of the King of England. Two years afterwards, Cabot proceeded on this voyage, and discovered the continent of North America, along which he sailed as far south as Virginia. To this discovery the English trace their title.[12]

McEachern concluded that it was obvious from the *outcome* of the last 200 years of history that the Crown had never ceased believing in its right to extinguish Aboriginal title and rights, and this itself was further evidence of the rightness of the initial assertion of sovereignty. Simply put, "in the beginning," Britain exercised its absolute prerogative to assert sovereignty. Subsequently, British, Canadian and American colonial courts consistently upheld this initial assertion, and colonial governments faithfully enacted legislation that took for granted the legitimacy of Crown sovereignty, and simply ignored any and all challenges brought forward by First Nations since contact. Each court's repetition of these principles, according to the law, resulted in a strengthening of their validity. In other words, in a court of law, the more often a lie is told, and more times a liar escapes reprimand, the closer the law comes to finding legal truth.

The Chief Justice explained his ruling:

> I think it unnecessary to continue this debate. In my view, it is part of the law of nations, which has become part of the common law, that discovery and occupation of the lands of this continent by European nations, or occupation and settlement, gave rise to a right of sovereignty. Such sovereignty in North America was established in part by Royal grant as with the Hudson's Bay Company in 1670; by conquest, as in Quebec in 1759; by treaty with other sovereign nations, as with the United States settling the international border; by occupation, as in many parts of Canada, particularly the prairies and British Columbia; and partly by the exercise of sovereignty by the British Crown in British Columbia though the creation of Crown Colonies on Vancouver Island and the mainland.[13]

In support of this assertion, the Chief Justice quoted at length from the work of the nineteenth-century Swiss theorist, Vattel:

> 'There is another celebrated question to which the discovery of the new world has principally given rise. It is asked whether a nation may lawfully take possession of some part of a vast country in which there are none but erratic nations, whose scanty population is incapable of occupying the whole? We have already observed, in establishing the obligation to cultivate the earth, that these nations cannot exclusively appropriate to themselves more land than they have occasion for, or more than they are able to settle and cultivate. Their unsettled habitation in those immense regions, cannot be accounted a true and legal possession, and the people of Europe, too closely pent up at home, finding land of which the Savage stood in no particular need, and of which they made no actual and constant use, were lawfully entitled to take possession of it and to settle in with Colonies. The earth, as we have already observed belongs to mankind in general, and was designed to furnish them with subsistence. If each nation had from the beginning resolved to appropriate to itself a

vast country, that the people might live only by hunting, fishing and wild fruits, our globe would not be sufficient to maintain a tenth part of its present inhabitants. We do not, therefore, deviate from the views of nature, in confining the Indians within narrower limits.[14]

Furthermore, the Chief Justice decreed, it was not legally necessary to find historical or legal evidence of the British Crown having expressly announced its "clear and plain intention" to extinguish Aboriginal title, as the Supreme Court of Canada's ruling in the *Sparrow* case had required. Rather, Chief Justice Allan McEachern offered his own unique interpretation of this precedent:

...the governing factor in extinguishment persuades me that intention in this context must relate not to a specific, isolated intention...[or to] a specific or precise state of mind on the part of the historical actors, but rather to the consequences they intended for their actions.... I therefore conclude that express statutory language is not a requirement for extinguishment.

In other words, the question is not did the Crown through its officers specifically intend to extinguish aboriginal rights...but rather did they plainly and clearly demonstrate an intention to create a legal regime from which it is necessary to infer that aboriginal interests were in fact extinguished.... Intention, in this context, must be a matter of implication...[from] an amalgam of thought, belief, planning and intention on the part of a number of officials who may all have had different knowledge, understanding and priorities. There was indeed an intention to manage Crown lands...[during the colonial period] throughout the colony by a system that was inconsistent with continuing aboriginal rights.[15]

To support his finding, the Chief Justice referred to the copious evidence presented by the Crown that demonstrated that the Province of British Columbia had, in fact, treated Aboriginal title and people as if they didn't exist, at least since 1871:

[The defendants in this case]...the province of British Columbia... introduced a large collection of documents which...record pervasive colonial and provincial Crown presence in the territory up to the date of the writ (1984)....

All this documentation demonstrates colonial and provincial dominion over the territory before and since Confederation by such diverse governmental and administrative activities as surveying, grants of land, leases and other tenures, land registry, schools and hospitals, rights of way for highways, power and pipe lines, grants in fee simple, forestry, mining, and guide out-fitting permits, various public works, the creation and governance of villages and municipalities, water and other placer rights and licences, trapline registration for all or almost all of the territory, fish and game regulation and conservation and a host of other legislatively authorized intrusions in the life and geography of the territory....

For its part, Canada also adduced extensive evidence of the federal presence in the territory....[16]

And, McEachern reiterated the cornerstone of the Crown's argument, and of his reasoning: the possibility of mutually-respectful co-existence between Aboriginal and non-Aboriginal property regimes is an absurdity not worthy of serious consideration:

> The province argues that it cannot rationally be asserted that, standing alongside this all-embracing structure, there are many parallel aboriginal governments and separate systems of ownership or rights to use a substantial portion of the province by what is now such a small segment of the population.[17]

Having asserted the British Crown's unfettered right to assert sovereignty, the Chief Justice went on to legitimate the arbitrariness of this exercise of power even more, by arguing that the date at which sovereignty may have been first declared was also irrelevant:

> Because of the view I have of this case, I do not think it is necessary to make a specific finding about a date of British sovereignty over the northern part of the province.... For practical purposes, especially in the territory it could well have been as early as the 1820's but legally it may not have been until the creation of the colony in 1858. 1846 was the date chosen by Judson J. in *Calder*. In my view the actual date of British sovereignty, whether it be the earliest date of 1803 or the latest date of 1858, or somewhere in between makes no difference...the Crown wished the island settled by British settlers...the establishment of the Colony of British Columbia, for example, should be classified as a displacement of one sovereignty by a different one which the law recognizes....[18]

> ...I do not believe there is any material difference, for the purposes of this case, between the date of contact and the date of sovereignty....[19]

> For my purposes it is sufficient to start with European expansion into this continent after the voyages of various navigators such as Columbus (1492), and Cabot, who according to Chief Justice Marshall discovered North America in 1498....[20]

> I am satisfied that at the date of British sovereignty the plaintiffs ancestors were living in their villages on the great rivers in a form of communal society, occupying or using fishing sites and adjacent lands as their ancestors had done for the purpose of hunting and gathering whatever they required for sustenance. They governed themselves in their villages and immediately surrounding areas to the extent necessary for communal living.

The judge went to some lengths to explain in no uncertain terms what he meant when he said that *whatever* may or may not have taken place historically was irrelevant to his judgment:

> Aboriginal persons and commentators often mention the fact that the Indians of this province were never conquered by force of arms, nor have they entered into treaties with the Crown. Unfair as it may seem to Indians or others on philosophical grounds, these are not relevant considerations. The events of the last 200 years are far more significant than any military conquest or treaties would have been. The reality of Crown ownership of the soil of all the lands of the province is not open to question and actual dominion for such a long period is far more pervasive than the outcome of a battle or a war would ever be. The law recognizes Crown ownership of the territory in a federal state now known as Canada pursuant to its Constitution and laws.[21]

> I fully understand the plaintiffs' wishful belief that their distinctive history entitles them to demand some form of constitutional independence from British Columbia. But neither this nor any Court has the jurisdiction to undo the establishment of the Colony, Confederation, or the constitutional arrangements which are now in place. Separate sovereignty or legislative authority, as a matter of law, is beyond the authority of any Court to award. I also understand the reasons why some aboriginal persons have spoken in strident and exaggerated terms about aboriginal ownership and sovereignty, and why they have asserted exemption from the laws of Canada and the province. They often refer to the fact that they were never conquered by military force. With respect, that is not a relevant consideration at this late date if it ever was. Similarly, the absence of treaties does not change the fact that Canadian and British Columbian sovereignty is a legal reality recognized both by the law of nations and by this Court.... In the language of the street, and in the contemplation of the law, the plaintiffs are subject to the same law and the same Constitution as everyone else. This is not to say that some form of self-government for aboriginal persons cannot be arranged. That, however, is possible only with the agreement of both levels of government under appropriate, lawful legislation. It cannot be achieved by litigation.... It follows, therefore, that the plaintiffs' claims for aboriginal jurisdiction or sovereignty over, and ownership of, the territory must be dismissed.[22]

In my judgment, the foregoing propositions are absolute. The real question is whether, within that constitutional framework, the plaintiffs have any aboriginal interests which the law recognizes as a burden upon the title of the Crown.[23]

Having confirmed that the absolute authority of the law is not bound by either place or time, the Chief Justice nevertheless took a moment to wander down a historical path:

> In my view...what happened in the territory...[is] that the aboriginal system, to the extent it constituted aboriginal jurisdiction or sovereignty, or ownership apart from occupation for residence and use, gave way to a new colonial form of government which the law recognizes to the exclusion of all other systems....[24]

> After that, aboriginal customs, to the extent they could be described as laws before the creation of the colony became customs which depended upon the willingness of the community to live and abide by them, but they ceased to have any force, as laws, within the colony.[25]

> To put it in a nutshell, I find that legislation passed in the colony and by the Imperial Parliament that all the land in the colony belonged to the Crown in fee, apart altogether from many other enactments, extinguished any possible right of ownership on the part of the Indians.[26]

To enter the Courthouses and Houses of Parliament built on their land without their consent, to negotiate the ownership and use of that same land and its resources, Aboriginal peoples must, according to the law and government policy, agree to ultimately surrender their title and rights. They must agree to "extinguishment." The alternative of co-existence, rather than domination by one and subordination of the other, is a possibility that cannot be argued within the Crown's interpretation of legal precedents, or negotiated within the federal government's extinguishment policy. In the legal forum, the process of surrender begins *before* Aboriginal litigants are permitted to launch a legal challenge, with the demand that they acknowledge that the "underlying title to all the land" in Canada is held by the hovering sovereign. Of course, if they go to court to establish the legitimacy of their claim that the hovering sovereign's title is invalid in the terms of British and Canadian law, this demand creates yet another double-bind. If they don't go to court, then their claim will never be acknowledged, and provincial governments may not be compelled to recognize or negotiate with them. If they do go to court, they have to surrender this basis of their claim first. Chief Justice McEachern explained this dilemma succinctly:

> In their pleadings and argument the plaintiffs admit that the underlying or radical or allodial title to the territory is in the Crown in Right of British Columbia. This reasonable admission was one which the plaintiffs could not avoid. It sets the legal basis for any discussion of title....[27] After much consideration, I am driven to find that jurisdiction and sovereignty are such absolute concepts that there is no half-way house.... The very fact that the

243

plaintiffs recognize the underlying title of the Crown precludes them from denying the sovereignty that created such title.[28]

Heads, the Crown wins. Tails, Indians lose.

A second significant legal ruling made by Chief Justice McEachern was his finding that the provincial government, as well as the federal government, have a fiduciary obligation to Aboriginal people. This has resulted in provincial governments having to institute consultation processes with First Nations before development takes place on what are designated their traditional lands.

Despite his protestations to the contrary, the Chief Justice's legal findings ultimately rely on historical and cultural interpretations. Were British and Indigenous peoples considered equal human beings, then or now, what possible rationale could there be for Britain simply having the right to assert sovereignty over another people without their consent, and for subsequent colonial governments to continue to do so?

In what follows I have reconstructed the *Reasons for Judgment*'s historical narrative by selecting excerpts from the text and organizing them according to a historical, chronological framework, in order to try to understand Chief Justice McEachern's "world view," as this is expressed through his narrative of the history and culture of Gitksan and Wet'suwet'en First Nations, British Columbia, and Aboriginal/non-Aboriginal relations in this province. I have concentrated on those historical and cultural interpretations upon which the legal findings of "fact" in McEachern's judgment rely most strongly to illustrate the culturally-specific underpinnings of the judge's reasoning, and the erroneous basis upon which his findings of "legal facts" depend. In so doing I have tried to be mindful of the context from which I have selected excerpts, and I have endeavoured not to intentionally misrepresent what the judge wrote. I have indicated by way of footnotes where the excerpts I have reproduced may be found in the original text of the *Reasons for Judgment*. I hope this will facilitate re-reading and re-interpretation by interested readers.

The text of Allan McEachern's *Reasons for Judgment* in *Delgamuukw v. R.*, is divided into 22 sections that include commentary on a range of legal, historical and cultural issues. The Chief Justice visited and revisited particular epochs and events in different sections of the *Reasons for Judgment*, in order to address various specific questions. An array of theories and diverse forms of argument are engaged by the judge. Frequently, the empirical evidence the Chief Justice draws on in his ruling is weak or absent, and the logics of interpretation he employs appear contradictory and inconsistent. The text makes sense only if the reader accepts its fundamental premises: First, that Aboriginal peoples are radically different from, *and inferior to*, Euro-Canadians, and that therefore a humanistic logic of equality does not apply in this case. This is most clearly evident in the "damned if you do and damned if you don't" nature of the law on Aboriginal issues, illustrated in many examples where it is clear that *whatever* Aboriginal people may do or say, the law has an interpretation waiting that judges can use, if it they so choose, to render that statement or practice evidence of justification to deny Aboriginal title and rights legal recognition. It goes without saying that judges also have the option of reconstructing a precedent narrative that *supports* recognition of Aboriginal title and rights. Second, in order to make sense of Chief Justice McEachern's text, a reader must assume that the British Crown was justified, historically, in asserting its sovereignty over First Nations without their consent; and that prolonged occupation on these grounds provides justification for continued political, economic and cultural domination. The legal argument that expresses this desire claims that non-Aboriginal settlers may now claim to hold common law title on the basis of long term use and occupancy. Third, readers must temporarily suspend their belief in common sense empiricism and everyday logic, and go along with law's imagining that the reality it creates in its own image is the truth.

My reading and reconstruction of the Chief Justice's text is unashamedly a critical interpretation. I am presenting an argument that begins from certain specific premises: I assume all human beings are fundamentally equal and that this principle should be reflected in law. I think that *Reasons for Judgment* that rely on historical and anthropological research should reflect contemporary research standards and knowledge in these fields. There are, and no doubt always will be, significant debates among academics on these topics. There are also, however, generally accepted standards by which courts *could* evaluate the relative reliability of expert evidence offered by academics and other researchers. I believe also that the "facts" a judge "finds" should be demonstrable as such to the average citizen. I think judges' arguments should be internally coherent, not illogical, on their own terms. I believe it is unjust and immoral that the Crown asserts its sovereignty and jurisdiction over First Nations peoples, their lands and resources *without their consent and in the face of their objections*. I take exception to the state of which I am a citizen, Canada, being based on the principle of the inequality of peoples. I believe that Canadian law has historically defended and reproduced a way of life based on a foundation of European male supremacy, economic inequality, and social injustice, and continues to.

No Writing, Horses or Wheeled Wagons

Having first reproduced law's narrative of discovery, sovereignty and extinguishment, the Chief Justice turned his attention to history. He began at the beginning:

> The evidence does not disclose the beginnings of the Gitksan and Wet'suwet'en people. Many of them believe God gave this land to them at

the beginning of time. While I have every respect for their beliefs, there is no evidence to support such a theory and much good reason to doubt it....[29] Most scientists believe the ancestors of our aboriginal people migrated to this continent from Asia, probably after, but possibly before, the last great Ice Age.... It is my conclusion, doing the best I can without the assistance of very much evidence, that the plaintiffs' ancestors...migrated from Asia, probably through Alaska, but not necessarily across the Bering Straits, after the last Ice Age, and spread south and west into the areas which they found livable...it is unlikely, or at least not proven, that any or all of the plaintiff groups have occupied the territory for all of the time since these post-glacial migrations.... For the purpose of this judgment it really does not matter where the plaintiffs' earlier ancestors came from....[30]

Although McEachern's ruling that Britain had the right to assert sovereignty anywhere, and anytime, and in any circumstances rendered the remainder of his judgement legally redundant, he proceeded to evaluate and interpret all the evidence and arguments he had heard in the course of four years of hearings. In so doing, he was providing an interpretation of this material for future appeal court judges, whose general practice is to privilege the "eye witness" account of the first judge in a case like this one. McEachern explained his role:

I have no doubt that what I am about to say will not be the last word on this case and that this judgment will be appealed to the Court of Appeal and perhaps to the Supreme Court of Canada. With this in mind I shall endeavour, for the assistance of the parties and the appeal process, to describe as best I can the facts and reasons upon which I have reached the conclusions I am about to state.[31]

And, although his ruling on the Crown's powers of extinguishment made consideration of any legal precedents unnecessary as well, Chief Justice McEachern acknowledged his judicial predecessors appropriately:

Although not binding upon me but deserving deference, is the opinion of the Privy Council in *Re: Southern Rhodesia.*... The right of the Imperial Crown to proceed with the settlement and development of North America without aboriginal concurrence was confirmed by the Privy Council in the *St. Catherine's Milling* case. This was expressed in practical terms by stating that 'Indian title' existed at the pleasure of the Crown.[32]

I think...there is much wisdom in the dictum of the Privy Council in *Re Southern Rhodesia:*...[to wit] 'The estimation of the rights of aboriginal tribes is always inherently difficult. Some tribes are so low in the scale of social organization that their usages and conceptions of rights and duties are not to be reconciled with the institutions or the legal ideas of civilized society.' ...I am quite unable to say there was much in the way of pre-contact social organization among the Gitksan and Wet'suwet'en simply because there is so little reliable evidence.[33]

The evidence suggests that the Indians of the territory were, by historical standards, a primitive people without any form of writing, horses, or wheeled wagons. Peter Skene Ogden, the controversial trader-explorer, visited Hotset in 1836 and noted their primitive condition in his journal.[34]

In 1919 Lord Sumner, in his ruling in *Re: Southern Rhodesia*, had decreed that only those Indigenous property laws that were based on concepts of private ownership were sufficiently "evolved" to be recognized by British imperial law. In 1921 Viscount Haldane, in *Amodu Tijani v. The Secretary, Southern Nigeria* had argued that many Indigenous land tenure systems were communally-based, as opposed to the British model of individual ownership in fee simple, and that such communal property regimes were worthy of respect by colonial law. McEachern concluded that Aboriginal title must, by definition, be communal, and he admonished the Gitksan and Wet'suwet'en Hereditary Chiefs for claiming a form of individual ownership:

> I do not understand the plaintiffs to allege or claim any 'people-wide' collective or communal ownership interest in any of the Gitksan or Wet'suwet'en territories, that is to say each chief claims ownership of specific territory or territories, and none of them claim any interest in any other territory....[35] I have already described the form of this action where some of the hereditary chiefs are advancing these claims for aboriginal interests on behalf of themselves or on behalf of their Houses or members. The authorities satisfy me that a claim for an aboriginal interest is a communal claim. Counsel for the Nishga in *Calder* (at p. 352) described it as a 'tribal interest' and Hall J. (at pp 401-402) said it was a 'communal right.' In *Sparrow* there are references to a collective rather than an individual, or sub-group interest.... The Crown's 'promise' of fair dealing must be classified as a communal or collective promise rather than separate or divided promises to a variety of individuals or sub-groups...the law cannot recognize discrete claims by small or sub groups within an aboriginal community.... The plaintiffs' case as pleaded, if established, could result in some Gitksan and Wet'suwet'en persons being treated substantially differently from other members of the larger aboriginal collective...any judgement to which they are entitled must be for the benefit of these peoples generally, and not piecemeal for the Hereditary Chiefs, their Houses, or their members.[36]

It is evidence of "our" advanced civilization that "we" have the right to kick our family off our property, so "they" must be communal. Otherwise, "they" are insufficiently different. Of course, if "they" are communal, "they" are less evolved than "we" are.

Chief Justice McEachern reached back to the nineteenth-century theories of Sir Henry Maine when he dismissed Gitksan and Wet'suwet'en law as mere "primitive custom" that resulted from the need to minimally regulate "instincts"; as opposed to "civilized law" that presumably emerges from the institutional consensus of rational thinkers:

> It became obvious during the course of the trial that what the Gitksan and Wet'suwet'en witnesses describe as law is really a most uncertain and highly flexible set of customs which are frequently not followed by the Indians themselves.... In my judgment, these rules are so flexible and uncertain that they cannot be classified as laws.[37] I have no difficulty finding that the Gitksan and Wet'suwet'en people developed tribal customs and practices relating to chiefs, clans and marriage and things like that, but I am not persuaded their ancestors practised universal or even uniform customs relating to land outside the villages. They may well have developed a priority system for their principal fishing sites at village locations. I expect it is probably so...[that the Gitksan and Wet'suwet'en] exercised their spiritual beliefs within the territory, but the evidence does not establish that their beliefs were necessarily common to all the people or that they were universal practices. I suspect customs were probably more widely followed. [38]

> The plaintiffs have indeed maintained institutions but I am not persuaded all their present institutions were recognized by their ancestors.... I do not accept the ancestors 'on the ground' behaved as they did because of 'institutions.' Rather I find they more likely acted as they did because of survival instincts which varied from village to village.[39] I do not question the importance of the feast system in the social organization of present-day Gitksan and I have no doubt it evolved from earlier practices but I have considerable doubt about how important a role it had in the management and allocation of lands, particularly after the start of the fur trade. I think not much....[40]

Having ruled out the possibility that such "primitive" peoples may have entered into treaties with their neighbours regarding rights to travel across and harvest resources from certain territories, the judge declared that there must not have been any borders worthy of the name:

> There seemed to be so many intrusions into the territory by other peoples that I cannot conclude the plaintiffs' ancestors actually maintained their boundaries or even their villages against invaders, although they usually resumed occupation of specific locations for obvious economic reasons....[41]

In a turn of logic particularly curious for a judge who, after all, spends his time adjudicating breaches in the law, the Chief Justice interpreted testimony that some Gitksan and Wet'suwet'en appeared at times to break their own laws as evidence that these were not laws in the first place:

While these are my findings, I am prepared to assume for the purpose of this part of my judgement that, in the legal and jurisdictional vacuum which existed prior to British sovereignty, the organization of these people was the only form of ownership and jurisdiction which existed in the areas of the villages. I would not make the same finding with respect to the rest of the territory.... In no sense could it be said that Gitksan or Wet'suwet'en law or title followed (or governed) these people except possibly in a social sense to the far reaches of the territory. Aboriginal life, in my view, was far from stable and it stretches credulity to believe that remote ancestors considered themselves bound to specific lands....[42]

The Judge concluded his findings on the question by referring to the stronger, in his estimation, case presented by the Crown:

The defendants, on the other hand, point to the absence of any written history, wheeled vehicles, or beasts of burden, and suggest the Gitksan and Wet'suwet'en civilizations, if they qualify for that description, fall within a much lower, even primitive order. I have no doubt life in the territory was extremely difficult, and many of the badges of civilization, as we of European culture understand that term, were indeed absent....[43] It is my conclusion that Gitksan and Wet'suwet'en laws and customs are not sufficiently certain to permit a finding that they or their ancestors governed the territory according to aboriginal laws even though some Indians may well have chosen to follow local customs when it was convenient to do so.[44]

And, the defendants, of course, relied upon *their* predecessors' accounts, which were validated by the Judge:

In July 1889 the Dominion...appointed an Agent to reside at Hazelton on what was called the Upper Skeena. The first incumbent was R. E. Loring who was then in the service of the province in the area. He seems to have been nominated for this position either by the Indians or by Mrs. Hankin, the widow of the first merchant at Hazelton whom Mr. Loring later married. She, being either an Indian woman or at least fluent in their language, acted as his translator. His many reports present a useful account of the Indians of the territory during his service there which continued until about 1920. In many cases, his reports present a far more realistic picture of what was happening on the ground than the careful language of government reports and diplomatic exchanges. Loring's 1889 reports describe a society in transit from what he regarded as 'heathen,' such as eating dogs and potlatching, and many disputes.[45]

Accounts based on the plaintiffs' ancestors' knowledge were not given the same credibility by Chief Justice McEachern:

The plaintiffs adduced a great deal of evidence directed towards establishing actual control of the territory.... The plaintiffs ask me to infer that the practices they describe were a continuation of long standing, pre-existing aboriginal ownership of and jurisdiction over territory. In fact, however, the plaintiffs seemed to have considerable difficulty with this claim for aboriginal sovereignty. Mr. Neil J. Sterritt is a Gitksan hereditary chief and a former President of the Gitksan-Wet'suwet'en Tribal Council. He is perhaps the most knowledgeable of the Gitksan chiefs on their claim in this action as he was, until 1988, involved directly with the preparation of the case for several years. In a brief submitted to the Penner Commission in 1983, Mr. Sterritt submitted: "Now, I want to talk to you about the Indian government of the past.... I want to tell you that the feast hall was our seat of government. It filled a legislative and judiciary function. It taught us how and why to govern.... The feast filled many functions. One of the functions was settling disputes. It was a place to do something about succession, passing on what was being done, passing on property, passing on title...." Brown's reports in the 1820s and Mr. Loring's reports, starting in about 1890, hardly mention the feast, particularly as a legislative body.... I am not persuaded that the feast has ever operated as a legislative institution in the regulation of land.[46]

I conclude...that there was indeed a rudimentary form of social organization in the Babine area, and it is reasonable to infer that similar levels of organization then existed in the territory.[47] There is no reason to believe the neighbouring Indians of the territory had any lesser degree of social organization at the same time. I therefore infer that the ancestors of a reasonable number of the plaintiffs were present in parts of the territory for a long, long time prior to sovereignty.[48]

Finders Keepers

The Chief Justice was convinced by the Crown's argument that the Royal Proclamation was never intended to recognize Aboriginal title or rights, and that, since British Columbia was not visible on British maps drawn in 1763, it did not exist in the eyes of the Crown. Hence the Proclamation, Allan McEachern agreed, does not apply to this province:

By 1700 there was little, if any European influence in western North America. Even horses were unknown to the plains Indians until mid-century, or in the territory until the middle of the 1800's.... Most maps show north-west America, including the territory, as "Terra Incognita" or "These parts Entirely Unknown." This state of relative ignorance about this part of the world remained that way for almost another century.[49]

The British were anxious to keep peace on the frontier, and for this and other mercantile reasons, Britain caused a Royal Proclamation to be issued in 1763....[50] One of the most interesting parts of the evidence and argument in this case concerned this famous Proclamation which was issued by George III, on the advice of his Ministers, on October 7, 1763.... It is therefore with much hesitation, and with the greatest possible respect both to the witnesses and to counsel who expended so much skill and energy on this question, that I find myself able to dispose of it quite summarily....[51]

I have no doubt that, apart from setting up governments for the new colonies, the underlying purposes of the Proclamation were firstly to pacify the frontier for defensive or military purposes, and secondly to secure the markets of the North American colonies for the manufactured products of the mother country....[52] The tenor of the Proclamation in its historical setting clearly relates to the practical problems facing the Crown in its then American colonies.... Even the language of the Royal Proclamation, 1763, makes it plain that the Crown did not consider it necessary to obtain the consent of the Indians to exclude their interests. Although the Crown set aside vast areas for hunting grounds at the Crown's 'pleasure'....[53]

The Crown had no connection with the Indian people west of the Rockies who owed the Crown, no actual or even notional allegiance, and were in no way under its protection.... There is nothing which persuades me that this Proclamation, either by is language or by the intention of the Crown, applies to the benefit of the plaintiffs or to the lands of present day British Columbia.[54]

1. Said 1975: 1.

2. *Reasons*, 1991: 1.

3. *Reasons*, 1991: 3.

4. *Reasons*, 1991: 5.

5. *Reasons*, 1991: 11.

6. *Reasons*, 1991: 11.

7. *Reasons*, 1991: 12.

8. *Reasons*, 1991: 12.

9. *Reasons*, 1991: 12.

10. *Reasons*, 1991: 2.

11. *Reasons*, 1991: 235.

12. *Reasons*, 1991: 80.

13. *Reasons*, 1991: 81.

14. *Reasons*, 1991: 80.

15. *Reasons*, 1991: 239; see also 241.

16. *Reasons*, 1991: 233.

17. *Reasons*, 1991: 233-234.

18. *Reasons*, 1991: 241.

19. *Reasons*, 1991: 212.

20. *Reasons*, 1991: 19.

21. *Reasons*, 1991: 81.

22. *Reasons*, 1991: 225.

23. *Reasons*, 1991: 81.

24. *Reasons*, 1991: 223.

25. *Reasons*, 1991: 224.

26. *Reasons*, 1991: 242.

27. *Reasons*, 1991: 19.

28. *Reasons*, 1991: 224.

29. *Reasons*, 1991: 15.

30. *Reasons*, 1991: 16.

31. *Reasons*, 1991: 3.

32. *Reasons*, 1991: 234.

33. *Reasons*, 1991: 227.

34. *Reasons*, 1991: 25.

35. *Reasons*, 1991: 15.

36. *Reasons*, 1991: 210.

37. *Reasons*, 1991: 219.

38. *Reasons*, 1991: 213.

39. *Reasons*, 1991: 213.

40. *Reasons*, 1991: 214.

41. *Reasons*, 1991: 213.

42. *Reasons*, 1991: 222-223.

43. *Reasons*, 1991: 31.

44. *Reasons*, 1991: 221.

45. *Reasons*, 1991: 168.

46. *Reasons*, 1991: 214.

47. *Reasons*, 1991: 74.

48. *Reasons*, 1991: 75.

49. *Reasons*, 1991: 21.

50. *Reasons*, 1991: 23.

51. *Reasons*, 1991: 83.

52. *Reasons*, 1991: 95.

53. *Reasons*, 1991: 234.

54. *Reasons*, 1991: 97.

Chapter 17: Reasons in the Public Eye

Pardon him, Theodutus: he is a barbarian, and thinks that the customs of his tribe and little island are the laws of nature.
—George Bernard Shaw, *Caesar and Cleopatra.*

Judgment Day

The banner headline on the front page of March 9th, 1991's Vancouver Sun announced: "INDIANS LOSE CASE." Pictures of the portly Chief Justice Allan McEachern ran in the daily papers over captions that said "Gut feelings ruled out," and "Emphasis on law and not gut feelings." Brief biographical notes included in the stories described the Chief Justice as a 64-year old, non-drinking, non-smoking, Coca-Cola addict and past president of the Canadian Football League. Born and raised on the middle class west side of Vancouver, the Judge and his family were now property-owning, tax-paying residents of Vancouver's elite Shaughnessy neighbourhood. The judge was described as "a jurist who has never allowed emotional considerations to shake his belief in the rule of law," and who "made it clear from the outset he would decide the case not on personal gut feelings, but according to the law."[1]

Gitksan and Wet'suwet'en Tribal Council President Mas Gak (Don Ryan) called for McEachern's removal from the bench, and vowed that "never again will the sacred boxes of our people be opened for the white man to look at." "The government has made fun of us," Gitksan chief, Maxlaxlex (Johnny David) said. Ernie Crey of the United Native Nations likened the text of the Chief Justice's *Reasons for Judgment* to a Stephen King horror novel. Larry Pootlas of Bella Coola said that when he heard the news he thought he was in South Africa. The Shuswap Nation Tribal Council called the judgment "brutal and hostile." "It's a travesty of justice," said Union of B.C. Indian Chiefs spokesman, Saul Terry. Ovide Mercredi, Grand Chief of the Assembly of First Nations of Canada, described McEachern's decision as "so demeaning it is breath-taking." "The Judgment stands on racism. It defines Indians as no better than the animals in the forest," protested Squamish chief Joe Mathias. "The corporate board rooms are probably saying, 'Thank God we had our brother on the bench,'" he added.[2]

Indeed, John Howard of Macmillan Bloedel, speaking for B.C.'s forest industry, said he was surprised by the ruling, but pleased. The Chief Justice's assessment that native issues constituted a "social problem that should be dealt with by the legislature," rather than a legal one to be determined by the courts, "has been our view at Macmillan Bloedel for a long time," he commented. A spokesman for the mining industry expressed relief that the status quo prevailed, and added that he hoped the decision would encourage Aboriginal peoples in the Yukon and Northwest Territories to bring their claims to "a final solution." Mike Hunter, representing the Fisheries Council of B.C. described the Chief Justice's ruling as "a common sense approach to settling." He agreed that the legislature was clearly a better place to deal with Native issues than the courtroom. Industry spokesmen also noted that they feared the court's decision might provoke another wave of Native militancy, which in turn would frighten away potential investors.[3]

Russ Fraser, Attorney-General in the Social Credit provincial government, said he hoped that British Columbians could now "put this whole era behind us." Federal Minister of Indian Affairs, Tom Siddon, stated that the decision gave the federal government an "important insight into the existence and meaning of aboriginal rights in Canada." New Democratic Party leader Mike Harcourt admonished all parties to "get out of court" where there must always be "winners and losers," and to come to the negotiating table where there could be "winners and winners." NDP Member of the Legislative Assembly for northwestern B.C. Jim Fulton called the decision "a declaration of cultural genocide by the B.C. Supreme Court. It's a legal neutron bomb."[4]

The British Columbia Government Employees' Union, the largest labour organization in the province, commented that: "In insulting and racist language, native people have been told they have no right to bring their disputes to court.... The provincial Crown is relentlessly seeking to grant large companies the unrestrained right to land without concern for aboriginal interests."[5]

Anglican Bishop Ronald Shepherd, Reverend William Howie of the United Church of Canada, and Roman Catholic Bishop J. Remi DeRoo issued a joint statement calling on their congregations to demonstrate solidarity with Aboriginal peoples. The Canadian Council of Churches issued a press release saying, "the judgment appears to reflect a colonial view of society towards aboriginal peoples which is not acceptable."[6] Commenting on the Chief Justice's dismissal of the validity of Native oral histories, and his uncritical acceptance of the literal truth of the written reports of nineteenth-century European fur traders, Sun columnist Stephen Hume reminded McEachern that the teachings of Jesus Christ had been communicated and transmitted by means of an oral, and not written, tradition for several centuries. "Eminent persons can be capable of the most loathsome claptrap if it serves their material interests," Hume observed.

The *Vancouver Sun* editorial of March 13, 1991, concluded that Chief Justice Allan McEachern had produced "a remarkable and crystal clear analysis of the law as he understands it," in the Gitksan and Wet'suwet'en case. They went on to quote the following passage from the *Reasons for Judgment*: "When plaintiffs bring legal proceedings, as these plaintiffs have, they must understand (as I believe they do), that our Courts are Courts of law which labour under disciplines which do not always permit judges to do what they might subjectively think (or feel) might be the right or the just thing to do in a particular case. Nor can judges impose politically sensitive non-legal solutions on the parties. That is what Legislatures do, and judges should leave such matters to them." "Hear! Hear!" the editorial cheered, adding that this was an appropriate response to "the likes of Don Ryan" of the Office of the Gitksan and Wet'suwet'en Hereditary Chiefs. A debate ensued in the *Sun*'s "Letters to the Editor" pages about whether or not it was appropriate, or even lawful, to call judges, or legal judgments, "racist."

"Call it whatever you want—ethnocentrism, eurocentrism, racism—you guys go ahead, go out in the hall and argue about what word you are going to use," Nuu-Chah-Nulth Chief, George Watts, thundered as he admonished an audience of lawyers and academics who gathered at the University of Victoria to review the *Delgamuukw* judgment, "We know what it is when we live with it."[7]

Another controversy about land in British Columbia competed with the Gitksan and Wet'suwet'en case for public attention in the Spring of 1991. Then provincial Premier Bill Vander Zalm, a tulip gardener who had emigrated from Holland after World War II, had amassed a considerable fortune by buying and selling real estate. The jewel in his family's crown was a large property on the outskirts of Vancouver that the Vander Zalms had developed into a theme park complete with windmills, tulip gardens, a miniature railroad, restaurants and gift shops. The premier and his family built a red brick replica of Captain George Vancouver's family home in Holland in the middle of the park. Vancouver was the explorer who is credited with having "discovered" the coast of British Columbia in the late eighteenth century. The Vander Zalms called their acreage "Fantasy Gardens" and made their home there until 1991 when they sold it all to a millionaire from Hong Kong, named Tan Yu. While Premier Vander Zalm insisted that his wife Lillian was the sole owner of Fantasy Gardens, legal documents concerning the transaction, and bearing the premier's signature, were leaked to the press. Further investigations revealed that the premier had met with Tan Yu's real estate agent, Fay Leung, late one night at a Vancouver hotel, where he had handed her a brown paper bag containing $20,000.00 in cash. The premier protested that there was nothing unusual about this meeting which he described as "a normal business practice." He complained that his own government's investigation of the events made him feel as though he was living in Nazi Germany. Throughout the spring and summer of 1991, the "Fantasy Gardens Affair," and the outcome of the Gitksan and Wet'suwet'en land claims case were hotly debated throughout British Columbia. Leung has since been convicted of real estate fraud, and Premier Vander Zalm resigned in 1992 when it was decided that he had, indeed, been in a conflict of interest position in relation to the sale of Fantasy Gardens.

Music is Lost on Me. I Have a Tin Ear

When I come to consider events long past, I am driven to conclude, on all the evidence, that much of the plaintiffs' historical evidence is not literally true.... I must assess the totality of the evidence in accordance with legal, not cultural principles....
—Chief Justice Allan McEachern, 1991, *Reasons for Judgment, Delgamuukw v. R.*

As a text, the *Reasons for Judgment* in *Delgamuukw v. R.* is structured predominantly by the questions set out in the legal tests for Aboriginal title developed by Justices Mahoney and Steele in the Baker Lake and Bear Island cases, respectively. The first, and the most fundamental of these questions was: did the Gitksan and Wet'suwet'en live in an "organized society" when Europeans first made contact with them? The authoritative sources of knowledge about this period of time presented to the judge were Gitksan and Wet'suwet'en oral histories—*adaawk* and *kungax*, supplemented by anthropological and historical research.

Chief Justice McEachern gave no weight to the oral tradition testimony except, minimally, where it could be supported by data from research conducted within the paradigm of western science: "I am not able to accept adaawk, kungax and oral traditions as reliable bases for detailed history.... Oral tradition may well provide useful information 'to fill in the gaps' left at the end of a purely scientific investigation," he wrote.[8]

It is important to understand what the Judge believed he was seeking, in a specifically legal sense, in the oral tradition evidence. He explains this most succinctly when he writes: "In a nutshell, they...[the Gitksan and Wet'suwet'en] sought first to establish both the present social organization of the Gitksan and Wet'suwet'en; secondly, that it exists today in the same or nearly the same form as at the time of contact; thirdly, that at that time, and since, the plaintiffs have used and occupied all of these separate and remote territories for aboriginal purposes; and fourthly, because of the way the plaintiffs have framed their case, they undertook also to prove the boundaries of these 133 separate territories and the distinct use made of them by the plaintiffs and their ancestors."

He went on to detail his reasons for rejecting *adaawk* and *kungax* as direct evidence of facts "except in a few cases where they could constitute confirmatory proof of early presence in the territory." "My reasons," the Chief Justice wrote, "are principally threefold.... First, I am far from satisfied that there is any consistent practice among the Gitksan and Wet'suwet'en Houses about these matters. The early witnesses suggested that the adaawk are well formulated and the contents constantly sifted and verified. I am not persuaded that this is so...Secondly, the adaawk are seriously lacking in detail about the specific lands to which they are said to relate."[9]

His third reason was that the attempt by the plaintiffs to authenticate their *adaawk* by reference to work on oral tradition among other peoples failed because this information did not "relate to the territory but they demonstrate the weakness of this kind of evidence." While acknowledging that the "objective validity" of oral traditions varies from culture to culture, and that Dr. Philip Drucker, among others, "believes oral histories on the north coast are usually correct," McEachern cites at length from Dr. Bruce Trigger's work that is based in Huron and other eastern Aboriginal peoples' oral history, in reference to which Trigger cautions that: "...oral traditions may supply valuable information about the not too distant past. Used uncritically, however, they can be a source of much confusion and misunderstanding in prehistoric studies."[10] In further support of his conclusions about oral history, McEachern cites two additional academics, Dr. Arthur Ray and Dr. Charles Bishop, who discuss problems of verification in "memory ethnography," a term that usually refers to the anecdotal recollections of ordinary individuals, rather than to oral traditions transmitted by specialists in institutionalized forum and in public ceremonies. McEachern quoted Ray and Bishop as saying that "memory ethnography" provides relatively accurate information "only to a depth of one hundred years."

Finally, the Chief Justice notes, and attaches an appendix provided by the Province of British Columbia for verification, that references to the historical—that is, post European contact—period are found in the *adaawk* and *kungax*. Specifically, McEachern points out one mention of moose (who, a provincial wildlife biologist estimated entered the territory after Europeans did); a story about a Chief Legaik who the Chief Justice assumes must be the same Legaik as the person who appears in "historical" written records; one allusion to guns and gun powder; and a remark about the Hudson's Bay Company. These references, in his opinion, render the oral histories changed in their representation of pre-contact, or "pre-historic" Aboriginal life. Chief Justice McEachern apparently could not, or would not, understand the explanation, offered repeatedly by Gitksan and Wet'suwet'en witnesses and other experts, that oral histories are dynamic and evolving accounts that pick up and include new elements as they arise in the lived experiences of the subjects of the accounts. In other words, the judge wanted to imagine "true" history as taking place in hermetically sealed time capsules that follow one after another in a linear progression. The oral histories, according to this way of thinking, should have been stored, like scrolls, in such capsules, and then regurgitated verbatim each time they were told. Twentieth-century listeners should, it follows, derive exactly the same interpretation from these accounts as did their eighteenth-century audiences. Accounts that reveal interconnections between speakers and listeners, and blurred boundaries between abstractly predetermined time periods are declared "untrue."

Having established, to his satisfaction, an intellectual and legal basis for rejecting oral tradition as valid evidence, the Chief Justice hastened to assure his readers that his conclusions were reached in the fullest spirit of cultural relativism. He wrote that he made this ruling reluctantly,

> ...without intending any affront to the beliefs of these peoples.... I am satisfied that the lay witnesses honestly believed everything they said was true and accurate. It was obvious to me, however, that very often they were recounting matters of faith which have become fact to them. If I do not accept their evidence it will seldom be because I think they are untruthful, but rather because I have a different view of what is fact and what is belief.... Much evidence must be discarded or discounted not because the witnesses are not decent, truthful persons but because their evidence fails to meet certain standards prescribed by law.... This in no way reflects upon adaawk and kungax for the spiritual use or value they have to Gitksan and Wet'suwet'en people. I do not purport to pass on that question in any way. All I say is that I do not find them helpful as evidence of the use of specific territories at particular times in the past.[11]

In addition to the Elders, several Gitksan and Wet'suwet'en testified as expert witnesses in a range of areas. In his *Reasons for Judgment* the Chief Justice gave mixed appraisals of their evidence. He interpreted Neil Sterritt's, and others, painstakingly detailed accounts of property transfers as evidence of inconsistency in the rules governing these transactions. While he commented that he "had a favourable impression of the competence and industry of Ms. Harris," and that "the only general discount I would apply to her work relates to the reliability of her informants...,"[12] he did not find the genealogies she collected could "establish House membership as an active force in the lives of the persons listed."[13] The Chief Justice was less complimentary towards Susan Marsden, who testified about evidence provided by the *adaawk* and *kungax* as to origins and migrations. McEachern wrote: "I am unable to accept Ms. Marsden's theory. I have no doubt it is put forward honestly and in good faith, but her qualifications are not adequate for such a study (Marsden holds a B.A. in Anthropology—ed.)"[14]

"In a case such as this," the Chief Justice wrote in his *Reasons for Judgment*:

> where the plaintiffs and their ancestors are the only sources of these histories, the Court may not be the best forum for resolving such difficult and controversial academic questions.... One cannot, however, disregard the 'indianness' of these people whose culture seems to pervade everything

in which they are involved. I have no doubt they are truly distinctive people with many unique qualities. For example...they have an unwritten history which they believe is literally true both in its origins and in its details.

A simple substitution of categorical labels reveals the ethnocentric bias of Allan McEachern's commentary, and its reflection in popular culture: Ask yourself why it would likely be read as humourous if an Aboriginal person surmised that "One cannot disregard the 'whiteness' of these people whose culture seems to pervade everything in which they are involved. Euro-Canadians are truly distinctive people with many unique qualities. For example, they have a written history which they believe is literally true both in its origins and in its details?"

Delgamuukw and the People Without Culture

> In the nations under discussion, full citizenship and cultural visibility appear to be inversely related. When one increases, the other decreases. Full citizens lack culture, and those most culturally endowed lack full citizenship. In Mexico, Indians have culture and 'ladinos'...do not. In the Philippines, 'cultural minorities' have culture, and lowlanders do not. Ladinos and lowlanders, on the other hand, are full citizens of the nation-state. They work for wages, pay taxes, and sell their wares in the local market. People in metropolitan centers classify them as civilized, in contrast with Indians and cultural minorities who are cultural, not 'rational'....
> ...People with culture have been confined to marginal lands.... In the Philippine case, the 'people without culture' occupy both ends of the social hierarchy. Roughly speaking, Negrito hunter-gatherer groups are on the bottom and lowlanders are on top. The difference between the two ends of the spectrum is that the Negritos are 'precultural' and the lowlanders are 'postcultural.'
> ...In this pseudoevolutionary ladder, people begin without culture and grow increasingly cultured until they reach that point where they become postcultural and therefore transparent to 'us.'
> —Anthropologist Renato Rosaldo, 1989, *Culture & Truth: The Remaking of Social Analysis*.

The *Reasons for Judgment* are characterized by inconsistency: the use of terms, concepts and logic are often internally incoherent and self-contradictory. Allan McEachern's use of the term "culture" is a case in point. In this instance he says: "Indian culture also pervades the evidence at this trial for nearly every word of testimony, given by expert and lay witnesses, has both a factual and a cultural perspective." The Chief Justice's use of the term "culture" as synonymous with subjectivity, emotion and irrationality reflects one of many contemporary meanings attached to the concept, in which "culture" is considered an attribute of subordinated categories of persons.

The judge's use of the term "culture," like that described by Rosaldo, simply replaces the word "race" but retains the same meaning as in archaic scientific racism.[15] This substitution of words is at the heart of what Henri Giroux calls the "nouveau racisme" of the late twentieth century.[16] In other places in his magnum opus, McEachern uses the term "culture" in relation to the Gitksan and Wet'suwet'en to convey the "ancienne racisme" premise that "indigenous behaviour patterns are based on instinct."[17] In this scheme, cultural traits are understood as genetically inherited, rather than learned through socialization.

Chief Justice McEachern concluded his remarks on oral tradition in his *Reasons for Judgment* by stating:

> I believe the plaintiffs have a romantic view of their history which leads them to believe their remote ancestors were always in specific parts of the territory, in perfect harmony with natural forces, actually doing what the plaintiffs remember their immediate ancestors were doing in the early years of this century. They believe the lands their grandparents used have been used by their ancestors from the beginning of time…. I do not accept the proposition that these people have been present on this land from the beginning of time…. In fact, I am not able to find that ancestors of the plaintiffs were using all of the territory for the length of time required for the creation of aboriginal rights, and I shall give my reasons in due course.

The judge could not understand the *adaawk* and *kungax* as subject to different but equally logical rules of validation *without first acknowledging the equality, and hence denying the superiority, of his own culture*, and, by extension, of "his people." His consistent failure to do so, and the concomitant impossibility of separating a critique of eurocentrism from an appreciation of other cultures becomes apparent. Simply put, the linchpin of McEachern's "world view" is that it is superior to all others, and particularly to Aboriginal world views. Mutual respect cannot emerge from such a foundation, as it denies—*a priori*—the possibility of considering other ways of life as different but equally valuable. When Chief Justice McEachern accepted the Crown's argument that Hugh Brody's testimony about "how white people see Indians" had "nothing to do with the matters before the bench," he rejected the first necessary condition for Aboriginal/non-Aboriginal dialogue. This can be seen, throughout the text of the *Reasons for Judgment*, in the way he repeats, in a variety of contexts, law's trap: difference constitutes evidence of failure to cease being Indian and thus to be ineligible for recognition as equal, rights-bearing legal subjects; similarity constitutes evidence of success in ceasing to be Indian and therefore ineligibility for recognition as distinct, rights-bearing legal subjects.

Insult and Injury

> *There's a serious contradiction going on in this country, and it has got a lot to do with who wields power. You haven't got us fooled about that. But we're not going to bite into this game...What you do is you react with violence or react with hate. We're not going to beat you with violence and we're not going to beat you with hate. We're going to beat you with our behaviour that we were taught by our grandparents.... We're going to beat you with logic because our logic is right, and I'll say that until my dying day.*
> —George Watts, Chairman, Nuu-chah-nulth Tribal Council, 1992, *The Law and Justice: A Contradiction?*

Whatever his intentions were, the Chief Justice's comments on oral tradition, the Chiefs and Elders, and their testimony, were heard by the Gitksan and Wet'suwet'en—and by many other people both Aboriginal and non-Aboriginal—as insults to the honesty of individual witnesses and to their collective integrity. "We did have certain expectations," Neil Sterritt wrote later. "The expectation was partly created by Judge McEachern himself. He sat in his chair and the witnesses were in their witness box, elders with whom he formed a relationship. They thought he was forming a friendly relationship...but you realize when you read his judgment that he saw our people as 'cute.'"[18]

"We talk about party line...," Sterritt continued. "If you're an elder, if you've been raised in the oral tradition to speak what you know, to speak the truth, there is no such thing as a party line.... There was no way we could go into court and say 'Don't say this.' Or 'Say this in this way,' or anything like that. Not a chance. The elders—and maybe it is part of how we bared our soul in the courtroom—went in and they said how they felt, what they knew about the land, what they wanted in the future, and where they came from in the past. It was that truth, ultimately that will be important...."[19]

"Our court case started with the elders," Sterritt wrote. "And one trait is universal amongst the elders—those who were born and raised on the land and know the land. That trait is optimism. At the bleakest of times, at the saddest of times, there's always a sense of humour and a sense of optimism about what's going on, and I think as younger people, as those who are picking up the torch and trying to carry on and win this struggle, we too have to be optimistic. Ultimately, we must be optimistic."[20]

Other Gitksan and Wet'suwet'en commentators agreed. Gitksan Chief Satsan (Herb George) expressed his frustration at the Court's arbitrary power: "The people who referee and umpire the game don't agree," Satsan explained. "And they don't agree because it's their right not to agree.... They set out the rules. We try to meet the rules, and they can just disagree with us.... They set out a test. 'You must be an organized society,' they say. So we look at what is an organized society in your terms. We find that out, and we say, 'Yes, we meet all of those different criteria as a society.' ...If you meet the test and you beat the test, then they change the test.... It's their game. We understand the game we're in. Make no mistake about that."[21]

Yagalahl (Dora Wilson) wrote: "The court case closed at 4:57 p.m. June 30th, 1990, my 370th day. This is a note I put down for myself in my note-book. 'My 370th day and there has been no document produced and no proof given that the Province or the federal government own this land....' It was a black day, March 8th, for the non-Aboriginal people in Canada, and it was sad because so many people know that we are telling the truth. We are right.... It is our land, and regardless of how many decisions come down, we will always say that because it is the truth. It will always be the truth."[22]

Dene Member of Parliament for the Western Arctic, Ethel Blondin-Andrews, was blunt in her response to Chief Justice McEachern's ruling. She said: "How much do you have to weigh, as an individual, when you deal with things like politics and law? How much of your principles and values do you want to prostitute or dilute? Well, I'll tell you something, I am willing to look at different definitions, but I am not willing to change one thing. I am not willing to forfeit the right that my people think they have to the land, the right that my people think they have to be who they are, the languages they speak, or their traditional forms of government.... Racism, even if you rationalize it, intellectualize it, tie it up in technological or technical terms, is still racism. Its impact cuts into the heart of a people. I'm calling it racist."[23]

Is There Intelligent Life in the Galaxy?

Imagine the situation of the inhabitants of Earth, visited and then taken over by space voyagers from Alpha Centauri, and required to defend their ownership of the planet entirely with reference, not to written documents, but to chants. The governments of the several countries of Europe would be left with whatever lands could be defended through citation of medieval sung liturgy. Farfetched? Certainly, but no more farfetched than what has actually happened to the Gitksan and Wet'suwet'en"
—Anthropologist Andrea Laforet, 1993.[24]

A number of critiques have been written by anthropologists about the Chief Justice's dismissal of oral tradition. For the most part, criticism has been directed at the judge's ethnocentrism, and his failure to respect the culturally different world view of Gitksan and Wet'suwet'en peoples, their particular conception of history and their oral tradition.

Lawyers for the Gitksan and Wet'suwet'en pointed to the "Catch 22" nature of Chief Justice McEachern's ruling on oral histories, arguing that: "The judge's rejection of oral histories effectively made the Gitksan and Wet'suwet'en 'peoples without history' before the first European records in the 1820s. The Gitksan and Wet'suwet'en oral histories are unusual in that there are great numbers of them, and they are very detailed. They have been accepted as reliable and used by anthropologists and archaeologists. If these oral histories are entitled, as the trial judge found, to little or no weight, it is doubtful if any Aboriginal people in Canada could rely on their oral history to establish the existence and character of their pre-contact societies...the judgement effectively makes the proof of Aboriginal rights impossible."[25]

The Chief Justice's words create an impression that he evaluated oral tradition by comparing it to written tradition and applying certain established rules of interpretation and analysis. Similarly, critics and supporters alike have, for the most part, responded to his rulings on oral tradition by commenting on whether or not the Chief Justice carried out this task competently. But, if we replace general and abstract language about concepts like "oral tradition" and "written tradition" with particular and concrete words that refer to living beings and experience, then it becomes clear that Allan McEachern did not believe what the Gitksan and Wet'suwet'en Elders said about their ways of life before the arrival of Europeans in the eighteenth century, but he did believe what *some* Europeans wrote about the same subject. His judgment of the validity of oral tradition reflects his judgment of the people whose tradition it is, not the application of abstract epistemological principles, or reason, or legitimate processes for validating different forms of knowledge.

Perhaps Allan McEachern's most revealing reflection on Gitksan and Wet'suwet'en oral tradition is his first, found on page 17 of his *Reasons for Judgment*. Here he laments that, with regard to those histories that "unfortunately, exist only in the memory of the plaintiffs.... I must leave it to the social scientists who are just beginning their journeys of discovery into the vast and largely uncharted *terra incognita* of the unwritten histories. I wish I could know what they will discover."

Like the "vast and empty land," the *terra nullius* "discovered" centuries ago, the voices of peoples deemed by law not to exist await European discovery, analysis and exploitation. The work of many social scientists who long ago began their "journey" into the study of oral tradition, and of those who testified in support of the Gitksan and Wet'suwet'en in this case, is also rendered invisible by the stroke of a pen inscribing a legal text.

---

1. Stills 1991: A12.

2. Glavin 1991: A1.

3. Glavin 1991: B8.

4. Stills 1991: B12.

5. BCGEU 1991: 1.

6. Glavin 1991: A2 & A11.

7. Watts 1992: 194.

8. *Reasons,* 1991: 48,75.

9. Ibid., 278.

10. Ibid., 47–48.

11. *Reasons,* 1991: 49.

12. *Reasons,* 1991: 67.

13. *Reasons,* 1991: 68.

14. *Reasons,* 1991: 68.

15. Kahn 1989.

16. Giroux 1993.

17. Asch 1992.

18. Sterritt 1992:306

19. Ibid., 305.

20. Ibid., 303.

21. Satsan 1992: 55.

22. Yagalahl 1992: 204–205.

23. Blondin 1992: 253, 255.

24. Laforet 1993.

25. *Delgamuukw v. R.*, Plaintiffs' Appeal Factum, 1991: 1.

PART IV:

TABULA RASA

(BLANK PAGE)

Chapter 18: Judging the Experts

I must briefly discuss the evidence of Drs. Daly and Mills and Mr. Brody because of the importance attached to it by the plaintiffs...apart from urging almost total acceptance of all Gitksan and Wet'suwet'en cultural values, the anthropologists add little to the important questions that must be decided in this case.... I am able to make the required important findings about the history of these people, sufficient for this case, without this evidence.
—Chief Justice Allan McEachern, 1991, *Reasons for Judgment, Delgamuukw v. R.*

Experts v. Advocates

The relationship between lawyers and anthropologists in Aboriginal title litigation is rife with problems. Law demands that stories be reduced to their simplest form so that a judgment can be made: true or false, guilty or innocent. Anthropology demands that stories be told in all their complexity, embedded in historical and cultural context.[1] Generally speaking, when lawyers and anthropologists work together, it is the lawyers who have the upper hand: the law sets out the parameters of what arguments can be made, the rules of the court determine how evidence can be presented, and the goal of winning a particular case dominates.[2]

Over the past twenty-five years in Canada, Aboriginal title litigation has provided considerable employment for many anthropologists and consultants at the same time as universities have "downsized" and the number of academic positions has dwindled. In this environment, anthropological knowledge has become increasingly commodified as "hungry" graduates of Ph.D. programs seek to sell bits and pieces of information and to solicit contracts in an ever more competitive market. When research is conducted and knowledge is produced through a piecework labour process that mimics the tabloid newspaper model, integrity is sacrificed to sales, and the customer often gets what s/he pays for. In contrast to the independence that can be demanded by some scholars with alternative employment in academic institutions and income from grants and publications like, for example, Arthur Ray, Richard Daly and Antonia Mills; or who, like writer and filmmaker Hugh Brody, enjoy independent financial success; contract researchers employed as expert witnesses must, to varying degrees, respond to the demands of their employers rather than to the demands of peer review or professional ethics. Imperfect as that academic process is, its procedures are less fickle than those of a buyer's market. When that marketplace is an adversarial courtroom governed by an "only winning counts" ethic, the predicament that expert witnesses find themselves in is even more exaggerated.

Given the adversarial nature of legal procedures, it would be naive in the extreme to suggest that anthropologists employed as expert witnesses do not tend to present interpretations that offer support for their employers' legal arguments. But this makes it even more crucial, by law's own professed standards of value neutrality, that the weight accorded to experts' testimonies be determined by applying the same reasonable assessment criteria equally to witnesses for both plaintiffs and defendants. An obvious place to begin would seem logically to be with a comparison of respective expert witnesses' education, experience and reputation within their professions.

The anthropologists who testified on behalf of the Gitksan and Wet'suwet'en hold degrees from some of the most prestigious universities in the Western world: Brody from Oxford; Daly from Manchester and Toronto; Mills from Harvard. Each of their careers spans approximately twenty years. Each has taught university courses. Each has published their research in peer-reviewed scholarly journals. Each, therefore, is a recognized expert in an area of specialized knowledge accredited by institutions charged with that authority within the judge's own culture. Each has had extensive professional experience working among the Gitksan and Wet'suwet'en and other Indigenous peoples. Each has a history of supporting Aboriginal land rights. None sought to hide this fact. Each submitted lengthy, well-documented opinion reports to the court that were based in research that involved combinations of extensive participant observation, archival research, and a review of previous historical and anthropological research.

While the Chief Justice set out in detail his reasons for dismissing the evidence of the anthropologists who testified on behalf of the Gitksan and Wet'suwet'en—with the exception of Hugh Brody's testimony which merited no reference at all by Allan McEachern—he only briefly mentioned the Crown's anthropologist, Sheila Robinson, once.

Since receiving her Ph.D. from the University of London in 1983, Sheila Robinson has been sporadically employed as a researcher and consultant by Parks Canada, primarily in Alberta, and has co-authored two published scholarly papers.[3] Robinson has never held an academic position. She was contracted by the federal government's Office of Native Claims to review the Kwakiutl Comprehensive Land Claim submission in 1984. She submitted an affidavit to the court in *Sparrow v. R.* on behalf of the Pacific Fishermen's Defence Alliance, an organization formed specifically to oppose Native fishing rights. Since testifying on behalf of the Crown in *Delgamuukw v. R.*, Robinson has appeared as an expert witness in anthropology in a number of other Aboriginal rights cases. On February 19, 1986, Geoffrey Plant of Russell & DuMoulin wrote to Sheila Robinson:

> Russell and DuMoulin wishes to retain you as a consultant to assist us in the conduct of litigation relating to certain Indian land claims. We wish to retain your services for four months. We may extend this agreement from time to time thereafter. Your fee would be $250.00 per day.... While we have not yet determined the nature of the assignments you will carry out, we confirm that your assistance will be in areas related to your professional and academic experience. We anticipate this will include, for example, research and evaluation of the anthropological aspects of Indian land claims.[3]

During the fifteen months that elapsed between the date of this initial contract and the submission of Sheila Robinson's final opinion report on May 12, 1987, Robinson corresponded regularly with Russell & DuMoulin, submitting at least two preliminary draft copies of her report for their comments, which she then incorporated into her final report. As late as May 4, 1987, Plant wrote to Robinson saying "I enclose the draft of your report.... You will see that I have made a considerable number of revisions and deletions.... What I would like you to do is to provide me with a final draft in a form which you are completely happy with (i.e. you would have no reservations about delivering it to a publisher)."[4]

A review of the curriculum vitae of the plaintiffs' anthropologists shows, therefore, a history of professional appointments by academic, public and private institutions, as well as a consistent pattern of employment by First Nations and Aboriginal organizations to do work in *support* of land rights. A parallel review of the Crown's anthropologist's career history shows a paucity of professional appointments, and a consistent pattern of employment by the state to do work in *opposition* to land rights. Only the anthropologists who testified in support of the Gitksan and Wet'suwet'en, however, were dismissed by Chief Justice McEachern as "advocates" who could therefore not be regarded as legitimate "experts."

Sheila Robinson has lived her entire life, received her education, and practiced her career among and within the cultural group to which she and her employers belong. And, she has chosen to professionally align herself with those particular political factions of that cultural group most actively opposed to Aboriginal rights. Both her short term and her long term livelihood depend, in many ways, upon the outcome of the cases in which she testifies. Why did the judge not appear to have been concerned about the possibility that Robinson could have been "urging the almost total acceptance" of Euro-Canadian cultural values?

Ethics v. License

The evidence of the anthropologists who testified for the Plaintiffs was seriously attacked on various grounds, particularly that they were too closely associated with the plaintiffs after the commencement of litigation.... It is always unfortunate when experts become too close to their clients, especially during litigation.

With regard to Dr. Daly, he made it abundantly plain that he was very much on the side of the plaintiffs. He was, in fact, more an advocate than a witness. The reason for this is perhaps found in the Statement of Ethics of the American Anthropological Association which Dr. Daly cites at p.29 of his report, as follows:

"Section 1: Relations with those studied; In research, an anthropologist's paramount responsibility is to those he studies. When there is a conflict of interest, these individuals must come first. The anthropologist must do everything within his power to protect their physical, social and psychological welfare and to honour their dignity and privacy."

—Chief Justice Allan McEachern, 1991, *Reasons for Judgment, Delgamuukw v. R.*

The Chief Justice interpreted the American Anthropological Association's ethical guidelines to mean that anthropologists must simply accept and regurgitate whatever representatives of the people they study say. But "...the Code of Ethics was not intended and cannot be appropriately interpreted to mean that... anthropologists are required to avoid telling the truth as they have come to know it."[5] Rather, guidelines reflecting similar principles as those articulated by the American Anthropological Association govern research carried out with human subjects under the auspices of major universities and public agencies such as the Social Sciences and Humanities Research Council of Canada. The judge's assumption that ethical guidelines aimed at insuring respect for human research subjects reduce social scientists to the status of "hired pens"—or human tape recorders—and prohibit them from conducting rigorous research, is clearly a legalistic assessment that seems to reflect case-building in an adversarial forum rather than scientific or interpretive approaches to research in the social sciences.

Sheila Robinson, while declared by the court to be an expert in anthropology, is not an anthropologist; and is therefore not bound by any professional code of ethics that might have led—by the logic the judge applied to Richard Daly—to her testimony being suspect. Nor was her lack of involvement in the academic arena of her profession challenged by the judge in the same way as he dismissed Susan Marsden's research on Gitksan and Wet'suwet'en origins and migrations because it "has not been published or subjected to academic or other learned scrutiny, she is an interested party, and she has ignored some verified facts and other learned opinions...."[6]

Revision v. Reversal

Dr. Mills, the plaintiffs' other principal anthropologist, also showed she was very much on the side of the plaintiffs. She has almost completely changed her opinion from that contained in her June 1986 draft where she attributed almost all Wet'suwet'en social organization, including the kungax, to borrowings from the Gitksan or some other coastal Indians. This is a startling departure from a large body of professional opinion on the part of a witness closely associated with the beneficiaries of her new opinion...

—Chief Justice Allan McEachern, 1991, *Reasons for Judgment, Delgamuukw v. R.*

Chief Justice McEachern's first criticism of Antonia Mills was directed to her having changed her opinion about the degree to which Wet'suwet'en social organization was derived from Gitksan and Tsimshian. He comments on this particular debate early, writing at page 32:

On the evidence, there are some, but not many, differences between the present social organization of the Gitksan and Wet'suwet'en people. This may well be because it is common for adjacent aboriginal people to "adopt" customs and practices from each other. That different people would have so many similar institutions and practices almost demonstrates the borrowing theory. Most of the experts believe the Wet'suwet'en adopted much of the culture of the Gitksan, but culture, like their languages, may well have travelled in both directions.

Mills explained, first under cross examination, and subsequently in a scholarly, peer-reviewed publication, that she had been led to change her opinion on the basis of research carried out by Isadore Dyen and David Aberle.[7] This scholarship challenged her earlier assumptions that had been based not on research among the Wet'suwet'en in particular, but among their neighbours, the Beaver. In "completely changing her opinion" then, Mills was following a normal scientific, and common sense, practice: revising knowledge on the basis of new information.[8] She was also reflecting a more general trend in contemporary anthropology away from relying on generalization and speculation from abstract theoretical models and towards valuing grounded knowledge understood within its local context and validated by the people whose cultures are the subject of study. Chief Justice McEachern appears to have taken exception to the fact that Mills *changed* her opinion, rather than whether her more recent thesis might more accurately reflect Wet'suwet'en cultural life.

Like Antonia Mills, Sheila Robinson, too, changed her opinion on several key issues during the period between 1983, when she completed her doctoral dissertation under academic direction, and 1987, when she began work as a witness for the Crown. In her Ph.D. thesis she argued against classical assumptions that hunting/fishing/gathering societies were insufficiently "evolved" to have practiced agriculture, claiming that Aboriginal peoples on the northwest coast were cultivating tobacco prior to the commencement of the fur trade. Robinson's dissertation reads:

> Implications of the relative neglect of prehistoric Indian agricultural practices go beyond correcting the record for academic purposes. Studies such as this one have direct relevance to modern political issues concerning aboriginal land claims. It has often been convenient for professionals other than scholars to 'forget' that Indians were farming in many parts of the Pacific Northwest region prehistorically and in the early historic period, or that they had well-developed systems of territorial property ownership. There is not room here to explore the unsatisfactory way most native people were treated after the mid-19th century with regards to their territorial claims: it is just mentioned in passing that when the lands the Indians had previously occupied and exploited were expropriated and then allotted to them after they had been 'adjusted' by government representatives to 'appropriately-sized' holdings for their future use, it was usually assumed that the Indians had no need for extensive acreage because they had not traditionally engaged in agricultural pursuits. This was especially the case on the coast of B.C., where territorial allocations (made without the Indians' formal agreement to allow any alienation of their lands) were, on the average, smaller than those recommended by the Dominion Government of Canada.[9]

The Province of British Columbia's legal argument rests principally on establishing that Indigenous peoples did NOT have well developed systems of territorial property ownership prior to the "historic" period (i.e. European arrival); and DID consent, implicitly and/or explicitly, to the alienation of their lands. In all her work as an expert witness, Robinson argues that, prior to contact, or "proto-contact," with Europeans, the practice of property ownership and resource management among Aboriginal peoples was simple and bore little if any resemblance to European concepts of property. She testifies that Aboriginal life was dramatically and irreversibly affected by the commencement of trade with Europeans during the eighteenth and nineteenth centuries to the point where these peoples ceased to live "truly aboriginal" lives, and that, since first contact, Aboriginal peoples have been assimilating into Canadian society, and have thus demonstrated their consent to the expropriation of their lands and the extinguishment of their Aboriginal title. Given that Robinson has not conducted new, original research in the field since writing her dissertation, and that contemporary literature supports the arguments advanced in her Ph.D. dissertation and not those put forward in her expert opinion evidence, it is fair to conclude that the changes in her opinion have not resulted from a normal scholarly process of rethinking and revising previous theories on the basis of new ideas. Sheila Robinson, expert witness, contradicts Sheila Robinson, scholar.

Politics v. Poetics

> *I found Dr. Daly's report exceedingly difficult to understand. It is highly theoretical and, I think, detached from what happens, 'on the ground'.... There are many passages which I do not understand.*
> —Chief Justice Allan McEachern, 1991, *Reasons for Judgment, Delgamuukw v. R.*

The Chief Justice continued his list of reasons for dismissing anthropologist, Richard Daly's evidence. He quoted a lengthy paragraph in which Daly describes "the world view of those living close to nature," as an example. In the section of his report that the Chief Justice cited, Daly challenged western readers to imagine a way of life very different from their own. He did so somewhat lyrically, juxtaposing the way "nature's life force" gives, as well as takes away, from human beings, and explaining the ongoing dynamic and constantly negotiated relationship between ownership and stewardship of lands and resources. The paragraph is unsettling in the way that poetry is: Daly brings diverse elements into unexpected and unfamiliar relationships with each other. He is, however, describing lived experiences, beliefs and practices taught to him by the Gitksan and Wet'suwet'en with whom he engaged in research. The Chief Justice infers that Daly's descriptions reflect a fictional, rather than a factual, account of Aboriginal relationships to nature. The judge does not entertain the possibility that the problem may lie in his own failure to understand cultures different from his own, or that fact and fiction may intermingle as much in his reading, as they do in Daly's writing, of cultural representation.

Sheila Robinson's text is highly theoretical: ironically, in precisely the sense that McEachern appears to be criticizing Daly. Robinson, using esoteric language, invokes abstract theoretical postulates inconsistently and sporadically to fill in gaps created by her dismissal of available empirical evidence and as a rhetorical device to help render her narrative, and the Crown's argument, convincing and authoritative.[10] This conflation can be read in her initial proposal to Russell & DuMoulin, where Robinson set out her understanding of the task they had assigned her as being:

> ...to develop theories showing that significant changes occurred in Gitksan and Wet'suwet'en socioeconomies during the late prehistoric and early historic eras and that these were the result of both indirect and direct European influence.

Peter Grant, lawyer for the Gitksan and Wet'suwet'en, pursued the question of Robinson's use of the term "theory" when he cross-examined her on this correspondence:

Grant: What do you mean by theory? What do you mean when you use the term theories as a social—as a cultural geographer?

Robinson: Theories are explanations or attempts at explanation that try to account for or resolve into a logical framework facts relating to a central issue or problem.

Grant: I would be correct to say that theories are not facts, you would agree with that?

Robinson: Yes.

Grant: And what you do when you have a theory is you test it?

Robinson: Sometimes.[11]

Grant questioned her again, asking her to differentiate between "theory" and "speculation." Robinson replied: "I use the word theorize…you use the word speculate. I think we are probably discussing the same thing.[12]

Chiefs v. Commoners

These anthropologists (Daly, Mills and Brody) studied the Gitksan and Wet'suwet'en people intensively. Drs. Daly and Mills actually lived with the Gitksan and Wet'suwet'en for 2 and 3 years respectively after the commencement of this action. Their type of study is called participant observation but the evidence shows they dealt almost exclusively with chiefs which, in my view, is fatal to the credibility and reliability of their conclusions…they did not conduct their investigations in accordance with accepted scientific practices.

Most significantly, Dr. Daly lived with these people for 2 years, while this litigation was under way making observations on their activities, listening, and, I think, accepting everything they said, without keeping notes.…

Further, he was not aware of a comprehensive survey of over 1,000 persons conducted by the Tribal Council in 1979 which achieved an 80% return. This survey disclosed, for example, that 32% of the sample attended no feasts, and only 29.6% and 8.7% engaged in hunting and trapping respectively.… Apart from admissibility as evidence of its contents (for I have no way of knowing if the survey is accurate or representative, although some of its results tend to confirm the view I obtained of present Indian life), its significance is more in the fact that it was kept from Dr. Daly. Many of his views of Indian life may have been markedly different if he had access to this substantial body of information in the possession of his clients. For these reasons, I place little reliance on Dr. Daly's report or evidence. This is unfortunate because he is clearly a well qualified, highly intelligent anthropologist.[14]

—Chief Justice Allan McEachern, 1991, *Reasons for Judgment, Delgamuukw v. R.*

Ethnographic fieldwork necessarily involves "intensively studying" people by "actually living" with them for a prolonged period of time. Allan McEachern's allegation that the anthropologists dealt primarily with Chiefs is only partially supported by their actual opinion reports which include interviews with, and descriptions of the life of, many Gitksan and Wet'suwet'en people who are not Chiefs. That they relied on the Chiefs as authorities on formal aspects of oral tradition, political and social organization and ceremonial life constitutes what seems an entirely reasonable way to go about researching these topics through consultations with experts in specialized areas of knowledge. Chief Justice McEachern referred again to Daly's reliance on the Chiefs to support his own conclusion that Daly's testimony, about the degree to which traditional feasting was economically supported by the community, "confuses the practice of chiefs making substantial contributions to feasts in which they are particularly interested with the day to day life of these people."[14] What the Chief Justice does not seem to have understood is that the event called "a feast" represents years of planning, hunting, fishing, gathering, preserving, storing, saving, amassing and making foods, goods, artwork and crafts by a wide range of house, clan and family members and as such is very much interwoven with everyday life. The fact that a Chief, representing her or his House and clan, makes the ceremonial presentation of collectively generated money and goods at a feast does not mean that he or she alone is responsible for having accumulated the entire contribution. Furthermore, the cultivation and maintenance by chiefly families of good relations within their own Houses and with the community at large requires much social labour in day to day life.

This having been said, I hasten to acknowledge that many anthropologists and Aboriginal people themselves have criticized some ethnographers for working with elites to the exclusion of ordinary members of communities. And, the focus on spectacular events like feasts and potlatches further tends to render much daily labour performed by women, particularly, invisible. However, the goal of these critiques is to develop more democratic and inclusive research methodologies. The Chief Justice's comments reflect a prevalent notion repeated throughout colonial history that the British imperial mission was a noble and civilizing one, aimed at liberating the common folk of Indigenous societies from the shackles of tradition, and the tyranny of their own despotic chiefs: Europeans saving Aboriginals from themselves.[15]

Contrary to the judge's criticism, Richard Daly did, in fact, take copious ethnographic fieldnotes. Typically, anthropologists maintain detailed journals that record technical data, descriptive observations, genealogies, formal interviews and other pertinent information. However, field journals also include anthropologists' personal reflections and interpretations, and information that research subjects specifically request anthropologists consider confidential. Anthropological fieldnotes are, therefore, private documents and on this basis Daly had, as journalists also do, refused to release his field journals to the court.

Chief Justice McEachern was strongly influenced by the results of the "comprehensive survey" that he cites in his *Reasons for Judgment*, despite claims by the Gitksan and Wet'suwet'en that the survey was poorly designed and conducted, and had been rejected by them on methodological grounds; and despite the judge's own admission that he could not evaluate the reliability of the study. The apparent significance of the survey for the Chief Justice was twofold. First, neither the plaintiffs, nor their expert witnesses, had entered the survey into evidence, or referred to it. This omission appears to have aroused the judge's suspicions, and led to his conclusion that it had been purposefully withheld because it showed that, contrary to what Chief Justice McEachern thought their claim was, many Gitksan and Wet'suwet'en are not actively and regularly involved in what the judge considers "aboriginal activities" like hunting, fishing, trapping, gathering and feasting. The judge elaborates on this theme throughout the *Reasons for Judgment*, juxtaposing participation in the contemporary economy in an either/or fashion with participation in the traditional economy, writing: "Daly placed far more weight on continuing aboriginal activities than I would from the evidence although he recognized the substantial participation of the Indians in the cash economy."[16] Apparently unable to conceptualize the possibility of a viable contemporary Aboriginal way of life that combines hunting, fishing and gathering on the land with wage labour and commercial business activities, the judge could only understand this integration as a contradiction. He rejected Daly's observation that "Gitksan and Wet'suwet'en persons regarded their land as 'their food box and their treasury' and young persons going hunting often say 'we are going to the Indian supermarket, to our land.'" In short, the survey confirmed the judge's view that a hunting, fishing and gathering economy and a capitalist economy cannot coexist, that contemporary Aboriginals have been assimilated, and they no longer live "truly Aboriginal" lives, identical to those of their ancestors.

Unlike the Gitksan and Wet'suwet'en's anthropologists, Sheila Robinson had conducted no fieldwork with the Gitksan and Wet'suwet'en or any other Aboriginal people. Hence, obviously, she could not be subjected to the same criticism of unscientific methodology that was levelled at Mills, Daly and Brody. The Chief Justice's thinking on this seems to reflect the notion that being a member of the dominant Euro-Canadian culture is evidence that the raw potential exists for an individual to develop an ability to discover the unmediated "truth" through the rational application of reason, learned in the process of professional education. Conversely, within this ideological framework, membership in a marginalized cultural group, like First Nations, is evidence of the opposite: they are considered *not* to have the raw potential to overcome subjectivity and achieve objectivity. In the place of reason and rationality, they have feelings and "culture." This was the rationale that lay behind the clause in the *Indian Act* that remained in effect until 1951 which automatically stripped legal Indian status away from any Aboriginal person upon graduation from university. Obtaining a university degree, which presumably evidences the capacity for rational thought, was considered antithetical to being Aboriginal. Two attributes: being white and being untutored in Aboriginal ways of life, worked in tandem to enhance Robinson's image as an "objective scientist," in contrast to the "subjective advocates" who testified on behalf of the Gitksan and Wet'suwet'en.

Just as by dismissing the validity of oral tradition the Chief Justice in effect ruled out the possibility of any Aboriginal history constituting valid evidence, by rejecting ethnographic fieldwork as inherently "unscientific" and unreliable, Chief Justice McEachern ruled out the possibility of any anthropological research ever being useful to a court. The important point is not that anthropologists may be offended by Chief Justice McEachern's contempt for their discipline, but that the Judge's findings that are based on his evaluation of the evidence affect the everyday lives of Aboriginal peoples. As Michael Asch has written, "Given the importance of the findings of fact to the judgment's decision about Gitksan and Wet'suwet'en aboriginal rights, it is fair to enquire as to the approach used for their determination.... If...the approach for determining the facts is not appropriate, this raises serious concerns about the judgement's findings in law."[17]

---

1. Geertz 1983.

2. For the record, however, Gitksan Elder Yagalahl (Dora Wilson) claims the Gitksan and Wet'suwet'en case may have been the exception that proves the rule. She wrote: "Alfred Joseph and I were chosen to represent the Gitksan and Wet'suwet'en—Alfred representing the Wet'suwet'en and I the Gitksan—to sit in the courtroom and monitor the court case, and also be in an advisory position with our lawyers. That's one thing, our lawyers were under our instruction. They don't instruct us. We instruct them. We tell them what to do. That's what they are getting paid for." (Yagalahl 1992: 200).

3. Letter G. Plant, Russell & DuMoulin to Sheila Robinson, February 19, 1986, Exhibit 1191-9, *Delgamuukw v. R.*, Supreme Court of British Columbia, Vancouver, B.C.

4. Letter G. Plant, Russell & DuMoulin to Sheila Robinson, May 4, 1987, Exhibit 1191-17, *Delgamuukw v. R.*, Supreme Court of British Columbia, Vancouver, B.C.

5. Asch 1992: 237; See also Daly and Mills 1993: 1,6.

6. *Reasons*, 1991: 68.

7. Dyen and Aberle 1974.

8. See Mills 1994 for a thorough discussion of Mills' testimony on this and other issues.

9. Robinson 1983: 405.

10. Robinson's "performance" is typical of court room ritual. See Brenneis 1988; Conley and O'Barr 1990; Levi and Walker 1990; Mertz 1988; O'Barr 1982; White 1985, 1990.

11. Transcripts,vol. 288: 21668.

12. Ibid., 22163.

13. *Reasons*, 1991: 50.

14. Ibid., 50.

15. For thorough discussions of this aspect of colonial ideology in other corners of the globe see Said 1992; Spivak 1988.

16. Ibid., 50.

17. Asch 1992: 222.

Chapter 19: How Do You Know Whose Story is True?

There is some conflict in the evidence about the start of this...[the protohistoric] period. Dr. Robinson believes that it was as early as 100 years before actual contact, mainly because of trade goods filtering into the territory both from the east and south as well as from known and unknown Russian (and possibly other) Asiatic travelers or traders who may have visited our coast. Other witnesses put the start of the protohistorical period later than Dr. Robinson, possibly about the time of the start of the sea otter trade in the last few years of the 18th or early 19th century...it would seem that the time of direct contact in the territory was not earlier than the early 1820's which is a reasonable date to select as the end of the protohistorical period....
—Chief Justice Allan McEachern, 1991, *Reasons for Judgment, Delgamuukw v. R.*

Sense v. Nonsense

The only reference Allan McEachern made to the Crown's leading expert witness was in relation to her rather extravagant dating of the protohistoric period. Sheila Robinson's influence, however, was reflected in the Chief Justice's *Reasons for Judgment* in a variety of ways and on a number of levels. Robinson rejected oral tradition and ethnographic fieldwork on methodological grounds, gave short shrift to linguistics and archaeology, ignored archival records and indirectly criticized the anthropologists who testified on behalf of the Gitksan and Wet'suwet'en. The Chief Justice's ruling repeats these dismissals. Allan McEachern made it clear in his comments during Hugh Brody's testimony that he did not believe that an examination of "what white people think," or "white frontier culture," had any bearing on this case. Nor, it would seem, did the Chief Justice think that academic credibility or professional reputation was relevant to the assessment of expert evidence. Perhaps this explains in part why the judge seemed to find it neither necessary nor appropriate to scrutinize the Crown's key expert witness with the same rigour that he applied to the experts who testified on behalf of the Gitksan and Wet'suwet'en.

Robinson provided a methodological blueprint for the Chief Justice to follow. Points presented as material "facts" by Robinson were marshalled and proclaimed "the truth" by the Chief Justice, as were many of the abstract theoretical postulates that Robinson frequently substituted for empirical evidence. Robinson's well-practiced performance skills as a professional witness, and the rhetorical flourishes of her technical and academic "bafflegab" created an aura of arcane expertise around her testimony. Her report and evidence are difficult to comprehend and critique, not because the subject matter she deals with is particularly complex, or her arguments especially sophisticated, but because she adopts an extraordinarily obfuscating style when she writes and testifies.

The historical description of non-literate Indigenous cultures as they were before written descriptions of them were recorded by Europeans is principally the subject matter of ethnohistory. Robinson's opinion report fell within the rubric of ethnohistory, and she claimed specific expertise in this field. Ethnohistorians strive to reconstruct a holistic picture of specific Aboriginal cultures by methodically combining data from a number of sources: oral tradition, archaeology, linguistics, historical documents and fieldwork.[1] Since these are the only possible data sources available for such reconstruction, the discipline of ethnohistory is largely defined by this methodology. In other words, ethnohistorical studies are based on interpretation and the discipline has treated the science of interpretation very seriously.

Robinson rejected oral tradition as unreliable. Readers will recall that her dismissal of oral tradition and ethnography stood as yet another oxymoron when it became clear that 47 of the 82 sources Robinson listed in the bibliography to her report based their work substantially on oral history and/or field work. Nonetheless, the judge agreed with Robinson's assessment and rejected oral histories as valid evidence.

Robinson's treatment of archaeological evidence as a whole was also highly selective. In her initial proposal to Russell & DuMoulin, Robinson suggested that "archaeological reports could be quite worthwhile," and she referred to archaeologists MacDonald, Allaire and Coupland as "usually forming sound opinions."[2] However, in her testimony at trial she changed her mind about this.[3] The Crown's case was based on the argument that social ranking among the Gitksan and Wet'suwet'en emerged in response to the European fur trade, and that the hunting territories outside the major villages were used only sporadically and incidentally prior to their "commercial" exploitation for the European-Aboriginal fur trade. Gary Coupland, whose work was cited by the Gitksan and Wet'suwet'en's expert in archaeology, had found that: "Archaeological evidence reflects the emergence of ranked society" approximately 1500-2500 years ago, that is between 500 B.C.-500 A.D.[4] Robinson dismissed Coupland's work, which did not support the Crown's argument.

Coupland's findings are not disputed in the research literature.[5] Where debate within archaeology does arise is on the question of migrations; that is, whether the present-day Gitksan and Wet'suwet'en are the direct, biological, descendants of the people who lived in the area at that time. Aboriginal oral traditions claim continuous occupation, but the archaeological jury is still out on the question. Chief Justice McEachern seized upon this debate in archaeology to support his conclusion that: "There is no doubt, in my view, that there has been human habitation at locations on the lower and middle Skeena River extending at least from Prince Rupert harbour in the west to Hagwilget canyon, and at Moricetown, for at least 3000 years or more. This has been established in the findings and conclusions of several reputable archaeologists.... The difficulty from the plaintiff's point of view, is that none of this evidence...relates distinctively to the plaintiffs. Any aboriginal people could have created these remains.... The archaeological evidence establishes early human habitation at some of these sites, but not necessarily occupation by Gitksan or Wet'suwet'en ancestors of the plaintiffs."[6] As he was disturbed by the appearance of post-contact phenomena like guns and the Hudson's Bay Company in what he thought should be "uncontaminated" oral histories, Allan McEachern was also concerned that the archaeological evidence was rendered "highly equivocal with findings of white man's garbage mixed with possible archaeological features...."[7] Robinson did not deal substantially with linguistic evidence. The Chief Justice found linguistics baffling but impressive, describing the discipline as: "a mysterious process only properly understood by very learned persons," and citing it as valid evidence that the descendants of the Gitksan and Wet'suwet'en had lived in the territory, if not since time began, at least for "a long, long time."[8]

Robinson declared that the historical record vis-à-vis the Gitksan and Wet'suwet'en was "virtually mute." Hence, she did not conduct any archival research in connection with her report. She claimed that the first written records kept by a European observer, Hudson's Bay trader William Brown who arrived in 1822, were irrelevant to her study because, she said, Brown was describing a Gitksan and Wet'suwet'en social organization that had radically changed as a result of the introduction of European commodities into Indigenous trade exchanges preceding Brown's arrival: "None of our contemporary knowledge is untainted by European influence which was manifested long before relevant written records were kept," she wrote. In other words, the only reliable information, according to Robinson would have to come from the written records of people who didn't write, or written records by Europeans who by their very presence—or, in this case, by the presence of commodities manufactured by them—would have so changed Aboriginal culture as to render it not "really aboriginal" anyway; or from a 300-year old person.[9] In short, Robinson denied the validity of all the sources of knowledge in the discipline in which she was qualified by the Court as an expert witness.

Robinson provided a facade of academic and putatively "scientific" legitimacy for the Crown's, and Chief Justice McEachern's, legal arguments, cultural beliefs and economic and political interests. Evolutionary supremacy is seen as being manifested in its purest form in the law as it has rationally developed over the course of western history, through the increasingly sophisticated application of reason to the resolution of disputes and the administration of civil life. To the Chief Justice's way of thinking he embodies justice, truth and common sense. In such an ideological framework, the grace of the Christian God, the will of the European sovereign, the security of the nation state and the best interests of the people are one and the same: woven together into a seamless whole. Just as the Crown's sovereignty is legitimized by reasoning backwards from consequences to causes, any lingering doubts about the obvious rightness of the status quo should be easily dispelled by referring back to the fact that the dominant culture is dominant. Were it not superior to those it imagines it has conquered, it would not have been victorious. Finally, the proof is in the pudding: Robinson drew no criticism because the truth of her story is evidenced by it being the story of those who claim exclusive monopoly over the truth.

Fact v. Fiction

> *The purpose of litigation is to settle a dispute with finality. Whether or not the decision is historically 'correct' is, from one perspective—that of the court—irrelevant.... Determining the truth of what happened is incidental to the courts role in society which is to secure peaceful settlement of economic, social, and political conflicts between two or more litigants.*
> —Historian Donald Bourgeois, 1986, *The Role of the Historian in the Litigation Process.*

Dr. Arthur Ray's evidence, as well as that of the archaeologists Drs. Ames and MacDonald, linguists Drs. Rigsby and Kari, Ms Heather Harris' genealogical evidence, and Brown's records, were cited by the judge in support of his conclusion that "the ancestors of a reasonable number of the plaintiffs were present in parts of the territory for a long, long time prior to sovereignty." The judge wrote that he had "no hesitation accepting the information contained in" William Brown's records,[10] and he acknowledged that Dr. Arthur Ray "has excellent qualifications in his special area of expertise." Allan McEachern went on to quote the following passage from Ray's opinion report as "the strongest statement supporting the plaintiffs' basic position which is to be found in any of the independent evidence adduced at trial:"

> When Europeans first reached the middle and upper Skeena River area in the 1820s they discovered that the local natives were settled in a number of relatively large villages. The people subsisted largely off their fisheries which, with about two months of work per year, allowed them to meet most of their food needs. Summer villages were located beside their fisheries. Large game

and fur bearers were hunted on surrounding, and sometimes, on more distant lands. Hunting territories were held by 'nobles' on behalf of the lineages they represented and these native leaders closely regulated the hunting of valued species. The various villages were linked into a regional exchange network. Indigenous commodities and European trade goods circulated within and between villages by feasting, trading and gambling activities.[11]

He went on to emphasize that "game was never really plentiful in the territory and fishing was the mainstay of the economy;" that Brown had noted that "the chief's control of territories was not exclusive...and was sometimes limited to beaver."

The Chief Justice continued:

> The foregoing must be considered in the context of the larger picture which emerged from the evidence. First, it would be incorrect to assume that the social organization which existed was a stable one. Warfare between neighbouring or distant tribes was constant, and the people were hardly amenable to obedience to anything but the most rudimentary form of custom. Brown held them in no high esteem, partly because of their addiction to gambling, and Ogden, about whom there are different views...described them most unkindly. I conclude from the foregoing, however, that there was indeed a rudimentary form of social organization....[12]

Sheila Robinson's evidence provided the rationale by which the judge was able to reconcile the apparent contradiction between his acceptance of the literal truth of William Brown's written reports that described the Gitksan and Wet'suwet'en as living in an organized, property-owning society in 1822, and his application of Lord Sumner's dictum in the *Re: Southern Rhodesia* precedent reserved for cases where "tribes are so low in the scale of social organization that their usages and conceptions of rights and duties are not to be reconciled with the institutions and legal ideas of civilized society." The resolution to this apparent paradox was provided by Robinson's argument that Gitksan and Wet'suwet'en cultures had changed rapidly and dramatically in the time just prior to Brown's arrival as a result of the impact of the European-Aboriginal fur trade. Therefore, the Crown and Robinson argued that Brown was describing not a "truly aboriginal" society, but rather one already significantly assimilating and inevitably disappearing. The Chief Justice agreed, and wrote in his *Reasons for Judgment*:

> In fact, active trade was underway at the coast and spreading inland for at least 30 years before trader Brown arrived at Babine Lake, probably converting a Gitksan and Wet'suwet'en aboriginal life into something quite different from what it had been....

> I find the weight of evidence supports the view that the fur trade materially changed aboriginal life before or around the time trader Brown was making

his records at Fort Kilmauers. That does not prevent me from accepting Dr. Ray's opinion that Indian social organization did not all arise by reason of the fur trade. I think the evidence supports that, by 1822, the Indians of the Babine Lake region had a structure of nobles or chiefs, commoners, kinship arrangements of some kind and priority relating to the trapping of beaver in the vicinity of the villages.[13]

Finally, he claimed he was presented with too much evidence to be able to do more than "extract from it an impression of what was going on."

Summarizing the historical evidence, the judge evaluated the particular historians who had testified as expert witnesses during the trial, writing:

Lastly, I wish to mention the historians. Generally speaking, I accept just about everything they put before me because they were largely collectors of archival, historical documents. In most cases they provided much useful information with minimal editorial comment. Their marvellous collections largely spoke for themselves. Each side was able to point out omissions in the collections advanced on behalf of others but nothing turns on that.

I do not accept that part of the evidence of...[the Crown's expert witness] Mr. Williams which suggests legal consequences from Gitksan or Wet'suwet'en compliance with Canadian law.... The honour of the Crown precludes me from giving effect to this defence. In my judgement, the plaintiffs have not directly or indirectly released their causes of action...I do not find, as a matter of law, that the acceptance of British Columbia law, or conformity with it, precludes them from advancing their claims for aboriginal interests. In my view, the Indians claims have not been discharged by any conduct on their part.[14]

Historian Robin Fisher has subsequently pointed out that, while at first glance Allan McEachern appears to respect historians, "a more careful examination of the evidence provided in the judgment will show that McEachern, in fact, paid very little attention to historians."[15] Fisher's argument is illustrated by the judge's characterization of historians as "largely collectors of documents," and his dismissal of their interpretations. In other words, McEachern heard the "facts" written in documents speaking directly to him, and he was grateful to the historians for bringing these written voices to his visual attention. The judge found debates among historians about various interpretations of documents "interesting," but not particularly relevant to the case at hand. Robin Fisher accused McEachern of having "failed to listen to the custodians of the past in his own culture."[34]

Fisher attributes many of McEachern's historical errors to what he describes as the judge's "xerox, scissors and paste" methodology. Fisher argues that the Judge appropriated historical evidence through a series of decontextualizing practices. "...The first step in this procedure is to pull the documents out of their original context by use of the xerox machine," Fisher began. "Thus, for example, a letter from Governor James Douglas to the British Colonial Secretary on Indian land policy is isolated from his numerous letters on other issues of the day. It is as if Douglas did his thinking in watertight compartments rather than as a busy governor dealing with a dozen overlapping questions at the same time." Fisher continued: "Individual documents are then cut to pieces so that excerpts can be quoted. The historical sections of the judgment consist of long successions of quotations from original sources strung together with commentary by the judge. The trouble with scissors and paste is that scissors cut things out of context and, once removed from their setting, all the bits of the document are of equal weight. After the individual pieces have been trimmed to a suitable shape, with the application of paste, the past can be stuck back together according to a new, and more acceptable, pattern."[17] Finally, Fisher concludes, McEachern's methodology can be reduced to arbitrariness. "But for McEachern, the best historians are not those who have done adequate research or drawn the most logical conclusions," he argues, "but simply those who appear to support his views."[18] Fisher claimed that, rather than being idiosyncratic, Chief Justice McEachern's use of history unfortunately represents common practice: "...there is also a developing tradition in this province of lawyers and judges presuming to be historians, whether in or out of the courtroom. Having made judgments about legal issues that have a historical dimension, they presumably feel that they are thereby qualified to write history. What these judges and lawyers are often doing is shaping the past to serve the needs of the present, which is not quite the same thing as writing history.... We can safely assume that none of these legal professionals, let alone the bar associations, would let an historian walk in off the street and take over one of their cases just for a change of pace...."[19]

A number of critiques of Chief Justice McEachern's use of both oral and written history have been written since the 1991 publication of his *Reasons for Judgment* in *Delgamuukw v. R.* Anthropologists Julie Cruikshank and Andrea Laforet and legal scholar Joel Fortune have discussed the judgment in the context of current academic debates on the nature of historical understanding. Citing anthropologist Arjun Appadurai, Laforet set out four criteria that she argued are universally applicable to the evaluation of historical validity. These are: authority, continuity, depth and interdependence. Laforet then analyzed both the *adaawk* and *kungax*, and what she calls "McEachern's history" according to Appandurai's four criteria, finding that, while radically different, both can be seen to formally fulfill these requirements in culturally-specific ways.

Julie Cruikshank argued that both oral traditions and written accounts are deeply embedded in social processes. "Written records do not 'speak for themselves,'" Cruikshank wrote, "and...like oral testimonies...must be understood within the context in which they were and are produced.... The lessons to be drawn from comparing oral with written accounts are not about the cultural relativity of texts," she concluded, "but about power and domination."[20]

Joel Fortune began with a review and assessment of the role played by history in land claims litigation in general, and in recent Supreme Court of Canada decisions in particular. Fortune put the central question succinctly: "In the context of history, philosophy and epistemology this illustrates a fundamental problem: how can past events or past cultures be retrieved from the intangible and present-ed to-day."[21] Both Aboriginal litigants and the Crown used history to support their positions, Fortune continued. Native litigants argued that original injustices, supposedly relegated to the past, continue into the present. This gives temporal depth to their grievances. Interpreting the history of Aboriginal/non-Aboriginal relations in this way also provided support for their argument that they have resisted domination and assimilation, and have persisted in exercising rights embedded in a distinct culture for "a long, long time." In these ways, the past and the present are linked in Aboriginal legal representations. However, past and present were uncoupled in First Nations' arguments when contemporary adaptation and cultural viability were highlighted. The Crown, for its part, separated the past and the present when they advanced arguments to legitimate the claim that the past should be forgotten, and "we can only be just in our time." Crown arguments that relied on assumptions of a radical break between pre-contact and post-contact, Aboriginal and non-Aboriginal cultures and practices, were also supported by a theoretical stance advocating significant differences between historical and contemporary conditions. The past and the present were joined in the Crown's arguments, however, when the past served the purposes of the present, as in the use of precedents. "In the end," Joel Fortune surmised in regard to Chief Justice McEachern's conclusions on historical evidence, "the dominant culture asserted its historical vision over that of the Gitksan and Wet'suwet'en."[22]

Arthur Ray charged that the Crown, by relying on documents written fifty or sixty years later than the time period being discussed, "attempted to interpret history backwards." He concluded that, "...after 374 days of trial covering all aspects of Gitksan and Wet'suwet'en history in depth, Justice McEachern still held the same eurocentric view of Native people that has been an unfortunate judicial and political tradition in British Columbia since the colonial era."[23]

The more important issue is, however, that the law is one of the most powerful institutions in Canadian society. The notion that we are governed by reason, logic and the intelligent evaluation of evidence is what legitimizes the state's and the courts' sole control over armed force and "the means of destruction." Fortune sets out the important problem pointed to by the numerous critiques of Chief Justice McEachern's judgment written by academics and intellectuals, when he writes: "The reason why the courts should critically examine the assumptions that underlie an unproblematic conception of historical knowledge is that these assumptions, as we have seen, inform the law. If the assumptions, when they are challenged, cannot be justified, neither can the law."[24]

The important problem regarding the evaluation of expert evidence in court is not what Sheila Robinson's, Richard Daly's, Hugh Brody's, Antonia Mills,' Arthur Ray's or any other individual expert's intentions or political sympathies may be, but rather whether judges should respect professional standards and integrity in their assessment of scholarly knowledge presented by expert witnesses in the courtroom. Not because these standards are infallible guarantees of any kind of absolute truth, but because *legal findings are based on historical and cultural interpretations*, and it therefore behooves the judiciary to at least respect the criteria for credibility adopted by the academic institutions of their own culture. The problem, in other words, is not that expert witnesses may mock the court, but rather that the courts make a mockery of expert witnessing.

Truth v. Lies

> Pointing up repeated failures to discover any but historically contingent foundations for thought does not in itself have to provoke a crisis of inquiry and understanding.... It requires rather that we acknowledge that all human inquiry is necessarily engaged in understanding the human world from within a specific situation. This situation is always and at once historical, moral and political.
> —Anthropologist Paul Rabinow, 1987, *Introduction: The Interpretive Turn, A Second Look.*[25]

In carrying out the Crown's first strategy as defendants—that is, attempting to undermine the credibility of the plaintiffs—Sheila Robinson continually reiterated and reinforced the notion that no valid or reliable knowledge about pre-contact Aboriginal societies exists, and that *all* theories and research findings are equally speculative. She then proceeded to offer an authoritative report on this very subject, using the same sources she had discredited. There is, thus, at the core of her argument, a logical fallacy that makes trying to understand her work feel like a descent into madness: she asserts a truth whose conditions of possibility she has already ruled out on *a priori* grounds. The Chief Justice, empowered by legal positivism's tradition of substituting law for fact, followed suit.

Philosopher Peter Dews describes these ideological contortions where the real and the imagined, and fact and fiction, are capriciously fused at one moment, and distinguished at another—not by principles of logic, reason, moral or ethical beliefs, or justice, nor by reference to culturally-specific rules of interpretation, or to observations of material phenomena, but according to the desires and interests of the powerful—as a feature of contemporary western culture.[26] Simply put, it is becoming increasingly acceptable to boldly follow the maxim that winning or losing is all that matters: playing the game with integrity is increasingly coming to be seen as naive at best, and irrelevant at worst.

Joel Fortune, in his analysis of Chief Justice McEachern's approach to history in his *Reasons for Judgment* in *Delgamuukw v. R.*, outlined three theoretical positions in contemporary historiography: interpretivism, postmodernism and positivism. He turned to British historian E. H. Carr's well-known book, *What Is History?*[27] as typical of the interpretivist school and quoted the following as representing the "essence" of Carr's argument: "What is the criterion which distinguishes the facts of history from other facts about the past?...The facts speak only when the historian calls on them: it is he who decides which facts to give the floor to, and in what order or context. It is the use to which certain facts are put that makes them historical."[28] Carr's book was cited by the Gitksan's and Wet'suwet'en's lawyers to support their argument that both oral and written histories should be subject to established criteria, standards and processes for validation.

In contemporary intellectual debates, arguments about subjectivity, objectivity and truth are often described as a battle between modernism and postmodernism.[29] Modernism refers to social theories that have arisen since the European Enlightenment that claim that the world exists independently of the human knower. The task of the modernist social scientist is to achieve objectivity by eliminating subjective biases like feelings and attitudes. This achieved, the researcher should be able to determine, and then reveal and explain, the single definitive truth that has awaited her or his discovery. Objectivist social science strives to emulate the natural and physical sciences that its methodologies mimic. Postmodernism refers to theories that have arisen, for the most part, during the last twenty-five years. Postmodernists argue that all knowledge is mediated through the culturally and historically specific lens of the knower, and whether or not there is a "reality" that exists outside of our apprehension of it we may never know for certain.

Fortune illustrated a postmodern approach by referring to the work of literary critic and historian Hayden White.[30] White's postmodern analysis of history argues that the meaning of historical texts is determined by the diverse contexts in which they are produced and interpreted. Texts, therefore, according to White, inevitably reveal their writers' and readers' interpretations of their subject matter, more than they describe observed events and "facts." "Recent literary theory...questions the notion that ancient documents, as 'texts' have any independent meaning at all," Fortune wrote.[31]

White's position and that of Carr are philosophically comparable in that both deny the possibility of "objective history" in a positivist sense. That is, both analyze historical documents as human creations that should not be understood outside of the social and political context in which they are written, read and analyzed. However, the two schools—interpretivism and postmodernism—differ on the question of whether or not a consensus can be achieved concerning criteria for what may constitute a "fact," and what standards may be sufficient to evaluate one account as being more valid than another. Fortune noted in regard to postmodernist theories that "for some historians, this proposition implies an especially pernicious relativism: the simultaneous interpretation of text and context appears to denude the past of any objective content."[32] In this book, I have critiqued the positivist ideology and modernist pretensions to exclusive possession of a single truth that the Crown's argument and the Chief Justice's *Reasons for Judgment* reveal. My first critique has been from *inside* the Crown's positivist ideology. I have argued that, within the terms of their own framework of analysis, the Crown and Chief Justice McEachern rejected what should constitute valid evidence: empirical data drawn from scientific studies. My second critique has been launched from *outside* the law, and I have argued that their framework of analysis is itself thoroughly eurocentric, and frequently crosses the line to racism. That is, the law demands that Aboriginal people present their claims within a European-derived discourse, and will not hear First Nations on their own cultural terms. I have tried to wage this critique, however, without making claims to a contrary but still universal and objective "truth"; that is, without acquiescing to the Crown's objectivist framework.

Objectivity and subjectivity—understood as absolute abstract concepts—are false opponents: two sides of the same coin.[33] They are abstractions marking the extreme poles on either end of a continuum. Moving the discussion out of philosophical abstractions and into lived experience makes this obvious. People in specific relationships with each other and in particular contexts in the course of their everyday living, move back and forth along this continuum from issues where there is a high degree of consensus on what is "true enough to be *true*," that is, where we can agree to shared meanings sufficiently to carry on conversation. For example, we can agree that a tree, is a tree, is a tree. However, as we move along this continuum, we find places where perspectives diverge significantly. For example, a tree represents profit; a tree offers a job; a tree symbolizes a sacred gift from the Creator. At this point, there are many *truths* that depend on the speaker's perspectives and interests, the context in which "the tree" is being talked about, and the purpose of the discussion.

In the case of the issues in dispute in the Gitksan and Wet'suwet'en trial, there is a high level of public, academic and cross-cultural consensus that it is empirically true that there were resources in the hunting territories and a significant degree of consensus on the likelihood that it is "true enough" that the Aboriginal peoples of the territory used these resources. There is less consensus that these two historical facts constitute justification for the recognition of contemporary legal Aboriginal rights. At this level of discussion multiple "truths" about the resources in the Gitksan and Wet'suwet'en hunting territories emerge. What is considered "truth" may be perpetually subject to review and change as new information, new perspectives, and new ways of understanding evolve. Claims to have "discovered" an unassailable "truth" at this level ultimately reflect points of view, experience, material conditions, and moral and political values. However, to reason backwards from the third level of debate to the first and second, and to argue then that all "facts" are equally contestable, and all interpretations equally valid, is spurious.

Truth in human relations is not a *thing* that can be discovered or revealed at either pole: in either "pure" objectivity or "pure subjectivity." Truth-seeking is an interactional process. How else could we come to know the *truth* about the meaning of land—or trees—or the value of a way of life, or what makes a joke funny, or what being in love is?[34] Truth in human relations emerges from within human relations, through conversation and dialogue, through conflict and debate. These truths are therefore always open to critical moral interrogation. The more important questions are what actions may people take, how may people be treated, according to particular "truths"? What are the consequences of believing, and organizing society on the basis of, one truth and not another? Whose interests are being served? At this point, truth becomes a moral question about justice, more than an empirical question about observations. Cultural differences present a major challenge to the search for such truths, the heart of which lies in communication. Power, of course, plays a significant role in this "intersubjective validation" process as well: whose truth will come to rule the day?

Many contemporary scholars and activists embrace postmodern critiques as shields against totalitarianism: if all points of view are necessarily partial, are constructed by human beings rather than by extra-human forces like God or Nature or Science or Culture, then all are ultimately open-ended and subject to critique, deconstruction and reconstruction.[35] In an increasingly multicultural world, postmodernist approaches in anthropology also mitigate against ethnocentrism in their critical stance towards its universalizing tendencies, and the demand that many points of view on a subject be taken into account when ascertaining meaning helps to displace the dominant culture's monopoly on defining meaning for everyone.[36] However, left within an abstract philosophical debate, postmodernism degenerates into a nihilistic, amoral kind of relativism: nobody's wrong if everybody's right.

That postmodern analyses are particularly difficult to translate into concrete strategy in the courtroom has been the subject of considerable debate among adherents of the critical legal studies movement.[37] I agree with Carlo Ginzburg who argues that: "There is an element in positivism that must be unequivocally rejected: the tendency to simplify the relationship between evidence and reality and to dismiss cultural mediation between the two.... [However,] Instead of dealing with the evidence as an open window, contemporary skeptics regard it as a wall, which by definition precludes any access to reality. This extreme anti-positivistic attitude, turns out to be a sort of inverted positivism.... Even if we reject positivism, we must still confront ourselves with notions like 'reality,' 'proof,' and 'truth'.... The fashionable injunction to study reality as a text," Ginzburg continues, "should be supplemented by the awareness that no text can be understood without a reference to extratextual realities."[38]

Based on a form of "inverted positivism," Robinson and McEachern appear to have concluded that there are no facts worthy of the name that can be told by anyone, except them. This approach leaves Robinson free to pursue theoretical speculation based on outmoded social science, while the Chief Justice is released to pursue his own speculations guided by legal positivism, archaic legal precedents and his own "common sense" nurtured by a lifetime's immersion in the "founding myths of White British Columbians."[39] Sheila Robinson's testimony, and Chief Justice McEachern's ruling, exemplify what critics of postmodernism fear most: that the adoption of a postmodern stance will result in the only "truth" being the one that power will tell.[40] Robinson's testimony and the Chief Justice's *Reasons for Judgment*, while claiming modernist and positivist authority, read like exemplaries of a "postmodern pastiche," where the writers seem to have imagined themselves gamblers in a carnival of "free-floating signifiers," where all possibilities are equally valid, where argument need not be grounded or falsifiable, and where the judicial market-place ultimately determines the truth value of any particular statement.

Contemporary life is lived within a social world structured by radically unequal, and often unjust, relations of power. There may be many perspectives, many stories, and many truths; but the story chosen and the truth proclaimed by the law has the might of the modern state, and ultimately the force of arms, behind it.[41]

1. Krech 1991; Ray 1991(a); Williams, S. 1988.

2. Exhibit 1191-2.

3. Transcripts, vol. 289: 21727-21730.

4. Coupland 1986: 18.

5. Ives 1987

6. *Reasons* 1991: 59-61.

7. *Reasons* 1991: 6.1

8. *Reasons* 1991: 68-72.

9. Yet, in her 1983 doctoral dissertation, Robinson criticized two other scholars for using a similar approach, writing: "...coming to grips with what is and what is not contained in the ethnographic and early historic records is a necessary precondition for further general theoretical investigations. There are already too many statements in Northwest Coast cultural historical research to this effect: When the documents are silent, I have chosen to rely on inference or speculation to provide an analysis that is systematic rather than piecemeal...[Taking these liberties] is, I believe, scientifically justifiable in that it provides hypotheses that can be tested by future documentary and/or field research."

10. *Reasons* 1991: 73.

11. Ray 1987: 55, quoted in Reasons 1991: 73.

12. *Reasons* 1991: 73-74.

13. *Reasons* 1991: 43.

14. McEachern is referring to the province's argument that the Gitksan and Wet'suwet'en, "by accepting and using reserves, and by conforming generally with the law of the province, have given up their Aboriginal rights."

15. Fisher 1992: 44

16. Fisher 1992: 44.

17. Ibid.,46.

18. Ibid., 48.

19. Ibid., 54.

20. Cruikshank 1992: 39.

21. Fortune 1993: 91.

22. Ibid., 116.

23. Ray 1991(a): 26.

24. Fortune 1993: 115.

25. Rabinow 1987: 21-24.

26. Dews 1987: 15-19.

27. Carr 1964.

28. Carr 1964: 10, quoted in Fortune 1993: 99.

29. Foster 1986; Nicolson 1990; Jameson 1984; Lyotard 1984.

30. White 1987: 185-203.

31. Fortune, 1993: 102.

32. 1993: 102.

33. See Rosaldo 1989.

34. See Ulin 1984 for an explication of the theory of "intersubjective validation" of truth statements.

35. See Boyle 1985; Coombes 1989; Cornell 1992; Derrida 1992; Frug 1992.

36. See McLaren 1993.

37. See, for example, Cornell 1992; Delgado 1988; Gordon 1984).

38. Ginzburg 1991: 83-84.

39. See Miller 1992

40. Callinicos, 1989; Hunt 1986; Pryce 1992; Ross 1988; Scott and Butler (eds.) 1992; Zavardadeh and Morton 1993.

41. See Terdiman 1987: "Unlike literary or philosophical hermeneutics...[the interpretation of texts. ed]...the practice of interpretation of legal texts is theoretically not an end in itself...but...is one way of appropriating the symbolic power which is potentially contained within the text. Control of the legal text is the prize to be won in interpretive struggles. (809)."

PART VII:

AD ARBITRIUM

(AT WILL)

Chapter 20: Moonlighting as an Anthropologist and an Historian

Drive-by Ethnography

Having discredited and erased all dissenting voices, Chief Justice McEachern saw before him a *tabula rasa* that mirrored law's image of *terra nullius*. He proceeded to write his own ethnography of the Gitksan and Wet'suwet'en, and his own history of British Columbia, on the blank pages he had created for this purpose.

Despite his apparent contempt for anthropological research methods, the Chief Justice took the opportunity to conduct an ethnographic excursion of his own, described by anthropologist Noel Dyck as an exercise in "drive-by ethnography." McEachern began with a stereotypical assertion of anthropological authority. He claimed for himself the unique expertise only achieved by personally experiencing fieldwork:

> Before I describe the magnificent country we viewed, I wish to say that no one can gain a proper appreciation of the overwhelming vastness and isolation of this magnificent but almost empty territory without spending at least the amount of time I spent there....

Combining his ethnographer's role with that of an eye-witness, the Chief Justice described a three-day trip during which he was "able to see about two-thirds of the territory":

> I visited many parts of the territory...during a 3-day helicopter and highway 'view' in June 1988.... I also took many automobile trips into the territory during many of the evenings of the nearly 50 days I sat in Smithers. These explorations were for the purpose of familiarizing myself, as best I could, with this beautiful, vast and almost empty part of the Province.

> I took the first six weeks of evidence in May-June 1987 at Smithers, a community situated in the Bulkley Valley in approximately the centre of the territory. Smithers is a community of about 7000 persons, mainly of European descent, who have made the Bulkley Valley into a fertile farming and dairy region....

> ...I usually took advantage of the long spring evenings to visit areas in the territory including several trips to each of Kitwancool, Gitwangaak,

Kitsegukla, Kispiox, the Hazeltons and Houston, plus evening trips by private logging roads to Smithers Landing on Babine Lake, Fulton and Topley Landing, and a single trip to Burns Lake. In this way I gained a good appreciation of the Bulkley and Skeena River corridors and their villages where at least 90% of the residents of the area, including most of the Gitksan and Wet'suwet'en, make their homes....

I was taken to and shown many of the remote northerly and southerly portions of the territory. On June 6th we visited the northern territories claimed by the Gitksan people and Mr. Neil Sterritt, a Gitksan Hereditary Chief, provided us with a running commentary on the important landmarks. On June 7th we visited the areas claimed by the Wet'suwet'en people and Mr. Alfred Joseph, a Wet'suwet'en Hereditary Chief, was our principal tour guide.... On June 8, 1988...I motored down the Skeena River from K'san to Kitwanga and beyond where many of the fishing sites I heard about in the evidence were pointed out to me....

I also wish to add that I wish I could have spent more time in the territory but helicopter travel is very expensive and although logging roads are pushing further and further into the territory, they are not always available for private traffic, and exploration by land in such country is a long, slow, tedious and often uncomfortable enterprise....

We started at Smithers and after a short detour to the west to avoid clouds in the Debenture Park area, we travelled north about 10 miles east of the westerly external boundary of the territory...to Kotine Mountain, where we stopped near its peak in a driving rainstorm to make observations of the Babine Range to the south-east and other landmarks of interest....

Allan McEachern's personal account was written in a style characteristic of explorers' journals and Victorian travelogues:[1]

We continued westerly along the Skeena. On this leg of our voyage of exploration we passed but did not stop at the ancient but now totally deserted village of Gitengas where there are no buildings still standing. We then left the Skeena and went north up the Slamgeesh River where we stopped for lunch at a point on the old Telegraph Trail where Chief William Backwater was born and grew up. There are no residents there now and only a few grave buildings and one small, totally uninhabitable building remains....

We then flew south to rejoin the Skeena.... We then flew a short distance east and then swung south down Shedin Creek to the confluence of the Babine and Skeena Rivers, which is the site of the ancient village of Kisgegas, which was once the largest of the Skeena villages. It is a large cleared area with the remains of a number of buildings including an almost fallen-down church built around 1930 but all the residents have left here although there are a few cabins on the other side of the river which I understand are occupied for part of the year by Joshua McLean. Access to Kisgegas is now possible by logging road from Kispiox but, except for the fish runs in the summer, the village has been largely empty since the 1940s...

When we reached the native village of Kitsequecla we stopped for fuel. We then proceeded south-east up the Kitsequecla River until we re-entered the rich Bulkley Valley on the south side of mighty Hudson Bay Mountain where the Bulkley River flows north, but we turned south up the valley to Smithers where we terminated a fascinating voyage of exploration and discovery.[2]

Civilization by Tautology[3]

Chief Justice McEachern's historical narrative was carefully divided into relevant time periods, and he returned repeatedly throughout his *Reasons for Judgment* to differentiate between them and to mark their legal significance:

The difference between the pre-historic, proto- and historic periods is relevant to the question of determining what are aboriginal as opposed to non-aboriginal practices. I find that the aboriginal practices of the plaintiffs' ancestors were, first residence, and secondly subsistence—the gathering of the products of the lands and waters of the territory for that purpose and also for ceremonial purposes. These both predated the historical period for a long, long time, and continue into the historic period (with new techniques) up to the time of sovereignty and since that time but with decreasing frequency.[4]

I find that the plaintiff's ancestors probably lived an aboriginal lifestyle mainly in the vicinity of their villages and during travel between their villages and this continued until sovereignty.... While there is no doubt the Indians harvested their subsistence requirements from parts of the territory, it is impossible to conclude from the evidence that these...activities...were anything more than common sense subsistence practices, and are entirely compatible with bare occupation for the purposes of subsistence. The evidence does not establish either a policy for management of the territory or concerted communal conservation.[5]

The testimony of the Gitksan and Wet'suwet'en Chiefs, and their expert witnesses in anthropology, archaeology, history, and ecology had been replete with such evidence. However, like Sheila Robinson, Chief Justice McEachern dismissed this research, and claimed that there is no reliable knowledge on the subject. He then ventured boldly into theoretical speculation to substantiate his position:

...it is likely, in my view, that the Indians in those early times would have searched for food and other products in the vicinity of their villages. There was no need for them to go very far for such purposes, and I know of no reason to suppose they did. It is likely that they visited, or made war with each other or with other peoples, using both the trails shown in some of the sketches adduced at trial, and by way of the great rivers both in summer and winter although there is little evidence they possessed boats. They must have had a way to cross rivers which would have been a formidable undertaking. I am sure they used some of the frozen rivers as cold weather sidewalks.

Creating fact from fictions of his own making, the judge then continued his speculation by determining a specific distance that people may have travelled from their villages:

It seems likely these early aboriginals would also have used the lands alongside the great rivers, between their villages, for aboriginal purposes. I do not question that some of these ancestors may well have lived and survived considerable distances from the villages and great rivers but they would be hardy, generational recluses whose personal preference to absent themselves from villages even for their lifetimes would not create aboriginal rights based upon indefinite, long time use.[6] Having regard to the difficulties of pre-contact travel in the territory it might be argued (I do not believe it was), that both the Gitksan and Wet'suwet'en would not have used lands and waters any great distance from their villages. Perhaps an area of 20 or 25 miles around their principal villages would be appropriate.... On the other hand, a hunter in reasonable country could comfortably walk 20 or 25 miles in a day....[7]

In some passages of his text, Chief Justice McEachern appeared to struggle with a desire to understand the Gitksan and Wet'suwet'en "on their own terms." He acknowledged, for example, that they continue to have attachments to their lands, even when they are not using them for "aboriginal purposes":

I do not think I should be quick to treat aboriginal use as abandoned, but common sense dictates that abandoned rights are no longer valid and land must be used or lost.[8] While recognizing that a right which is not used can be treated as abandoned, the law does not like the principle because it lacks certainty. It also requires the Court to look objectively at what may well be a subjective state of mind...I do not think I can safely conclude that the intention to use these lands for aboriginal purposes has been abandoned even though many Indians have not used them for many years.[9]

Chief Justice McEachern did not, however, struggle with any questions concerning his definition of what an "aboriginal life," or "aboriginal purposes" might be. Nor, of course, did he question his right, or his power, to define:

The evidence satisfies me that most Gitksan and Wet'suwet'en people do not now live an aboriginal life. They have been gradually moving away from it since contact....[10]

Reasons to Travel

Moving on to the protohistoric era, the Chief Justice upheld the Crown's and Sheila Robinson's analysis of this period as the one during which the Gitksan and Wet'suwet'en ceased to live a "truly aboriginal life" by virtue of the fact that a few European trade goods had filtered into their territories through trade with their Coast Tsimshian neighbours.

> It is not possible to speak with much confidence about the commencement of the protohistoric period in the territory but some historical facts are known which at least permit informed estimates....[11]

> Doing the best I can, it appears to me that after a period of unknown duration prior to about 1700...major population destabilization began to occur at the coast which probably spread to the interior; warfare became common, if it had not always been present; and within about 10 years of Cook's arrival at Nootka and his discovery of the potential for an ocean fur trade in 1778...a cruel sea otter trade started in the north Pacific in the 1780s with British, American, Russian and possibly other nationals almost extinguishing the sea otter until this trade fell into a sharp decline because of over-hunting just after the turn of the century. This made it necessary for traders to find other kinds of furs, and the interior fur trade was their natural response....

> By the early 1800's, Russian traders had established an outpost at Sitka, and the Tsimshian and Carriers had established trade networks with the Gitksan in the north and with the Bella Coola people in the south. The Gitksan became middlemen for the Tsimshian traders.... I doubt if the commencement of European influence in the territory was earlier than Cook's landfall in 1778 and it was more probably around or after the turn of the century. There may have been isolated intrusions of trade goods from unknown directions at a slightly earlier period but not in any significant quantity.... I also doubt if commercial trapping started in the territory before 1805 or 1806 and probably a few years later than that. Then with the introduction of metal or mechanical traps and a market for excess furs, I believe some of the ancestors of the plaintiffs found it advantageous to spread out from their villages into distant territories for the purpose of commercial trapping.

The judge reiterated in very clear terms, throughout his *Reasons for Judgment*, his support for the Crown's position that Aboriginal rights are "frozen" rights: arrested at the moment of contact with Europeans, and sealed in time capsules:

While the Supreme Court of Canada will ultimately be called upon finally to settle this important question, I am not able to avoid expressing an early judicial opinion. In my view the purpose of aboriginal rights was to sustain existence in an aboriginal society, that is to hunt and fish and collect the products of the land and waters for the survival of the communal group...land-based commercial enterprise cannot be regarded as an aboriginal right. Notwithstanding the complexity of mixed land use in the province, I think aboriginal rights, to the extent recognized by law, have always been sustenance user rights practised for a very long time in a specific territory. These rights do not include commercial activities, even those related to land or water resource gathering, except in compliance with the general law of the province.

According to Chief Justice McEachern's frozen rights theory, the only practices that may be recognized by section 35(1) of the *Constitution Act 1982* as eligible for constitutional protection as "Aboriginal rights" should be those that can be identified as activities that the Aboriginal litigants' ancestors carried out before Europeans arrived in the eighteenth century, and are still carrying out to-day. The judge agreed that the use of modern technology—like guns for hunting—should not disqualify a practice from classification as an "Aboriginal right." The defining characteristic that differentiated, for example, an "aboriginal" hunting practice from a "non-aboriginal hunting practice," was neither the intention of the hunter, nor the technology used, nor the species of prey. Rather, the law took a post-mortem approach and decreed that the final destination of the hunted animal's carcass and remains would define its legal status, retrospectively. If a hunter exchanged her or his catch with another Aboriginal person for another product of the land, then the previous act of hunting would be posthumously classified as the practice of an "aboriginal right." If, on the other hand, the same hunter exchanged the same carcass with an Aboriginal or non-Aboriginal person for either a commodity of European manufacture, or cash, then the result would be that, consciously or intentionally or not, the Aboriginal hunter would be deemed to have been engaging in "non-Aboriginal practices."

Given the tautological nature of the judge's reasoning, the important legal findings that were based on interpretations of actual events that may have occurred during the protohistoric period did not require empirical support. Since he had determined that "aboriginal practices" in relation to land and resources were only those that were engaged in prior to the arrival of Europeans, it followed inevitably that trapping in conjunction with the European-Aboriginal fur trade must have been a "non-aboriginal" practice by definition. What actually happened "on the ground" is irrelevant within this framework in which the answers are pre-determined by the premises of the questions:

In my view, commercial trapping was not an aboriginal practice prior to contact with European influences and it did not become an aboriginal practice after that time even if lands habitually used for aboriginal purposes were also used for commercial trapping after contact.... With regard to new lands used after contact for commercial trapping, particularly in the far North and south extremities of the territory, it is my view that such would not be an aboriginal use and those new lands would not be aboriginal lands even if they were also used for sustenance after contact. This is because, firstly, commercial trapping is not an aboriginal practice, and secondly because the use of these new lands, even partly for aboriginal purposes under European influences after contact, does not constitute the kind of indefinite long time use which is required for aboriginal rights....[12]

Apart from this, and the gradual accommodation of Indians to European trade goods and civilization (which did not change the nature of aboriginal activities), I doubt whether anything relevant to this action occurred in the territory between early European influences and the assertion of British sovereignty whenever that may have been.

Although his ruling on the legitimacy of British sovereignty and the extinguishment of Aboriginal title precluded consideration of any Aboriginal rights whatsoever, in a number of places in the *Reasons for Judgment* the Chief Justice stressed his concurrence with the provincial Crown's argument that the only lands "used and occupied" by the Gitksan and Wet'suwet'en with any regularity were the village sites on the major salmon-producing rivers, pieces of which became federally administered Indian reserves. The judge went to great lengths to argue that the provincial crown lands between villages that include miles of valuable timber, and are currently leased to giant forest companies, could not possibly be subject to any Aboriginal claim:

I believe some Gitksan moved into these areas...[outside the major villages] after the start of the fur trade, or later...[and] particularly in the last 150 years when there was a reason to be there....

Allan McEachern relied on the Crown's "social theory" of simplistic economic determinism to reiterate over and over again that the Gitksan and Wet'suwet'en had "no reason to travel" to these parts of their territories before becoming involved in the European-Aboriginal fur trade, trapping for which, the Judge decreed, was a "non-Aboriginal" and an "economic" practice. Chief Justice McEachern's rulings depended on the validity of his foundational assumption that repeats the Crown's argument: the only "reason" for people to travel into their territories was for "economic" purposes. And, "economic" activities are defined as only those that were engaged in as part of the European-Aboriginal fur trade:

There was no reason for them to travel other than between the villages or far from the great rivers for these or other aboriginal purposes, or to take more animals than were needed for subsistence although it is also reasonable to assume they would have travelled as far as was necessary for such purposes....[13]

There was little reason for the Gitksan to stray far from their villages...except to visit other villages and for journeys along the grease trail...to get oolichan oil.... Similarly, there was little reason for the Wet'suwet'en to stray far from their canyon fisheries at Hagwilget.... There was, in fact, little reason for the Wet'suwet'en to have lived far from the Bulkley villages with which they all seemed to have connections.... There was no reason, until the fur trade, for these people to have any boundaries....

The question of boundaries elicited a ruling by the Chief Justice that expressed the double-bind nature of legal reasoning on Aboriginal matters. First he confessed that the irregular shape of Gitksan and Wet'suwet'en hereditary chiefs' territories led him to think they were gerrymandered. But, he reflected, gerrymandering requires rational intent to deceive, an intellectual capacity only acquired through evolutionary development and the achievement of civilization. The judge thought such calculated, "rational" duplicity uncharacteristic of Aboriginal societies:

The unusual shape of some of the territories leads me to doubt their authenticity.... They and many others appear to be excessively gerrymandered or artificial which seems inappropriate for an aboriginal society.... Further, I am troubled by the fact that so many chiefs claim so many different, widely scattered territories....

Momentarily adopting a culturally relativistic view, the Chief Justice allowed that what *he* might see as *duplicity*, might *really* be a feature of Aboriginal culture:

It would not be fair for me to conclude that the above is inconsistent with Indian custom or practice for there is no evidence to that effect, and I must not see with uncultured eyes what may not be there. Viewed with judicial eyes, however, these considerations alert me to be cautious....[14]

In the end, regardless of evidence viewed by cultured or uncultured eyes, the legal point was made:

It is unlikely that the plaintiffs' ancestors, prior to the fur trade, would occupy territories so far from the villages, particularly in fierce Canadian winters.[15]

Accompanying the arrival of William Brown in 1822, who brought history with him, the stereotypical image of the "lazy Indian" made its first appearance in the Chief Justice's narrative:

Thus, it would seem that the time of direct contact in the territory was not earlier than the early 1820's which is a reasonable date to select as the end of the protohistorical period.[16]

In 1822...William Brown of the Hudson's Bay Company—one of our most useful historians—established Fort Kilmaurs on Babine Lake.... Brown reports some minimal levels of social organization but the primitive condition of the natives described by early observers was not impressive.... By the time trader Brown arrived...the coastal sea otter trade was finished but the taste for trade made new initiatives necessary....[17] Throughout his Journals Brown frequently recognized that he was having great difficulty competing with the traders from the coast, and that beaver returns were never what he hoped they would be. He had great difficulty getting the Indians in his area to be as industrious in their trapping as he wished they would be.[18]

Legal Rights and Social Wrongs

In his description of the early colonial period in British Columbia, the Chief Justice reiterates all the key points made in the Crown's legal argument:

It seems indisputable that the historic period began in the territory with the establishment of Fort Kilmaurs on Babine Lake by Trader Brown in 1822.[19]

Nothing of much political importance occurred in what is now the province for some time following the voyages of Cook, Vancouver, Dixon, Barkley and others. The Hudson's Bay Company was headquartered near the mouth of the Columbia River where James Douglas had been its Chief Factor since 1839.... In 1849 the Company was given a 5-year monopoly on the fur trade on Vancouver Island on the understanding that it would foster the settlement of the Island leading to the establishment of a colony.... Douglas remained as Chief Factor for the Company and in that capacity he negotiated 11 of a total of 14 treaties with Indians on Vancouver Island, mainly in the vicinity of what is now the City of Victoria. No treaties were ever negotiated on the mainland. Douglas became Governor of the Colony of Vancouver Island in 1851.... An Act of the Imperial Parliament dated August 2, 1858 provided for the Government of the Colony of British Columbia which was proclaimed November 19, 1858.

The Chief Justice began to stress the participation of Gitksan and Wet'suwet'en in the Euro-Canadian controlled economy when he came to describe mid-nineteenth-century British Columbia. This focus supported the Crown's "assimilation" and "implicit extinguishment" arguments:

As early as the 1850s The Gitksan, who had not previously seen a horse, quickly became adept at packing for the construction of the Collins Overland Telegraph, for the Yukon Telegraph, for the Omineca and Cassiar

Gold Rushes, and for the construction of the Grand Trunk Pacific Railroad in the first decade of this century. At the same time, the Indians increasingly participated in commercial fishing at the coast, and in the logging and lumbering industries which became the economic mainstays of the region.

The Chief Justice was unequivocal in his assessment of the legal importance of the Douglas Treaties:

As James Douglas was a principal actor in setting the stage for much of the misunderstanding about Indian rights which later developed, it will be useful to mention that his policy for the mainland, as described in several pronouncements and correspondence with the Colonial Office in London, was that the colony would be opened up for settlement quickly so as to establish a British as opposed to an American community here.... It seems to be accepted by scholars that concern about American influences, mainly miners and Mormons, was indeed the principal reason for the establishment of a mainland colony.... Unlike the American experience where Indians were being confined by force to reserves, Indians in the Colony were entitled to the free use of all unoccupied lands.[20]

The plaintiffs argue that the willingness of the Crown, the Hudson's Bay Company, Governor Douglas, and the Legislative Assembly of Vancouver Island to purchase aboriginal lands or interests is evidence of the existence of Indian ownership of the entire province.... With respect, I think too much has been made of these treaties as there is no clear understanding of what was involved, and the reasons which motivated the parties to act as they did. The Hudson's Bay Company apparently decided to acquire aboriginal interests in land in which it was interested, and obtained such land for a few blankets. The Vancouver Island treaties may represent no more than the surrender of the Indians of whatever rights they had in exchange for the modest consideration they received together with the substitution of a treaty right to continue to use the land. It cannot be inferred that the Indians owned the land or that the Crown was obliged by law to enter into these or further treaties.... It is not clear whether the acquired lands included village sites, or cultivated fields or surrounding hunting grounds....

This is all so uncertain and equivocal that I am unable to attach any legal consequences to these treaties.... I am more impressed by the unequivocal fact that the Crown, while recognizing aboriginal possession of village sites, was both setting aside reserves and marketing the unoccupied balance of the colony.[21]

...It would certainly have come as a surprise to Governor Douglas and his colleagues, and to the Colonial Secretaries and the Imperial Privy Councillors if it had been suggested to them that the consent of the Indians was required before the settlement of any part of the colony could be under-taken....[22]

The Chief Justice acknowledged that Aboriginal people may not have been treated *justly*, but he was certain they had been treated *legally*; and the good intentions of the colonial officials were never in doubt:

> It would not be accurate to assume the colonial officials, or their masters in London, chose wilfully to ignore aboriginal interests...their intention was to allot generous reserves, and to satisfy the requirements of the Indians in that way...it is obvious none of these colonial officers believed the settle-ment of the colony depended in any way upon Indian consent.... While the foregoing describes the state of mind of colonial officials at the start of the colonial period, the social disadvantage of the Indians was ongoing and largely but not entirely unrecognized. For this reason it is difficult, but nec-essary, to keep the difference between legal rights and social wrongs very much in mind.[23]

The Chief Justice stressed, in a number of places in his *Reasons for Judgment*, that Aboriginal people had been permitted, for a short time, to pre-empt land on the same terms and conditions as settlers:

> Douglas retired in 1864, and was replaced by Joseph Trutch. In 1866 the two colonies of Vancouver Island and British Columbia were amalgamated into the Colony of British Columbia....[24] Until 1866 Indians had equal rights to pre-empt land for cultivation in the same way as all other subjects of the Crown.... Trutch revoked this, prohibiting Aboriginal pre-emption of land without special permission. The historical explanation for this is that speculators were unfairly accumulating land pre-empted by Indians.... This provision remained in the law until 1953. This, of course, marked an unfortunate departure from the policy established by Governor Douglas, which had contemplated Indians having the same rights and privileges, except for their protected reserves, as everyone else.[25]

In his account of the colonial period, the Chief Justice reiterates his theory that essential "cultural differences" are the cause of conflicts between First Nations and colonial governments:

> Notwithstanding the policy enunciated by Governor Douglas, the anticipated equality of life and opportunity with the white community quickly turned (even before Confederation) into the same depressing, continuing and paternalistic inequality experienced in most areas of North America. The prohibition of Indian pre-emption of land is but one example, but possibly not a significant one because they probably would have sought only infrequently to obtain land in this way. Also, I doubt if they would have long retained any land they might have obtained by pre-emption because their culture had not prepared them for the disciplined life of a tax paying

agriculturist.... This undoubtedly illustrates the difficulties then encountered, (and which continue), in accommodating the two cultures.[26]

McEachern concluded that, in the long run, Aboriginal people were responsible for their own problems, having failed to take advantage of the opportunities made available to them:

> Although Governor Douglas intended the Indians would be treated equally with white settlers, it did not work out that way. Indian reserves were established in or near the settled areas, and the Indians had free access to all unoccupied Crown lands instead of being confined to reserves. Otherwise, the Indians were, as later stated by Trutch, more or less left alone. Being reticent people, and benefiting in some respects from the industry and trade goods of the settlers, they often did not object to the inroads made into the geography of the Colony.... In fact, white and immigrant populations in the province grew from the 5000 mentioned by Governor Douglas in 1859 to perhaps 12,000 at the time of Confederation, while the Indian population probably remained more or less the same, estimated from 25,000 to 40,000 with the great majority of them on or near the coast living off the sea, rivers and land to which they had free access. They were often thought not to have any need for reserves much larger than their village sites.[27]

> It is...regrettable that the Indians themselves did not take more effective steps to secure larger reserves if they really wished to have larger tracts of land allotted to them.[28]

Chief Justice McEachern described the federal-provincial dispute about British Columbia Indian policy at the time of Confederation as a difference of opinion about "theories of history":

> Generally speaking, Canada at this time was negotiating treaties with nomadic or semi-nomadic Indians on the prairies which included the surrender of aboriginal 'title,' the payment of annuities or other payments, and Indian Reserves comprising hundreds and thousands of acres. Canada originally believed the same procedure should be followed in British Columbia. The province, on the other hand, believed Canada's position was unrealistic, and that its own policy...was entirely adequate given the different history and geographic circumstances of the province.... It is apparent that a theory of history was operating at this time to create a mind-set in the Government of Canada which was, to say the least, different from what some colonial officials in British Columbia then believed about Indian interests. Neither was entirely consistent and neither was necessarily right or wrong.[29]

Communicating Deeds and Legislating Greed

By the late nineteenth century, according to the Chief Justice's historical narrative, First Nations had become insatiable and unreasonable in their demands. And, problems of cross-cultural communication worsened:

> In August 1887 Commissioner O'Reilly[30] of the Indian Reserve Commission went to the north-west coast and met with Indians at various locations.... His notes make fascinating reading, particularly his repeated request to the Indians to let him know what lands they wished; but generally the story was the same. The Indians claimed either huge reserves and payment for all lands outside their reserves, or just the former, and declined to participate in the process if they did not receive a favourable response. Mr. O'Reilly repeatedly urged the Indians to tell him what they required in the way of land, forestry resources and fishing stations, but often to no avail. As is so often the case...the two cultures do not always communicate well with each other.[31]

The judge took exception to allegations that Joseph Trutch had intentionally deceived the federal government. He defended the actions of the provincial politicians:

> In their argument plaintiff's counsel make serious allegations against many Colonial officials including Trutch, Robson, Crease and Governor Musgrave. They allege Trutch 'purposely lied' in the discussions on Confederation and that he participated in a scheme of misinformation which led to the 'impoverishment of the people.' Counsel allege a 'perversion of history'.... The evidence does not prove that Trutch himself was not convinced that the Indian policy of the province was anything but in the best interests of both the Indians and the white settlers, but it does suggest that he was not anxious to have the details of that policy known to the dominion authorities...the evidence about the character of Trutch is equivocal and, there being no need to do so, I think it best not to enter into that controversy. Such matters are better left to historians.[32]

In the context of the consequences of colonial policy for Aboriginal peoples, Chief Justice McEachern was uncharacteristically reluctant to reason from results to causes:

> However much one may regret the failure of the colonists to recognize or react to the differences between the two communities, the legal consequences arising from the rights of the parties must be determined objectively from the constitutional and legal measures taken in that period rather than from social and economic failures.[33]

Rather, he argued, let sleeping dogs lie:

Undoubtedly there was a measure not of assimilation, but rather of conformity on the part of many Indians with the growing white population. This was particularly evident in the larger centres such as Victoria and New Westminster and in the various mining camps throughout the limited areas affected by mining activity or settlement. Even in the territory the Indians were understandably taking whatever advantage they could of the white economy, particularly by utilizing its market for their furs and by working for wages. It is impossible to say if they were better or worse off as result of these changes. I suspect they would hardly be aware of the policies described by Trutch.[34].

For reasons which seemed sufficient at the time, but which have caused great resentment, the federal government made the Indian potlatch illegal in 1884....[35]

By to-day's morality, the foregoing will be regarded by many as an attempt to destroy Indian culture and identity. By the standard of the day, compared with the rest of the world, it was probably enlightened. I need not pronounce on that question....[36]

The Chief Justice reiterated his view that historic truth could never really be known, and repeated his lamentation about cross-cultural misunderstanding and the failure of Indians to help themselves. And, while having rejected the value of anthropology in settling legal disputes, McEachern suggested that the discipline might be more useful in explaining other problems:

For reasons which can only be answered by anthropology, if at all, the Indians of the colony, while accepting many of the advantages of European civilization, did not prosper proportionately with the white community as expected. No one can speak with much certainty or confidence about what really went wrong in the relations between the Indians and the colonists...In my view the Indians' lack of cultural preparation for the new regime was indeed the probable cause of the debilitating dependence from which few Indians in North America have yet escaped.

It would be overly simplistic, and probably inaccurate, to say that the white settlers were either too kind or too cruel, and that the Indians should either have been given more support, and the dependence increased, or no support at all so that a dependence would not have arisen. So long as Indians had access to white communities there was bound to be a mixing of incompatible cultures. Being of a culture where everyone looked after himself or perished, the Indians knew how to survive (in most years). But they were not as industrious in the new economic climate as was thought to be necessary by the newcomers in the Colony. In addition, the Indians were a greatly weakened people by reason of foreign diseases which took a fearful toll, and by the ravages of alcohol. They became a conquered people, not by force of arms, for that was not necessary, but by an invading culture and a relentless energy with which they would not, or could not compete....

Many have said with some truth, but not much understanding, that the Indians did not do as much for themselves a they might have done. For their part, the Indians probably did not understand what was happening to them.

Although there is much, the Chief Justice claimed, that cannot be known with any certainty about the colonial period, he was confident about at least one thing:

This mutual solitude of misunderstanding became, and remains, a dreadful problem for them and for everyone. What seems clear, however, is that the source of Indian difficulty was not the loss of land for aboriginal purposes. So far as the evidence shows, they were largely left in their villages and an aboriginal life was available to them for a long time after the 'Indian problem' was identified....

If the settlers could be faulted for anything, it might be for poor time management practices. The Chief Justice wrote that they were busy, and failed to make time to cultivate more benevolence:

Preoccupied with the business of getting a new colony started, and of scratching out a hard life in a hard land, the new white settlers, and particularly their leaders, did not pay sufficient attention to the real and potential sociological, cultural, and economic difficulties the Indians were experiencing. They became a problem seen through European eyes to be dealt with bureaucratically—an Ordinance here, a dollar there, and tragedy almost everywhere. I suspect the white community understood what was happening to the Indians but did not have the resources, or the knowledge, to respond appropriately....

Even to-day, it is difficult to say what should have been done short of abandoning the settlement of the colony.... Even a division of the colony between settlers and Indians was not possible for there was no part of the colony where Indians did not have a presence. Much larger reserves may have helped, but probably not without segregation which would have been severely criticized on other grounds. As in so many other parts of the world, the seeds of present difficulties were sown, not intentionally I am sure, but by mixing two cultures, and by indifference, during the colonial period.[37]

Driven to Drink...

As he began to describe the early years of the twentieth century, Chief Justice McEachern concentrated on how the Gitksan and Wet'suwet'en had voluntarily acquiesced to Euro-Canadian political and economic domination, and how eagerly—if imperfectly—they had tried to assimilate:

Disease and other misfortune arrived in the territory 70 years or so before the settlers or the railway.... The evidence suggests the land was seldom able to provide the Indians with anything more than a primitive existence.... There was no massive physical interference with Indian access to non-reserve land sustenance in the territory, and there was no forced or encouraged migration away from the land towards the villages. Migration away from the land has been an Indian initiative and it started before there was any substantial settlement in the territory.[38]

At this point in his narrative he introduced a still familiar theme in contemporary analyses of Aboriginal communities where questions are framed as debates about what single causal factor best explains wide-spread poor health, demoralization and alcohol abuse among Aboriginal people. This is, of course, a very contentious political question and arguments abound about whether "alcoholism" is a medical disease or a social problem. Most contemporary health care professionals in the field recognize the complexity of this issue, and focus on seeking ways of healing, rather than pursuing the futile task of seeking to assign blame simplistically. In a legalistic ideology, "cause" and "liability" are frequently conflated and substituted for understanding and responsibility:

The introduction of alcohol, disastrous epidemics and limited economic opportunities did not result from a lack of access to land.... This is not to say that European influences upon Indian life were not pervasive, but when I consider the effects of disease, alcohol and other social insults upon the Indian community, it is apparent that interference with aboriginal use of land, except for actual dispossessions, was not a principal cause of Indian misfortune.[39]

And, again, in the final analysis, Chief Justice McEachern determined that Aboriginal people are to blame for having become "dependent" upon Euro-Canadians. Further assistance would only exacerbate the situation now:

Settlement, which did not begin in the territory until the beginning of this century, was initially confined to the Bulkley and Kispiox valleys where land cultivation had not been pursued vigorously by many Indians...yet there were some dispossessions and almost from the beginning of the colony, and from the time of settlement in the territory, it must have been obvious that the Indian population was falling into disadvantage when compared with the then white non-Indian community. The condition of the Indians in the territory throughout the entire history of their association with the European settlers has been an unhappy one with alcohol abuse, disease, infant mortality, poverty, and a lack of many of the benefits of civilization, particularly health, education and economic opportunities, and the ubiquitous dependence being usually the most serious social problems....[40]

They cannot be helped, but must help themselves.

Compliance with Euro-Canadian law, according to the judge, was evidence of the Gitksan and Wet'suwet'en having implicitly acquiesced in the extinguishment of their Aboriginal title:

> The first farmers moved into the area around 1900 and there was much resentment, which continues to this day, about pre-emption of land occupied by Indians and over the issue of land script for veterans of the Boer War…. The construction of the Grand Truck Pacific Railroad from 1908 to 1914 provided some employment for the Indians, but also opened up this inviting country to further settlers.[41] When there were disputes with settlers or governments…the Indians often accepted solutions which denied aboriginal ownership….

Resistance to Euro-Canadian law, according to the judge, was evidence of the Gitksan and Wet'suwet'en having implicitly acquiesced in the extinguishment of their Aboriginal title:

> In the meantime the dispute about Indian rights continued to simmer. The federal government was anxious to resolve the 'rights' issue but the province was adamant that no such rights existed except claims to village sites and cultivated fields. As a result a Royal Commission known as the McKenna-McBride Commission was established in 1913 to adjust Indian reserves in the province. In order to deal with reserves, the representative of the federal government, McKenna, agreed to 'drop' the question of title, believing that the Courts…would settle the rights problem in due course. Unfortunately, it never did. The commissioners unquestionably gave assurances to the Indians in the territory that the reserve adjustment process in which they were engaged could not deal with aboriginal rights or prejudice their claims which, the commissioners said, would be looked after by other means, more particularly the proposed reference to the Exchequer Court.

> In 1927 a Special Joint Committee of the House of Commons and Senate inquired into 'Indian affairs' and rejected all the claims of the Indians of British Columbia to anything except the reserves which had been allotted to them.[42]

Infantile Disorders

> *I do not consider it necessary to mention anything else which occurred between 1927 and the commencement of this action in 1984.*
> —Chief Justice Allan McEachern, 1991, *Reasons for Judgment, Delgamuukw v. R.*[43]

Like a toddler who cannot understand why, when she closes her eyes, everyone else can still see her, Chief Justice McEachern seemed to mistake the law for reality in this statement. He did, however, go on to comment extensively on events that occurred between 1927 and 1984.

Reasoning backwards from the present to the past, the Chief Justice made the somewhat alarming claim that the observations he made in 1987 allowed him to simultaneously view what was happening in the territory hundreds of years ago:

> If the land is substantially empty now, as I believe it is except for non aboriginal purposes such as commercial trapping, mining or logging, then I believe it was also empty for aboriginal purposes at the time of contact....[44] As it is empty now, it was probably empty both at the time of contact and, except possibly for some limited commercial trapping, at the time of sovereignty.[45]

Just as the Judge had observed the "vast emptiness" of the Gitksan and Wet'suwet'en territories, so too had other non-Aboriginal eye-witnesses seen an unoccupied land stretching before them:

> In this century, long time settlers such as Mr. Shelford were, until very recently, unaware of any claim to aboriginal ownership or control of the territory or of any claim to an interest inconsistent with the activities of himself and other white settlers.... Mr. Shelford...has been living near the west end of Francois Lake since the 1920's. Much of this area is known as the Shelford Hills. He did not know until recently that the few Indians in his neighbourhood, with whom he was always on friendly terms, claimed to be the owners of both his trapline as well as their own and all the other lands in the area. This seriously questions the existence of an undisputed, settled reputation[46] sufficient to found a declaration of any kind of interest in land...it is impossible to infer a community reputation for an interest in land when a prominent, life long resident in the area like Mr. Shelford, a Member of the Legislature for many years, and a Cabinet Minister for a time, who acknowledges hearing about general land claims for a long time, has never heard until very recently of claims of ownership or jurisdiction, or claims to specific lands, including his own,[47] by Chiefs whose families he has known personally for most of his life.[48]

The Chief Justice considered the possibility that, actually, the Gitksan and Wet'suwet'en didn't even really understand their own claims:

> It seems to me that there has always been much uncertainty about the true nature of 'Indian title' in the province. Even some Indians have not always been completely consistent because there are references in the historical record to suggestions that enlarged reserves were their primary concern. In this respect, of course, the speakers, whoever they may have been, did not speak for anyone but themselves.

Although he admitted they have taken a consistent position on the subject for at least 100 years:

> I think it is fair to conclude that the basic position of most Indians, at least since 1880, was that the various Indian tribes or peoples owned all or most of the province.... It is not difficult to summarize the position of the province. Since Confederation, the position of the province has been consistent, even unyielding, on the question of 'Indian title'....[49]

Unlike legal decisions that become more true with each utterance, the Chief Justice concluded that, because Aboriginal people have consistently taken every opportunity to assert their Aboriginal title, and their argument has not changed since contact, and because they have discussed their case for over a century, their claim has ceased to be based on "objective evidence." Its validity has been *weakened* by time and repetition. The Gitksan and Wet'suwet'en, it would seem, are not blessed—as are Judge McEachern and Mr. Shelford—with the ability to see the past in the present:

> What happened is that, beginning in 1973, following the *Calder* case, the plaintiffs began thinking about their boundaries....[50] During this process, there has been much discussion within the Indian communities about the collection of this information for land claim purposes. This deprives the process of the objectivity which would have added confidence to it....[51] The plaintiffs and their ancestors have been actively discussing land claims for many years, long before the McKenna-McBride Commission in 1914. This has been a very current issue with the plaintiffs for a very long time. The collection of evidence in such a climate deprives it of the independence and objectivity expected for reputation evidence.[52] I find that, except for occasional political statements, the plaintiffs in the post sovereignty period seldom conducted themselves as if they believed they were owners of such vast areas.[53]

Camp Potlatch

Chief Justice McEachern repeated his opinion that cultural assimilation and economic integration were the answers to "the Indian problem" in a variety of passages in his *Reasons for Judgment*. However, the judge also ruled in favour of the Crown's position that nothing resembling an "economy" existed before European colonization, therefore Aboriginal people could not, by definition, engage in "economic" activities. If they did, they were, *ipso facto*, engaging in "non-Aboriginal" practices. Just as trading with the Hudson's Bay Company had brought an end to their historic identity as Aboriginal peoples, so too the judge interpreted participation in the Euro-Canadian controlled-economy as evidence that cast doubt on the legitimacy of contemporary Gitksan and Wet'suwet'en claims to "Aboriginal" rights:

Witness after witness admitted participation in the wage or cash economy. Art Matthews Jr., (Tenimyget) for example, is an enthusiastic, weekend aboriginal hunter. But at the time of trial, he was also head saw filer at the Westar sawmill at Gitwangak where he had been steadily employed for 15 years, a graduate of the B.C. Institute of Technology, a shop steward, and a member of the Negotiating Committee of the Industrial Woodworkers of America. Pete Muldoe (Gitludahl) has followed a variety of non-aboriginal vocations including logging on the lands claimed by another chief; Joan Ryan (Hanamuxw) teaches school in Prince Rupert.... Even in their aboriginal pursuits...the plaintiffs do not seem to consider themselves tied to particular territories....[54]

The judge bemoaned the passing of the "aboriginal" way of life of his fantasies:

I have no doubt aboriginal activities have fallen very much into disuse in many areas. This was admitted by several Indian witnesses who observed that many of their young people have very little interest in aboriginal pursuits. Eventually, the Indians must decide how best they can combine the advantages the reserves afford them with the opportunities they have to share and participate in the larger economy, but it is obvious they must make their way off the reserves.... Care must always be taken to ensure that the good things of community life are not sacrificed just on economic grounds....[55] Without intending any offence, I have driven through some of the reserves which demonstrate disadvantages, and I have witnessed first-hand how some of them live. It is interesting to note that housing on reserves seems to be much better where there is (or was) a payroll such as from the sawmill at Kitwangak.[56]

The Chief Justice did recommend a way for Aboriginal and non-Aboriginal practices to be reconciled:

The Crown's obligation, in my judgment, is to permit aboriginal people, but subject to the general law of the province, to use any unoccupied or vacant Crown land for subsistence purposes until such time as the land is dedicated to another purpose.... Land that is conveyed away, but later returned to the Crown, becomes again usable by Indians. Crown lands that are leased or licensed, such as for clear-cut logging to use an extreme example, become usable again after logging operations are completed or abandoned.[57]

McEachern's comments recall a familiar adage, often voiced by actors playing demoralized settlers in old western movies: "This land ain't good for nothin' no more. Might as well give the country back to the Indians." The fact that second-class treatment of Aboriginal peoples is considered justifiable at many levels of Canadian society is not, however, a joke. Neither is there anything funny about the clear-cutting of British Columbia forests, that the law permits.

On another matter of considerable contemporary political significance, the judge took the time to remind his readers that a disproportionate number of Indian people are, like himself, dependent for their income on the public purse. He urged Aboriginal people to take their citizenship responsibilities more seriously and to be generous and public-spirited:

> The plaintiffs are also troubled because they have not progressed equally with some of the 'newcomers,' and because they have not been able, for many real and intangible reasons, to share the opportunities they think they should have to the commercial use of the land and to the prosperity they think should accrue to them from the land they truly believe is their own.... At the same time, the Indians must realize the importance of creating public wealth from the territory as they, like so many members of the non-Indian community, are heavily dependent upon public funding for every day sustenance....[58]

> The worst thing that has happened to our Indian people was our joint inability to react to failure and to make adjustments when things were not going well...the answer to these social questions, ultimately, will be found in the good health and education of young Indian people, and the removal of the conditions that have made poverty and dependence upon public funding their normal way of life...the difficulties of adapting to changing circumstances, not limited land use, is the principal cause of Indian misfortune....[59]

> The Indians have remained dependent for too long. Even a national annual payment of billions of dollars on Indian problems, which undoubtedly ameliorates some hardship, will not likely break this debilitating cycle of dependence.[60]

The Chief Justice then turned his attention to the issue of spirituality:

> There is a further dimension to this question, however, which must also be considered. I refer to the obvious spiritual connection some Indians have with the land. I accept this as a real concern to the plaintiffs worthy of as much consideration as actual sustenance use.... Except in rare cases, there should be no difficulty obtaining sufficient fish, game and other products from most areas of the territory...for spiritual purposes.

The judge continued along this path, noting that, in fact, First Nations people were greatly aided in their spiritual growth by colonization and modern technology:

> I believe the Indians of the territory are probably now much more united and cohesive as peoples, and they are more culturally sensitive to their aboriginal birthright than they were when life was so harsh and communication so difficult. I cannot find lack of access to aboriginal land has seriously harmed the identity of these peoples....[61]

In this respect I pause to mention that the salmon of the great rivers pass right alongside the principal villages and one need not travel far from the villages to reach wilderness areas were game can usually be taken. There is much wood in the territory and it can be obtained far more easily with chain saws, snowmobiles and 4 x 4's than in earlier days. Anyone can now travel with much greater ease to whatever parts of the territory he or she may wish for the purpose of gathering what is required for sustenance or ceremonial purposes....[62]

Reflecting on contemporary practices later in his text, the judge surmised:

The aboriginal activities that are being pursued now may be indistinguishable in many cases from the wilderness activities enjoyed by many non-Indian citizens of the province.[63]

Chief Justice McEachern's point of view is not uncommon. It repeated an opinion that is frequently expressed in British Columbia by people who argue that Aboriginal people are not different enough to claim distinct rights. The equating of Aboriginal hunting, fishing and gathering with recreational camping decontextualizes and reduces these practices to their most simplistic form, as behaviours and commodities: one of many experiences that can be purchased in the leisure and entertainment market place.

And, he concluded, the market place does not discriminate on the basis of race or culture as it sifts the wheat from the chaff:

There is no doubt, as I have said, that many of the present male and female population trapped and hunted for economic reasons in their youth. However, most of them discontinued trapping years ago before or at the time the price of furs collapsed in the 1950's, and they have gradually moved into other segments of the cash economy even though the price of furs has recovered. There is very little, and decreasing, interest in pursuing these activities at the present time.[64]

Many aboriginals are directly engaged in the wage economy, and few—not enough but some—participate as entrepreneurs. Mr. Pete Muldoe, a prominent Gitksan hereditary chief, has engaged in logging and sawmilling in the territory, as has the Moricetown Band Council. The aboriginal communities, like the provincial community, have their economic successes and failures.[65]

The Battle of Britain

Chief Justice McEachern's *Reasons for Judgment* in *Delgamuukw v. R.*, ended with a proposal for resolving outstanding Aboriginal title and rights claims. Not surprisingly, his prescription for the future reflected his analysis of the past:

It is my conclusion, reached upon a consideration of the evidence which is not conveniently available to many, that the difficulties facing the Indian population of the territory, and probably throughout Canada, will not be solved in the context of legal rights. Legal proceedings have been useful in raising awareness levels about a serious national problem....

The parties have concentrated for too long on legal and constitutional questions such as ownership, sovereignty, and 'rights,' which are fascinating legal concepts. Important as these questions are, answers to legal questions will not solve the underlying social and economic problems which have disadvantaged Indian peoples from the earliest times. Indians have had many opportunities to join mainstream Canadian economic and social life. Some Indians do not wish to join, but many cannot....

This increasingly cacophonous dialogue about legal rights and social wrongs has created a positional attitude with many exaggerated allegations and arguments, and a serious lack of reality. Surely it must be obvious that there have been failings on both sides. It is not the law, or common sense, nor is it in the interest of people of the province or of the plaintiffs that the development, business and economy of the province and its citizens should constantly be burdened by litigation or be injunctioned into abeyance by endless or successive legal proceedings.[66]

While he ruled that they had occupied a low rung on the theoretical ladder of social evolutionary development when Europeans had arrived, Chief Justice McEachern found that the Gitksan and Wet'suwet'en had progressed over the last two hundred years:

Compared with many Indian Bands in the province, the Gitksan and Wet'suwet'en peoples have already achieved a relatively high level of social organization. They have a number of promising leaders, a sense of purpose and a likely ability to move away from dependence if they get the additional assistance they require. I cannot, of course, speak with confidence about other Indian peoples because I have not studied them.

I am impressed that the Gitksan and Wet'suwet'en are ready for an intelligent new arrangement with both levels of government. I am not persuaded that the answers to the problems facing the Indians will be found in the reserve system which has created fishing footholds, and ethnic enclaves. Some of these reserves in the territory are so minuscule, or abandoned, that they are of little or no use or value.... It must be recognized...that most of the reserves in the territory are not economic units and it is not likely that they can be made so without serious disruption to the entire area....[67]

The judge credited himself, and the Canadian legal system, with having saved the day, and the people:

I wish to say...that I shall leave this case with the settled conviction that, in the long run, the greatest value of this case, apart from being the first stage in the settlement of legal rights, may well be the enhancement of interest in Gitksan and Wet'suwet'en languages, traditions and cultures. This is because the evidence satisfies me this case has been a 'Battle of Britain' for these peoples and it has inspired them to renew (an accurate word, in my view) what was a declining interest in their aboriginal heritage. The interest and activity generated by this law suit assures the survival of these peoples as distinct societies. This may at one time have been doubtful but I now believe it is a certainty.[68]

---

1. Pratt 1992.

2. McEachern, Allan (1991) "Schedule 1. Itinerary of View of Territory June, 1988," *Reasons for Judgment in Delgamuukw v. R.*, 305-307.

3. Tautology: true by virtue of its local form alone.

4. *Reasons*, 1991: 211-212.

5. *Reasons*, 1991: 213.

6. *Reasons*, 1991: 274.

7. *Reasons*, 1991: 275.

8. *Reasons*, 1991: 284.

9. *Reasons*, 1991: 291.

10. *Reasons*, 1991: 56.

11. *Reasons*, 1991: 23.

12. *Reasons*, 1991: 210-212.

13. Arthur Ray has pointed out that the judge accepted as valid Ray's evidence that the Chiefs owned and regulated beaver trapping sites, and did not eat the meat of the beaver but rather prized their pelts for trade: that is, they exercised ownership and control over a resource they did *not* use for subsistence but rather produced for exchange. Given that the judge accepted this as "fact," his conclusion that the Gitksan and Wet'suwet'en had no interest in non-subsistence harvesting before European arrival is illogical (Ray, 1991(b): 312).

14. *Reasons*, 1991: 262.

15. *Reasons*, 1991: 261.

16. *Reasons*, 1991: 75.

17. *Reasons*, 1991: 74.

18. *Reasons*, 1991: 26.

19. *Reasons*, 1991: 25.

20. *Reasons*, 1991: 26.

21. *Reasons*, 1991: 124.

22. *Reasons*, 1991: 234.

23. *Reasons*, 1991: 235.

24. *Reasons*, 1991: 26.

25. *Reasons*, 1991: 126.

26. *Reasons*, 1991: 126.

27. *Reasons*, 1991: 128.

28. *Reasons*, 1991: 221.

29. *Reasons*, 1991: 28.

30. Governor Joseph Trutch's brother-in-law, and appointee to the Indian Reserve Commission.

31. *Reasons*, 1991: 167.

32. *Reasons*, 1991: 132.

33. *Reasons*, 1991: 235.

34. *Reasons*, 1991: 133.

35. *Reasons*, 1991: 28.

36. *Reasons*, 1991: 128.

37. *Reasons*, 1991: 129.

38. *Reasons*, 1991: 250.

39. *Reasons*, 1991: 251.

40. *Reasons*, 1991: 250.

41. *Reasons*, 1991: 28.

42. *Reasons*, 1991: 28-29.

43. *Reasons*, 1991: 182.

44. *Reasons*, 1991: 275.

45. *Reasons*, 1991: 276.

46. In common law, a "reputation" of ownership—that is, common knowledge within one's community that one is the owner of a particular plot—is considered valid evidence of proof of ownership. Chief Justice McEachern, in rejecting oral tradition as valid evidence of a "reputation of ownership," in effect racialized this "common" law principle. He rejected reputation of ownership confirmed by the Aboriginal community, in favour of reputation of ownership asserted by Euro-Canadian settlers.

47. But, note that neither the Gitksan and Wet'suwet'en or any other First Nation in British Columbia has included privately owned homes and lots in its claim. Chief

Justice McEachern acknowledged this at page 10, writing: "The plaintiffs, in what I understand they regard as a matter of grace on their part, do not seek to recover pre-Writ (1984) privately owned (fee simple) lands within the territory. Instead, they claim compensation from the province for the value of whatever territorial interests have been transferred to other ownership. They claim the right to terminate all less than fee simple legal interests in the territory, such as logging, mining and other leases or licenses.

48. *Reasons*, 1991: 222.

49. *Reasons*, 1991: 182.

50. *Reasons*, 1991: 263.

51. *Reasons*, 1991: 264.

52. *Reasons*, 1991: 266.

53. *Reasons*, 1991: 222.

54. *Reasons*, 1991: 56.

55. *Reasons*, 1991: 291-292.

56. *Reasons*, 1991: 184.

57. *Reasons*, 1991: 248.

58. *Reasons*, 1991: 252.

59. *Reasons*, 1991: 248.

60. *Reasons*, 1991: 299.

61. *Reasons*, 1991: 37.

62. *Reasons*, 1991: 251.

63. *Reasons*, 1991: 291.

64. *Reasons*, 1991: 56.

65. *Reasons*, 1991: 228-229.

66. *Reasons*, 1991: 253-254.

67. *Reasons*, 1991: 248.

68. *Reasons*, 1991: 37.

PART VIII:

AD INFINITUM

(GOING ON FOREVER, INTO INFINITY)

Chapter 21: *Delgamuukw* at the British Columbia Court of Appeal, 1993

...The reason why courts have had no difficulty taking judicial notice of the facts of history is that historical fact is not a matter of opinion when dealt with by the courts. The doctrine of judicial notice is firmly grounded in the court's recognition of its general ability to deal with matters of history without the assistance of experts. Historians revise history.... The Chief Justice's ruling is consistent with the doctrine of judicial notice...and is based firmly on the difference between the way historians approach history and judges approach history.[1]
—Province of British Columbia, 1991, Defendant's Appeal Factum.

We Own Therefore We Are

It was on the question of extinguishment that the Chief Justice's ruling elicited the most surprise within the legal community as a whole. Critics argued that the Chief Justice's findings in law were as archaic and, in some cases, as questionable in terms of fact and reasoning as his findings on oral tradition, anthropology and history.[2] The legal test for extinguishment that had been developing since *Calder* was affirmed by the Supreme Court of Canada's decision in *R. v. Sparrow* in these words: "The test for extinguishment to be adopted, in our opinion, is that the Sovereign's intention must be clear and plain if it is to extinguish an aboriginal right."[3] Chief Justice McEachern's interpretation that such expressions of a "clear and plain intention" could be inferred post hoc and reasoned backwards in time from the contemporary consequences of colonial domination, flew in the face of contemporary legal thinking. Furthermore, the Supreme Court of Canada had suggested that the "honour of the Crown" would be well served by reasonable attempts to obtain Aboriginal consent to extinguishment as well. McEachern's crude "to the victors go the spoils" analysis shocked several of his own peers.

Second, legal critics were taken aback by McEachern's ruling that Aboriginal jurisdiction and customary law "gave way" to colonial law upon the establishment of the colonies of Vancouver Island and the mainland in the mid-nineteenth centuries. The problem, scholars pointed out, was that British colonial law had no provision for Indigenous legal systems to simply "give way." The direction of the Memorandum of the Privy Council of 1722, and subsequent proclamations and treaties had stipulated clearly that British imperial law required that a choice be made between two options: either Indigenous people were there living in an organized society with recognizable forms of government in which case the doctrine of conquest applied, and Indigenous laws were to continue until expressly extinguished by the conquering sovereign through military force and/or treaty; or, if no Indigenous people were "discovered" living in the lands desired by the sovereign; or were deemed not to be living in an organized society and their land declared *terra nullius*, the doctrine of discovery/occupation/settlement applied, and the sovereign's laws could be superimposed at the moment of discovery. Chief Justice McEachern invented new law by finding *both* that underlying title was vested in the British Crown since the sixteenth century by virtue of the doctrine of discovery, based on *terra nullius; and* that the Gitksan and Wet'suwet'en lived in an organized society at whatever moments in time Britain may have *post hoc* and *de facto* asserted sovereignty between 1774 and 1860.[4] As anticipated, Chief Justice McEachern's decision was appealed by the Gitksan and Wet'suwet'en, and the appeal was responded to by the provincial and federal governments.

In November 1991, six months before Chief Justice McEachern's ruling in *Delgamuukw v. R.* had been rendered, the left-leaning, social democratic New Democratic Party (NDP) had been voted into office on a platform that included promises that they would recognize Aboriginal title and commence negotiations of Aboriginal rights. With the exception of the years 1974-1976, British Columbia had been governed since 1953 by the right-leaning, free-enterprise Social Credit party who had, until 1990, staunchly opposed any recognition of, or negotiations with, Aboriginal peoples on the land question. It was a Social Credit "provincial crown" who, with the law firm of Russell & Dumoulin, had argued the cases from *Calder* to *Delgamuukw*. However, it was an NDP government that was forced to make a decision about what do to when the Gitksan and Wet'suwet'en appealed Judge McEachern's ruling to the British Columbia Court of Appeal. The Crown had changed heads.

The NDP and the Gitksan and Wet'suwet'en Hereditary Chiefs negotiated an agreement to request that the B.C. Court of Appeal be asked to decide only some of the questions that arose from Chief Justice McEachern's decision. Outstanding questions would be left for the Supreme Court of Canada to decide if, by the time an appeal of *Delgamuukw v. R.* came before them, the Gitksan and Wet'suwet'en had been unable to reach negotiated agreements with the federal and provincial governments. The NDP government put forward the following position in its appeal factum:

(1) The trial judge (McEachern) erred in making a finding of "blanket extinguishment" on the basis of colonial instruments enacted prior to 1871.
(2) The Plaintiffs (Gitksan and Wet'suwet'en) do not have a right to ownership of, or a proprietary interest in, the lands and resources which they claim.

(3) The Plaintiffs do not have the right of self-government or jurisdiction as claimed.... But it is understood that aboriginal peoples who lived in an organized society governed themselves by their own system of laws and customs. Certain rights or freedoms to self-government may continue to exist, but are subject to the laws of Canada and of the Province.

(4) The Province does not generally disagree with the factual findings of the trial judge on the question of ownership and jurisdiction.

(5) The Province supports the findings of the trial judge with respect to the effect to be given to the expert evidence.... It does not take the position the trial judge ignored or improperly rejected evidence. It supports the trial judge's conclusions as to the value of oral histories.

(6) The trial judge was correct to characterize the plaintiff's aboriginal rights as *sui generis*. But the precise location, scope, content, and consequences of the plaintiffs' aboriginal rights is a matter for negotiation, and further judicial consideration.[5]

The New Democratic Party government supported all Chief Justice McEachern's rulings on expert evidence, including the dismissal of oral history, and the testimony by anthropologists and historians. While the B.C. Court of Appeal's panel of five judges were divided on many of the issues before them, they all supported the Chief Justice's rulings on this evidence. One of them, Justice Lambert, mentioned that more weight should have been given to the oral histories and the testimony of the Chiefs and Elders. However, the judges were unanimous in their finding that the volume of evidence was such that they could not reasonably be expected to review it; and, they were satisfied that no "palpable and overriding error in fact" was evident in McEachern's assessment of the expert evidence, or his findings in law that were based on them. They said that, even if they were to review all the evidence and the transcripts, "The Court of Appeal could not be exposed to all the nuances in the evidence or be in as good a position as the trial judge to weigh the credibility...."[6]

The panel of five appeal court judges—Macfarlane, Taggart, Wallace, Hutcheon and Lambert— found unanimously that there was no blanket extinguishment of Aboriginal title as a result of Britain's colonization of what is now British Columbia; that the introduction of a land settlement scheme by the colonial government prior to 1871 did not show a "clear and plain intention to extinguish" Aboriginal title; that, after British Columbia joined Confederation in 1871, Aboriginal rights could not be extinguished by a provincial government; that there was no evidence that the federal Crown extinguished Aboriginal rights between 1871 and 1982; and, finally, that after 1982, not even the federal government has the power to extinguish Aboriginal rights because of their entrenchment in Section 35 of the Constitution. The Appeal court ruled that Aboriginal rights existed in British Columbia prior to Britain asserting sovereignty, had not been extinguished, and therefore continued to exist. In other words, the B.C. Court of Appeal found in favour of the (new) Crown's (new) position. In overruling the Chief Justice's decision on blanket extinguishment, the Court of Appeal strategically "cleaned up" the worst of McEachern's judgment, in a legal sense, and brought it up to date and in line with directions taken in Supreme Court of Canada decisions on extinguishment in particular rendered during the 1980s and 1990s, and within the framework of federal and provincial government perspectives that support the recognition of some form of Aboriginal rights. This course of action rendered unnecessary any explicit critique of the Chief Justice's ruling which would have been an embarrassment to the judiciary as a whole, and the B.C. judiciary in particular. Explicit disavowal of Chief Justice McEachern's "findings of fact," and his tautological reasoning would have challenged one of the most important social and political roles of the law: in order to legitimate the exercise of power law must present itself as being guided by the objective, neutral application of reason, free of racialist and other biases, and serving the interests of society as a whole, and not simply the needs of the rich and powerful.

While the Appeal Court did not define what these rights are, they were clear about what they are NOT: Aboriginal title and rights, they said, are not proprietary or commercial. Furthermore, they ruled that evidence in support of Aboriginal rights would have to be "site-specific" and drawn from documentation about the cultural practices of the specific First Nation making the claim.

We Buy Therefore We Are

> It is worth recalling that while British policy toward the native population was based on respect for their right to occupy their traditional lands, a proposition to which the Royal Proclamation of 1763 bears witness, there was from the outset never any doubt that sovereign and legislative power, and indeed the underlying title, to such lands vested in the Crown....
>
> The nature and content of an aboriginal right is determined by asking what the organized aboriginal society regarded as "an integral part of their distinctive culture."...To be so regarded those practices must have been integral to the distinctive culture of the aboriginal society from which they are said to have arisen. A modernized form of such a practice would be no less an aboriginal right.... A practice which had not been integral to the organized society and its distinctive culture, but which became prevalent as a result of European influences would not qualify for protection as an aboriginal right....
>
> The content of aboriginal rights is to be determined not by reference to whether executives or legislative action conferred such a right on the people in question, but rather by reference to that which is essential to or inherent in the unique relations that native people have with nature, each other, and other communities....
>
> —1990, *Reasons for Judgment, R. v. Sparrow.*

The existence and persistence of Aboriginal title and rights upheld by the British Columbia Court of Appeal's ruling, meant that the legal question remaining to be resolved was "what is the nature and scope of these existing Aboriginal rights?" The Appeal Court judges failed to reach a consensus on answers to this question. Mr. Justice Macfarlane, supported by Taggart, Wallace and Hutcheon, relied on the "new test" enunciated in the Supreme Court of Canada's decision in *R. v. Sparrow* that identified four questions to be decided by Courts in determining whether a particular practice should be protected as an Aboriginal right. First, what discrete practices, such as harvesting and exchanging fish, were to be identified as "aboriginal" practices? Second, was this practice integral to the distinctive culture of the Aboriginal society in which some of the ancestors of the present plaintiffs were members? That is, the legal definition of Aboriginality was now dependent on evidence that described practices which could be shown to have been carried out prior to European contact; and which were, then and now, "integral to the distinctive culture" of the particular Aboriginal nation bringing forward a claim. The critical defining difference—in law—between Aboriginal and non-Aboriginal "practices"—and therefore between Aboriginal and non-Aboriginal peoples—was to be determined on the basis of the courts' analysis of what a "distinctive culture" is. If the first and second questions were answered in the affirmative, then third and fourth questions could be posed: was the practice existing as an Aboriginal right at the date when sovereignty was asserted; and was it unextinguished prior to 1982?[7] Affirmative and negative responses to these questions, respectively, would legally establish the existence of a constitutionally protected Aboriginal right.

There are several important aspects to the British Columbia Court of Appeal Justice Macfarlane's definition of Aboriginal rights. First, the focus of the question is what lands did the people occupy and how were these lands and resources used before contact? Claimants wishing to pass this part of the test were required to bring forth evidence on the specific customs and practices of their people in occupying particular pieces of land, and/or in using particular resources. Given the Appeal Court's endorsement of Chief Justice McEachern's dismissal of oral history and expert academic evidence, the issue of "proof" remained problematic. Furthermore, "occupation" was defined as use to the exclusion of others. This meant that First Nations had to show they had actively excluded others from their territory, and maintained exclusive possession of the same territory. Failure to do so, either prior to the arrival of Europeans, or even in the face of force of arms and numbers of settlers after contact, could jeopardize the Aboriginal claim. Second, the use of the land and resources must be "integral to the distinctive culture," and deemed by the court to be "truly Indian." Aboriginality, and the Aboriginal "other" remained firmly frozen in the past.

But, what if an Aboriginal society engages in practices, and develops traditions and customs *after* contact with Europeans, and they continue for a long, long time before the assertion of sovereignty? This issue of time and the continuation of "Aboriginality" into the present and future divided the appeal panel. Justices Macfarlane and Wallace took an historical approach. They tried to look to the past, to find something they could identify as "traditional," or "distinctively Indian" and "integral to the culture."

Judge Lambert dissented from the majority. He viewed Aboriginal title, and the rights flowing from it, to be contemporaneous, allowing "a blossoming in the present and into the future" of the rights. Lambert represented a minority position when he cited a recent Australian precedent—the *Mabo* decision— handed down by Mr. Justice Brennan of the Supreme Court of Australia in 1992, that dispensed with the assertion of *terra nullius* as a foundation for Australian law.[8] Lambert accused the other members of the Appeal Court panel of supporting a "frozen rights" thesis. He wrote: "Once it is recognized that aboriginal societies were societies capable of change, the notion that there is an 'aboriginal' use which can be discovered only on the basis of evidence of long-time use must be rejected."[9] "The purpose of s.35…[of the Canadian Constitution] when it was prepared in 1982," Lambert continued, "cannot have been to protect the rights of Indians to live as they lived in 1778…. Its purpose must have been to secure to Indian people, without any further erosion, a modern unfolding of the rights." He chastised Chief Justice McEachern for finding that "commercial trapping is not an aboriginal practice," saying: "In my opinion…this…is to adopt the settlers' point of view of the classification of aboriginal title rather than the aboriginals' point of view…. If the Indians used land in 1820 in accordance with their aboriginal title but the use was a new one in 1820, then the important point is that at that time, namely 1820, the aboriginal right represented by the aboriginal title was taking on an 1820 contemporary form."[10]

The question of jurisdiction, or an inherent right to self-government, further divided the B.C. Court of Appeal judges. Macfarlane, for the majority, rejected this aspect of the Gitksan's and Wet'suwet'en's claim, calling it incompatible with federal and provincial jurisdiction: "Rights of self-government encompassing a power to make general laws governing the land and resources in the territory, and the people in that territory, can only be described as legislative powers…the jurisdiction of the plaintiffs would diminish the provincial and federal share of the total distribution of legislative power in Canada," he wrote.[11] To bolster their claim that such a sharing of political authority was legally impossible, Macfarlane, on behalf of the majority, offered four arguments. First, he wrote, "on the date that the legislative power of the Sovereign was imposed…any vestige of aboriginal law-making competence was superseded." Britain had the absolute right to assert sovereignty. Second, "…if this is wrong (in law) then a continuing aboriginal legislative power is inconsistent with the division of powers found in the *Constitution Act* of 1867." Even if Britain's original assertion of sovereignty was illegal, it became legal when the *Constitution Act 1867* reaffirmed the initial violation of British colonial law. Third, "the plaintiffs failed to establish the necessary ownership needed to support such a jurisdiction." The oral history testimony and the other expert evidence was not valid or reliable. But, he concluded, "the establishment of some form of Indian self-government…is ripe for negotiation and reconciliation."[12] Now that the terms, conditions, limits and possibilities have been circumscribed by law, political negotiations may be initiated.

Judge Lambert, again, disagreed. In his minority finding he argued, based on the "doctrine of continuity" provided for under British common law, that Aboriginal rights survived both the assertion of sovereignty and the division of legislative powers. Justice Hutcheon also took an independent position on this question, placing himself between the majority and Lambert. He transformed "self-government" into a more limited concept of "self regulation" by removing any concept of law-making by Gitksan or Wet'suwet'en institutions. A minimal range of jurisdiction, he argued, could be granted: "The appellants have a right of self-regulation exercisable through their own institutions to preserve and enhance their social, political, cultural, linguistic and spiritual identity."[13]

Finally, the Appeal Court panel dealt with the logical conclusion of their findings: if Aboriginal title and rights have not been extinguished, then what is the status of titles in fee simple that have been granted to non-Aboriginal citizens by the province for the past 123 years? In other words, if British and Canadian laws have not been obeyed by the governments, can any non-Aboriginal land titles be truly legal? They declined to give a definitive answer but made a range of suggestions about situations in which Aboriginal title and Crown and/or fee simple title could co-exist. Justice Macfarlane, for example, concluded that: "Uncultivated, unfenced, vacant land held in fee simple does not necessarily preclude the exercise of hunting rights…. On the other hand the building of a school on land usually occupied for aboriginal purposes will impair or suspend a right of occupation…." In essence, this is little different from Chief Justice McEachern's suggestion that land could be returned to Aboriginal use after it had been clear cut. Aboriginal people may use whatever lands and resources non-Aboriginal governments and corporations don't want or need, until they desire it again.

During the course of the *Delgamuukw* trial several other Aboriginal rights cases were winding their way through the lower courts in British Columbia. These additional cases were: *R. v. Alphonse, R. v. Dick, R. v. Van Der Peet, R. v. Gladstone, R. v. N.T.C. Smokehouse, R. v. Lewis* and *R. v. Nikal,* and all dealt in one way or another with the question of whether or not Aboriginal title could be proprietary, and Aboriginal rights could be commercial. Since *Delgamuukw v. R.* addressed issues fundamental to all of these cases, particularly whether Aboriginal rights had been extinguished or are now protected by the Canadian Constitution, the Appeal Court decided to rule on all these cases at the same time.

Their majority rulings on these cases were consistent: Aboriginal title is not "proprietary" and does not constitute ownership; and Aboriginal rights are not commercial ones. Concretely, this abstract debate can be reduced to the question of whether Aboriginal title is a form of property ownership that is equal and valid in comparison to Euro-Canadian title in fee simple. This is what the legal term "proprietary interest" refers to. Questions about the nature and scope of Aboriginal rights have quickly boiled down to debates about whether Aboriginal rights may be commercial ones or not, defined as equal and valid in comparison to production for exchange in a capitalist market-place. For example, if Aboriginal peoples traded fish for hides prior to contact with Europeans, and subsequently traded fish for cash, is their trade in fish an "Aboriginal practice"? If they own the fish in the first place, do they not have the right to dispose of it in any way they see fit? If their ownership of resources, like fish, has, like their title to land, never been surrendered or extinguished, then don't Aboriginal peoples still own the fish? What criteria establishes a radical and significant difference between the first exchange for hides, and the second for cash? The contemporary question of the legal effect of "European influences" is really a debate about whether or not Aboriginal peoples can use the lands and resources they claim to own and have never surrendered, to enter into and compete in the capitalist market-place as self-governing owners of resources; or whether they are to be forced to join the race empty-handed, with nothing but their labour to exchange. Litigation and treaty negotiations are, after all, sites at which First Nations are endeavouring to negotiate a mutually-respectful *relationship* with the Canadian state and within that state. They are not battlegrounds in a struggle for national liberation or political separation. It is the terms of the future relationships that are at stake, not the question of whether there will be a relationship or not.

In summary, the majority of B.C. Court of Appeal judges found that the Gitksan and Wet'suwet'en had Aboriginal rights that were not proprietary or commercial, but otherwise remained undefined; and that these rights had not been extinguished because the Crown has failed to demonstrate a "clear and plain intention" to do so. "In the end," Justice Macfarlane concluded, "the aboriginal interest is a right of use and occupation of a special nature—best described as *sui generis*. To stretch and strain property law concepts in an attempt to find a place for these unusual concepts which have arisen in a special context, is in my opinion, an unproductive task…. Whatever protection is required to sustain the *sui generis* interest of the descendants of the aboriginal peoples is now afforded by the Constitution, and in my view we should struggle no more to find a place in English property law for that interest."[14]

The *sui generis* theory of Aboriginal rights, in terms of Aboriginal interests is, however, a double-edged sword, another now familiar double-bind. On the one hand, it recognizes the "cultural distinctiveness" of Aboriginal title and does not try to force it to conform to European categories or definition. On the other hand, as long as Canadian law, and Canadian popular culture, are dominated by beliefs in European racial or cultural supremacy, then saying Aboriginal rights are different in theory can be expected to result in these rights being considered "lesser" ones in practice. Cultural difference may be recognized, but interpreted as justification for inequality. Heads, the Crown wins. Tails, Indians lose.

From the point of view of a dualist perspective rooted in notions of binary oppositions, when judges define communal property and non-profit barter as "integral to the distinctive culture" of First Nations—that is, as the most legally significant differences between Aboriginals and non-Aboriginals—they are simultaneously proclaiming that individual, private property, and profit-making commerce, are "integral to the distinctive culture" of non-Aboriginal Canadians. Simply put, the key cultural difference, according to the law, is that private property and money are integral to the distinctive culture of non-Aboriginals; and communal property and cashless barter are the distinctive characteristics of Aboriginal cultures. "We" have land and money. "They" do not. Cynics might ask if this is news? Skeptics may question the wisdom of spending vast sums of public funds on legal proceedings over the last several hundred years to arrive at this conclusion.

---

1. Court of Appeal of British Columbia, *Delgamuukw v. R.*, Defendant's Appeal Factum, III 1991: 12-14.

2. See Burns 1992; Burton and Kellock 1992; Doyle-Bedwell 1993; Fortune 1993; Foster 1992; Macklem 1993; Sanders 1992; Slattery 1992; Walters 1993.

3. See Bowker 1995 for a thorough analysis of the *Sparrow* decision, its interpretation by the B.C. Court of Appeal, and its implications.

4. Walters 1993: 410.

5. Court of Appeal of British Columbia, *Delgamuukw v. R., Reasons for Judgment*: 1993: 15.

6. Court of Appeal of British Columbia 1992 *Delgamuukw v. R.*, Defendant's Appeal Factum.

7. Court of Appeal of B.C. 1992 *Delgamuukw v. R., Reasons for Judgment*: 18.

8. Stephenson and Ratnapala (eds.) 1993.

9. Court of Appeal of British Columbia, *Delgamuukw v. R., Reasons for Judgment:* 172.

10. Ibid., 189.

11. Ibid., 34.

12. Ibid., 43-44.

13. Ibid., 268.

14. Ibid., 130-131.

Chapter 22: The British Columbia Treaty Process and the Supreme Court of Canada, 1996

How did the strategy of litigation fit with other strategies to bring about change? No one could suggest that the Gitksan and Wet'suwet'en put all their eggs in one basket. They used every strategy available—roadblocks, fish-ins, marshmallow fights, participation in the First Minister's conferences, a play (that toured the province, the country, and the world), a film, links to academics...buttons, shirts, posters, T-shirts. Is such litigation a bad strategy? Only if the litigation is seen in isolation from other actions and strategies. We need to get over our idolatry of the courts and judges.... The cases were attempts to get the courts to kick governments.[1]
—Legal scholar Douglas Sanders, 1992, *Getting Back to Rights.*

From Negotiation to Litigation to Negotiation to Litigation to Negotiation to Litigation to...

Neither Aboriginal peoples in B.C. nor the Crown have looked primarily to the courts for resolution of the Aboriginal title and rights issue in the years since the *Delgamuukw* judgment was handed down in 1991. Rather, attention has focussed on the British Columbia Treaty Commission (BCTC). Just as the *Calder* decision encouraged the federal government to initiate the Comprehensive Claims Policy, and to negotiate with the Nishga; the *Sparrow, Delgamuukw* and other 1993 B.C. Court of Appeal decisions have all recommended that the issues be resolved politically, and have recommended negotiation rather than litigation. Although not often stated frankly, the courts, bound as they are by their colonial inheritance and archaic powers of truth creation, have been shown unwilling to, or incapable of, resolving these issues.

On June 28, 1991, about three months after the *Delgamuukw* decision was released, the B.C. Claims Task Force, which had been made up of representatives of federal, provincial and Aboriginal governments, academics and "third party" labour and business interests, published their report. It contained 19 recommendations for developing a process for negotiations amongst the parties. The Task Force report called for casting aside the historically troubled relationship between Aboriginal and non-Aboriginal peoples, rooted in an imperial past. A contemporary "made-in-BC" solution was required. This new relationship would be realized through the negotiation of "modern day treaties," and would be based on "recognition and respect for First Nations as self-determining and distinct nations with their own spiritual values, histories, languages, territories, political institutions and ways of life."[2]

In September, 1992, representatives of the federal and provincial governments and the First Nations' Summit, signed an agreement creating the B.C. Treaty Commission, which would serve as a watchdog over and facilitator of the six stage process of treaty making. On June 21, 1993, the federal and provincial governments finalized a *Memorandum of Understanding between Canada and British Columbia* respecting the sharing of pre-treaty costs, settlement costs, implementation costs, and the costs of self-government, in which Canada agreed to provide the cash, and B.C. the land, required by any subsequent treaty agreement. The Gitksan and Wet'suwet'en signed a *Memorandum of Understanding* with the Province and the Federal Government in 1992, agreeing to postpone their appeal of the *Delgamuukw* decision to the Supreme Court of Canada in order to enter treaty negotiations under the auspices of the BCTC.

Appealing Culture

What our Chiefs don't understand, what they have difficulty with, is that when we compare the case law that is put forward in Delgamuukw with our own laws, our chiefs say, 'That's really funny. Look at that. They can just change their law anytime they want. Where our laws have remained unchanged for centuries.' They can't understand that.
—Satsan (Herb George), 1992, *The Fire Within Us.*

The British Columbia Treaty Commission is ultimately bound by legal decisions since the law remains the "court of last resort" in settling differences that cannot be reconciled through the negotiation process. In November of 1996, the Supreme Court of Canada handed down landmark rulings on three of the cases that the British Columbia Court of Appeal had heard simultaneously with the *Delgamuukw* appeal: *R. v. Gladstone, R. v. Van Der Peet*, and *R. v. NTC Smokehouse*.

Dorothy Van Der Peet, a member of the Sto:lo Nation of Southwestern British Columbia, sold 10 Fraser River salmon for $50.00 to her neighbour. She was arrested and charged under a clause in the *Fisheries Act* that prohibits selling, bartering or offering to sell or barter any fish caught under Indian Food Fish licenses. The Crown called Dr. Gordon Stryd, an archaeologist, as an expert witness in anthropology, and the Sto:lo called Dr. Richard Daly. Stryd argued that bartering and trading fish had been an "occasional, incidental and opportunistic" occurrence prior to contact and was not central to Sto:lo life the way fishing for food and ceremony was. Daly argued that the Sto:lo had produced, preserved and traded surplus fish prior to contact, and had sold large amounts of fish, for cash, to the British between 1820 and 1846 when British sovereignty was established. Therefore, the selling of fish was an Aboriginal right protected under section 35(1) of the Canadian Constitution. This was a case where a practice had become "traditional," "unique," and "integral to the distinctive culture" of an Aboriginal people *after* contact with Europeans and for a long, long time *before* the assertion of sovereignty.

B.C. Provincial Court judge Scarlett was the first to hear the case. He agreed with Gordon Stryd and found Dorothy Van Der Peet guilty. Scarlett ruled that "*Natives did not fish to supply a market, there being no regularized trading system,* nor were they able to preserve and store fish for extended periods of time (emphasis in original). A market as such for salmon was not present but created by European traders, primarily the Hudson's Bay Company. At Fort Langley the Sto:lo were able to catch and deliver fresh salmon to the traders where it was salted and exported. This use was clearly different in nature and quantity from Aboriginal activity."

When the case was heard by the Supreme Court of B.C., Judge Selbie disagreed with Judge Scarlett, and found Dorothy Van Der Peet *not* guilty. Judge Selbie wrote in his *Reasons for Judgment*: "In my view, the evidence in this case, oral, historical and opinion, looked at in the light of the principles of interpreting aboriginal rights...*is more consistent with the aboriginal right to fish including the right to sell, barter or exchange than otherwise and must be found so.* We are, after all, basically considering the existence in antiquity of an aboriginal's right to dispose of his fish other than by eating it himself or using it for ceremonial purposes—the words 'sell', 'barter', 'exchange,' 'share,' are but variations on the theme of 'disposing.' It defies common sense to think that if the aboriginal did not want the fish for himself there would be some stricture against him disposing of it by some other means to his advantage.... I am satisfied that when the first Indian caught the first salmon he had the 'right' to do anything he wanted with it—eat it, trade it for deer meat, throw it back or keep it against a hungrier time. As time went on and for an infinite variety of reasons that 'right' to catch the fish and do anything he wanted with it became hedged in....One of the social changes that occurred was the coming of the white-man.... A money economy eventually developed and...Indians...adjusted to that also—he traded his fish for money. *This was a long way from his ancient sharing, bartering and trading practices but it was the logical progression of such.* It has been held that the aboriginal right to hunt is not frozen in time so that only the bow and arrow can be used in exercising it.... The Indian right to trade his fish is not frozen in time to doing so only by the medium of the potlatch and the like...(emphasis in the original.)"[3]

Justices Macfarlane and Taggart of the B.C. Court of Appeal, however, disagreed with Judge Selbie and reversed his decision. They ruled that the first trial judge, Scarlett, was correct. Applying the *Sparrow* test, the B.C. Court of Appeal judges wrote: "Fishing was a integral part of the distinctive culture of the aborigines. Fish had a religious significance. Fish were revered. They were used for food, but played a significant role in ceremonial and social ways.... But that is not to say the purpose of fishing was to engage in commerce. In our opinion, trade with the British was not of the same nature and quality as the aboriginal traditions disclosed by the evidence...the question of what is an aboriginal right deserving protection is not determined necessarily by reference to the activities in which aboriginal persons were engaged in 1846. The test is whether such activities or practices were integral to the distinctive culture of the aborigines...."[4] Justice Wallace agreed.

Justice Lambert, writing on his own, concluded that "Mrs. Van Der Peet was exercising an aboriginal right when she sold ten salmon to Mrs. Lugsdin for $50.00."[5] Lambert argued that when the Sto:lo began selling fish to the first Europeans who arrived in the early nineteenth century, "all they were doing was exploiting a new opportunity....a response to a new circumstance in the carrying out of the existing practice."[6] Justice Lambert supported his reasoning by arguing for a "social perspective" on the definition of Aboriginal rights. "I think the 'social' perspective is the correct one," he wrote, "because rights are not defined in terms of the purpose for which they are to be exercised, but in the way the rights may be employed in a social context."[7] He continued: "The fact that non-aboriginal people now engage in or formerly engaged in the same practices as aboriginal people does not indicate that the practice was not or is not an aboriginal practice. No doubt the Hudson's Bay traders who arrived at the Fort Langley post in the early 19th century had fished for salmon in their boyhood in the Tay or the Dee. A practice, tradition or custom may be integral to the distinctive culture of an aboriginal people even if a similar custom is integral to the distinctive culture of many other peoples as well."[8]

Another B.C. Court of Appeal panel member, Justice Hutcheon, agreed with Mr. Justice Selbie's decision that the Aboriginal right to sell fish includes the right to sell, trade or barter. He based his decision on the fact that the evidence showed that Sto:lo had been engaged in the "commercial exchange of fish" for at least 26 years when, in 1846, British sovereignty was declared. He rejected Chief Justice McEachern's extension of the test for Aboriginal rights to include that Aboriginal rights must have been in effect for a "long, long time" prior to British sovereignty. And, he rejected the Crown's argument that "aboriginal rights must describe pre-contact life."

The B.C. Court of Appeal decision on *R. v. Van Der Peet* was appealed to the Supreme Court of Canada, who handed down its decision in November, 1996. Again, the court was divided. The majority ruled that "the exchange of fish among the Sto:lo was 'incidental,'" and "the trade with Europeans was quantitatively different from what was typical of Sto:lo culture prior to contact."[9] Therefore the exchange of fish for money or other goods is not an integral part of the distinctive Sto:lo culture, and is not protected by the Constitution.

In a dissenting judgment, Justice L'Heureux-Dubé followed B.C. Court of Appeal Justice Lambert's reasoning. She chastised her fellow jurists for assuming that the arrival of Europeans was necessarily a pivotal and determining feature of history, and for ultimately upholding a "frozen rights" approach to the determination of Aboriginal rights. The Judge went on to criticize her colleagues for misconstruing the words "distinctive culture" in the *Sparrow* test, and interpreting them to mean "distinct culture," or "that which is left over after features of non-aboriginal culture have been taken away." L'Heureux-Dubé added that "culture" should be understood as an interrelated whole, and not a catalogue of individualized practices. She proposed a delineation between three different categories of Aboriginal harvesting rights: subsistence, social and ceremonial; the provision of a modest livelihood; and commercial. Each category should have a unique bundle of rights, she argued.[10]

A second judge, Justice Mclachlin, also took an independent stand, writing her own minority judgment. She argued that Aboriginal rights should be defined "through an empirical approach" and should be "drawn from history." This would be more practical than Courts repeatedly trying to describe *a priori* what an Aboriginal right is. She agreed with L'Heureux-Dubé that there is "no justification for extending the right beyond what is required to provide the people with reasonable substitutes for what they traditionally obtained from the resource—basic housing, transportation, clothing and amenities."[11] By this reasoning, it may now be "Aboriginal"—in the eyes of the law—to be lower middle class, but it remains "non-Aboriginal" to be any wealthier than that. Neither L'Heureux-Dubé nor Mclachlin addressed how the historical information that their proposed tests relied upon should be evaluated by the law.

A second case decided by the Supreme Court of Canada in November 1996, *R. v. Gladstone and Gladstone*, arose from a "sting" operation wherein Department of Fisheries' officers attempted to entrap two members of the Heiltsuk First Nation of Waglisla (Bella Bella). The Crown first told the story to the Supreme Court of British Columbia as follows:

> Donald and William Gladstone are members of the Heiltsuk Indian Band of Bella Bella. They arranged to ship to Vancouver approximately 4200 pounds of herring spawn on kelp. The fisheries officers were alerted by an informant and they kept under surveillance the transportation of the crates from the freight carrier in Vancouver to a warehouse in Richmond.... Later that day, William Gladstone arrived with a U-haul truck to pick up the crates. He drove into Vancouver and parked in a lot at Seymour and Nelson Streets. William and Donald Gladstone then drove in a Javelin automobile

to the premises of Seaborn Enterprises Limited, a retail fish store at 1310 West 73rd Avenue in Vancouver. They had with them one white container of herring spawn which they took into the store. William Gladstone spoke to Mr. Katsu Hirose, the owner, and asked, according to Hirose, if he was 'interested in herring on kelp' to which he replied he 'never touched herring on kelp from native Indians'. They left and returned to the parking lot where they were arrested. Subsequently, the herring spawn on kelp was sold by the fisheries officials for $143,944.00

This case involved complicated charges and defences under the Criminal Code having to do with entrapment, search warrants and evidence. At the first trial, the judge acknowledged that the Heiltsuk had harvested herring spawn on kelp for hundreds of years. Alexander Mackenzie's 1793 journal recorded his having traded with them for this foodstuff. Therefore, Judge Lemiski of the Supreme Court of British Columbia found that the right to trade and barter herring roe was an Aboriginal right that the *Fisheries Act* regulations, in *general,* unjustly interfered with. However, he concluded that this interference was valid in this *particular* case because the Gladstones had attempted "to sell a relatively large quantity of spawn in a surreptitious manner to a foreign buyer in a location far removed from the Heiltsuk Band's region."[12]

When the *Gladstone* case was appealed to the B.C. Court of Appeal, Judge Anderson agreed with the trial judge, although he found the *Fisheries Act* regulations did not, in general, interfere with an Aboriginal right to fish. He was adamant, however, that selling 4800 pounds of herring roe for several hundred thousand dollars was "inconsistent with a 'traditional aboriginal right'." Justices Macfarlane, Taggart and Wallace agreed that "the activity in question could not be viewed as an integral part of the distinctive culture of the Heiltsuk people...the activity is different in nature and quality than the aboriginal right...."[13] They continued: "The case is not one that turns on quantity, although both judges took account of the quantity involved. There was evidence of considerable quantities being transported to other Indians in aboriginal times. But the quality and character of the activity in aboriginal times was quite different from that disclosed by the evidence in this case. The aboriginal activity was rooted in a culture which gave significance to sharing a resource, to which one nation had ready access, while other Indian peoples did not.... The appellants were not exercising an aboriginal right when they attempted to sell herring spawn on kelp to a Japanese fish product buyer in Vancouver."[14] The "non-Aboriginal" characteristics of the exchange in this case included the large amount of money involved, the style of doing business, the location of the exchange, and the race/culture/nationality of the purchaser.

Again, Mr. Justice Lambert took an independent position. He argued: "...that the aboriginal rights of the Heiltsuk people to harvest herring spawn and to trade their herring spawn extensively and in quantities measured in tons, subject only to the need for conservation of the resource...have been established...."[15]

The Supreme Court of Canada overturned the B.C. Court of Appeal's decision, and ruled that the evidence supported a finding that "the exchange of herring spawn on kelp for money or other goods was to an extent a central, significant and defining feature of the culture of the Heiltsuk prior to contact and is best characterized as commercial. This exchange and trade was an integral part of the distinctive culture of the Heiltsuk...."[16] Justice LaForest, however, dissented. He argued that the significance of barter in herring roe to the Heiltsuk prior to contact was based on a cultural value of sharing resources, and that such values were not demonstrated by the Gladstone brothers whose activities, LaForest claimed, "were done in a completely different context."[17]

On the one hand, the Supreme Court of Canada ruled that the attempted sale by members of the Heiltsuk Nation of thousands of pounds of herring roe, *is* a constitutionally protected Aboriginal right because they were satisfied by the evidence that such commerce was "integral to the distinctive culture" of the Heiltsuk before contact with Europeans. The judges argued that their decision was based on the evidence presented. On the other hand, the Supreme Court found that Dorothy Van Der Peet's sale of 10 fish for $50.00 to her non-Aboriginal neighbour was *not* within her constitutionally protected Aboriginal rights because the oral history testimony of the Sto:lo, and their expert witnesses in history and anthropology did not supply convincing evidence that pre-contact trade and exchange was sufficiently similar to capitalist commerce. In the absence of a developed critique of, and recommendations for specific alternatives to, Chief Justice McEachern's assessment of Aboriginal oral histories and his approach to expert evidence provided by anthropologists, archaeologists and historians, these latest rulings result in the possibility that the rights of different First Nations, with diverse histories of relationships with academics—particularly archaeologists and historic ethnographers—could be determined by the presence or absence, reliability or weakness, of the academic record. More to the point, the law retains the absolute power to arbitrarily interpret and evaluate expert evidence according to its own rules, at its pleasure.

Contrary to Chief Justice McEachern's claim that judges are bound by the letter of the law, and by tradition-bound precedent, a majority of the Supreme Court of Canada judges, in their 1996 rulings, stated clearly that the Court's role was not only to make decisions based on the determination of "facts," but that it was also incumbent upon them to facilitate the goal of reconciliation between sectors of the population in dispute with each other. "In pursuing the goal of reconciliation...limits are equally a necessary part as much as recognition," Judges Lamer, Sopinka, Gonthier, Cory, Iacobucci and Major wrote. "With regards to the distribution of the fisheries resource after conservation goals have been met, objectives such as the pursuit of economic and regional fairness, and the recognition of the historical reliance upon, and participation in, the fishery by non-aboriginal groups, are the type of objectives which can (at least in the right circumstances) satisfy this standard," they concluded.[18] Dorothy Van Der Peet's ten fish were sockeye salmon, harvested from the profitable Fraser River run. This bounty, and the opportunity to harvest it, is sought after and contested by Aboriginal and non-Aboriginal fishers, and local and international fish processors. The Gladstone's thousands of pounds of herring roe, on the other hand, represent a delicacy eaten only by coastal First Nations and Japanese people. While the Japanese consumer market is a lucrative and captive one—their own herring resources having been overfished to extinction—there is little competition among harvesters; and no sports, recreation or tourist interests involved as there are in relation to the salmon industry. There is, in other words, no need for the Court to concern itself with the reconciliation of competing interests in the herring roe industry.

---

1. Sanders 1992: 281-283.

2. Province of British Columbia 1991: 16. See McKee 1996 for a comprehensive overview and analysis of the treaty process.

3. Court of Appeal for British Columbia, 1993 *R. v. Dorothy Marie Van Der Peet, Reasons for Judgment*: 91.

4. Ibid., 92.

5. Ibid., 134.

6. Ibid., 134.

7. Ibid., 134.

8. Ibid., 136.

9. Supreme Court of Canada, *R. v. Van Der Peet, Reasons for Judgment*: 140.

10. Ibid., 144.

11. Ibid., 150.

12. Court of Appeal for British Columbia, *R. v. Gladstone, Reasons for Judgment*: 158.

13. Ibid., 168.

14. Ibid., 158.

15. Ibid., 180.

16. Ibid., 184.

17. Ibid., 167.

18. Supreme Court of Canada, *R. v. Gladstone, Reasons for Judgment*: 11.

Part IX:

In Futuro

(In the Future)

Chapter 23: The Past In the Present, In the Future

Just Another Day in Lotus Land

Chief Justice Allan McEachern addressed the Canadian Bar Association's Annual Meeting in Vancouver in September, 1996. He used the occasion to rail against people he called "agendists," who "place themselves firmly on the side of the angels" and have made "outrage" a "common and effective debating technique." The Chief Justice lashed out at the media who, he charged, "prefer an exaggerated or controversial outburst to rational analysis."

"One of the most serious misconceptions that troubles the judiciary," McEachern said, "is the apparent belief on the part of many that judges decide cases in accordance with personal views or values.... Anyone who takes the time to read reasons for judgment knows that judges are not 'free spirits' who can decide cases any way they wish.... The relentless disciplines of evidence, law and appellate review all operate to require decisions to be rational within a much larger context than just the case under consideration."

Representatives of the United Native Nations organization, who were also invited to attend the Bar Association's meetings, suggested that a good place to start looking for the "relentless disciplines" under which judges make decisions in this province might be in big law firms' long-standing business ties with forestry companies. In 1997, Allan McEachern was replaced as Chief Justice of B.C. by Bryan Williams. McEachern now sits on the British Columbia Court of Appeal.

Justice. Then Peace

British Columbia's primary resource-based economy is suffering the consequences of globalization: multi-national logging, mining and fishing companies are moving their operations to Third and other Fourth world locations. Unemployment has increased, wages have been depressed, and trade unions undermined. The commercial fishing industry's existence is threatened by declining salmon stocks. Hundreds of unionized cannery workers have lost their jobs in recent years as processors moved to Alaska and Washington, taking advantage of the lower wage opportunities afforded by the North American Free Trade Agreement. The fishing fleet has been cut in half in the last two years by the infamous federal government restructuring scheme named "the Mifflin Plan," after the Liberal Fisheries Minister, Fred Mifflin, who administered the fleet reduction policy. Already marginalized, First Nations fishers have suffered the brunt of this new policy. Aboriginal and non-Aboriginal peoples living in coastal communities economically dependent on the fishery have seen the bases of their livelihoods and ways of life disappear during the last two years.

Tensions exist between Aboriginal peoples who have demanded moratoria on logging until their claims are settled, and workers and labour unions who rely on the forestry industry for their livelihood. The fishing industry is also a site of sometimes violent confrontations between Aboriginal fishers who claim ownership of the resource, and the right to harvest and sell their fish, and non-Aboriginal fishers who argue that the fish stocks are the "common property" of all Canadian citizens, and that Aboriginal people have no unique claim to it. Poverty has increased throughout the province, and social services have been cut back dramatically as the welfare state "retreats:" joblessness and economic insecurity, hopelessness and despair characterize life for more and more people—Aboriginal and non-Aboriginal—in contemporary British Columbia.

Right wing political parties such as Reform and the B.C. Liberal Party scapegoat Aboriginal peoples and the land rights movement, identifying it as the cause of economic instability and mounting unemployment. They claim that disputes about Aboriginal title that frequently involve roadblocks, injunctions and blockades—along with widely-publicized protests against logging by environmentalists—create a "chilly climate" in B.C. for potential investors. When called upon to support their arguments, opponents of Aboriginal land rights repeat the ethnocentric historical narrative, and eurocentric cultural beliefs articulated by Chief Justice McEachern in his *Reasons for Judgment* and upheld by some judges in the B.C. Court of Appeal and the Supreme Court of Canada: the tried—and untrue—"founding myth of white British Columbians."[1] This, briefly, is the social and political context in which the British Columbia Treaty Commission (BCTC) has, since 1992, been engaged in a "modern-day treaty-making process."

As of this writing, forty-four First Nations in British Columbia have opted to become involved in negotiations with the federal and provincial governments in the context of the British Columbia Treaty Commission (BCTC). The BCTC's treaty-making process has been plagued by bureaucratic red tape, opposition by non-Aboriginals, conflicts between Aboriginal groups, shifting government positions and inequities in access to resources. For example: any costs incurred by First Nations in preparing for and carrying out negotiations will be deducted from final settlements. Governments, corporations and "third party interests" of course, have considerably more non-repayable resources at their disposal.

Not all First Nations who are participating in the treaty process are enthusiastic. Some are cautiously optimistic. Many feel there are no other options and *anything* is worth a try. An alliance of eighteen First Nations in the interior of British Columbia has consistently refused to participate in the treaty process unless, or until the government drops its demand that extinguishment of Aboriginal title must be the inevitable outcome of treaty negotiations. Recent precedents for modern-day treaties like the James Bay Northern Quebec Agreement and the Yukon Land Claim settlement have made recognition of Aboriginal title dependent upon extinguishment: at precisely the same moment that the Crown recognizes title, Aboriginal peoples must surrender it.

Representatives of off-reserve, urban and Metis Aboriginal peoples have launched an increasingly vocal critique of the B.C. treaty process. They claim that their unique situations and interests are being ignored in favour of a narrowly construed, legalistic definition of First Nations limited to on-reserve populations represented by Band and Tribal Councils sanctioned by the *Indian Act*.

Another grouping of Aboriginal people excluded from, and without faith in, either the treaty process or leaders sanctioned by the *Indian Act*, became involved in an armed stand-off at Gustafsen Lake in central British Columbia during the summer of 1995. Their political/legal relationship, they argue, is with the British Crown as articulated in the Royal Proclamation of 1763. They have never surrendered their title to Britain, and they do not recognize the authority of the federal or the provincial governments to negotiate with them on a nation-to-nation basis. Given that this premise results in the logical conclusion that Canadian courts have no jurisdiction over Aboriginal lands or peoples, when their lawyer, Bruce Clark, attempted to put forward this argument, he was, of course, thrown out of the court whose legitimacy he refused to recognize. The NDP's Attorney-General, Ujjal Dosanjh, called in the Royal Canadian Mounted Police and alerted the Canadian army. Sixteen Aboriginal people were arrested and tried on criminal charges ranging from attempted murder to mischief.

Resource companies, small businesses, wildlife and tourist industries, municipal governments and trade unions are represented in the treaty process as "third party interests." Members of these groups argue that they should play a greater role in decision-making, and that they have been excluded from the treaty process even though they will experience the consequences of any agreements that are made. First Nations, and representatives of the federal and provincial governments, argue that "third parties" are represented, as voting citizens, by the government's negotiators. "Third parties" have mounted concerted and successful campaigns to pressure the provincial government into narrowing the terms and conditions of treaty negotiation.

Since coming to power in 1991, the New Democratic Party provincial government has steadily retreated from its initial position of recognizing

Aboriginal title. The Nishga Tribal Council commissioned the prestigious accounting firm of Price Waterhouse to conduct an audit of their traditional territories in the Fall of 1994. The accountants' report estimated that non-Aboriginal "stakeholders" had gleaned between $2 billion and $4 billion in resources from Nishga ancestral lands since the mid-nineteenth century. In May, 1995, the provincial NDP government announced a new policy for treaty settlement that would be based on First Nations' "future needs" rather than "past injustices." "If treaties are to be meaningful in a contemporary world, they cannot be based solely on evidence from the past," the Province's position paper explained. "The current and future interests of *all* parties will determine the final land area of each treaty."

The Supreme Court of Canada's 1996 decisions in *Van Der Peet* and *Gladstone* demand that Aboriginal claimants bring forward detailed, site-specific historical evidence to prove their case. The British Columbia Treaty Commission now appears to be saying history doesn't matter, at least where compensation is concerned.

Provincial treaty negotiators were advised that their mandate specifically excluded discussions of compensation based on "calculations of damages arising from past use and alienation of the lands and resources within traditional territories." Instead, the province announced a seven point formula for determining treaty settlements: the goals of the particular First Nation; the quantity and quality of Indian reserve land already held; the availability of Crown land in the treaty area and the value of lands and resources on them; local economic opportunities; the nature and extent of provincial and public interest in the area; the nature and extent of private interests (such as leases and tree-farm licenses) in lands and resources in the treaty area; and, finally, the amount of cash in the treaty settlement after the costs of treaty negotiations have been deducted. Any disputes that may arise concerning the application of the treaty should be settled by mediation, but the parties may bring conflicts to the Supreme Court of B.C. for resolution. The law and its precedents, including those created by Chief Justice McEachern in *Delgamuukw v. R.* will constitute the court of last resort.[2]

Very early on May 12, 1995, the day they later released their new policy to the press, the NDP's Minister of Aboriginal Affairs, Rev. John Cashore, addressed a breakfast meeting of the Master Members of the Business Council of B.C., who are influential representatives of "Third Party Interests" in the treaty process. Cashore assured his audience that the NDP government was committed to attracting foreign investment and supporting the business sector. The social democratic government pledged to "get out of the way" in the relationship between Aboriginal peoples and corporate interests. First Nations would be liberated from paternalistic government protection, and released to sink or swim in the shark-infested waters of the global marketplace. Furthermore, the Minister promised, Aboriginal peoples would no longer be a "burden" on the public purse.

"We won't…we can't support tax havens and ghettoes," Reverend Cashore added. "Self-determination means responsibility to pay taxes."[3]

Only one treaty has reached the final stages of negotiation, and it is not officially a part of the BCTC process but is, rather, a conclusion of negotiations begun over twenty years ago in response to the Supreme Court of Canada's *Calder* decision. Talks had been stalled until 1991 by the B.C. provincial government's refusal to participate. An Agreement in Principle (AIP) between the Nisga'a First Nation Tribal Council, and the federal and provincial governments was signed in 1995, but remains to be ratified and passed into legislation. The key terms of this proposed "modern-day treaty" include: the hovering sovereign will retain "underlying title" to all the lands; 1,930 square kilometers of lands in the Lower Nass River area will be designated as communally-owned "Nisga'a lands"; the lands within 18 reserves and an additional 2.5 square kilometres will be reclassified as "fee simple lands" to be used for economic development, subject to provincial laws. The Nisga'a will be able to implement forest management standards, and there will be public access to Nisga'a lands for hunting, fishing and recreation. Nisga'a will be entitled to hunt moose and other designated species, and they will participate in the administration of a wildlife management area. They will not be permitted to sell wildlife, but may trade or barter it among themselves or with other Aboriginal peoples. The Nisga'a will be able to make laws governing such things as culture and language, employment, public works, regulation of traffic and transportation, land use and solemnization of marriage. They will provide health, child welfare and education services, and will exercise local policing powers similar to those of municipalities. The Nisga'a will receive $190 million over a period of years, will levy taxes on their members and will enter into taxation agreements with Canada and B.C., as municipalities do.[4]

A complex agreement on fisheries that will form a part of the proposed treaty was announced on August 22, 1996. Under the terms of this agreement, the Nisga'a will receive an annual treaty entitlement of approximately 18% of the Canadian Nass River salmon run, which they will be allowed to sell ("the priority entitlement"). This represents somewhat less than what Nisga'a already involved in the commercial fishery already catch. However, "the Nisga'a will not have any preferential commercial rights in respect of the sale of fish…. If in any year there are no directed commercial or recreational harvests of Nass Area stocks by non Nisga'a, there will be no Nisga'a commercial fishery of those stocks, in that year…. In exchange for agreeing to a ceiling on the priority salmon fishery…the Nisga'a will receive an additional entitlement to be delivered through a Harvest Agreement outside of the treaty, and which will have exactly the same priority as commercial or recreational fisheries…. By definition, there must be harvesting by others, before there will be any Nisga'a entitlement above the priority entitlement set forth in the Treaty."[5]

The Nisga'a Agreement in Principle (AIP) has opponents and supporters in both Aboriginal and non-Aboriginal populations. Chief Joe Gosnell, Sr., President of the Nisga'a Tribal Council, was circumspect in his announcement of the AIP. "This represents a hard-fought compromise that has seen a generation of Nisga'a growing old at the negotiating table, but we are making that compromise in order to become full and active participants in the social, political and economic life of this country," Gosnell explained.[6] Minister of Indian Affairs Ron Irwin was bombastic: "Today we make history," he proclaimed. "We are forging a new relationship based on partnership and mutual respect." Provincial Minister of Aboriginal Affairs Reverend John Cashore praised the Agreement-in-Principle, calling it "a fair and honourable resolution."

Milton K. Wong, Vice-President of the Hong Kong Bank of Canada, made a submission to the provincial government's Select Standing Committee on Aboriginal Affairs in 1997 urging ratification of the Nisga'a AIP and other treaties. Citing the results of a recent benefits and costs analysis of potential treaty settlements conducted by the Vancouver accounting firm KPMG, Wong argued that treaties would establish the necessary framework within which "we can establish a social, political and economic certainty that will encourage investment in British Columbia and therefore be of enormous help to business communities across the province."[7]

In 1996, the federal Liberal government proposed significant changes to the *Indian Act*. The direction of these initiatives, too, is towards encouraging and facilitating relations between multi-national corporations, the private sector, and First Nations who, along with their lands, will no longer be wards of the Crown. Aboriginal leaders are divided in their responses to the Liberals' proposals. Critics charge that the consequences of these changes will be the emergence of late twentieth century "company towns" on Indian land, reminiscent of the monopolies granted to the Hudson's Bay Company in the nineteenth century. They say that the federal government is using the rhetoric of self-government and the currently fashionable lure of entrepreneurialism to legitimate abandoning their historical responsibilities and legal obligations— especially their fiduciary obligations— to Aboriginal peoples. Supporters of the proposed *Indian Act* revisions argue that First Nations must be pragmatic, and position themselves competitively in the world market.

In the context of the increasing dominance of international capital and the declining economic or political power exercised by governments of nation states, it is interesting to recall the debates that gave rise to the cases that constituted the "Marshall trilogy" in nineteenth-century America, when "suddenly, even the most hardened land-market capitalist assumed the mantle of zealous advocate of the Indians'…right to engage in unregulated real-estate transactions."[8] A persistent theme in the struggle over land has been the competing interests of Crown(s), state(s), and private capital(s) when each sought to appropriate Indian lands. We are currently moving out of a historical era dominated by state/Crown monopoly on the purchase and administration of Indian land, government intervention in economic development on behalf of citizens' well-being, and publicly-funded social programs that protected people against the worst ravages of the mercurial market. We are moving into an era of rapid privatization and corporatization where the federal government is decentralizing and rolling up "the social safety net." Paralleling the gross reductions in government spending on health, education and social services throughout the country, critics charge that new federal Indian policy represents the application of the same neo-conservative agenda to Aboriginal peoples. The federal government calls their new approach "the devolution policy," and they claim they are supporting Aboriginal self-government by transferring responsibility for local government to Band Councils and Tribal Councils. Critics call it "the de-evolution policy" and "cutbacks with feathers." They charge that what the government calls "self-government" is really "self-administration." And, as "transfers of responsibility" have been accompanied by reduced transfers of resources, some First Nations leaders say they are being "given the right to administer our own misery."

Since 1990, and immediately preceding the province of British Columbia's historical policy change from non-recognition to qualified recognition of Aboriginal rights, major corporations have shown an interest in promoting reconciliation between Aboriginal peoples and governments, and in engaging in negotiations with Aboriginal groups directly. Leading Canadian banks and law firms now all have departments and personnel devoted exclusively to promoting Aboriginal businesses. The nexus of the relationship between Aboriginal and non-Aboriginal peoples is shifting from the political to the corporate arena. Aboriginal lands, culture, art, and even spirituality are being rapidly commodified. Increasingly, Indigenous peoples in Canada and throughout the world are faced with difficult choices about what direction to take regarding "economic development." If First Nations communities were to lose their Aboriginal title to lands and to become pseudo-independent enclaves in a global capitalist economy this may provide some short-term economic benefits for members of existing Indigenous elites, or individually successful entrepreneurs, but the fate of peoples here and around the world whose lands have been expropriated and communities displaced, stands as a warning of where a journey directed by the profit motive may lead. Vancouver's Downtown Eastside neighbourhood is home to thousands of young Aboriginal people, many of them dislocated from their homes, detached from their communities and veterans of the foster care system. These are the children walking the streets selling their bodies. These are the young people dealing drugs destined to quell rebellion on the streets, and to soothe alienation in the corporate boardrooms and lawyers' lounges that litter the landscape of the "vast emptiness." As I write, public health officials have declared the Downtown

Eastside to be a "medical state of emergency": its residents are suffering the worst pandemic of HIV+/AIDS in the "developed" world.

On September 10, 1996, the province of British Columbia withdrew from treaty negotiations with the Gitksan and applied to have the appeal of *Delgamuukw v. R.* heard by the Supreme Court of Canada. Intervention by the British Columbia Treaty Commission to attempt to restart negotiations failed to bring the province back to the table. Although treaty negotiations with the Wet'suwet'en had not broken down, the Wet'suwet'en decided as well to proceed with the appeal and negotiations within the B.C. treaty process were suspended. The federal government agreed to provide minimal funding—insufficient to cover real costs—in support of the appeal. The appeal was heard in June, 1997. The Supreme Court of Canada allowed only one and a half days for arguments to be presented.

For the purposes of their appeal, the Gitksan and Wet'suwet'en agreed to compromise on two issues. They changed the wording of their claim from one seeking recognition of "ownership" and "jurisdiction," to one claiming "Aboriginal title" and "self-government." Second, they changed their claim from one made on behalf of specific chiefs and houses to a communal claim on behalf of all. The province and the federal government both argued that the test to prove Aboriginal title should be based on evidence of actual, continuous, physical occupation of specific land sites since time immemorial, and that Aboriginal rights should be limited to those that were "integral to the distinctive culture" of the First Nation applying to the court for recognition. Lawyers for both federal and provincial governments supported Chief Justice McEachern's findings on expert evidence. The Gitksan and Wet'suwet'en argued that an application of this test would result in the only lands enjoying Aboriginal title today being those already designated as reserves. The Province of British Columbia and "third party" intervenors argued that Aboriginal title had been extinguished, and that Chief Justice McEachern's findings of fact should be accepted. The Hereditary Chiefs had failed to prove their case, they claimed. The Gitksan and Wet'suwet'en replied that they had proven their essential connection to all their land in their oral history evidence that demonstrated cultural, historical, physical and spiritual relationships to the territory from time immemorial. Proof of site-specific and continuous use and occupation should not be required to prove Aboriginal title, they said. Such evidence is not required of the Crown or non-Aboriginal people wishing to prove ownership.

All parties awaited the decision of the Supreme Court of Canada.

---

1. For an articulation of this political position see See Smith, M., 1995, and Lippert 1995. For a critique of the same see Bateman 1997.

2. Province of British Columbia, Ministry of Aboriginal Affairs, "B.C.'s Approach to Treaty Settlements: Lands and Resources," Victoria, B.C.: May 12, 1995.

3. Business Council of B.C., "Presentation on Draft Position Paper on Treaty Negotiations in British Columbia", Vancouver: May 12, 1995; and Culhane, Dara, unpublished fieldnotes, May 12, 1995.

4. Nisga'a Tribal Council, "Agreement-in-Principle In Brief," Vancouver: February 15, 1996.

5. Nisga'a Tribal Council, "Backgrounder: Nisga'a Agreement in Principle, Fisheries Component," Vancouver: August 27, 1996.

6. Nisga'a Tribal Council, Government of Canada, Government of British Columbia, "Tripartite Press Release: Nisga'a, British Columbia and Canada Release Historic Agreement-In-Principle," Vancouver: February 15, 1996.

7. Wong, Milton (1997) "Economic Imperatives to Settle A Nisga'a Treaty," letter to B.C. Select Standing Committee on Aboriginal Affairs," March, 1997.

8. Williams R. A. 1990(b): 72.

Chapter 24: Back to the Future

...We wish to begin by clearly stating that in our view the extinguishment policy is harmful and counterproductive.... Instead, the focus of negotiations between the Canadian government and Aboriginal peoples should be on reconciliation based on an affirmation of Aboriginal title and rights, according to the principle of equitable sharing of ownership and jurisdiction.... The present approach does damage to Canada's ethical core, for it founds negotiations on the premise that one party is inherently superior to the other....

We argue that without a legitimate Aboriginal title there cannot be a legitimate Canadian state, for without the recognition of Aboriginal title we would have a state based on colonial rationalizations. The model we propose bases the relationship between Aboriginal peoples and Canada on the recognition of a permanent Aboriginal title that sustains all of us. It represents a direction that can ultimately take Canada from a state founded on colonialism, into the twenty-first century as a state with roots going back to time immemorial.[1]

—Anthropologist Michael Asch, and Lawyer Norman Zlotkin, 1997, *Affirming Aboriginal Title: A New Basis for Comprehensive Claims Negotiations.*

Colouring Outside the Lines

And so here we are, on the eve of what the Julian calendar marks as a "millennium." We are about to embark on a new century: the twenty-first, in the year of Our Lord. Jesus Christ. Countless numbers of people, Aboriginal and non-Aboriginal, have lived and died since 1774, pursuing just and unjust resolutions to the "Aboriginal title issue" in British Columbia and Canada. A generation has passed on, another has reached middle-age, and a new one has been born since Frank Calder and the Chiefs of the Nisga'a went to court in 1969. Millions and more millions of dollars have been spent on trials, hearings, research, studies and proposals. Learned people have combed the texts of western law, philosophy and politics and have developed blueprints for change. They have provided interpretations of precedents, models of logical arguments, and readings of history that would allow Canadian judges to recognize and codify, within their own terms, a new legal and political relationship between Aboriginal and non-Aboriginal peoples.[2] These possibilities, however inevitably limited, exist, as they always have, within the parameters of the law as it exists. The judicial will to realize this potential that has been absent.

Contemporary Canadian legal and political positions and cultural beliefs that continue to uphold the doctrine of discovery/occupation/settlement, and the concept of *terra nullius* refuse to acknowledge the legitimacy of First Nations' existence. This position prohibits any possibility of dialogue or negotiation. The bully simply asserts his will through the power of force, and justifies it by denying the existence of the other. Positions that rely on the doctrine of conquest begin with a demand for the extinguishment of Aboriginal sovereignty, the recognition of the hovering sovereign's underlying title to all the land, and his omnipotent jurisdiction over all the peoples. In this scenario, the bully recognizes the existence of the other, holds his gun to their heads, and offers options for surrender.

A Royal Commission on Aboriginal Peoples released its report in November 1996, after consulting, researching and deliberating for almost five years, at a cost of approximately 56 million dollars. Their extensive recommendations begin by proposing alternatives to the extinguishment policy to facilitate Nation-to-Nation negotiations between Aboriginal and non-Aboriginal Canadians. The Commissioners advocate a concept of dual-citizenship for Aboriginal peoples in Canada, and outline a 20-year plan for redressing historic injustices and achieving social, economic and political equality. To date, the federal government has ignored the Royal Commission's report. The political will to implement their recommendations is absent.

Contemporary Aboriginal legal and political representatives who advocate what is referred to as the "sovereignty argument" begin their story in the times before Europeans arrived. Aboriginal people who identify with the "sovereignty position," and self-described "traditionalist" groupings, argue that Aboriginal sovereignty over lands and resources is a sacred trust entered into by the Creator and their ancestors that cannot be altered or negotiated away by mere mortals but must endure for all time. People committed to this position are open to negotiating agreements regarding sharing lands and resources with other sovereign peoples, but the prospect of surrendering sovereignty, or "Aboriginal title," would constitute a betrayal of what they believe is their sacred covenant with the Creator to be stewards of the land. It is, literally, unthinkable.

Many Aboriginal representatives who are involved in the treaty process and litigation make it very clear that they do not reject the sovereignty position in principle, but see themselves as being involved in processes that demand pragmatism and the making of strategic compromises. Remember that Chief Justice McEachern set out this double bind when he asked the absurd question whether the Gitksan and Wet'suwet'en themselves really believed in their own assertions of title because they acknowledged—within the framework of meaning of the law—the Crown's underlying title to all the land. Although the Chief Justice simultaneously argued that such recognition of Crown sovereignty constituted the non-negotiable terms and conditions under which the courts would hear the Gitksan's and Wet'suwet'en's case in the first place. Damned if you do. Damned if you don't.

Any future coexistence between Aboriginal and non-Aboriginal Canadians must be built on a strong and just foundation, and for this to be possible the old one must first be dismantled. Canadians must return to the first moment in the relationship: to the initial assertion of brute force and demonstration of raw power when the Crown declared the land *terra nullius* and asserted its dominion as if the Aboriginal peoples already living on the land did not exist. We must face the fact that this was justified then, and continues to be justified today, on the basis of an equally crude and violent assertion: that Europeans are superior human beings and Aboriginal peoples are inferior human beings. This was and is wrong: wrong according to British law then and now, and morally repugnant and politically indefensible according to Canadian ideals of justice, then and now. So the first reciprocal step towards reconciliation *must* be for judges, through law; and political representatives, through legislation; and institutions, through inclusion and respect for autonomy; and Canadians, through intelligence and decency, to recognize this historical truth publicly and plainly for what it was, and is. Coming to terms with this truth of Canadian history requires that Canadians understand this legacy not as a series of historical errors or anomalies, but as consistent with the underlying foundations and principles of the colonial project. This means too that those who inherit the benefits of these practices must also be prepared to change and act responsibly. These truths must be acknowledged, without rationalizations. Justice must be done, and must be seen to be done, before any just future can begin to be built.

A new generation of Aboriginal political activists and legal academics, and non-Aboriginal supporters have been engaged in the study of historical reinterpretation and revision and complex reconstructions of dialogues between European and Aboriginal philosophies.[3] From their work have emerged sophisticated proposals and directions for legal, political and cultural reconciliation based on shared morality, ethics and justice. For example, Ojibway legal scholar John Borrows has revisited the Royal Proclamation of 1763 through studying Aboriginal oral histories. He argues that "First Nations were not passive objects, but active participants, in the formulation and ratification of the Royal Proclamation.... In these early confrontations with the Crown, First Nations possessed their own power and a range of choices to which they could bring their own considerations and alternatives."[4] Foremost among Aboriginal understandings of these agreements was the notion of continuity into perpetuity of their relationship to their lands, and of coexistence with other peoples. The Royal Proclamation of 1763, according to Aboriginal interpretations, guaranteed that negotiations would be required in order to change use of lands, and to determine the relative jurisdictions of Aboriginal and Canadian law and governments. This interpretation can provide for a relationship based on the assumption that Crown sovereignty and Aboriginal sovereignty may co-exist unless or until changes in this relationship are legitimately agreed upon by both parties. Read in this way, as a Nation-to-Nation treaty between First Nations and the Crown, Borrows argues, the Royal Proclamation could serve as a model for modern-day treaty-making.

The first step in creating the necessary conditions for intercultural communication is to agree to converse within a shared framework. Borrows' interpretation of the Royal Proclamation of 1763 as the outcome of intercultural negotiations, whose written *and* oral history must be given equal weight, and whose contemporary meaning must be found in continuing dialogue, signals a significant gesture towards reconciliation with non-Aboriginal Canadians. Aboriginal peoples have also agreed to a shared language of negotiation, and accept, as sufficient for the purposes of communication, the translation of their histories and aspirations into English and French words.

A Crown response that acknowledges that the Royal Proclamation *recognizes* rather than *creates* Aboriginal rights; that agrees to take into account the intentions and understandings of both British and Aboriginal authors of the Proclamation; that interprets the Royal Proclamation as recognizing the existence of sovereign Aboriginal *nations*; that, following from this, acknowledges the obligation for Britain, and now for Canada, to negotiate with Aboriginal Peoples on a *nation to nation* basis; and that agrees to negotiate the nature of the Aboriginal rights so recognized, would constitute a reciprocal step towards dialogue and reconciliation.

In British Columbia, as elsewhere, an intangible yet palpable anticipation that we are standing at a cross-roads, or on the edge of a cliff, pervades the general sense of things: structures the feelings of our times. We know we are experiencing a social and cultural sea change, but we are uncertain what the future may hold. While parties to Aboriginal title litigation contest the details of history, they also dispute each other's visions of moral and social universes. Understanding "culture" as being most deeply rooted in theories of human nature and visions of what constitutes a "good society," a "good life," and a "good person," rather than as a collection of traits, or a blueprint people carry around in their heads that, like a computer program, determines how they will interpret experiential "input," allows the discussion to go beyond dualist, binary oppositions, hierarchal competitions for cultural supremacy, and essentialist notions of culture as naturally or divinely given. Many contemporary supporters of universal human rights argue for proposals that are not limited to the individual rights prized by the dominant western culture, but also address collective cultural rights, including the "right to belong."[5] Various concepts of "the self" and what it means to be a person in different cultural contexts serve as windows onto the broader political landscape. The self embedded in the Crown's legal arguments, in Sheila Robinson's anthropology, in Chief Justice

McEachern's ruling, and in the Supreme Court of Canada's precedents, is the self of nineteenth-century European political theory. It is an idealized male self, unencumbered by obligations to family; freed from dependence on, or responsibility for, others; released from the mercy of time and tides. It is a self moved around by the demands of global capital in the international marketplace: the multinational corporate executive for whom home is where the profit is, and the migrant worker for whom home must be where the paycheque is. A self with "reasons to travel." It is the self of the atomistic individual: the soldier in the war of all against all, the warrior in the battle of the fittest to survive. These theories of human nature embodied in aggressive, competitive individualists have been contested throughout western European history, from both inside and outside this intellectual tradition. The Crown's vision does not describe a natural or universal way of being human; nor a consensus on what it ought to mean, or could mean, to be human.[6]

Contrary to the dominant image represented by the Crown, its opponents argue that human beings should be conceptualized as essentially and irreducibly social beings, and that individuals exist always already in relationships with others. As social beings we are constituted by our relationships. We need others in order to be ourselves. Within such a vision of human life we do not feed ourselves, we feed each other. If people are hungry, we have failed in our responsibilities as human beings. We do not shelter ourselves, we shelter each other. If people are homeless, we have failed in our responsibilities as human beings. If justice does not prevail, it is because we choose to practice injustice. Neither Nature nor God nor Culture—nor "The Deficit"—compel us to make the choices we make. As social beings we are, or ought to be, responsible to and for each other, and for our collective future.

Clearly, there are places within European legal, philosophical and cultural traditions from which openings to Aboriginal traditions are possible, and sites where bridges can be built. Many Aboriginal leaders and their supporters, of necessity, have been absorbed in responding to agendas set by the courts that have, as law dictates, focussed on competing interpretations of the past. Political negotiations follow the law, however unevenly or erratically. Until responsibility for the past is recognized, and fair reparations made, dreaming outside possibilities framed by existing legal and political structures seems to some a luxury that Aboriginal peoples and their allies cannot yet afford. This has inadvertently encouraged a kind of legalization of political imagination where justification for social change and visions of the future are sought in the past: in Lockean or Hobbesian political theory, or in romanticized images of pre-contact Aboriginal Gardens of Eden.

Others argue that none of us—Aboriginal or non-Aboriginal—can afford *not* to dream. While we may draw on history, it is the future that we are constructing in the present. Societies will always reflect their histories, but need not be limited by them. Cultures are inevitably shaped by traditions, but are dynamic and creative too. Must we remain obedient to the tyranny of precedent? Why consider history to be normative, why allow it to be normalizing? Why hold the future a prisoner of the past? What does it mean, after all, to create human(e) communities? What is required to build a just world? These are ultimately moral and political challenges that must address economic structures and technology, but should not be determined by them. The answers to these questions will not be found in empirical studies of population to resources ratios, nor in abstract theoretical premises. These are questions that require moral and political dialogue, and solutions that must be lived and experienced in the everyday world, within relationships between people, not within contracts between things.

There are those who suggest more radical possibilities than the law, or the mainstream political imagination, currently envisions. They propose that Aboriginal title be recognized as the "underlying title to all the lands." A living, breathing Mother Earth would displace the abstract, hovering sovereign. This title would be defined as a relationship to land and resources that constitutes a sacred trust held by the living for the not-yet-born. Such visions of possible futures see human beings as inextricably part of interdependent and mutually-sustaining relationships with all of nature. "Man" need not seek dominion over all he surveys; need not build fences or evict his family. Neither may he destroy at his whim that which shelters and sustains fellow beings. If land and resources were to be conceptualized and codified in law on such philosophical premises, then perhaps we could cease energy-devouring and soul-destroying battles in courtrooms, at negotiating tables, and on logging roads. Rather than competing in expensive contests of abstract legal acrobatics and arguing about who has the right to exploit the land, we could begin to discuss who has the responsibility to nurture the land. Perhaps we could all survive. Together. On this land.

Easier said than done? Of course. Utopian idealism in the face of global capitalism and the ever-encroaching New World Order? Perhaps. But when are dreams most necessary if not in times like these? When should morality be celebrated if not when "pragmatism" terrorizes? Why should such a vision *not* be possible to realize? Who says it could never be?

---

1. Asch and Zlotkin 1997.

2. Macklem 1991, 1993; McNeil 1979; Slattery 1992.

3. Henderson J. Y 1985; Monture-Okanee 1993; Turpel 1991; Venne 1997.

4. Borrows 1997.

5. Marcus and Fisher 1986; Turner 1993, 1997.

6. Benhabib and Cornell 1989; Taylor 1991.

POSTSCRIPT: DECEMBER 11, 1997

I have mixed emotions today. I am filled with joy and also with remembrance of people who have worked so hard. I remember our Elders who passed on with broken hearts and the words of Chief Justice McEachern in their ears. Today's decision begins to heal the wounds. The Supreme Court of Canada has come out on the side of justice and humanity.
—Ray Jones, December 11, 1997.

I was there. I sat through the whole trial. I saw how our elders and witnesses were treated. I remember their tears that day that Chief Justice McEachern made his judgment. Now, at last, our truth has been heard.
—Yagalahl (Dora Wilson), December 11, 1997.

We've been given a diamond for Christmas...instead of a lump of coal.
—Satsan (Herb George), December 11, 1997.

The Dawn of a New Day?

On December 11, 1997, Gitksan and Wet'suwet'en representatives, Aboriginal rights supporters and members of the media gathered at the Vancouver Aboriginal Friendship Centre to hear the Supreme Court of Canada's ruling on the *Delgamuukw v. R.* appeal. Most people had been taken by surprise a week earlier when it had been announced that this decision, not expected until the Spring of 1998, was to be handed down before Christmas.[1]

Cautious anticipation turned into celebration as the contents of the Supreme Court's ruling were revealed: Allan McEachern had erred when he dismissed the oral history evidence of the Gitksan and Wet'suwet'en Chiefs and Elders, his own superiors determined. "The trial judge, after refusing to admit, or giving no independent weight to these oral histories, reached the conclusion that the appellants had not demonstrated the requisite degree of occupation for 'ownership,'" wrote the Right Honourable Antonio Lamer, Chief Justice of the Supreme Court of Canada. "Had the trial judge assessed the oral histories correctly," Lamer continued, "his conclusions on these issues of fact might have been very different." The depth and breadth of McEachern's errors led the Supreme Court of Canada to order a new trial. For the same reasons, the Supreme Court also stated that they could not rule on the Gitksan's and Wet'suwet'en's claims for self-government rights.[2]

Appeal courts are normally loathe to contradict findings of fact made by lower court judges, and do so only when they are convinced that the trial judge has made a "palpable and overriding error" in his findings of fact. Usually, such a conclusion may arise from three possible bases: (1) where it can be demonstrated that there was no evidence to support a material finding of fact made by the trial judge; (2) when the trial judge wrongly overlooked admissible evidence relevant and material to the issue before the court; or, (3) where the trial judge's findings of fact cannot be supported as reasonable. Chief Justice Lamer added a fourth, new, condition to this list: "In cases involving the determination of aboriginal rights," he wrote, "appellate intervention is also warranted by the failure of a trial court to appreciate the evidentiary difficulties inherent in adjudicating aboriginal claims when, first, applying the rules of evidence and, second, interpreting the evidence before it."[3]

Lamer detailed his court's criticisms of McEachern's decision on this matter, devoting eight full pages of text to the issue:

Although he...[McEachern] had earlier recognized, when making his ruling on admissibility, that it was impossible to make an easy distinction between the mythological and "real" aspects of these oral histories, he discounted the adaawk and kungax because they were not 'literally true,' confounded 'what is fact and what is belief,' 'included some material which might be classified as mythology,' and projected a 'romantic view' of the history of the Gitksan and Wet'suwet'en. He also cast doubt on the authenticity of these special oral histories because...'the verifying group is so small that they cannot safely be regarded as expressing the reputation of even the Indian community, let alone the larger community whose opportunity to dispute territorial claims would be essential to weight.' Finally, he questioned the utility of the adaawk and kungax to demonstrate use and occupation because they were 'seriously lacking in detail about the specific lands to which they are said to relate.'[4]

Although he framed his ruling in terms of the specific oral histories before him, in my respectful opinion, the trial judge...[McEachern] in reality based his decision on some general concerns with the use of oral histories as evidence in aboriginal rights cases. In summary, the trial judge gave no independent weight to these special oral histories because they did not accurately convey historical truth, because knowledge about those oral histories was confined to the communities whose histories they were and because those oral histories were insufficiently detailed. However...these are features to a greater or lesser extent, of all oral histories.... The implication of the trial judge's reasoning is that oral histories should never be given any independent weight and are only useful as confirmatory evidence in aboriginal rights litigation. I fear that if this reasoning were followed, the oral histories of aboriginal peoples would be consistently and systematically undervalued by the Canadian legal system.[5]

The trial judge also erred when he discounted the "recollections of aboriginal life" offered by various members of the appellant nations...he effectively held that this evidence did not demonstrate the requisite continuity between present occupation and past occupation in order to ground a claim for aboriginal title. In my opinion, the trial judge expected too much of the oral history of the appellants, as expressed in the recollections of aboriginal life of members of the appellant nations. He expected that evidence to provide definitive and precise evidence of pre-contact aboriginal activities on the territory in question.... Rather, if oral history cannot conclusively establish pre-sovereignty occupation of land, it may still be relevant to demonstrate that current occupation has its origins prior to sovereignty. This is exactly what the appellants sought to do.[6]

The trial judge also erred in his treatment of the territorial affidavits filed by the appellant chiefs.... He questioned the degree to which the declarations amounted to a reputation because they were largely confined to the appellants' communities.... Furthermore, the trial judge reasoned that since the subject-matter of the affidavits was disputed, its reliability was doubtful. Finally, the trial judge questioned...the 'independence and objectivity' of the information contained in the affidavits, because the appellants and their ancestors 'have been actively discussing land claims for many years.'[7]

The requirement that a reputation be known in the general community ...ignores the fact that oral histories...generally relate to particular locations, and refer to particular families and communities and may, as a result, be unknown outside of that community, even to other aboriginal nations. Excluding the territorial affidavits because the claims to which they relate are disputed does not acknowledge that claims to aboriginal rights, and aboriginal title in particular, are almost always disputed and contested.... Casting doubt on the reliability of the territorial affidavits because land claims had been actively discussed for many years also fails to take account of the special context surrounding aboriginal claims, in two ways. First, those claims have been discussed for so long because of British Columbia's persistent refusal to acknowledge the existence of aboriginal title in that province until relatively recently.... It would be perverse, to say the least, to use the refusal of the province to acknowledge the rights of its aboriginal inhabitants as a reason for excluding evidence which may prove the existence of those rights. Second, this rationale for exclusion places aboriginal claimants whose societies record their past through oral history in a grave dilemma. In order for the oral history of a community to amount to a form of reputation, and to be admissible in court, it must remain alive through the discussions of members of that community; those discussions are the very basis of that reputation. But if those histories are discussed too much, and too close to the date of litigation, they may be discounted as being suspect, and may be held to be inadmissible. The net effect may be that a society with such an oral tradition would never be able to establish a historical claim through the use of oral history in court.[8]

Finally, Chief Justice Lamer concluded:

In the circumstances, the factual findings cannot stand. However, given the enormous complexity of the factual issues at hand, it would be impossible for the Court to do justice to the parties by sifting through the record itself and making new factual findings. A new trial is warranted, at which the evidence may be considered in light of the principles...elaborated upon here. In applying these principles, the new trial judge might well share some or all of the findings of fact of McEachern C.J.[9]

Patience Is a Virtue

This struggle began when the first Europeans arrived on our land. We have been waiting 130 years for this day. We are no longer invisible.
—Joan Ryan, Gitksan, December 11, 1997

"Aboriginal title is a right to the land itself," the Supreme Court's ruling stated, and this right is protected by Section 35(1) of the Canadian Constitution. The purpose of Section 35(1), the Supreme Court decreed, "is to reconcile the prior presence of aboriginal peoples with the assertion of Crown sovereignty." Therefore both aspects of that prior presence—the occupation of land, and the prior social organization and distinctive cultures of Aboriginal peoples on that land—must be recognized and affirmed.

The Supreme Court proceeded to define, for the first time, the exact content of Aboriginal title that the law would legitimate. Chief Justice Lamer noted that it was necessary to do this because, he said, "I believe that all of the parties have characterized the content of aboriginal title incorrectly."[10]

Aboriginal title, the judgment continued, is inalienable; it must be communal; it cannot be transferred, sold or surrendered to anyone other than the Crown; and it finds its source in recognition (not creation) by the Royal Proclamation of 1763; in the common law principle that occupation constitutes proof of possession; and in laws that pre-existed the assertion of British sovereignty. Aboriginal title in law, the Supreme Court explained, is *sui generis:* it represents a reconciliation of common law and aboriginal law and cannot be reduced to either.

The Supreme Court modified the "frozen rights" position adopted by previous judicial panels. Aboriginal title, the judges decreed, is not restricted to practices whose origins can be traced to pre-contact times. Legally codified Aboriginal title now encompasses the right to exclusive use and occupation of the land for a variety of purposes which need not be aspects of those practices, customs and traditions "integral to the claimant group's distinctive aboriginal culture" as had been required by the *Sparrow* test. "The nature of the Indian interest is very broad and incorporates present-day needs," the Supreme Court declared. "Aboriginal title encompasses mineral rights and lands held pursuant to aboriginal title should be capable of exploitation. Such a use is certainly not a traditional one."[11] However, "practices, customs or traditions that arose solely as a response to European influences do not meet the standard for recognition."[12]

In order to "prove" Aboriginal title in court, First Nations must present evidence that they used and occupied the lands claimed on the date British sovereignty was asserted. In British Columbia, this date has been established as 1846. Or, in the alternative, they may present evidence of present occupation as proof of pre-sovereignty possession as long as there is "a continuity between present and pre-sovereignty occupation."

The Supreme Court distinguished between general Aboriginal *title* and specific Aboriginal *rights*. While the relevant time period for establishing Aboriginal title is the date of British sovereignty, Aboriginal rights must be traced to the date of first contact with Europeans. Aboriginal rights are identified with particular practices, customs, and traditions that exist on a continuum related to the degree of connection with land.

The Supreme Court went on to develop the principle that Aboriginal title contains an "inherent limit." In so doing, they clarified the legal definition of Aboriginal title more precisely:

> Lands held pursuant to aboriginal title cannot be used in a manner that is irreconcilable with the nature of the claimants' attachment to those lands. This inherent limit arises because the relationship of an aboriginal community with its land should not be prevented from continuing into the future. Occupancy...[the "proof" required to establish Aboriginal title at law] is determined by reference to the activities that have taken place on the land and the uses to which the land has been put by the particular group. If lands are so occupied, there will exist a special bond between the group and the land in question such that the land will be part of the definition of the group's distinctive culture. Land held by virtue of aboriginal title may not be alienated because the land has an inherent and unique value in itself which is enjoyed by the community with aboriginal title to it. The community cannot put the land to uses which would destroy that value.

> For example, if occupation is established with reference to the use of the land as a hunting ground, then the group that successfully claims aboriginal title to

that land may not use it in such a fashion as to destroy its value for such a use (e.g. by strip mining it). Similarly, if a group claims a special bond with the land because of its ceremonial or cultural significance, it may not use the land in such a way as to destroy that relationship (e.g. by developing it in such a way that the bond is destroyed, perhaps by turning it into a parking lot.)[13]

Finally…the importance of the continuity of the relationship between an aboriginal community and its land, and the non-economic or inherent value of that land, should not be taken to detract from the possibility of surrender to the Crown in exchange for valuable consideration. On the contrary, the idea of surrender reinforces the conclusion that aboriginal title is limited in the way I have described. If aboriginal peoples wish to use their lands in a way that aboriginal title does not permit, then they must surrender those lands and convert them into non-title lands to do so…. This is not, I must emphasize, a limitation that restricts the use of the land to those activities that have traditionally been carried out on it. That would amount to a legal straightjacket on aboriginal peoples who have a legitimate legal claim to the land. The approach I have outlined above allows for a full range of uses of the land, subject only to an overarching limit, defined by the special nature of the aboriginal title in that land.

The courts maintain the power to determine what constitutes a "truly aboriginal" use of land and what does not, and that limiting distinction continues to turn on degrees of commercial exploitation and development.

Chief Justice Lamer dispensed with the "old" question of extinguishment of aboriginal title by declaring that provincial governments could not extinguish Aboriginal title or rights prior to 1982 when they were entrenched in the Constitution. Therefore, Aboriginal title and rights in British Columbia arise from long term use and occupation prior to European arrival, have never been extinguished, and still exist today. The possibility of legal extinguishment of Aboriginal title remains, but it has been projected into the future, rather than into the past; and could now involve Aboriginal initiative, participation and consent.

The judges of the Supreme Court of Canada upheld Allan McEachern's dismissal of the evidence provided by non-Aboriginal expert witnesses. Claiming that the Gitksan's and Wet'suwet'en's objections to McEachern's rulings on historical, anthropological, and archaeological evidence represented "mere disagreement," rather than any "palpable and overriding errors," and that the Province of British Columbia and the Government of Canada had established that "there was some contradictory evidence that supported the trial judge's conclusions" in these areas, Chief Justice Lamer concluded that "the appellants have failed to demonstrate that the trial judge erred in this respect."[15]

Justice Lamer continued, emphasizing his court's support for Allan McEachern's dismissal of Richard Daly and Antonia Mills, and erasure of Hugh Brody:

One objection that I would like to mention specifically, albeit in passing, is the trial judge's refusal to accept the testimony of two anthropologists who were brought in as expert witnesses by the appellants. This aspect of the trial judge's reasons was hotly contested by the appellants in their written submissions. However, I need only reiterate what I have stated above, that findings of credibility, including the credibility of expert witnesses, are for the trial judge to make, and should warrant considerable deference from appellate courts.[16]

Chief Justice Lamer and the Supreme Court of Canada panel is to be commended for respecting Aboriginal self-representation, and for finally acknowledging what First Nations have always known: that oral tradition is the preeminent, legitimate source of knowledge about Aboriginal culture and history, and must be understood and validated on its own terms. Rules for historical interpretation drawn from the mainstream, western, academic study of written history are not appropriate to the understanding of marginalized, non-western, oral histories. Neither should the law require Aboriginal peoples' representations to be mediated by anthropologists.

However, Allan McEachern's "findings of fact" did not arise purely out of thin air, or his own imagination. They echoed the Crown's legal arguments in *Delgamuukw v. R.* These in turn drew on the evidence presented by the Crown's expert witnesses in history and anthropology, and on the unreflected upon "common sense" of Canadian colonial culture. The question that logically arises is: had the Crown and their witnesses "assessed the oral histories correctly [would] their conclusions on...issues of fact...have been very different"? In short, the Supreme Court of Canada appears to be saying, rather contradictorily, that Allan McEachern erred in his assessment of the oral histories, but the Crown and its witnesses who advised him to make the evaluation he did were not also wrong, but were merely expressing a difference of opinion arising from academic debates.

The problem with the Supreme Court's failure to find "palpable and overriding errors" in Allan McEachern's evaluation of the academic historical and anthropological testimony is not that it insults anthropologists and historians, but that such evidence will still continue to figure prominently in Aboriginal title litigation even if Aboriginal oral tradition is considered more appropriately and respectfully. In future litigation, questions about research standards and methodologies, about the evaluation of expertise, about ethnocentric biases in the historical and ethnographic record, and about the problems and complexities involved in cross-cultural interpretation and communication will continue to be at issue. If such considerations were taken seriously by the Supreme Court, in tandem with culturally-appropriate analyses of Aboriginal oral histories, such methodological rigour might mitigate against the possibility of a "new trial judge...[sharing] some or all of the findings of fact of McEachern C.J." in this or any other cases.

The Way Forward

This judgment restores a measure of faith in the legal system. The rule of law applies to all British Columbians now. The federal and provincial governments should come back to the treaty negotiation table in a fair and honest manner.
—Chief Joe Mathias, Squamish First Nation, December 11, 1997.

"Aboriginal title is a right to the land itself!" Premier Clark and Prime Minister Chretien, take note! You can no longer make trade deals with the Asia Pacific countries or anyone else without us.
—Chief Ed John, First Nations Summit, December 11, 1997.

Finally, the Supreme Court of Canada judges turned their attention to determining how—once Aboriginal title and/or Aboriginal rights are established at law—federal and provincial governments could justifiably infringe upon them. The Aboriginal title codified by the Supreme Court's ruling remains a subordinate one that constitutes a burden on the Crown's underlying, radical title. The hovering sovereign's hegemony remains paramount. This principle is most clearly spelled out in the judgment's articulation of legal tests for the justification of infringement. The satisfaction of two conditions would constitute legally sanctioned infringement of aboriginal title and rights: (1) that the infringement furthers a compelling and substantial legislative objective; and/or (2) that the infringement is consistent with the special fiduciary relationship between the Crown and the Aboriginal peoples. The ruling sets out the following as "compelling and substantial legislative objectives":

> The development of agriculture, forestry, mining and hydroelectric power, the general economic development of the interior of British Columbia, protection of the environment or endangered species, and the building of infrastructure and the settlement of foreign populations to support those aims....[17]

Legitimate government objectives also include "the pursuit of economic and regional fairness;" and in relation to specific resources like salmon, "the recognition of the historical reliance upon, and participation in, the fishery by non-aboriginal groups." Attainment of these objectives constitute legally justifiable reasons for infringement. The Supreme Court of Canada explained their reasoning:

> Because distinctive aboriginal societies exist within, and are part of, a broader social, political and economic community over which the Crown is sovereign, there are circumstances in which, in order to pursue objectives of compelling and substantial importance to that community as a whole

(taking into account the fact that aboriginal societies are part of that community), some limitation of those rights will be justifiable. Aboriginal rights are a necessary part of the reconciliation of aboriginal society with the broader political community of which they are a part; limits placed on those rights are, where the objectives furthered by those limits are of sufficient importance to the broader community as a whole, equally a necessary part of that reconciliation. [18]

However, such infringement should not be arbitrary or unfair within the terms established by the court. Aboriginal peoples must be consulted, included, and compensated, according to the fiduciary obligation owed by the Crown to Aboriginal peoples. The Supreme Court explained their interpretation of this second part of the test for justifiable infringement:

The fiduciary duty does not demand that aboriginal rights always be given priority. Each case is different...The form the fiduciary obligation can take is also variable...Within the analysis of justification, there are further questions to be addressed, depending on the circumstances of the inquiry. These include the questions of whether there has been as little infringement as possible in order to effect the desired result; whether, in a situation of expropriation, fair compensation is available; and, whether the aboriginal group in question has been consulted....[19]

The nature and scope of the duty of consultation will vary with the circumstances. In occasional cases, when the breach is less serious or relatively minor, it will be no more than a duty to discuss important decisions that will be taken with respect to lands pursuant to aboriginal title. Of course, even in the rare cases when the minimum acceptable standard is consultation, this consultation must be in good faith, and with the intention of substantially addressing the concerns of the aboriginal peoples whose lands are at issue. In most cases, it will be significantly deeper than mere consultation. Some cases may even require the full consent of an aboriginal nation, particularly when provinces enact hunting and fishing regulations in relation to aboriginal lands. [20]

...In keeping with the duty of honour and good faith on the Crown, fair compensation will ordinarily be required when aboriginal title is infringed. The amount of compensation payable will vary with the nature of the particular aboriginal title affected and with the nature and severity of the infringement and the extent to which aboriginal interests were accommodated. [21]

Answers to all these questions will be determined on a case-by-case basis.

The Irony of Ironies

It is not open to the appellants to challenge the trial judge's findings of fact merely because they disagree with them. I fear that a significant number of the appellants' objections fall into this category.... The bulk of these objections, at best, relate to alleged instances of misapprehension or oversight of material evidence by the trial judge.
—Chief Justice Lamer, 1997, *Reasons for Judgment*: para 90.

While the Supreme Court of Canada ruled that Allan McEachern's errors were so fundamental as to be beyond the scope of an appeal court to repair, and that a new trial was therefore warranted, the judges recommended that disputes concerning land title and jurisdiction between First Nations in British Columbia and the federal and provincial governments should be settled through negotiations and not through further litigation. In so doing, they reiterated a position that has become increasingly influential in contemporary Canadian politics and was clearly articulated by the Supreme Court's recent decisions in the *Van Der Peet* and *Gladstone* cases: appointed judges simultaneously proclaiming the omnipotent independence of the law from society, while explicitly and intentionally shaping and directing public policy that is, theoretically, the job of elected politicians. Law advances, democracy retreats. The Supreme Court of Canada's ruling in the appeal of *Delgamuukw v. R.* is specifically directed to treaty negotiations in British Columbia, and it significantly strengthens the position of First Nations in this process. Specifically, by recognizing unextinguished Aboriginal title to *all* of British Columbia, by insisting on consultation with First Nations regarding development on their lands, and by requiring that compensation be paid for historical and future exploitation of Aboriginally-owned resources, the Supreme Court of Canada undermined the positions that the Province of British Columbia and the Government of Canada have brought to the treaty negotiation table. The governments have argued there that Aboriginal jurisdiction should be limited to specific lands, such as those already designated as Indian reserves; and that no entitlement to compensation for resource exploitation should be considered. Law advances minority rights that democracy has retreated from protecting.

Public opinion and the electoral process also affects what the future of treaty negotiations may be. The Supreme Court's validation of Aboriginal title and rights, and their recognition of the legitimacy of oral histories contradicts the still popular "founding myth of White British Columbians" that was presented by the Crown, and articulated by former Chief Justice McEachern in *Delgamuukw v. R.* This continues to be the "historical myth of choice" of significant sectors of the B.C. population, particularly of the provincial Liberal and Reform parties, who threaten to form the next government and to dismantle the treaty process if they do.

Tomorrow Today

> *Legal orders may embody asymmetrical power relations, but power is always an interactional process. Dominant groups enjoy legally protected privileges, but they are also constrained by the law. And subordinated groups that suffer under particular legal systems may find that law offers them, the less powerful, a measure of protection from the powerful, just as it sometimes offers them resources for action.*
> —Anthropologists June Starr and Jane Collier, 1989, "Introduction," *History and Power in the Study of Law.*

That the Supreme Court of Canada's December, 1997, ruling on the *Delgamuukw v. R.* appeal significantly changes the legal landscape in which Aboriginal title and rights litigation is adjudicated in Canada and in other colonial contexts worldwide is beyond question. While initial public responses to the judgment by representatives of industry and federal and provincial governments have tended to minimize its significance and potential impact on treaty negotiations, clearly this is truly a "landmark judgment" whose consequences will be many and varied. We will live in interesting times in the years to come.

For now, for today, First Nations of British Columbia are deservedly celebrating an historic turning point in a long, hard-fought, hard-won battle. Theirs has been a victory for humanity, for social justice and for the land: a triumph of spirit. They deserve the admiration, the respect and the gratitude of good people the world over.

People make history. Not under conditions of their own choosing and against great odds.

Dara Culhane
Vancouver, B.C.
December 12, 1997

1. This book was in press and scheduled for release in December 1997, when the Supreme Court of Canada announced that they would release their judgment in the *Delgamuukw* appeal. This postscript describes first impressions of the key features of this very complex and detailed 200-page judgment. I had intended to write an addendum and publish a revised edition of this book following the handing down of the appeal judgment originally expected in 1998. Time will tell the extent to which, and the speed with which, this work becomes a documentation of "historical times," and of questions no longer asked or answered.

2. Supreme Court of Canada, 1997, Reasons for Judgment in the Appeal of *Delgamuukw v. R.*: para 107.

3. Ibid., para 80.

4. Ibid., para 97.

5. Ibid., para 98.

6. Ibid., para 99-101.

7. Ibid., para 104.

8. Ibid., para 106.

9. Ibid., para 108.

10. Ibid., para 90.

11. Ibid., para 91.

12. Ibid., para 110.

13. Supreme Court of Canada, 1997, Judgment in the Appeal of *Delgamuukw v. R.*: 4.

14. Reasons 1997:para 144.

15. Ibid., para 128.

16. Ibid., para 131.

17. Judgment 1997:14.

18. Reasons 1997:para 161.

19. Ibid., para 162.

20. Ibid., para 168.

21. Ibid., para 169.

BIBLIOGRAPHY

Abu-Lughod, Lila and Catherine A. Lutz, eds. 1990. Introduction: emotion, discourse, and the politics of everyday life. In *Language and the politics of emotion*, 1-23. Cambridge: Cambridge University Press.

Acheson, Steve. 1995. Culture contact, demography and health among the aboriginal peoples of British Columbia. In *A persistent spirit: Towards understanding aboriginal health in British Columbia*, Stephenson, P. H., S. J. Elliott, L. T. Foster and Jill Harris, eds., Canadian Western Geographical Series, 31:1-41. Victoria, B.C.: University of Victoria, Department of Geography.

Adachi, Ken. 1976. *The enemy that never was: A history of the Japanese-Canadians.* Toronto: McClelland and Stewart.

Adams, John Winthrop. 1969. The politics of feasting among the Gitksan. Unpublished Ph.D. dissertation. Harvard University, Department of Anthropology.

Adams, John Winthrop. 1973. *The Gitksan potlatch: Population flux, resource ownership, and reciprocity.* Montreal: Holt, Rinehart and Winston.

Adams, John W. 1987. Introduction. *Arctic Anthropology* 24(1): 67-71.

Adelberg, E. and C. Currie, eds. 1993. *In conflict with the law: Women and the Canadian justice system.* Vancouver: Press Gang.

Alexander, Ken and Avis Glaze. 1996. *Towards freedom: The African-Canadian experience.* Toronto: Umbrella Press.

Altman, A. 1990. *Critical legal studies: A liberal critique.* Princeton, N.J.: Princeton University Press.

Ames, Michael M. 1988. The liberation of anthropology: A rejoinder to Professor Trigger's *A present of their past. Culture* 8(1): 81-85.

Andrews, K.R., N.P. Canny and P.E.H. Hair, eds. 1973. *The westward enterprise: English activities in Ireland, the Atlantic and America 1480-1650.* Detroit: Wayne State University Press.

Aronowitz, Stanley. 1993. *Roll over Beethoven: The return of cultural strife.* New England: Wesleyan University Press.

Asad, Talal, ed. 1973. *Anthropology and the colonial encounter.* London: Ithaca Press.

Asad, Talal. 1986. The concept of cultural translation in British social anthropology. In *Writing culture: The poetics and politics of ethnography*, 141-164. Berkeley: University of California Press.

Asch, Michael. 1984. *Home and native land: Aboriginal rights and the Canadian Constitution.* Toronto: Methuen.

Asch, Michael. 1989. To negotiate into Confederation: Canadian aboriginal views on their political rights. In *We are here: Politics of aboriginal land tenure*, Wilmsen, Edwin N., ed., 118-137. Berkeley: University of California Press.

Asch, Michael and Patrick Macklem. 1991. Aboriginal rights and Canadian sovereignty: An essay on *R. v. Sparrow. Alberta Law Review* XXIX(2): 498-517.

Bibliography

Asch, Michael. 1992 (a). *Aboriginal self-government and the construction of Canadian Constitutional identity.* Alberta Law Review XXX(2): 465-491.

Asch, Michael. 1992 (b). Errors in *Delgamuukw:* An anthropological perspective. In *Aboriginal title in British Columbia: Delgamuukw v. The Queen,* Cassidy, F., ed., 221-244. Lantzville: Oolichan Books and Institute for Research on Public Policy.

Asch, Michael, ed. 1997 (a). *Aboriginal and treaty rights in Canada: Essays on law, equality, and respect for difference.* Vancouver: University of British Columbia Press.

Asch, Michael. 1997 (b). Introduction. In *Aboriginal and treaty rights in Canada: Essays on law, equality, and respect for difference,* ix-xv. Vancouver: University of British Columbia Press.

Asch, Michael and Norman Zlotkin. 1997 (c). Affirming Aboriginal Title: A New Basis for Comprehensive Claims Negotiations. In *Aboriginal and treaty rights in Canada: Essays on law, equality, and respect for difference,* 208-2310. Vancouver: University of British Columbia Press.

Backhouse, Constance. 1991. *Petticoats and prejudice: Women and the law in 19th Century Canada.* Toronto: Women's Press, for the Osgoode Society.

Barbeau, C. Marius. 1929. *Totem poles of the Gitksan, Upper Skeena River, British Columbia,* National Museum of Canada, Bulletin No. 61, Anthropological Series No. 12. Ottawa: King's Printer.

Barnett, S. and M. Silverman. 1979. *Ideology and everyday life: Anthropology, neomarxist thought, and the problem of ideology and the social whole.* Ann Arbor: University of Michigan Press.

Barsh, Russell and James Youngblood Henderson. 1980. *The road: Indian tribes and political liberty.* Berkeley: University of California Press.

Bartlett, Richard. 1990. *Indian reserves and aboriginal lands in Canada: A homeland.* Saskatoon: University of Saskatchewan Native Law Centre.

Bateman, Rebecca. 1997. Comparative thoughts on the politics of aboriginal assimilation. *B.C. Studies* Summer 1997, No. 114.

Bauman, Zygmunt. 1987. *Legislators and interpreters: On modernity, postmodernity and the intellectuals.* Cambridge: Polity Press.

Bauman, Zygmunt. 1992. *Intimations of postmodernity.* London: Routledge.

Beals, Ralph. 1985. The anthropologist as expert witness: Illustrations from the California Indian land claims case. In *Irredeemable America: The Indians' estate and land claims,* Sutton, Imre, ed., 133-138. New Mexico: University of New Mexico Press and Institute for Native American Studies.

Behar, R. and D. Gordon, eds. 1996. *Women writing culture.* Berkeley: University of California Press.

Bell, Catherine and Michael Asch. 1997. Challenging assumptions: The impact of precedent in aboriginal rights litigation. In *Aboriginal and treaty rights in Canada: Essays on law, equality, and respect for difference,* Asch, Michael, ed., 38-74. Vancouver: University of British Columbia Press.

Benhabib, Seyla. 1992. *Situating the self: Gender, community and postmodernism in contemporary ethics.* New York: Routledge.

Benhabib, Seyla and Drucilla Cornell, eds. 1989. *Feminism as critique.* Minneapolis: University of Minnesota Press.

Berger, Thomas. 1981. Wilson Duff and native land claims. In *The world is as sharp as a knife*, Abbott, D., ed., 49-64. Victoria: B.C. Provincial Museum.

Berger, Thomas. 1983. Native history, native claims and self determination, *B.C. Studies* No. 57: 10-23.

Berger, Thomas. 1991. A long and terrible shadow: White values, native rights in the Americas, 1492-1992. Vancouver: Douglas and McIntyre.

Bibeau, Gilles. 1988. A step toward thick thinking: From webs of significance to connections across dimensions. *Medical Anthropology Quarterly* 2(4): 402-425.

Bishop, Charles A. and Arthur J. Ray. 1976. Ethnohistoric research in the central subarctic: Some conceptual and methodological problems. In *Western Canadian Journal of Anthropology* 6(1): 116-44.

Bishop, Charles. 1979. Limiting access to limited goods: The origin of stratification in interior British Columbia. In *The development of political organization in native North America*, Tooker, E. ed., 148-161. New York: American Ethnological Society.

Bishop, Charles. 1987. Introduction. *Anthropologica* 28(1-2): 7-9.

Blackman, Margaret, ed. 1982. *During my time: Florence Edenshaw Davidson, a Haida woman.* Seattle: University of Washington Press.

Bleich, David. 1988. *The double perspective: Language, literacy, and social relations.* New York: Oxford University Press.

Blomley, N. 1996. 'Shut the province down!' First Nations blockades in British Columbia, 1984-1995. *B.C. Studies* 3:5-35.

Blondin, Ethel. 1992. Our rights will not be forfeited. In *Aboriginal title in British Columbia: Delgamuukw v. the Queen*, Cassidy, F. ed., 253-258. Lantzville: Oolichan Books and Institute for Research on Public Policy.

Boas, Franz [1916]. 1970. *Tsimshian Mythology.* New York: Johnston Reprint Co.

Boldt, Menno and J. A. Long, eds., in association with LeRoy Little Bear. 1986. *The quest for justice: Aboriginal peoples and aboriginal rights.* Toronto: University of Toronto Press.

Bologh, Roslyn. 1979. *Dialectical phenomenology: Marx's method.* London: Routledge and Kegan Paul.

Borrows, John. 1992. A genealogy of law: Inherent sovereignty and First Nations self-government, *Osgoode Hall Law Journal*, 29, 291.

Borrows, John. 1997. Wampum at Niagara: The royal proclamation, Canadian legal history, and self-government. In *Aboriginal and treaty rights in Canada: Essays on law, equality, and respect for difference*, Asch, Michael, ed., 155-172. Vancouver: University of British Columbia Press.

Bourdieu, Pierre. 1987. The force of law: Toward a sociology of the juridical field. *Hastings Law Journal* 39(3): 805-853.

Bourdieu, Pierre. 1990. *In other words: Essays towards a reflexive sociology.* Stanford, California: Stanford University Press.

Bourgeois, Donald J. 1986. The role of the historian in the litigation process. *Canadian Historical Review* 67(2): 195-205.

Bowker, Andrea. 1995. Sparrow's promise: Aboriginal rights in the British Columbia Court of Appeal, *University of Toronto Faculty of Law Review* 53, 1:1-48.

Bowsfield, C. and M. Ormsby, eds. 1979. *Fort Victoria Letters (1846-1851).* Winnipeg: Hudsons Bay Record Society.

Boyarin, Jonathan, ed. 1992. *The ethnography of reading.* Berkeley: University of California Press.

Boyd, R. 1990. Demographic history, 1774-1874. In *Handbook of North American Indians: Northwest coast,* Suttles, W., ed., Vol. 7, 135-148. Washington, D.C.: Smithsonian Institution.

Boyle, James. 1985. The politics of reason: Critical legal theory and local social thought. *University of Pennsylvania Law Review,* 133.

Bray, M. and Thompson, A., eds. 1990. *Temagami: A debate on wilderness.* Toronto: Dundurn Press.

Brenneis, D. 1988. Language and disputing. *Annual Review of Anthropology* 17:221-237.

British Columbia. [1875] 1987. *Papers connected with the land question (1850-1875).* Victoria, B.C.: Richard Wolfenden Government Printer. Reprinted 1987, Victoria: Crown Publishers. [Herein referred to as "The Papers"].

Brodkey, Linda. 1987. *Academic writing as social practice.* Philadelphia: Temple University Press.

Brody, Hugh. 1975. *The peoples land: Eskimos and whites in the eastern Arctic.* Markham, Ontario: Penguin Books.

Brody, Hugh. 1983. *Maps and dreams: Indians and the British Columbia frontier.* Ontario: Penguin Books.

Brody, Hugh. 1987 (a). *The living Arctic.* Vancouver: Douglas and McIntyre.

Brody, Hugh. 1987 (b). The nature of cultural continuity among the Gitksan and Wet'suwet'en of northwest British Columbia. Opinion report prepared for the Office of the Gitksan and Wet'suwet'en Hereditary Chiefs in the matter of *Delgamuukw v. R.*

Burns, Peter T. 1992. Delgamuukw: A summary of the judgment. In *Aboriginal title in British Columbia: Delgamuukw v. the Queen,* Cassidy, F., ed., 21-34. Lantzville: Oolichan Books and Institute for Research on Public Policy.

Butler, Judith and Joan W. Scott, eds. 1992. *Feminists theorize the political.* New York: Routledge.

Callinicos, Alex. 1989. *Against postmodernism: A Marxist critique.* London: Polity Press.

Campisi, Jack. 1991. *The Mashpee Indians: Tribe on trial.* Syracuse, N.Y.: Syracuse University Press.

Canada. 1969. Department of Indian Affairs, Policy Statement.

Canada. 1983. First Ministers' Conference on Aboriginal Constitutional Matters, unofficial and unverified verbatim transcript, March 15, 1983, 1:115. Cited in Asch 1989.

Canada. 1989. Royal Commission on the Donald Marshall Jr. Prosecution. *Digest of Findings and Recommendations.* Halifax: The Commission.

Canada. 1993. Partners in Confederation: Aboriginal peoples, self-government and the Constitution. Royal Commission on Aboriginal Peoples. Ottawa: Supply and Services Canada.

Canada. 1995. Aboriginal Self-Government: Legal and Constitutional Issues, Macklem, Patrick et al. Royal Commission on Aboriginal Peoples. Ottawa: Canada Communications Group.

Canada. 1996 (a). Bridging the cultural divide: A report on Aboriginal peoples and criminal justice in Canada. Royal Commission on Aboriginal Peoples. Ottawa: Canada Communications Group.

Canada. 1996 (b). Treaty-making in the spirit of co-existence: An alternative to extinguishment. Royal Commission on Aboriginal Peoples. Ottawa: Canada Communications Group.

Canada. 1996 (c). Report of the Royal Commission on Aboriginal Peoples. Ottawa: The Commission.

Canada. 1996 (d). People to people, nation to nation: Highlights from the report of the Royal Commission on Aboriginal Peoples. Royal Commission on Aboriginal Peoples. Ottawa: Ministry of Supply and Services.

Canny, Nicholas P. 1973. The Ideology of Colonization: From Ireland to America. *William and Mary Quarterly* October, 30 (575): 575-598.

Caplan, Patricia, ed. 1987. *The cultural construction of sexuality.* London: Tavistock Press.

Caputo, John and Mark Yount. 1993 (a). Introduction: Institutions, normalization, and power. In *Foucault and the critique of institutions,* Caputo, J. and M. Yount, eds., 3-26. Pennsylvania: Pennsylvania State University Press.

Caputo, John and M. Yount, eds. 1993 (b). *Foucault and the critique of institutions.* Pennsylvania: Pennsylvania State University Press.

Carr, E. H. 1964. *What is history?.* New York: Vintage Books.

Cassidy, F., ed. 1992 (a). *Aboriginal title in British Columbia: Delgamuukw v. the Queen.* Lantzville: Oolichan Books and Institute for Research on Public Policy.

Cassidy, F. 1992 (b). Introduction: Rethinking British Columbia: The challenge of *Delgamuukw.* In *Aboriginal title in British Columbia: Delgamuukw v. the Queen,* Cassidy, F., ed., 5-19. Lantzville;: Oolichan Books and Institute for Research on Public Policy.

Chamberlin, J. E. 1997. Culture and anarchy in Indian country. In *Aboriginal and treaty rights in Canada: Essays on law, equity, and respect for difference,* Asch, Michael, ed., 3-36. Vancouver: University of British Columbia Press.

Chatterjee, P. 1989. Colonialism, nationalism, and colonized women: The context in India. *American Ethnologist*, 16:622-633.

Chunn, Dorothy and Dany Lacombe, eds. 1998 (forthcoming). *Law as a gendering practice: Canadian perspectives*. Toronto: Oxford University Press.

Clark, Bruce. 1990. *Native liberty, Crown sovereignty: The existing aboriginal right of self-government in Canada*. Kingston: McGill-Queen's University Press.

Clarke, Loreene M. 1992. Women and the state:Oasis or desert island. *Canadian Journal of Women and the Law* 5:166-179.

Clifford, J. 1986 (a). Introduction: Partial truths. In *Writing culture: The poetics and politics of ethnography*, Clifford J. and G. E. Marcus, eds., 1-26 Berkeley, California: University of California Press.

Clifford, J. 1986 (b). On ethnographic authority. In *Writing culture: The poetics and politics of ethnography*, Clifford J. and G. E. Marcus, eds., 98-121. Berkeley, California: University of California Press.

Clifford, J. 1988 (a). *The predicament of culture: Twentieth-Century ethnography, literature and art*. Cambridge: Harvard University Press.

Clifford, J. 1988 (b). Identity in Mashpee. In *The predicament of culture: Twentieth Century ethnography, literature and art*, 277-346. Cambridge: Harvard University Press.

Clifford, J. and G. Marcus, eds. 1986. *Writing culture: The poetics and politics of ethnography*. Berkeley: University of California Press.

Cohen, Anthony P. 1992. Self-conscious anthropology. In *Anthropology & Autobiography*, Okeley, Judith and Helen Callaway, eds., 221-241. London: Routledge.

Cohn, Bernard S. 1989. Law and the colonial state in India. In *History and power in the study of law: New directions in legal anthropology*, Collier, Jane and June Starr, eds., 131-152. Ithaca: Cornell University Press.

Collison, W. H. 1915. *In the wake of the war canoe*. London: Seeley, Service and Co.

Comaroff, John and Simon Roberts. 1981. *Rules and processes: The cultural logic of disputes in an African context*. Chicago: University of Chicago Press.

Coolichan, Murray. 1985. *Living treaties: Lasting agreements: Report of the task force to review comprehensive claims policy*. Canada, Government of, Department of Indian Affairs and Northern Development, Ottawa.

Conley, John and William O'Barr. 1990. *Rules versus relationships: The ethnography of legal discourse*. Chicago: University of Chicago Press;

Coombe, Rosemary. 1989. Toward a theory of practice in critical legal studies. *Law and Social Inquiry* 69.

Coombe, Rosemary. 1989. *Room for manoeuvre: Toward a theory of practice in critical legal studies*. American Bar Foundation.

Coombe, Rosemary. 1991. Encountering the postmodern: New directions in cultural anthropology. *Canadian Review of Sociology and Anthropology* 28(2): 188-205.

Cornell, Drucilla, Michael Rosenfeld and David G. Carlson, eds. 1992. *Deconstruction and the possibility of justice: Gender, sex and equivalent rights.* London: Routledge.

Cornell, Drucilla. 1992. The philosophy of the limit: Systems theory and feminist legal reform. In *The sociology of law: An introduction,* Cornell Cotterrell, R. (1984) 10. London: Butterworths. [Quoted in Burtch, Brian, 1992. *The sociology of law: Critical approaches to social control,* p. 3. Toronto: Harcourt Brace Jovanovich Canada Inc.]

Coupland, Gary. 1986. The evolution of the prehistoric lower Skeena cultural system. Unpublished Ph.D dissertation. Department of Anthropology and Sociology, University of British Columbia.

Court of Appeal for British Columbia. 1992. Defendant's/Respondent's Appeal Factum, *Delgamuukw v. R.*

Court of Appeal for British Columbia. 1992. Plaintiff's/Appellants' Appeal Factum, *Delgamuukw v. R.* Vancouver Registry No. CA013770.

Court of Appeal for British Columbia. 1993. *Reasons for judgment,* in *Delgamuukw v. R.* Vancouver Registry No. CA 013770. [Referenced in the text as Reasons *Delgamuukw* Appeal 1993].

Court of Appeal for British Columbia. 1993. *Reasons for judgment,* in *R. v. William Alphonse.* Vancouver Registry No. CA 010153. [Referenced in the text as Reasons, *Alphonse* Appeal 1993].

Court of Appeal for British Columbia. 1993. *Reasons for judgment,* in *R. v. Harry Thomas Dick.* Vancouver Registry No. CA 011223. [Referenced in the text as Reasons *Dick* Appeal 1993].

Court of Appeal for British Columbia. 1993. *Reasons for judgment,* in *R. v. Dorothy Marie Van Der Peet.* Vancouver Registry Nos. CA 014436, CA 014458. [Referenced as Reasons *Van Der Peet* Appeal 1993].

Court of Appeal for British Columbia. 1993. *Reasons for judgment,* in *R. v. William Gladstone and Donald Gladstone.* Vancouver Registry No. CA 014389. [Referenced as Reasons, *Gladstone* Appeal 1993].

Court of Appeal for British Columbia. 1993. *Reasons for judgment,* in *R. v. N.T.C. Smokehouse Ltd.* Vancouver Registry No.CA 011962. [Referenced as Reasons *N.T.C.Smokehouse* Appeal 1993].

Court of Appeal for British Columbia. 1993. *Reasons for judgment,* in *R. v. Allen Jacob Lewis, Allen Frances Lewis, Jacob Kenneth Lewis.* Vancouver Registry Nos. CA 011419, CA 011420, CA 011428. [Referenced as Reasons: *Lewis* Appeal 1993].

Court of Appeal for British Columbia. 1993. *Reasons for judgment,* in *R. v. Jerry Benjamin Nikal.*Vancouver Registry No. CA 013216. [Referenced as Reasons *Nikal* 1993].

Cove, John. 1996. Playing the devil's advocate: Anthropology in *Delgamuukw.* *POLAR: Political and Legal Anthropology Review* 19(2): 53-58.

Critical Legal Studies Symp.984. *Stanford Law Review* 36 (Jan): 1.2.

Crook, Stephen. 1991. *Modernist radicalism and its aftermath.* London: Routledge.

Cruikshank, Julie, in collaboration with Angela Sidney, Kitty Smith & Annie Ned. 1990. *Life lived like a story*. Lincoln: University of Nebraska Press.

Cruikshank, Julie. 1992. Invention of anthropology in British Columbia's Supreme Court: Oral tradition as evidence in *Delgamuukw v. B.C. B.C. Studies*, Special Issue No. 95:25-42.

Cruikshank, Julie. 1993. Oral tradition and oral history: Reviewing some issues. *Canadian Historical Review* LXXV 3:403-418.

Culhane Speck, Dara. 1987. *An error in judgement: The politics of medical care in an Indian/White community*. Vancouver: Talon Books.

Culhane Speck, Dara. 1989. Revenge of the hidden agenda or a step in the right direction? The native health transfer policy. *Native Studies Review* 5(1): 187-213.

Culhane, Dara. 1991. Review of *Dancing With Daddy* by Betsy Petersen. *New York Times Book Review*, August 8, B12.

Culhane, Dara. 1992. Adding insult to injury: Her Majesty's loyal anthropologist. *B.C. Studies*, Theme Issue: Anthropology and History in the Courts No. 95:66-92.

Culhane, Dara. 1994. *Delgamuukw* and the people without history: Anthropology and the Crown. Unpublished Ph.D. thesis, Department of Sociology and Anthropology, Simon Fraser University, Burnaby, B.C.

Cumming, P. A. and N. H. Mickenberg, eds. 1972. *Native rights in Canada*. 2nd ed. Toronto: University of Toronto Press.

Currie, Dawn. 1992. Feminist encounters with postmodernism: Exploring the impasse of debates on patriarchy and law. *Canadian Journal of Women and The Law* 5(2): 63-86.

Daly, Richard. 1988 (March). *Our box was full: Opinion evidence on the Gitksan and Wet'suwet'en economy*. Expert opinion report prepared for the Gitksan and Wet'suwet'en Tribal Council in the matter of *Delgamuukw v. R.*

Daly, Richard and A. Mills. 1993. Ethics and objectivity: AAA principles of responsibility discredit testimony. *American Anthropology Association Newsletter* 34(8): 1, 6.

Danielson, Dan and Karen Engle, eds. 1995. *After identity: A reader in law and culture*. New York: Routledge.

Dauenhauer, Nora M. and R. Dauenhauer, eds. 1994. *Haa kusteeyi, our culture: Tlingit life stories*. Seattle: University of Washington Press.

Delgado, Richard. 1988. Critical legal studies and the realities of race: Does the fundamental contradiction have a corollary?. *23 Harv. C.R.-C.L.L.R.*, 407.

Deloria, Vine Jr. 1969. *Custer died for your sins: An Indian manifesto*. New York: Macmillan.

Derrida, Jacques. 1992. Force of law: The 'Mystical Foundation of Authority'. In *Deconstruction and the possibility of justice: Gender, sex, and equivalent rights*, Cornell, D., Michael Rosenfeld and David G. Carlson, eds. New York: Routledge: 3-67.

Dews, Peter. 1987. *Logics of disintegration: Post-structuralist thought and the claims of critical theory.* Cambridge: Cambridge University Press.

Diamond, Irene and Lee Quinby, eds. 1988. *Feminism & Foucault: Reflections on resistance.* Boston: Northeastern University Press.

di Leonardo, M., ed. 1991. *Feminist anthropology at the crossroads of knowledge: Political economy, culture and postmodernism.* Berkeley: University of California Press.

Dickason, Olive Patricia. 1992. *Canada's first nations, a history of founding peoples from earliest times.* Toronto: McClelland & Stewart Inc.

Dobyns, H. F. 1978. Taking the witness stand. In *Applied Anthropology in America,* Eddy, E. M. and W. L. Partridge, eds., 261-275. New York: Columbia University Press.

Doyle-Bedwell, Patricia. 1993. Case comments: The evolution of the legal test of extinguishment: From Sparrow to Gitksan. *Canadian Journal of Women and the Law* 6(1): 193-204.

Dreyfus, Hubert and Stuart Dreyfus. 1979. From Socrates to expert systems: The limits of calculative rationality. In *Interpretive social science: A second look,* P. Rabinow and W. Sullivan, eds., 327-350. Berkeley: University of California Press.

Duff, Wilson, ed. 1951. Notes on Carrier social organizations. *Anthropology in British Columbia* (Victoria) 2:28-34.

Duff, Wilson, ed. 1959. Histories, territories, and laws of the Kitwancool. *Anthropology in British Columbia* Memoir No.4. Victoria: British Columbia Provincial Museum.

Duff, Wilson,ed. 1964. The Indian history of British Columbia. Vol.1 The impact of the white man. *Anthropology in British Columbia* 5. Victoria: British Columbia Provincial Museum.

Dumont, Louis. 1977. *From Mandeville to Marx.* Chicago: University of Chicago Press.

Durham, William H. 1990. Advances in evolutionary culture theory. *Annual Review of Anthropology,* Annual Reviews Inc. (Palo Alto, California) Vol.19:187-210.

Dyck, Noel. 1985. Introduction. In *Indigenous peoples and the nation-state: Fourth world politics and Canada, Australia and Norway,* N. Dyck,ed., 1-26. St. John's: Institute of Social and Economic Research, Memorial University of Newfoundland.

Dyck, Noel. 1991. *What is the Indian 'problem': Tutelage and resistance in Canadian Indian administration.* St. John's: Institute of Social and Economic Research, Memorial University of Newfoundland.

Dyck, Noel and James B. Waldram, eds. 1993 (a). *Anthropology, public policy and native peoples in Canada.* Montreal: McGill-Queen's University Press.

Dyck, Noel. 1993 (b). 'Telling it like it is:' Some dilemmas of fourth world ethnography and advocacy. In *Anthropology, public policy and native peoples in Canada,* Dyck, Noel and James B. Waldram eds., 192-212. Montreal, Quebec: McGill-Queen's University Press.

Dyen, Isadore and David Aberle. 1974. *Lexical reconstruction: The case of the proto-Athabaskan kinship system*. London: Cambridge University Press.

Edwards. E.R.A. 1992. Delgamuukw and the fiduciary duty of the Crown. In *Aboriginal title in British Columbia: Delgamuukw v. The Queen*, Cassidy, F., ed., 35-43. Lantzville: Oolichan Books and Institute for Research on Public Policy.

Elias, Peter Douglas. 1993. Anthropology and aboriginal claims research. In *Anthropology, public policy and native peoples in Canada*, Dyck, Noel and James B.Waldram, eds., 233-270. Montreal, Quebec: McGill-Queen's University Press.

Eagleton, Terry. 1983. *Literary theory: An introduction*. Minneapolis: University of Minnesota Press.

Eagleton, Terry. 1984. *The function of criticism: From the spectator to post-structuralism*. London: Verso.

Escobar. Arturo. 1992. Culture, practice and politics: Anthropology and the study of social movements. *Critique of Anthropology* 12(4): 395-432.

Fabian, Johannes. 1983. *Time and the other: How anthropology makes its object*. New York: Columbia University Press.

Fahim, Hussein, ed. 1982. *Indigenous anthropology in non-western countries*. Durham: University of North Carolina Press.

Falkowski, J. E. 1992. *Indian law / race law: A 500-year history*. New York: Praeger.

Fanon, Frantz. 1963. *The wretched of the earth*. New York: Grove Press Inc.

Feit, Harvey. 1982. The future of hunters within nation-states: Anthropology and the James Bay Cree. In Politics and history in band societies ,E. Leacock and R. B. Lee, eds., 373-411. Cambridge: Cambridge University Press.

Feldman, K. D. 1980. Ethnology and the anthropologist as expert witness in legal disputes: A southwestern Alaskan case. *Journal of Anthropological Research* 36:245-257.

Ferguson, Russell, M. Gever, T. M. H.Trinh, C. West, eds. 1990. *Out there: Marginalization and contemporary cultures*. Cambridge: Massachusetts Institute of Technology Press.

Finnegan, Ruth. 1992. *Oral traditions and the verbal arts*. London: Routledge.

Fisher, Robin. 1977. *Contact and conflict: Indian-European relations in British Columbia, 1774-1890*. Vancouver: University of British Columbia Press.

Fisher, Robin. 1992. Judging history: Reflections on the Reasons for Judgment in *Delgamuukw v. B.C. B.C. Studies* Issue No. 95:43-54.

Forgacs, David and Geoffrey Nowell-Smith, eds. 1985. *Antonio Gramsci: Selections from cultural writings*. London: Lawrence and Wishart.

Fortune, Joel. 1993. Construing Delgamuukw: Legal arguments, historical argumentation, and the philosophy of history. *University of Toronto Faculty of Law Review* 51(1): 80-117.

Foster, Hal, ed. 1986. *Postmodern culture*. London: Pluto Press.

Foster, Hamar. 1981. The Kamloops outlaws and commissions to assize in nineteenth-century British Columbia. In *Essays on the history of Canadian law*, Flaherty, D. H,. ed., 311-351. Toronto: Carswell.

Foster, Hamar. 1992 (a). It goes without saying: The doctrine of extinguishment by implication in *Delgamuukw*. In *Aboriginal title in British Columbia: Delgamuukw v. The Queen*, Cassidy, F., ed., 133-160. Lantzville: Oolichan Books and Institute for Research on Public Policy.

Foster, Hamar. 1992 (b). Forgotten arguments: Aboriginal title and sovereignty in Canada, jurisdiction act cases. *Manitoba Law Journal* 21:343.

Foster, Hamar and A. Groves. 1993. Looking behind the masks: A land claims discussion paper for researchers, lawyers and their employers. *University of British Columbia Law Review* 27(2): 213-255.

Foucault, Michel. 1973. *The order of things: An archaeology of the human sciences*. New York: Vintage Books.

Foucault, Michel. 1975. *The birth of the clinic*. New York: Vintage Books.

Foucault, Michel. 1979. *Discipline & punishment: The birth of the prison*. New York: Vintage Books.

Fox-Genovese, Elizabeth. 1991. *Feminism without illusions: A critique of individualism*. Chapel Hill: University of North Carolina Press.

Fox, Richard, ed. 1991 *Recapturing anthropology: Working in the present*. School of American Research Advanced Seminar Series. Santa Fe, NM: School of American Research Press.

Francis, Daniel. 1992. *The imaginary Indian*. Vancouver: Arsenal Pulp Press.

Fraser, Nancy. 1989. *Unruly practices: Power, discourse and gender in contemporary social theory*. Minneapolis: University of Minnesota Press.

Frug, Mary Joe. 1992. *Postmodern legal feminism*. New York: Routledge.

Gailey, C., ed. 1992. *The politics of culture and creativity: A critique of civilization*. Gainesville: University Press of Florida.

Galois, Robert. 1987. *Patterns of tension: History of the Gitksan and Wet'suwet'en*. Expert opinion report prepared for the Office of the Gitksan and Wet'suwet'en Hereditary Chiefs.

Galois, Robert. 1992. The Indian rights association, native protest activity and the 'land question' in British Columbia. *Native Studies Review* 8(2): 1-34.

Garfield, Viola E. 1950 (1). The Tsimshian and their neighbours. In *The Tsimshian Indians and their arts*, Viola E.Garfield and Paul S.Wingert, eds., 1-72. Vancouver: Douglas & McIntyre. [Originally published as part 1 of *The Tsimshian: their arts and music*. Publication 18 of the American Ethnological Society. New York: J.J. Augustin.]

Gartrell, Beverley. 1986. 'Colonialism' and the fourth world: Notes on variations in colonial situations. *Culture* VI(1): 3-17.

Gates Jr., Henry Louis. 1991. Critical fanonism. *Critical Inquiry* 17 (Spring 1991). Chicago: University of Chicago.

Gavignan, Shelley A.M. 1988. Law, gender and ideology. In *Legal theory meets legal practice*, Bayefsky, J., ed. Edmonton: Academic Press.

Geertz, C. 1973. *The interpretation of cultures*. New York: Basic Books Inc.

Geertz, C. 1983 (a). *Local knowledge: Further essays in interpretive anthropology*. New York: Basic Books Inc.

Geertz. C. 1983 (b). Local knowledge: Fact and law in comparative perspective. In Local knowledge: Further essays in interpretive anthropology, Geertz, C., 167-234. New York: Basic Books Inc.

Geertz, C. 1984. Distinguished lecture: Anti anti-relativism. *American Anthropologist* 86:263-278.

Ginzburg, Carlo. 1991. Checking the evidence: The judge and the historian. *Critical Inquiry* 19 (Autumn 1991), 79-92. Chicago: University of Chicago.

Giroux, Henry A. 1993. Living dangerously: Identity politics and the new cultural racism: Towards a critical pedagogy of representation. *Cultural Studies* 7(1): 1-27.

Gisday Wa and Delgam Uukw. 1987. The opening statement of the Gitksan and Wet'suwet'en hereditary chiefs in the Supreme Court of British Columbia, May 11, 1987, Smithers, B.C. Ms. in author's possession.

Gisday Wa and Delgam Uukw. 1989. *The spirit in the land: The opening statement of the Gitksan and Wet'suwet'en hereditary chiefs in the Supreme Court of British Columbia*. Gabriola Island: Reflections Press.

Gisday Wa and Delgam Uukw. 1992. *The spirit in the land: Excerpts from the testimony of the Gitksan and Wet'suwet'en hereditary chiefs in the Supreme Court of Canada, 1987-1991*. Gabriola Island: Reflections Press.

Glavin, Terry. 1990. *A death feast in Dimlahamid*. Vancouver: New Star Books.

Glavin, Terry. 1991. Mood somber even as claims win expected. *Vancouver Sun* March 7, B3.

Godelier, Maurice. 1972. *Rationality and irrationality in economics*. New York: Monthly Review Press.

Goldman, Irving. 1940. The Alkatcho Carrier of British Columbia. In *Acculturation of seven American Indian tribes*, Linton, Ralph, ed., 333-389. New York: Appleton Century.

Goldman, Irving. 1941. The Alkatcho Carrier: Historical background of crest prerogatives. *American Anthropologist* 43 (n.s.) 396-421.

Goldman, Irving. 1975. *The mouth of heaven: An introduction to Kwakiutl religious thought*. New York: Wiley and Sons.

Gordon, Deborah R. 1988. Tenacious assumptions in western medicine. In *Biomedicine examined*, Lock, M. and D. Gordon, eds., 19-56. Dordrecht: Kluwer Academic Publishers.

Gordon, R. 1984. Critical legal histories. *Stanford Legal Review* 36:57.

Gough, Kathleen. 1968. Anthropology: child of imperialism. *Monthly Review* Vol. 19(11): 12-27.

Gramsci, Antonio. 1971. *Selections from prison notebooks*. London: Lawrence and Wisehart.

Grant, Judith. 1987. I feel therefore I am: A critique of female experience as the basis for a feminist epistemology. *Women and Politics* 7(3): 99-114.

Green, L. C. 1989. Claims to territory in colonial America. In *The law of nations and the new world*, Green, L. C. and O. P. Dickason, eds., 1-131. Edmonton: University of Alberta Press.

Gyamk, Medig'm [Neil Sterritt]. 1992. It doesn't matter what the judge said. In *Aboriginal title in British Columbia: Delgamuukw v. The Queen*, Cassidy, F., ed., 303-309. Lantzville: Oolichan Books and Institute for Research on Public Policy.

Haig-Brown, Celia. 1928. *Resistance and renewal: Surviving the Indian residential school*. Vancouver, B.C.: Tillicum Library.

Halliday, W. 1935. *Potlatch and totem: Memoirs of an Indian agent*. Toronto: J. M. Dent & Sons Ltd.

Hamilton, A.C. and M. Sinclair, eds. 1991. *Report of the Aboriginal Justice Enquiry of Manitoba: The justice system and aboriginal people*, Vols. 1 & 2. Winnipeg: Province of Manitoba.

Hammersley, Martin and Paul Atkinson. 1983. *Ethnography, principles in practice*. London:Tavistock.

Handler, Richard. 1984. On sociocultural discontinuity: Nationalism and cultural objectification in Quebec. *Current Anthropology* 25(1): 55-71.

Handler, Richard. 1985. On dialogue and destructive analysis: Problems in narrating nationalism and ethnicity. *Journal of Anthropological Research* 41(2): 171-181.

Hanke, Lewis. 1974. *All mankind is one: A study of the disputation between Bartolomeo de Las Casas and Juan Gines De Sepulveda in 1550 on the intellectual and religious capacity of the American Indian*. Delkalb: Northern Illinois University Press.

Harries-Jones, Peter. 1985. From cultural translator to advocate: Changing circles of interpretation. In *Advocacy and anthropology, first encounters*, Paine, Robert, ed., 224-248.St. John's: Institute of Social and Economic Research, Memorial University of Newfoundland.

Hart, Jonathan and Richard W. Bauman, eds. 1996. *Explorations in difference: Law, culture and politics*. Toronto: University of Toronto Press.

Hartsock, Nancy. 1990. Foucault on power: A theory for women?. In *Feminism / Postmodernism*, Nicholson, L. J., ed., 157-175. New York: Routledge.

Hawkes, David, ed. 1989. *Aboriginal peoples and government responsibility: Exploring federal and provincial roles*. Ottawa: Carleton University Press.

Hawkesworth, Mary E. 1989. Knowers, knowing, known: Feminist theory and claims of truth. *Signs: Journal of Women in Culture and Society* (University of Chicago) 14(3): 533-557.

Healey, Elizabeth. 1958. *History of Alert Bay and district, 1958.* Comox: Alert Bay Centennial Committee, E. W. Bickie Ltd.

Hedican, Edward J. 1986. Anthropologists and social involvement: Some issues and problems. *Canadian Review of Sociology and Anthropology* 23(4): 544-58.

Hedley, Max J. 1986. Community based research: The dilemma of contract. *Canadian Journal of Native Studies* 6(1): 91-103.

Henderson, William B. and James Youngblood. 1985 (a). The doctrine of aboriginal rights in western legal tradition. In *The quest for justice: Aboriginal peoples and aboriginal rights,* Boldt, Menno and J. Anthony Long, eds., in association with Leroy Little Bear, 185-220. Toronto: University of Toronto Press.

Henderson, William B. and James Youngblood. 1985 (b). Canadian legal and judicial philosophies on the doctrine of aboriginal rights. In *The quest for justice: Aboriginal peoples and aboriginal rights,* Boldt, Menno and J. Anthony Long, eds., in association with Leroy Little Bear, 221-229. Toronto: University of Toronto Press.

Henderson, William B. 1991. Evidentiary problems in aboriginal title cases. *Law Society of Upper Canada: Special Lecture* Ottawa: September 19, 1991.

Henry, Alexander. 1809. *Travels and adventures in Canada and the Indian Territories between the years 1760 and 1776.* New York: Riley. Quoted in Jones, Dorothy V. 1982. *License for empire: Colonialism by treaty in early America.* Chicago: University of Chicago Press.

Herbert, R. G. 1954. A brief history of the introduction of English law into British Columbia. *U.B.C. Legal Notes* Vol. 35(1): 94-112.

Henige, David. 1982. *Oral historiography.* Essex: Longman Group Limited.

Hill, Christopher. 1958. *Puritanism and revolution.* New York: Penguin.

Hirsch, Susan and Mindie Lazarus-Black. 1994. Introduction: Performance and paradox: Exploring law's role in hegemony and resistance. In *Contested states: Law, hegemony and resistance,* Lazarus-Black, Mindie and Susan Hirsch, eds., 1-31. New York: Routledge.

Humphreys, Sally. 1985. Law as discourse. *History and Anthropology* 1:241-264.

Hunt, Alan. 1981. Marxism and the analysis of law. In *Marxism and law,* Bierne, Piers and R. Quinney, eds. New York: Wiley & Sons.

Hunt, Alan. 1990. The big fear: Law confronts postmodernism. *McGill Law Journal* 35:507.

Hunt, Alan. 1993. *Explorations in law and society: Towards a constitutive theory of law.* New York: Routledge.

Hymes, Dell, ed. 1974. *Reinventing anthropology.* New York: Random House Vintage Books.

Ignatiev, Noel. 1995. *How the Irish became white.* New York: Routledge.

Inglis, Richard and George MacDonald. 1979. Skeena River prehistory. National Museum of Man Mercury Series. Archaeological Survey of Canada, Paper No. 87. Ottawa: National Museums of Canada.

Isaac, Rhys. 1993. On explanation, text, and terrifying power in ethnographic history. *Yale Journal of Criticism* 6(1): 217-236.

Isaac, Thomas. 1992. Discarding the rose-coloured glasses: A commentary on Asch and Macklem. *Alberta Law Review* Vol. XXX(2): 708-712.

Ives, John W. 1990. *A theory of northern Athabaskan prehistory.* Boulder, CO: Westview.

Jackson, Michael. 1984. The articulation of native rights in Canadian law. *University of British Columbia Law Review* 18(2): 235-263.

Jameson, Fredric. 1984. Postmodernism, or the cultural logic of late capitalism. *New Left Review* 146.

Jenness, Diamond. 1934. Myths of the Carrier Indians of British Columbia. *Journal of American Folklore* 47 (nos. 184-5): 97-257.

Jenness, Diamond. 1943. The Carrier Indians of the Bulkley River: Their social and religious life. *Bureau of American Ethnology* Bulletin 133, Anthropological Papers No. 25. New York: Smithsonian Institution.

Johnston, J. J. M. 1989. *The voyage of the Komagata Maru.* Vancouver: University of British Columbia Press.

Jones, Dorothy V. 1982. *License for empire: Colonialism by treaty in early America.* Chicago: University of Chicago Press.

Just, Peter. 1992. History, power, ideology and culture: Current directions in the anthropology of law. *Law & Society Review* 26(2): 373-412.

Kahn, Joel. 1989. Culture, demise, resurrection?. *Critique of Anthropology* Vol.IX: 5-26.

Kellock, Burton H. and F. C. M. Anderson. 1992. A theory of aboriginal rights. In *Aboriginal title in British Columbia: Delgamuukw v. The Queen*, Cassidy, F., ed., 97-112. Lantzville: Oolichan Books and Institute for Research on Public Policy.

Kenny, Anthony. 1983. The expert in court. *The Law Quarterly Review* 99 (April): 197-216.

Kenny, Michael G. 1986. *The passion of Ansel Bourne.* Washington, D.C.: Smithsonian Institution.

Kew, Michael. 1993-94. Anthropologists and first nations in British Columbia. *B.C. Studies* No. 100:78-105

Klamer, Arjo. 1987. As if economists and their subjects were rational. In *The rhetoric of the human sciences: Language and argument in scholarship and public affairs*, Nelson, J. S., A. Megill and D. N. McCloskey, eds. Madison: University of Wisconsin Press.

Kline, Marlee. 1989. Race, racism, and feminist legal theory. *Harvard Women's Law Review* 11:115-134.

Knafla, Louis A. 1986 (a). From oral to written memory: The common law tradition in western Canada. In *Law & justice in a new land: Essays in western Canadian legal history*, Knafla, Louis A., ed. Toronto:, 31-77. Carswell.

Knafla, Louis A., ed. 1986 (b). *Law & justice in a new land: Essays in western Canadian legal history*. Toronto: Carswell.

Knight, Rolf. 1978. *Indians at work*. Vancouver: New Star Books.

Kobkrinsky, Vernon. 1977. The Tsimshianization of the Carrier Indians. In *Problems in the prehistory of the North American subarctic: The Athabaskan question*, 201-210. Calgary: University of Calgary, Department of Archaeology.

Koppel, Tom. 1995. *Kanaka: The untold story of Hawaiian pioneers in British Columbia and the Pacific northwest*. Vancouver: Whitecap Books.

Korsmo, F. L. 1996. Claiming memory in British Columbia: Aboriginal rights and the state. *American Indian Culture and Research Journal* Vol. 26(4): 71-87.

Kousser, J. M. 1983. Are expert witnesses whores? Reflections on objectivity in scholarship and expert witnesses. *The Public Historian* (Winter) 6:5-19.

Krech, Shepard III. 1991. The state of ethnohistory. *Annual Reviews of Anthropology* Vol. 20:345-375. Palo Alto, California: Annual Reviews Inc.

Kulchyski, Peter, ed. 1994. *Unjust relations: Aboriginal rights in Canadian courts*. Toronto: Oxford University Press.

Labov, W. 1969. The logic of nonstandard English. *Georgetown Monographs on Language and Linguistics* 22:179-214.

Laforet, Andrea. 1993. Competing concepts of the past: The Gitksan-Wet'suwet'en case. Unpublished ms.

LaRusic, I. 1985. Expert witness?. In *Advocacy and anthropology: First encounters*, Paine, Robert, ed., 165-169 St. John's: Institute of Social and Economic Research, Memorial University of Newfoundland.

Lash, Scott. 1990. *Sociology of postmodernism*. London: Routledge.

Laslett, Peter, ed. 1964. *John Locke: Two treatises on government: A critical edition with an introduction and apparatus criticus*. Cambridge: Cambridge University Press.

Lassiter, C. 1987. Relocation and illness. In *Pathologies of the modern self: Postmodern studies on narcissism, schizophrenia, and depression*, Levin, David M., ed., 212-238. New York: New York University Press.

LaViolette, Forrest Emmanuel. 1973. *The struggle for survival, Indian cultures and the protestant ethic in British Columbia*. Toronto: University of Toronto Press.

Lazarus-Black, Mindie and Susan F. Hirsch, eds. 1994. *Contested states: Law, hegemony and resistance*. New York: Routledge.

Lee, Richard and I. DeVore. 1966. *Man the hunter*. Chicago: Aldine Publishing Co.

Leonard, Jerry, ed. 1995. *Legal studies as cultural studies: A reader in (post)modern critical theory*. New York: State University of New York Press.

Lester, Geoffrey S. 1977. Primitivism v. civilization: A basic question in the law of aboriginal rights to land. In *Our footprints are everywhere*, C. Brice-Bennett, ed., 351-376. Newfoundland: Labrador Inuit Association.

Lester, Geoffrey S. 1981. The territorial rights of the Inuit of the Canadian Northwest Territories: A legal argument. Unpublished Ph.D. dissertation. York University, Toronto.

Levi, Judith and Anne Grafam Walker. 1990. *Language in the judicial process.* New York: Plenum Press.

Li, Peter. 1988. *The Chinese in Canada.* Toronto: University of Toronto Press.

Lippert, Owen. 1995. Change and choice: A policy vision for British Columbia. In *Out of Our Past: A New Perspective on Aboriginal Land Claims in British Columbia.* Vancouver: Fraser Institute.

Lips, Julius. 1966. *The savage hits back.* New Hyde Park, NY: University Books.

Lock, M. and D.Gordon, eds. 1988. *Biomedicine examined.* Dordrecht: Kluwer Academic Publishers.

Lock, Margaret. 1988. Introduction. In *Biomedicine examined*, Lock, M. and D. Gordon, eds., 3-10. Dordrecht: Kluwer Academic Publishers.

Lorde, Audre. 1984. The master's tools will never dismantle the master's house. In *Sister Outsider: essays and speeches*, 101-113. Trumensberg, NY: Crossings Press.

Lurie, N. O. 1956. A reply to `the land claims case': Anthropologists in conflict. *Ethnohistory* 3:256-279.

Lurie, N. O. 1985. Epilogue. In *Irredeemable America: The Indians' estate and land claims*, Sutton, Imre, ed., 363-382. New Mexico: University of New Mexico Press and Institute for Native American Studies.

Lutz, Catherine A. 1988. *Unnatural emotions.* Chicago: University of Chicago Press.

Lutz, Catherine A. and Lila Abu-Lughod, eds. 1990. *Language and the politics of emotions.* Cambridge: Cambridge University Press.

Lyons, Oren. 1985. Traditional native philosophies relating to aboriginal rights. In *The quest for justice: Aboriginal peoples and aboriginal rights*, Boldt, Menno and J. Anthony Long, eds., in association with Leroy Little Bear, 19-23. Toronto: University of Toronto Press.

Lyotard, Jean-Francois. 1984. *The postmodern condition: A report on knowledge.* Minneapolis: University of Minnesota Press.

MacKinnon, Catherine. 1987. *Feminism unmodified: Discourses on life and law.* Cambridge: Cambridge University Press.

MacDonald, George F. 1979. Kitwanga Fort national historic site, Skeena River, British Columbia, Historical research and analysis of structural remains. Parks Canada. Manuscript Report No. 341. Ottawa: Department of the Environment.

MacDonald, George F. 1984. The epic of Nekt: The archaeology of metaphor. In *The Tsimshian, images of the past: Views for the present*, Margaret Seguin, ed., 65-81. Vancouver: University of British Columbia Press.

MacDonald, James A. 1984. Images of the nineteenth-Century economy of the Tsimshian. In *The Tsimshian, images of the past: Views for the present*, Margaret Seguin, ed., 40-54. Vancouver: University of British Columbia Press.

MacDonald, Maryon, and Elizabeth Tonkin. 1989. Introduction. In *History and Ethnicity* [provisional title], Macdonald, Maryon and Elizabeth Tonkin, eds. ASA Monograph Series. London: Tavistock.

Macklem, Patrick. 1991. First nations self-government and the borders of the Canadian legal imagination. *McGill Law Journal* 36:382-456.

Macklem, Patrick. 1993. Distributing sovereignty: Indian nations and equality of peoples. *Stanford Law Review* 45:1309-1367.

Maclean, Ian, A. Montefiore, P. Winch, eds. 1990. *The political responsibility of intellectuals.* Cambridge: Cambridge University Press.

Macpherson, C. B. 1962. *The political theory of possessive individualism: Hobbes to Locke.* Oxford: Oxford University Press.

Maddock, Kenneth. 1989. Involved anthropologists. In *We are here: Politics of aboriginal land tenure*, Wilmsen, Edwin N., 155-176. Berkeley: University of California Press.

Madill, Dennis F. K. 1981. British Columbia Indian treaties in historical perspective. Ottawa: Research Branch, Department of Indian and Northern Affairs.

Maine, Henry Sumner. 1861, 1970. *Ancient law: Its connection with the early history of society and its relation to modern ideas.* With introduction and notes by Frederick Pollock, pref. to the Beacon paperback ed. by Raymond Firth. Gloucester, Mass.: Beacon Press.

Mandell, Louise. 1987. Native culture on trial. In *Equality and judicial neutrality*, Martin, J. and M. Mahoney, eds. Toronto: Carswell:358-365.

Manganaro, Marc., ed. 1990. *Modern anthropology from fieldwork to text.* Princeton: Princeton University Press.

Manners, Robert A. 1956. The land claims cases: Anthropologists in conflict. *Ethnohistory* 3:72-81.

Markchak, Patricia, N. Guppy, J. McMullan, eds. 1987. *Uncommon property: The fishing and fish-processing industries in British Columbia.* Toronto, Methuen Publications.

Marcus, George E. and M .J.Fischer, eds. 1986. *Anthropology as cultural critique: An experimental moment in the human sciences.* Chicago: University of Chicago Press.

Marx, Karl. [1867] 1973. *Capital, Vol. 1.* Selections reprinted in *The Marx-Engels reader*, Tucker, R., ed., 3092-304. New York, NY: W. W. Norton & Co.

McGrane Bernard. 1989. *Beyond anthropology: Society and the other.* New York: Columbia University Press.

McHugh, P. G. 1987. The aboriginal rights of the New Zealand Maori at common law. Unpublished doctorate dissertation, Cambridge University, Faculty of Law.

McKee, Christopher. 1996. *Treaty talks in British Columbia: Negotiating a mutually beneficial future.* Vancouver: University of British Columbia Press.

McLaren, John, H. Foster, C. Orloff, eds. 1992. *Law for the elephant, law for the beaver: Essays in the legal history of the North American west*. Regina: Canadian Plains Research Center, University of Regina, and Pasadena, CA: Ninth Judicial Circuit Historical Society.

McLaren, Peter. 1993. Multiculturalism and the postmodern critique: Towards a pedagogy of resistance and transformation. *Cultural Studies* 7.1.

McNeil, Kent. 1989. *Common law aboriginal title*. Oxford: Clarendon Press.

Medig'm Gyamk [Neil Sterrit]. 1992. It doesn't matter what the judge said. In *Aboriginal title in British Columbia: Delgamuukw v. the Queen*, Cassidy, F., ed., 303-308. Lantzville: Oolichan Books and Institute for Research on Public Policy.

Menkel-Meadow, C. 1988. Feminist legal theory, critical legal studies, and legal education or 'The fem-crits go to law school'. *Journal of Legal Education* 38:47-63.

Merry, Sally Engle. 1992. Anthropology, law, and transnational processes. *Annual Review of Anthropology* 21:357-379.

Mertz, Elizabeth. 1988. The uses of history: Language, ideology, and law in the United States and South Africa. *Law and Society Review* 22(4): 661-185.

Mertz, Elizabeth. 1992. Review essay: Language, law, and social meanings: Linguistic / anthropological contributions to the study of law. *Law and Society Review* Vol. 26(2): 413-445.

Mertz, Elizabeth. 1994. Pragmatics, poetics, and social power. *Annual Review of Anthropology* 231:435-55.

Messerschmidt, Donald A., ed. 1981. *Anthropologists at home in North America: Methods and issues in the study of one's own society*. Cambridge: University of Cambridge.

Miles, Robert. 1989. *Racism*. London: Routledge.

Miller, Bruce. 1992. Common sense and plain language. *B.C. Studies* Special Issue: Anthropology and History in the Courts, No. 95, Autumn, 55-65.

Miluulak [Alice Jeffrey]. 1992. Remove not the landmark. In *Aboriginal title in British Columbia: Delgamuukw v. the Queen*, Cassidy, F.,ed., 58-61. Lantzville: Oolichan Books and Institute for Research on Public Policy.

Mills, Antonia. 1987. The feasts, institutions and laws of the Wet'suwet'en. Expert opinion report prepared for the Office of the Gitksan and Wet'suwet'en Hereditary Chiefs in the matter of *Delgamuukw v. R.*

Mills, Antonia. 1995. *Eagle down is our law: Witsuwit'en law, feasts, and land claims*. Vancouver: University of British Columbia Press.

Mills, Antonia. 1996. Problems of establishing authority in testifying on behalf of the Witsuwit'en. *POLAR: Political and Legal Anthropology Review* Vol. 19(2): 39-51.

Monet, D. and Skanu'u [Ardythe Wilson]. 1992. *Colonialism on trial: Indigenous land rights and the Gitksan and Wet'suwet'en sovereignty case*. Gabriola Island: New Society Publishers.

Monture, Patricia. 1986. Ka-nin-geh-heh-gah-e-sa-nonh-yah-gah. *Canadian Journal of Women and the Law* 2:148-163.

Monture-Okanee, Patricia. 1992. The violence we women do: A first nations view. In *Challenging times: The women's movement in Canada and the United States*, David H.Flaherty and Constance Backhouse, eds. Montreal: McGill-Queen's University Press.

Moore, Henrietta. 1988. *Feminism and anthropology*. Cambridge: Cambridge University Press.

Moore, Sally F. 1986. *Social facts and fabrications: 'Customary law' on Kilimanjaro, 1880-1980*. Cambridge,England: Cambridge University Press.

Morice, Father A. G. 1970. *The history of the northern interior of British Columbia*. Smithers: Smithers Interior Stationery.

Morris, Alexander. 1979. *The treaties of Canada with the Indians*. Toronto: Coles Publishing Co.

Morris, Glenn. 1992. International law and politics. In *The state of native America: Genocide, colonization and resistance*, Jaimes, Annette, ed., 55-86. Boston: South End Press.

Morris, James. 1973. *Heaven's command: An imperial progress*. London: Penguin Books.

Morse, Bradford W. and G. R.Woodman, eds. 1985. *Indigenous law and the state*. Ottawa: Dordrecht, Holland:Foris Publications.

Mossman, M. J. 1985. Toward `new property' and `new scholarship': An assessment of Canadian property scholarship. *Osgoode Hall Law Journal* 23:633.

Nader, Laura. 1969 (a). Introduction. In *Law in culture and society*, Nader, L., ed., 1-17. Chicago: Aldine.

Nader, Laura. [1969 (b)] 1974. Up the anthropologist—perspectives gained from studying up. In *Reinventing anthropology*, Hymes, Dell, ed. New York: Random House Vintage Books.

Nencel, Lorraine and Peter Pels, eds. 1991. *Constructing knowledge: Authority and critique in social science*. London: Sage Publications.

Nicolson, Linda, ed. 1991. *Feminism / Postmodernism*. New York: Routledge.

Nightingale, Margo L. 1992. Judicial attitudes and differential treatment: Native women in sexual assault cases. *Ottawa Law Review* 23(1): 71-98.

Norcross, E. Blanche, ed. 1983. *The company on the coast*. Nanaimo: Nanaimo Historical Society.

O'Barr, William M. 1982. *Linguistic evidence: Language, power, and strategy in the courtroom*. Durham, NC: Academic Press.

Obeysekere, Gananath. 1992. *The apotheosis of James Cook: European mythmaking in the Pacific*. Princeton, NJ: Princeton University Press.

Okely, J. 1992. Anthropology and autobiography: Participatory experience and embodied knowledge. In *Anthropology and autobiography*, Okely, J. and H. Callaway, eds., 1-28. London, Routledge.

Okely, Judith and Helen Callaway, eds. 1992. *Anthropology and autobiography*. London: Routledge.

Ong, Walter J. 1982. *Orality and literacy: The technologizing of the word*. London and New York: Methuen.

Orlove, B. S. 1980. Ecological anthropology. *Annual Review of Anthropology* 9:235-273.

Paine, Robert, ed. 1977. *The white Arctic: Anthropological essays on tutelage and ethnicity*. St. John's: Institute of Social and Economic Research, Memorial University of Newfoundland.

Paine, Robert, ed. 1981. *Politically speaking: Cross-cultural studies of rhetoric*. Philadelphia: Institute for the Study of Human Issues, Inc.

Paine, Robert, ed. 1985. *Advocacy and anthropology: First encounters*. St. John's: Institute of Social and Economic Research, Memorial University of Newfoundland.

Paine, Robert. 1996. In Chief Justice McEachern's shoes: Anthropology's ineffectiveness in court. *POLAR: Political and Legal Anthropology Review* Vol. 19(2): 59-70.

Palmer, Vaughn. February 26, 1990. *Vancouver Sun*. Quoted in *Aboriginal peoples and politics: The land question in British Columbia, 1849-1989*, Tennant, P., (1990), 237. Vancouver: University of British Columbia Press.

Parker, Graham. 1986. Canadian legal culture. In *Law & justice in a new land: Essays in western Canadian legal history*, Knafla, Louis A., ed., 3-29. Toronto: Carswell.

Parry, J. H. 1979. Introduction: The English in the new world. In *The westward enterprise: English activities in Ireland, the Atlantic and America 1480-1650*, Andrews, K. R., N. P. Canny and P. E. H. Hair, eds., 1-16. Detroit: Wayne State University Press.

Penner, Roland. 1992. Power, the law and Constitution-making. In *Aboriginal title in British Columbia: Delgamuukw v. the Queen*, Cassidy, F., ed., 247-252. Lantzville: Oolichan Books and Institute for Research on Public Policy.

Phillipson, Chris. 1982. *Capitalism and the construction of old age*. London: MacMillan.

Pinder, Leslie Hall. 1991. *The Carriers of no: After the land claims trial*. Vancouver: Lazara Press.

Postema, Gerald J. 1991. On the moral presence of our past. *McGill Law Journal* 36(4): 1154-1180.

Pratt, M. L. 1986. On fieldwork in common places. In *Writing culture: The poetics and politics of ethnography*, Clifford J. and G. E. Marcus, eds., 27-50. Berkeley, California: University of California Press.

Pratt, M. L. 1992. *Imperial eyes*. New York: Routledge.

Province of British Columbia. 1991. *Report of the B.C. Claims Task Force*. Victoria, British Columbia.

Pryce, Paula. 1992. The manipulation of culture and history: A critique of two expert witnesses. *Native Studies Review* 8(1): 35-46.

Rabinow, Paul. 1986. Representations are social facts: Modernity and post-modernity in anthropology. In *Writing culture: The poetics and politics of ethnography*, James Clifford and Marcus, George E., eds., 234-261. Berkeley: University of California Press.

Rabinow, Paul and W. M. Sullivan. 1987. Introduction: The interpretive turn, a second look. In *Interpretive social science: A second look*, Rabinow, P. and W. M. Sullivan, eds., 1-30. Berkeley: University of California Press.

Ray, Arthur. 1987. The early economic history of the Gitksan and Wet'suwet'en territory. Opinion report, prepared for the Gitksan and Wet'suwet'en Tribal Council.

Ray, Arthur. 1990. Creating the image of the savage in defence of the Crown: The ethnohistorian in court. *Native Studies Review* 6(2): 13-29.

Ray, Arthur. 1991 (a). Fur trade history and the Gitksan-Wet'suwet'en comprehensive claim: Men of property and the exercise of title. In *Aboriginal resource use in Canada: Historical and legal aspects*, Abel, Kerry and Jean Friesen, eds., 303-315. Winnipeg: University of Manitoba Press.

Ray, Arthur J. 1991 (b). Creating the image of the savage in defence of the Crown: The ethnohistorian in court. *Native Studies Review* 23(1): 71-78.

Razack, Sherene. 1991. *Feminism and the law: The women's legal education and action fund and the pursuit of equality in the eighties*. Toronto: Second Story Press.

Reid, John Phillip. 1992. Introduction: The layers of western legal history. In *Law for the elephant, law for the beaver: Essays in the legal history of the North American west*, McLaren, John, Hamar Foster and Chet Orloff, eds., 23-73. Regina: Canadian Plains Research Center, University of Regina, and Pasadena, CA: Ninth Judicial Circuit Historical Society.

Richardson, Boyce. 1975. *Strangers devour the land: The Cree hunters of the James Bay area versus Premier Bourassa and the James Bay Development Corporation*. Toronto: Macmillan.

Richardson, Boyce. 1993. *Terra nullius*. Toronto: MacMillan.

Ridington, Robin. 1992. Fieldwork in Courtroom 53: A witness to *Delgamuukw v. B.C. B.C. Studies* Special Issue No. 95:12-24.

Robbins, Bruce, ed. 1990. *Intellectuals: Aesthetics, politics, academics*. Minneapolis: University of Minnesota Press.

Robinson, Sheila P. 1983. Men and resources on the northern northwest coast. Unpublished Ph.D. dissertation. London: University of London.

Robinson, Sheila P. 1987 (a). Protohistoric developments in Gitksan and Wet'suwet'en territories. Expert witness opinion report, *Delgamuukw v. R.*, Supreme Court of British Columbia, Vancouver, British Columbia.

Robinson, Sheila P. 1987 (b). Affidavit of Sheila P. Robinson. *Sparrow v. R.*, Supreme Court of Canada, Vancouver, British Columbia.

Robinson, Sheila P. 1990. Traditional and historic ways of Life in British Columbia's central coast. Expert witness opinion report, *Reid et al v. R.*, Supreme Court of British Columbia, Vancouver, British Columbia.

Robinson, Sheila P. 1991. Aboriginal gambling relating to the Bulkley River Carrier. Expert witness opinion report, *R. v. Victor Jim*, Supreme Court of British Columbia, Smithers, British Columbia.

Rogers, Edward. 1986. Epilogue: Reevaluations and future considerations. *Anthropologica* N.S. 28(1-2): 203-216.

Rosaldo, Renate. 1980. Doing oral history. *Social Analysis* 4:89-99.

Rosaldo, R. 1986. From the door of his tent: The fieldworker and the inquisitor. In *Writing culture: The poetics and politics of ethnography*, J. Clifford and G. E. Marcus, eds. Berkeley, California: University of California Press.

Rosaldo, R. 1989. *Culture & truth: The remaking of social analysis.* Boston: Beacon Press.

Rose, T. F. 1972. *From shaman to modern medicine: A century of the healing arts in British Columbia.* Vancouver: Mitchell Press.

Roseberry, William. 1989. *Anthropologies and histories: Essays in culture, history, and political economy.* New Brunswick and London: Rutgers University Press.

Rosen, Lawrence. 1977. The anthropologist as expert witness. *American Anthropologist* 79:55-578.

Rosen, Lawrence. 1989. Islamic law and the logic of consequences. In *History and power in the study of law: New directions in legal anthropology*, Starr, J. and J. Collier, eds., 302-319. Ithaca: Cornell University Press.

Rosman, Abraham and Paula G. Rubel. 1971. *Feasting with mine enemy: Rank and exchange among northwest coast societies.* New York: Columbia University Press.

Ross, Andrew, ed. 1988. *Universal abandon? The politics of postmodernism.* Minneapolis: University of Minnesota Press.

Roy, Patricia E. 1989. *A white man's province: British Columbia politicians and Chinese and Japanese immigrants, 1858-1914.* Vancouver: University of British Columbia Press.

Ruby, Jay, ed. 1982. *A crack in the mirror: Reflexive perspectives in anthropology.* Philadelphia: University of Pennsylvania Press.

Rush, Stuart. 1991. The role of anthropological evidence in land claims litigation: The Gitksan-Wet'suwet'en case as an illustration. Unpublished paper, delivered to C.A.S.C.A. Meeting, University of Western Ontario, May 10, 1991, in author's possession.

Ryan, Joan. 1978. *Wall of words: The betrayal of the urban Indian.* Toronto: Peter Martin Associates.

Ryan, Joan. 1985. Decolonizing anthropology. In *Advocacy and anthropology: First encounters*, R.Paine, ed., 208-214. St.John's: Institute of Social and Economic Research, Memorial University of Newfoundland.

Ryan, Joan. 1990. Implementing participatory, action research in the Canadian north: A case study of the Gwich'in language and culture project. *Culture* 10(2): 57-65.

Ryan, Joan. 1992. Dene traditional justice:A case study. *Canadian Journal of Criminology* 34(3/4): 523-528.

Ryan, Joan. 1995. *Doing things the right way: Dene traditional justice in Lac La Martre, NWT.* Calgary: University of Calgary Press.

Ryan, Michael. 1982. *Marxism and deconstruction: A critical articulation.* Baltimore: John Hopkins University Press.

Sahlins, Marshall. 1972. *Stone age economics.* Chicago: Aldine Atherton.

Said, Edward. 1975. *Beginnings: intention and method.* New York: Basic Books.

Said, Edward. 1978. *Orientalism.* New York: Pantheon.

Said, Edward. 1983. *The world, the text, the critic.* Cambridge: Harvard University Press.

Said, Edward. 1992. *Culture and imperialism.* Cambridge: Harvard University Press.

Salisbury, Richard. 1976. The anthropologist as societal ombudsman. In *Development from below: Anthropologists and development situations*, David C. Pitt, ed., 255-265. The Hague: Mouton.

Sampson, Tom. 1992. Canada on trial. In *Aboriginal title in British Columbia: Delgamuukw v. the Queen*, Cassidy, F., ed., 95-97. Lantzville: Oolichan Books and Institute for Research on Public Policy.

Sandel, Michael J.,ed. 1984. *Liberalism and its critics.* New York: New York University Press.

Sanders, Douglas. 1980. Lawyers and Indians. Unpublished ms.

Sanders, Douglas. 1983 (a). The Indian lobby. In *And no one cheered*, Simeon, Richard and K. Banting, eds. Toronto: Methuen.

Sanders, Douglas. 1983 (b). The rights of the aboriginal peoples of Canada. *Canadian Bar Review* 61:314-354.

Sanders, Douglas. 1985 (a). Aboriginal rights: The search for recognition in international law. In *The quest for justice: Aboriginal peoples and aboriginal rights*, Boldt, Menno and J. Anthony Long, eds. in association with Leroy Little Bear, 292-304. Toronto: University of Toronto Press.

Sanders, Dougals. 1985 (b). The Queen's promises. In *Law & justice in a new land: Essays in western Canadian legal history*, Knafla, Louis A., ed. 1986 (b). Toronto: Carswell.

Sanders, Douglas. 1989. Pre-existing rights: The aboriginal peoples of Canada. In *The Canadian charter of rights and freedoms*, Beaudoin, Gerald and Ed Ratushny, eds. Toronto: Carswell

Sanders, Douglas. 1992. Getting back to rights. In *Aboriginal title in British Columbia: Delgamuukw v. the Queen*, Cassidy, F., ed., 261-287. Lantzville: Oolichan Books and Institute for Research on Public Policy.

Sangren, P. S. 1988. Rhetoric and the authority of ethnography: `Postmodernism' and the social reproduction of texts. *Current Anthropology* 29(3): 405-435.

Sanjek, Roger. 1990. *Fieldnotes: The makings of anthropology*. Ithaca: Cornell University Press.

Sansom, B. 1985. Cross-examination: W. E. H. Stanner versus the Solicitor General of Australia. In *Advocacy and anthropology: First encounters*, Paine, R., ed., 174-198. St. John's: Institute of Social and Economic Research, Memorial University.

Satsan [Herb George]. 1992. The fire within us. In *Aboriginal title in British Columbia: Delgamuukw v. the Queen*, Cassidy, F., ed., 21-34. Lantzville: Oolichan Books and Institute for Research on Public Policy.

Sayer, Derek. 1987. *The violence of abstraction: The analytic foundations of historical materialism*. Oxford: Basil Blackwell.

Schwartz, Bryan. 1986. *First principles, second thoughts: Aboriginal peoples, Constitutional reform, and Canadian statecraft*. Montreal: Institute for Research and Public Policy.

Schwartz, Bryan. 1992. The general sense of things: *Delgamuukw* and the Courts. In *Aboriginal title in British Columbia: Delgamuukw v. the Queen*, Cassidy, F., ed., 161-177. Lantzville: Oolichan Books and Institute for Research on Public Policy.

Scott, Colin. 1989. Ideology of reciprocity between the James Bay Cree and the whiteman state. In *Outwitting the state*, P.Skalnik, ed., 89-108. New Brunswick: Transaction Publishers.

Scott, Colin H. 1993. Customs, tradition, and the politics of culture: Aboriginal self-government in Canada. In *Anthropology, public policy and native peoples in Canada*, Dyck, Noel and James B. Waldram, eds., 311-333. Montreal: McGill-Queen's University Press.

Scott, David. 1992. Criticism and culture: Theory and post-colonial claims on anthropological disciplinarity. *Critique of Anthropology* 12(4): 371-394.

Seidler, Victor J. 1987. Reason, desire, and male sexuality. In *The cultural construction of sexuality*, Pat Caplan, ed., 82-112. London: Tavistock Publications Ltd.

Silverman, Robert A. and Marianne O. Nielsen, eds. 1992. *Aboriginal peoples and Canadian criminal justice*. Vancouver: Butterworths Canada Ltd.

Simmel, Georg. 1978. *The philosophy of money*. Translated by T. Bottomore and D. Frisby with an introduction by D. Frisby. London/Boston: Routledge.

Slattery, Brian. 1979. The land rights of indigenous Canadian peoples, as affected by the Crown's acquisition of their territory. Unpublished Ph.D. dissertation. University of Oxford.

Slattery, Brian. 1983. *Ancestral lands, alien laws: Judicial perspectives on aboriginal title*. Saskatoon: Native Law Centre, University of Saskatchewan.

Slattery, Brian. 1985. The hidden Constitution: Aboriginal rights in Canada. In *The quest for justice: Aboriginal peoples and aboriginal rights*, Boldt, Menno and J.Anthony Long, eds. in association with Leroy Little Bear, Toronto: University of Toronto Press.

Slattery, Brian. 1987. Understanding aboriginal rights. *Canadian Bar Review* 66:727.

Slattery, Brian. 1991. Aboriginal sovereignty and imperial claims: Reconstructing North American history. In *Aboriginal self-determination*, Cassidy, F., ed., 197-218. Lantzville, B.C.: Oolichan Books and Institute for Research on Public Policy.

Slattery, Brian. 1992. The legal basis of aboriginal title. In *Aboriginal title in British Columbia: Delgamuukw v. the Queen*, Cassidy, F., ed., 113-132. Lantzville,B.C.: Oolichan Books and Institute for Research on Public Policy.

Smart, Barry. 1992. *Modern conditions, postmodern controversies*. London: Routledge.

Smart, Carol. 1989. *Feminism and the power of law*. London: Routledge.

Smith, Melvin. 1995. *Our home or native land? What governments' aboriginal policy is doing to Canada*. Victoria, B.C.: Crown Western.

Smith, Michael D. 1993. Language, law and social power: Seaboyer; Gayme v. R. and a critical theory of ideology. *University of Toronto Faculty of Law Review*, 51(1): 118-155.

Snyder, Francis. 1981. *Capitalism and legal change: An African tradition*. New York: Academic Press.

Spivak, Gayatri Chakravorty. 1988 *In other worlds: Essays in cultural politics*. New York: Routledge.

Starr, June and Jane F. Collier, eds. 1989. *History and power in the study of law: New directions in legal anthropology*. Ithaca: Cornell University Press.

Stephenson, M.A. and S.Ratnapala, eds. 1993. *Mabo: A judicial revolution: The aboriginal land rights decision and its impact on Australian law*. Queensland: University of Queensland Press.

Steward, Julian. 1955. Theory and application in social science. *Ethnohistory* 2:292-302.

Steward, Julian. 1961. Carrier acculturation: The direct historical approach. In *Evolution and ecology: Essays on social transformation*, Steward, Jane and R. Murphy, eds., 188-99. Chicago: University of Illinois Press.

Steward, Julian. 1968. The limitations of applied anthropology: The case of the Indian new deal. *Journal of the Steward Society* 1(1): 1-17.

Steward, Julian. 1970. Determinism in primitive society?. In *Cultural ecology*, B. Cox, ed. Toronto: McLelland & Stewart.

Steward. Julian. 1977 (a). Carrier acculturation: The direct historical approach. In *Evolution and ecology: Essays on social transformation*, Steward, Jane C. and Robert F. Murphy, eds., 188-200. London: University of Illinois Press. [First published in Stanley, Diamond, ed. 1960. *Culture in history: Essays in honor of Paul Radin*. Columbia University Press, 732-744].

Steward. Julian. 1977 (b) .Determinism in primitive society?. In *Evolution and ecology: Essays on social transformation*, Steward, Jane C. and Robert F. Murphy, eds., 180-187. London: University of Illinois Press. [First published in *Scientific Monthly* 1941, 53:491-501].

Stocking, George. 1987. *Victorian anthropology*. New York: The Free Press.

Stocking, G. Jr., ed. 1991. *Colonial situations: Essays on the contextualization of ethnographic knowledge*. Madison: University of Wisconsin Press.

Stocking, G.Jr., ed. 1992. *The ethnographer's magic and other essays in the history of anthropology*. Madison: University of Wisconsin Press.

Stocking, G. Jr. 1995. *After Tylor: British social anthropology, 1888-1951*. Madison: University of Wisconsin Press.

Storrow, Marvin and Michael J. Bryant, eds. 1992. Litigating aboriginal rights cases. In *Aboriginal title in British Columbia: Delgamuukw v. the Queen*, Cassidy, F., ed., 178-192. Lantzville: Oolichan Books and Institute for Research on Public Policy.

Supreme Court of British Columbia. 1987. *Delgamuukw et al v. The Queen*. 40 D.L.R. (4th) 685. [Referenced in the text as *Reasons: Delgamuukw: oral history*].

Supreme Court of British Columbia. 1989. *Delgamuukw et al v. The Queen*. 38 B.C.L.R. (2d) 165. [Referenced in the text as *Reasons: Delgamuukw: documents*].

Supreme Court of British Columbia. 1989. *Delgamuukw et al v. The Queen*. 38 B.C.L.R. (2d) 176 [referenced in the text *Reasons: Delgamuukw: treatises*].

Supreme Court of British Columbia. 1991 (a). *Delgamuukw et. al. v. The Queen. Reasons for Judgment of the Honourable Chief Justice Allan McEachern*. Number 0843, Smithers Registry. [Referenced in the text as *Reasons, 1991*].

Supreme Court of Canada. *Judgment and Reasons for Judgment in Gladstone v. R.* File no. 23801, Ottawa.

Supreme Court of Canada. *Judgment and Reasons for Judgment in Van Der Peet v. R.* File no. 23803, Ottawa.

Supreme Court of Canada. *Judgment and Reasons for Judgment in N.T.C. Smokehouse Ltd.* File no. 23800, Ottawa.

Supreme Court of Canada. *Judgment and Reasons for Judgment in Delgamuukw v. R.* File no. 23799, Ottawa.

Sutton, Imre, ed. 1985. *Irredeemable America: The Indians' estate and land claims*. New Mexico: University of New Mexico Press and Institute for Native American Studies.

Sutton, Imre. 1985. Prolegomena. In *Irredeemable America: The Indians' estate and land claims*, Sutton, Imre, ed., 3-15. New Mexico: University of New Mexico Press and Institute for Native American Studies.

Tanner, A. 1979. *Bringing home animals*. St. John's: Institute of Social and Economic Research, Memorial University of Newfoundland.

Tanner, Adrian, ed. 1983. *The politics of Indianness in Canadian society*. St.John's: Institute of Social and Economic Research, Memorial University of Newfoundland.

Taussig, Michael. 1980. *The devil and commodity fetishism in South America*. Chapel Hill, North Carolina: University of North Carolina Press.

Taylor, Charles. 1985. Introduction. In *Philosophy and the Human Sciences*. Cambridge: Cambridge University Press.

Taylor, Charles. 1987. Interpretation and the sciences of man. In *Interpretive social science: A second look*, Rabinow, P. and W. M. Sullivan, eds., 33-81. Berkeley: University of California Press.

Taylor, Charles. 1991. *The malaise of modernity*. Concord, Ontario: Anansi.

Tennant, Paul. 1990. *Aboriginal peoples and politics: The Indian land question in British Columbia, 1849-1989*. Vancouver: University of British Columbia Press.

Tennant, Paul. 1992 (a). The place of *Delgamuukw* in British Columbia history and politics—and vice versa. In *Aboriginal title in British Columbia: Delgamuukw v. the Queen*, Cassidy, F., ed., 73-91. Lantzville, B.C.: Oolichan Books and The Institute for Research on Public Policy.

Tennant, Paul. 1992 (b). Aboriginal rights and the Canadian legal system: The west coast anomaly. In *Law for the elephant, law for the beaver: Essays in the legal history of the North American west*, McLaren, John, H. Foster, C. Orloff, eds., 110-126. Regina: Canadian Plains Research Centre.

Terdiman, Richard. 1987. Translator's introduction to *The force of law: Toward a sociology of the juridical field* by Pierre Bourdieu. *Hastings Law Journal* 38(3): 805-813.

Tesh, Sylvia. 1988. *Hidden arguments: Political ideology and disease prevention policy*. New Brunswick: Rutgers University Press.

Thomas, Nicolas. 1994. *Colonialism's culture: Anthropology, travel and government*. Princeton: Princeton University Press.

Thompson, E. P. 1978. Eighteenth-century English society: Class struggle without class. *Social History* 3:133-161. Quoted in Starr, June and Jane F. Collier, eds. 1989. *History and power*, 25. Ithaca: Cornell University Press.

Titley, E. Brian. 1986. *A narrow vision*. Vancouver: University of British Columbia Press.

Tobey, Margaret L. 1981. Carrier. In *Handbook of North American Indians, Vol.6 Subarctic*, Sturtevant, William, ed. and June Helm, vol.ed., 413-432. New York: G.P.O. for the Smithsonian Institution.

Todorov, Tzvetan. 1982. *The conquest of America: The question of the other*. New York: Harper and Row.

Torres, Gerald and Kathryn Milan. 1990. Translating Yonnondio by precedent and evidence: The Mashpee Indian case. *Duke Law Journal* 625.

1987-1991. Transcripts of Proceedings, *Delgamuukw et al v. R.*, Supreme Court of British Columbia. Smithers and Vancouver, British Columbia. [Referenced in the text as Transcripts].

Tremblay, M.A. 1983. Anthropology in question: What knowledge and knowledge for what?. In *Consciousness and inquiry: Ethnology and Canadian realities*. F. Manning, ed., 332-347. Ottawa: National Museums of Canada.

Trigger, Bruce G. 1985. *Natives and newcomers: Canada's 'heroic age,' reconsidered*. Kingston: McGill-Queen's University Press.

Trigger, Bruce G. 1985. The past as power: Anthropology and the North American Indian. In *Who owns the past?*, Isabel McBryde, ed., 11-40. Melbourne: Oxford University Press.

Trigger, Bruce G. 1988. A present of their past? Anthropologists, native people and their heritage. *Culture* 8(1)71: 79.

Trinh T. Minh-ha. 1989. *Woman native other.* Bloomington: Indiana University Press.

Trouhillot, Michel-Rolph. 1991. The savage slot. In *Recapturing anthropology*, Fox, Richard G., ed. Sante Fe, NM: School of American Research Press. Distributed by the University of Washington Press.

Tully, James, ed. 1993 (a). *An approach to political philosophy: Locke in contexts.* Cambridge: Cambridge University Press.

Tully, James. 1993 (b). Rediscovering America: The two treatises and aboriginal rights. In *An approach to political philosophy: Locke in contexts*, Tully, J., ed., 253-282. Cambridge: Cambridge University Press.

Tully, James. 1993 (c). Aboriginal property and western theory: Recovering a middle ground. Department of Philosophy, McGill University. Paper delivered to Conference on property rights, Social philosophy and policy section. Palo Alto, California, April 15-18, 1993.

Turner, Terence. 1993. Anthropology and multiculturalism: What is anthropology that multiculturalists should be mindful of?. *Cultural Anthropology: Journal of Society* Vol. 8(4): 411-442.

Turner, Terence. 1997. Human rights, human differences: Anthropology's contribution to an emancipatory cultural politics. *Journal of Anthropological Research* Vol. 53(3): 273-287.

Turpel, Mary Ellen. 1991 (a). Aboriginal peoples and the Canadian charter: Interpretive monopolies, cultural differences. In *First nations issues*, Devlin, R. F., ed. Toronto: Edmond Montgomery Publications Limited.

Turpel, Mary Ellen. 1991 (b). The judged and the judging: Locating innocence in a fallen legal world. *University of New Brunswick Law Journal* 40:281-288.

Turpel, Mary Ellen. 1991 (c). Further travails of Canada's human rights record: The Marshall Report. *International Journal of Canadian Studies* 3, 27:133-154.

Tyler, Kenneth. 1981. A modest proposal for legislative reform to facilitate the settlement of specific Indian claims. *Canadian Native Law Reporter* 3:27.

Tyler, Stephen. 1986. Post-modern ethnography: From document of the occult to occult document. In *Writing culture: The poetics and politics of ethnography*, James Clifford and Marcus, George E., eds., 122-140. Berkeley: University of California Press.

Ulin, Robert. 1984. *Understanding cultures: Perspectives in anthropology and social theory.* Austin: University of Texas.

Ulin, Robert. 1991. Critical anthropology twenty years later: Modernism and postmodernism in anthropology. *Critique of Anthropology* 11(1): 81.

Van Esterik, P. 1985. Confronting advocacy confronting anthropology. In *Advocacy and anthropology*, Paine, R., ed., 59-77. St. John's: Institute of Social and Economic Research, Memorial University of Newfoundland.

Vansina, Jan. 1965. *Oral tradition: A study in historical methodology*. Chicago: Aldine.

Vansina, Jan. 1985. *Oral tradition as history*. Madison: University of Wisconsin Press.

Venne, Sharon. 1997. Understanding Treaty 6: An indigenous perspective. In *Aboriginal and treaty rights in Canada: Essays on law, equity, and respect for difference*, Asch, Michael, ed., 173-207. Vancouver: University of British Columbia Press.

Vincent, Joan. 1989. Contours of change: Agrarian law in colonial Uganda, 1895-1962. In *History and power in the study of law: New directions in legal anthropology*, Collier, Jane and June Starr, eds., 153-167. Ithaca: Cornell University Press.

Vincent, Joan. 1990. *Anthropology and politics: Visions, traditions, and trends*. Tucson: University of Arizona Press.

Vincent, Joan. 1994. On law and hegemonic moments: Looking behind the law in early modern Uganda. In *Contested states: Law, hegemony and resistance*, Lazarus-Black, Mindie and Susan Hirsch, eds., 118-137. New York: Routledge.

Waldram, James B. 1993. Some limits to advocacy anthropology in the native Canadian context. In *Anthropology, public policy and native peoples in Canada*, Noel Dyck and Waldram,James B., eds., 293-310 Montreal: McGill-Queen's University Press.

Walters, Mark. 1993. British Imperial Constitutional law and aboriginal rights: A Comment on *Delgamuukw v. B.C. Queen's Law Journal* 17:350-413.

Ward, William Peter. 1978. *White Canada forever: Popular attitudes and public policy toward orientals in British Columbia*. Montreal: McGill-Queen's University Press.

Warry, Wayne. 1990. Doing unto others: Applied anthropology, collaborative research, and native self-determination. *Culture* Vol. 10(1): 61-73.

Watts, T.George. 1992. The law and justice: A contradiction?. In *Aboriginal title in British Columbia: Delgamuukw v. the Queen*, Cassidy, F., ed., 193-196. Lantzville: Oolichan Books and Institute for Research on Public Policy.

Weaver, Sally M. 1981. *Making Canadian Indian policy: The hidden agenda 1968-1970*. Toronto: University of Toronto Press.

Weaver, Sally M. 1984. Struggles of the nation-state to define aboriginal ethnicity: Canada and Australia. In *Minority and mother country imagery*, Gold, Gerald L., ed., 182-210. St.John's: Institute of Social and Economic Research, Memorial University, Newfoundland.

Webster's New Collegiate Dictionary. 1981. Toronto, Ontario: Thomas Allen & Son Ltd.

West, Cornel. 1993. *Race matters*. Boston: Beacon Press.

White, Hayden. 1987. The context in the text: Method and ideology in intellectual history. In *The content of the form: Narrative discourse and historical representation*, 185-203. Baltimore: John Hopkins University Press.

White, James Boyd. 1985. *Heracles' bow: Essays on the rhetoric and poetics of the law*. Madison: University of Wisconsin Press;

White, James Boyd. 1990. *Justice as translation: An essay in cultural and legal criticism*. Chicago: University of Chicago Press.

Wickwire, Wendy. 1994. To see ourselves as the other's other: Nlaka'pamnx contact narratives. *Canadian Historical Review* Vol. LXXV: 1, 1-20.

Wigetimstochol [Dan Michell]. 1992. Deep within our spirit. In *Aboriginal title in British Columbia: Delgamuukw v. the Queen*, Cassidy, F., ed., 62-66 Lantzville: Oolichan Books and Institute for Research on Public Policy.

Wike, J. A. 1951. The effect of the maritime fur trade on northwest coast Indian society. Unpublished Ph.D. dissertation, Columbia University.

William, S. 1988. Culture theory in contemporary ethnohistory. *Ethnohistory* 35(1): 1-14.

Williams, Brett, ed. 1991. *The politics of culture*. Washington: Smithsonian Institution Press.

Williams, David Ricardo. 1987. Imposition and acceptance of law and order within the claims area. Expert opinion report prepared for Russell DuMoulin and the Ministry of the Attorney-General of British Columbia in the matter of *Delgamuukw v. R.*

Williams, P. J. 1987. Alchemical notes: Reconstructing ideals from deconstructed rights. *Harvard Law Review* 22, 22:401-444.

Williams, P. J. 1990. *The alchemy of race and rights: Diary of a law professor*. Cambridge: Harvard University Press.

Williams, R. A. 1987. Taking rights aggressively: The perils and promise of critical legal theory for people of colour. *Law & Inequality* 1(3): 112-134.

Williams, R. A. 1989. Documents of barbarism: The contemporary legacy of European racism and colonialism in the narrative tradition of federal Indian law. *Arizona Law Review* 31(2): 237-278.

Williams, R. A. Jr. 1990 (a). Gendered checks and balances: Understanding the legacy of white patriarchy in an American Indian cultural context. *Georgia Law Review* 34(8): 1019-1067.

Williams, R. A. Jr. 1990 (b). *The American Indian in western legal thought: Discourses of conquest*. New York: Oxford University Press.

Williams, S. 1988. Culture theory in contemporary ethnohistory. *Ethnohistory* 35(1): 1-44.

Williamson, Barbara. 1989. The pizza syndrome. *Project North (Aboriginal Rights Coalition) Newsletter* Fall 1989, Vol. 1(3).

Wilmsen, Edwin N.,ed. 1989. *We are here: Politics of aboriginal land tenure*. Berkeley: University of California Press.

Wolf, Eric. 1983. *Europe and the people without history*. Berkeley: University of California Press.

Worthen, Kevin J. 1991. Sword or shield: The past and future impact of western legal thought on American Indian sovereignty. A review of *The American Indian in Western Legal Thought: Discourses of Conquest* by R. A.Williams. *Harvard Law Review* 104:1372-1392.

Wright, Robin M. 1988. Anthropological presuppositions of indigenous advocacy. *Annual Review of Anthropology* 17:365-390.

Yagalahl [Dora Wilson]. 1992. It will always be the truth. Member, Gitksan-Wet'suwet'en Litigation Team, in *Aboriginal title in British Columbia: Delgamuukw v. the Queen*, Cassidy, F., ed., 199-205. Lantzville: Oolichan Books and Institute for Research on Public Policy.

Yerbury, John Collin. 1975. An ethnohistorical reconstruction of the social organization of Athabaskan Indians in the Alaskan Subarctic and in the Canadian western Subarctic and Pacific Drainage. M.A. thesis, Simon Fraser University.

Young, Allan. 1980. The discourse on stress and the reproduction of conventional knowledge. *Social Science Medicine* 14B:133-146.

Young, Iris, ed. 1991. *Justice and the politics of difference.* Princeton: Princeton University Press.

Zavardadeh, Mas'ud and Donald Morton. 1993. *Theory as resistance: Politics and Culture after (post)structuralism.* New York: Guilford Publications.

TABLE OF CASES *

Calvin's Case (1608), 7 Co Rep 1a, 2 State Tr 559, Moore KB 790, Jenk 306, 77 ER 377 at 398.

Fletcher v. Peck, 10 U.S. (6 Cranch) 87 (1810) at 146.

Johnson v. M'Intosh 21 U.S. (8 Wheat) 543 (1823) at 573.

Worcester v. Georgia 34 U.S. (4 S.G.U.S.) 762 (1832) at 843.

St. Catherine's Milling and Lumber Co. v. R. (1885), 10 or 196 (Ont.Ch.); (1886) 13 OAR 148 (Ont.CAO); (1887) SCR 577(SCC); (1888) 14 AC 46 (PC).

Re: Southern Rhodesia [1919], A.C. 211 at 233-4.

Amodu Tijani v. Southern Nigeria [1921], 2 A.C. 399(p.c.) at 403.

R. v. White & Bob (50) D. L. R. (2d) [1965], 620.

Calder et al v. Attorney-General of B.C. (1969), 8 D.L.R. (3d), 59-83, [S.C.B.C.]

Calder v. Attorney-General of B.C. [1973], S.C.R. 313.

Kruger and Manual v. The Queen [1977], 4 WWR 300, [1978] 1 SCR 104, 75 DLR (3d) 434, 14 NR 495, 34 CCC (2d) 377.

Hamlet of Baker Lake et al v. Minister of Indian Affairs and Northern Development et al [1980], 5 WWR 193, 50 CCC (2d) 377 (FCTD).

R. v. Simon (1985) 24 D.L.R. (4 th) 390 (S.C.C.).

A.G. Ontario v. Bear Island Foundation [1985], 49 O.R. (2d) 353, 15 D.L.R. (4th 321 (Ont. H.C.).

A.G. Ontario v. Bear Island Foundation [1989], 68 O.R. (2d) 394, 38 D.L.R. (4th) 117 (Ont.C.A.).

A.G. Ontario v. Bear Island Foundation [1991], 83 D.L.R. (4th) 381.

Guerin v. R. [1984], 2 S.C.R. 335.

R. v. Sparrow [1990], 1 S.C.R. 1075.

Mabo v. Queensland (1992), 107 A.L.R. 1.

R. v. N.T.C. Smokehouse Ltd. [1996], 2 S.C.R. 672. (Supreme Court of Canada Appeal).

R. v. Gladstone Provincial Court of British Columbia, Lemiski Prov. Ct.J., October 3, 1990. (Original trial.)

R. v. Gladstone B.C.S.C. (Anderson J.): (1991), 13. W.C.B. (2d) 601. (British Columbia Supreme Court.)

R. v. Gladstone B.C.C.A. (1993), 80 B.C.L.R. (2d) 133. 29 B.C.A.C. 253. 48 W.A.C. 253. [1993] 5 W.W.R. 517 [1993] 4 C.N.L.R. 75. (B.C. Court of Appea)

R. v. Gladstone [1996], 2 S.C.R. 723. (Supreme Court of Canada Appeal).

R. v. Van Der Peet, British Columbia Provincial Court: [1991], 3 C.N.L.R. 155. (Original trial.)

R. v. Van Der Peet British Columbia Supreme Court: (1991), 58 B.C.L.R. (2d) 392, [1991] 3 C.N.L.R. 161. (British Columbia Supreme Court.)

R. v. Van Der Peet, British Columbia Court of Appeal: (1993), 80 B.C.L.R. (2d) 75, 29 B.C.A.C. 209, 48 W.A.C. 209, 83 C.C.C. (3d) 289, [1993] 5 W.W.R. 459, [1993] 4 C.N.L.R. 221. (B.C. Court of Appeal.)

R. v. Van Der Peet, [1996], 2 S.C.R. 507. (Supreme Court of Canada Appeal.)

Delgamuukw v. R. (1987), 40 D.L.R. (4th) 698. (Judgment on admissibility of oral tradition as an exception to the "hearsay rule.")

Delgamuukw v. B.C. (1989), 38 B.C.L.R. (2d) 165. (Judgment on the admissibility of historical documents.)

Delgamuukw v. B.C. (1989), 38 B.C.L.R. (2d) 176. (Judgment on the admissibility of treatises.)

Delgamuukw v. B.C. [1991], 3 W.W.R. 97, [1991] C.N.L.R. xii, (1991), 79 D.L.R. (4th) 185, [1991] b.c.j. nO. 535 (QL). (Original trial.)

Delgamuukw v. B.C. (1993), 30 B.C.A.C. 1, 49 W.A.C. 1, 104 D.L.R. (4th) 470, [1993] 5 W.W. R. 97 [1993] 5 C.N.L.R. 1, [1993] B.C.J. No. 1395 (QL). (B.C. Court of Appeal.)

* Key:

A.L.R. (Australian Law Reports)

B.C.L.R. (British Columbia Law Reports)

C.C.C. (Canadian Criminal Courts)

C.N.L.R. (Canadian Native Law Reports)

D.L.R. (Dominion Law Reports)

F.C.T.D. (Federal Court Trial Division)

S.C.R. (Supreme Court Reports)

S.C.C. (Supreme Court of Canada)

W.A.C. (Western Appeal Courts)

W.W.R. (Western Weekly Reports)

ACKNOWLEDGEMENTS

It seems appropriate to end by acknowledging that all stories are *about* the activities of people: history ultimately belongs to those who create it. If the participants in the events I have chronicled didn't choose to put their case before the courts and the public, this document would not exist. So my first bow is to the "Plaintiffs" and their supporters in *Delgamuukw v. R.* for having the courage to take a stand, and for working hard to defend it. I feel arrogant at this moment, facing you as a critic working after the fact and out of the fray. I do not expect that everyone will appreciate my effort. I hope most will at least agree that this book constitutes a worthwhile project, as one account of a historical moment that continues to have far-reaching effects.

So many people's thoughts, comments, questions and criticisms have gone into this project over the course of the last six years that it is impossible to name everyone. This book's first incarnation was as a Ph.D. thesis and I am grateful to those who assisted and supported me in producing that document: my supervisor, Professor Noel Dyck; members of my thesis committee, Professors Michael Kenny and Arlene McLaren; examiners Dr. Ian Angus and Dr. Robert Paine. For a lot of practical assistance, and for the endless patience and support that I do not believe anyone could ever produce a doctoral thesis without, I am grateful to Fran Gillis, and to my late mother, Claire Culhane.

Without Gary Fisher's incisive editing, bounteous encouragement, and great sense of humour, the thesis would not have become a book. Thank you. Thank you.

Several readers' comments and critiques transformed a draft into a manuscript: Thank you: Leslie Butt, Phil Russell, Roisin Sheehy-Culhane; and two anonymous peer reviewers. Thanks to Ann Vanderbijl for meticulously verifying references and polishing the bibliography. Other people from whom I have learned much that is relevant to this book: Frances Abele, Julie Cruikshank, Lori Gabrielson, Dan Gillis, Fran Gillis, Miki Maeba, Renee Taylor, Barbara Williamson. None are responsible for errors, omissions, or opinions expressed in the text: any of those are mine alone.

And last, but never least, I thank my children Carey Speck, and Lori Speck, for sustaining me, always.